Decolonizing Tradition

Decolonizing Tradition

New Views of Twentieth-Century
"British" Literary Canons

Edited by

KAREN R. LAWRENCE

University of Illinois Press   *Urbana & Chicago*

© 1992 by the Board of Trustees of the University of Illinois
Manufactured in the United States of America

1 2 3 4 5 C P 5 4 3 2 1

This book is printed on acid-free paper.

Library of Congress Cataloging-in-Publication Data

Decolonizing tradition : new views of twentieth-century "British"
   literary canons / edited by Karen R. Lawrence.
      p.   cm.
   Includes bibliographical references and index.
      ISBN 0-252-01821-4 (alk. paper).—ISBN 0-252-06193-4 (pbk.:
alk. paper)
      1. English literature—20th century—History and criticism.
   2. English literature—Minority authors—History and criticism.
   3. Commonwealth of Nations literature (English)—History and
   criticism. 4. English literature—Women authors—History and
   criticism. 5. Women and literature—History—20th century.
   6. Decolonization in literature. 7. Minorities in literature.
   8. Canon (Literature) I. Lawrence, Karen, 1949–
   PR473.D43 1992
   820.9′0091—dc20   91-15006
                                                              CIP

Contents

PART 3. Postcolonial Configurations

Acknowledgments

I am indebted to a number of people for their help with this project. Anyone who has edited a book with multiple authors knows how crucial is the coordination of the project, and I would like to thank Toula Leventis and Mary Looser for their assistance. My friend and colleague Barry Weller offered invaluable advice about copyediting. Finally, I am grateful to Ann Lowry, at the University of Illinois Press, who shepherded the manuscript with care and persistence.

"Snapshots of a Daughter-in-Law," from *The Fact of a Doorframe: Poems Selected and New,* 1950–1984 by Adrienne Rich, copyright © 1984 by Adrienne Rich; copyright © 1975, 1978 by W. W. Norton and Co., Inc.; copyright © 1981 by Adrienne Rich. Reprinted by permission of the author and W. W. Norton and Co., Inc.

Maria Banus, "Wedding." Reprinted by permission of the author and the translator.

Mary Barnard, *Sappho: A New Translation,* fragments 27, 32, 34, and 36, copyright © 1958 by The Regents of the University of California; © renewed 1984 by Mary Barnard.

Pamela Hadas, "Post-Thalamion," first published in *Webster Review* 3, no. 2 (Spring 1987). Reprinted by permission of the author.

Patricia Storace, "Pamina's Marriage Speech," from *Heredity,* copyright © 1987 by Beacon Press. Reprinted by permission of the author.

Pamela Stewart, "Prothalamion," from *Nightblind,* copyright © 1985 by Ion Books, Inc.

Phyllis Janowitz, "The Arrangement" and "The Funeral Director's Wedding," from *Visiting Rites,* copyright © 1982 by Princeton University Press.

Sandra Hochman, "The Eyes of Flesh," from *Manhattan Pastures,* copyright © 1963 by Yale University Press.

Susan Donovan, "Why the Bride Kept a Bear," *Massachusetts Review* 24, no. 2 (Summer 1983), © 1984 (corrected) by The Massachusetts Review, Inc.

Ann Stanford, "Ceremonies," in *"High Wedlock Then Be Honoured": Wedding Poems from Nineteen Countries and Twenty-five Centuries,* ed. Virginia Tufte, New York: Viking, 1970. Reprinted by permission of the author.

Pat Murphy, *Maeve.* Permission to quote from the typescript granted by the author.

Eavan Boland, "The Achill Woman," first published in the *Atlantic Monthly,* Aug. 1988. Reprinted by permission of the author.

"Canon Fathers and Myth Universe" is reprinted with minor changes from *New Literary History* 19 (1987–88): 23–35 by permission of the publisher.

Decolonizing Tradition

KAREN R. LAWRENCE

Introduction

The Cultural Politics of Canons

It seems that everyone is talking about canons today, but the debate has entered a new phase. On the one hand, we have reached a point where canonical reconsideration has become fashionable within academe. A colleague who is editing a book on canons recently wrote to me, "Canons to the left of us, canons to the right. I'm used to being in the vanguard and not on the bandwagon." Indeed, the genesis of this collection is a certain legitimation in the American academy of the kind of discourse it proposes, for a number of essays gathered here were presented at three sessions on "Reconsidering the Canon," sponsored by the Modern Language Association Division of Twentieth-Century English Literature. On the other hand, one can say that within the academy critique of the canon is both established and still urgently seeking a foothold. Recent academic transformations of the canon have succeeded perhaps in establishing a new list of great works rather than in keeping open to question the process of canon formation itself. Moreover, increasing the urgency and complicating the dynamic of reconsidering canon formation is the fact that the ideological struggles over the canon are now raging openly beyond the halls of academe. The fate of the canon is argued not only on the pages of *Critical Inquiry* and *ELH* but in the *New York Times* and the *London Times* as well. Books by academics, such as Allan Bloom's *Closing of the American Mind* and E. D. Hirsch's *Cultural Literacy,* have captured the popular imagination as well as the attention of those in conservative governments. Paradoxically, academic elitists like Bloom and Hirsch make the best-seller list with their pleas for preserving Western high culture. One can say that the authority to critique the canon has established itself well enough to mount challenges from within, but has now found itself meeting a challenge from "authorities" outside the academy who have launched a neoconservative critique of the humanities that is recorded in the press.[1]

As if in answer to former Secretary of Education William Bennett and to Stephen Balch, president of a conservative organization called the National Association of Scholars, who attribute a violence to those who would "open" the canon and thereby destroy the citadel of tradition, this book explores the conflicts that produce the august edifice itself. The essays share an assumption that the formation and revision of literary tradition and the canon reflect ideological struggle rather than a natural aesthetic order. Perhaps it is more accurate to say that these essays explore the way literary canons disguise their own histories of violence, for the "cover story" of canons, both within the academy and in Bennett and Balch, is that they transcend ideology. If tradition is regarded as a form of cultural imperialism, then these essays seek to decolonize the empire's literary territory.

The conflicts that produce the canon occur on the levels of production and reception; they involve writers' confrontations with inherited tradition and the evaluation of texts in relation to it. Although diverse, these essays seek to analyze and complicate the geometry of cultural inclusion and exclusion in twentieth-century British literature. They take up challenges to the British literary tradition which have been mounted on a number of fronts: by writers interrogating the cultural implications of generic boundaries; by feminist writers plotting gender in relation to tradition, often in conjunction with other categories such as race and class; by multicultural writers whose work emerges from and addresses the postcolonial condition. The essays consider how the postcolonial has reshaped the field of writing in English, and how this new configuration prompts revaluation and reinterpretation of more familiar authors. Indeed, the contested word "British" is used in the title to evoke the global colonial and postcolonial context of the literary formation, and thus the politics implicit in the putatively "disinterested" world of the literary canon. The resurgence of the term in Britain to represent indigenous nonwhite populations in England, such as in "Black British" writing, is another important indication of the postcolonial context.[2] What makes the discussion of the workings of ideology particularly fascinating in a modern British context is precisely the contradictions one finds between the myth of disinterestedness and gentlemanly civility in the realm of aesthetics and the more openly hegemonic ideologies of imperialism and patriarchy. Presented here are new narratives of the twentieth-century British literary tradition that examine the repression not only of specific texts and ideologies but of the role of ideology in relation to aesthetics. They seek not to collapse the distinctions between various kinds of repressions but to analyze the multiple forms of repression in the processes of canonicity, involving writers white and black, male and female, of English and colonial origin.

The erasure, or neutralization, of conflict is a general feature of aesthetic culture in capitalist societies. In an issue of *Cultural Critique* devoted to minority discourse, David Lloyd writes that aesthetic culture in bourgeois capitalist societies provides "a site of reconciliation which transcends continuing political differences and accordingly furnishes the domain of human freedom promised in theory by bourgeois states but belied in all but form by their practices" ("Genet's Genealogy" 171). Speaking of the British literary tradition in particular, the authors of *Rewriting English: Cultural Politics of Gender and Class* cite the "strong and central position occupied in [the intellectual culture of class societies] by literary discourse, a position that enables it to displace and supplant historical, social and, above all, political analysis of cultural activity as too narrow, parochial and partisan and to offer itself as a 'totalizing' explanation, ecumenical, disinterested and classless" (27). The authors maintain that "the ruling culture of Englishness—white, male and (whatever its electoral habits) conservative—remains profoundly mistrustful of politics . . . and resistant to its infiltration into everyday life" (9). For Matthew Arnold, the authors contend, "the 'culture' to which we must look to redeem the inevitable 'anarchy' of class interest was, virtually, the national literature" (20). One must note, however, the contradictions within this idea of the apolitical nature of British culture, since it is apparent that Arnold's mistrust of politics coexists with a progressive view of the civilizing, instrumental functions of literature and criticism. Interestingly, this notion of the transcendence of politics by literary culture has had the effect of excluding specific ideologies of the right as well as of the left. Although Marxist critics correctly focus on the literary-critical neutralization of class struggle and the exclusion of the marginal and disenfranchised, in his essay on male adventure stories from 1876 to 1914, Martin Green points out that the liberal ideology of British aesthetic culture has excluded as well certain writers and genres whose politics of imperialism were insufficiently disguised. Green looks at the other side of the transforming power of the great tradition, which expunges literature that is too nakedly imperialistic as well as too radical.

Feminist criticism and theory have been most instrumental in focusing attention on the gender- as well as class-inflected processes of aesthetic legitimation.[3] In a seminal essay on the canon, one of the contributors to this collection, Lillian Robinson, compares the canon to a "gentlemen's agreement," invoking the class and gender bias disguised behind the gentility of canonization (106). Further, as contemporary analyses of colonial discourse have demonstrated, definitions of Englishness and English literature in the nineteenth and twentieth centuries have been constructed in part in opposition to England's racial "others" (see, e.g., Spivak, "Three Women's Texts"). Thus, contemporary theory and criticism have forced the recognition that literary tradition and canon formation have always involved cultural narratives, disguised as aesthetic principles but constructed upon assumptions about class, gender, language, and race.

But if the effacement of ideology is a feature of aesthetic culture in general, this collection presents the ways in which modern and contemporary British texts offer specific and particularly interesting versions of this phenomenon, for during its modern phase, the British tradition fetishized its own disinterestedness. The separation between art and politics was fueled by many of the manifestos of modernism, which stress the formal properties of art and discredit the ties between literature and immediate political and social concerns. As Robert L. Caserio says in his essay on H. G. Wells, ideological representations and discourse have been marginalized in the canonization of modernist literature. In a *Critical Inquiry* essay on appropriation in modern narrative, Robert Weimann argues that modernism, with its "erosion of representational form" (441), presents a heightened form of the disorientation between art and the social "world."[4]

And yet, to expose the repression of ideology within canonical texts, and the workings of ideology in the process of canonization, does not necessarily suggest how complicated these processes are. These general statements on the sociology of canon formation may lead to two different simplifications or overemphases. The first is a too institutional and deterministic view of literary history and canon formation that fails to account for, as Jerome McGann puts it, the "specific and worlded engagements in which meaning is rendered and used" (72). Most of the essays in this collection analyze specific textual representations of cultural ideology and the ideological assumptions underlying aesthetic reception. They attend to the micro- as well as the macro-level of literary production and do not dismiss the idea of "agency" for the writer within ideology.[5] The second distortion lies at the opposite pole and is represented by a view that reifies canonizers and "neglecters" by overemphasizing the power of specific agents who intentionally include and exclude certain texts. It seems that both those who decry the recent "opening" of the canon and those who advocate change in the established order simplify the idea of the "they" who are either the gatekeepers or gatecrashers of the hall of fame. The problem inherent in an analogy between theological and literary canonization is nowhere more apparent than in regard to this issue of the authority to legitimate. By what authority is the authority of the canon invested or withheld? We can identify the authority responsible for the canonization of St. Theresa, as well as the loss of status suffered by St. Christopher and St. Philomena, but it is more difficult to pinpoint just who determines the rise and fall of literary fortunes. By what cultural authority is John Donne accorded a place in the canon after years of neglect? By what authority did Beaumont and Fletcher lose their claims to a place in the pantheon?

Without losing the sense of power available to certain actors within the literary, cultural, and political drama, it is helpful to refine our notions of "authorizers" of the canon. First, we have come to see the way in which "strong" acts of literary rescue or legitimation by individual critics depend upon cultural arguments and are themselves part of larger cultural scripts. Middleton Murry's attempt to secure a place for Keats in the British literary tradition and F. R. Leavis's advocacy of D. H. Lawrence are two prominent examples. Defending Keats from the charge of effeminacy, Murry attempts to show Keats as a legitimate heir of Shakespeare—healthy, manly, and English. A similar cultural scripting is involved in Leavis's claim that Lawrence was "sane to the point of genius," in which a kind of British seriousness and "maturity" determine the assignment of aesthetic value. Indeed, as Alan Sinfield points out, in arguing for these national characteristics Leavis set British virtues against the stylistic virtuosity of continental modernism, which he felt negated literature's cultural mission (182).

Second, recent analyses have rightly stressed the complexity of the cultural mediation involved in canon formation and reformation. In a fine discussion of the mechanisms of canonization in modern American poetry, Michael Berubé questions the notion of "neglecters," that is, "people actively and willingly neglecting [certain writers] as they go about their business doing something else" (178). Berubé and others focus on the complexity of the ways in which critical conversations "are formed, joined, or allowed to sputter" (181). In other words, the critique of the subject so crucial to postmodern theory necessarily affects the conception of canonizers and neglecters. In examining cultural scripts, critics are looking at who writes, who publishes, who reads, who interprets, who teaches, at particular times in particular places. A focus on the multiplicity of social forces affecting and affected by the canon is not meant to dissipate the power of the critique of canon formation but to concentrate it, to regionalize it in order to understand the processes and to intervene in them. Pierre Bourdieu describes the dynamics of struggle within the literary field, and although his comments are more directed to the production of literature than to the canonization of texts, they apply to those who help legitimate as well as produce texts:

> the strategies of actors and institutions involved in literary or artistic struggles depend on the position that they occupy in the structure of the field, that is, within the structure of distribution of capital of the prestige (institutionalized or not) accorded them by their peers and by the public at large, and by their interest in preserving or transforming this structure, in maintaining the rules of the game or subverting them. Conversely, the stakes of the struggle between those in control and the claimants to control, the questions that set them against each other, the theses and even the antitheses contested by both sides, depend on the state of the accepted problematic, that is, on the space of possibilities inherited from preceding struggles, because this space orients the search for solutions and, hence, present and future production. (545)

This emphasis on the currency of social relations affecting literary production and evaluation broadens the implications of a theory of the "interested" nature of canonization without subscribing to a narrow theory of conspiracy. Bourdieu's work seems promising because it accounts for struggles that produce change in the literary field, while acknowledging the force of the inherited structure that renders certain possibilities "thinkable" or "unthinkable," both in terms of the production of works and in the configuration of the canon.

It is the "accepted problematic" for academic discourse to include a reconsideration of the canon, and it has become equally "thinkable" for a vociferous public and government response. To illustrate Bourdieu's point about the complexity of the ideological struggles played out in the Ideological State Apparatus, one could point to some of the paradoxes of the recent furor over the canon and the strange coalitions it has spawned.[6] For example, two Reagan appointees mounted their attacks on the humanities on very different fronts. William Bennett, then secretary of education, castigated leftist professors who threaten "our" cultural heritage by advocating the opening of the canon to marginal and subliterary texts. (Bennett went on to a more fitting target for his venom over the collapse of societal standards. In his position as drug czar, he battled drug lords with gusto and rhetoric similar to those he displayed in his crusade against "leftist" professors subverting the process of higher education.) On the other hand, Lynne Cheney, the chair of the National Endowment for the Humanities, blasted higher education for its neglect of "the people" in its emphasis on rarified specialization; and she proposed a new kind of popularism for the humanities. Indeed, some liberals within the academy joined the neoconservatives in this latter charge, bemoaning the destruction of humanism.

Such unlikely coalitions may reveal that the common "enemy" in all these criticisms is the radical questioning of what Antonio Gramsci calls "the common sense" of bourgeois culture, which allows us so comfortably to posit humanism's "free" and unified individual. Postmodern theories of varied kinds require us to question the accepted wisdom of "our" culture, high, low, and middle. Indeed, both Bennett's fear of losing "high" culture and Cheney's fear of losing the culture of the people unite in a fear of losing our white middle-class assumptions about writers and readers. This radical critique, aimed at the idea of the subject, argues for theorizing various "subject positions" rather than unified subjectivity. Mas'ud Zavarzadeh and Donald Morton point out in their provocative essay "Theory Pedagogy Politics: The Crisis of 'The Subject' in the Humanities," that we are participating in a fundamental reunderstanding of the subject in postmodern theory (and this includes theory from various disciplines, such as philosophy, linguistics, psychoanalysis, literature, film, and gender, race, and class studies [2]). It is worth observing that the question of the subject is vexed even for different groups represented above as postmodern. As feminists know, strategically it is hard to abandon a voice and a "self" that one has never fully "possessed." And, as Marilyn Reizbaum shows in her essay "Canonical Double Cross: Scottish and Irish Women's Writing," questions of "voice" and "representation" that hark back to the vocabulary of the liberal subject are complicated by the politics of colonial and ex-colonial literatures still waging battles for their "rights." She shows how the discourses of feminism and Marxism may reveal competing agendas, subtended by differing notions of the subject and subjection.[7]

The strategic difficulties that attend the politics of the critique of the subject affect the critique of the canon as well. The desire for a place in the canon for previously marginalized texts may lead to a greater pluralism that nevertheless does not fundamentally alter our thinking about canonicity. The diverse essays in this collection seek to theorize about canon formation, then, not merely by adding to an anthology of criticism some essays on new cultural territories but by questioning the notion of marginality itself. Although none of the essays labels itself "deconstructive," many attempt to overturn the binary oppositions between center and margin upon which most ideas of the canon depend. Although deconstruction has tended to focus on canonical texts in the Western tradition, showing how the hierarchies within these texts can be deconstructed, it has provided a powerful theory for rigorously overturning the very patterns of our thinking about the center and the margin. Allied with feminist or Marxist theory, as in the work of Gayatri Spivak, a deconstructive approach to the canon would recognize that the center and the periphery collapse back into each other, as Spivak puts it, though never fully "undoing . . . the canon-apocrypha opposition" ("Scattered Speculations" 154).

This rethinking, which amounts to a redrawing of the geometry of inclusion and exclusion, might be fruitfully approached by way of recent discussions of the categories of major and minor. Race, class, and gender studies have exposed the investment that bourgeois, patriarchal, white culture has in maintaining a separation between the "major" and the "minor." They have fruitfully engaged in a dialogue about the relation between "minor" literature and "major" texts, as well as that between "minor" and "minority" literature, a relation that bears upon the crucial area of postcolonial discourse.

A special issue of *Cultural Critique* focuses on these relationships; many of the articles explicitly or implicitly draw on an important study by Gilles Deleuze and Felix Guattari called *Kafka: Toward a Minor Literature* which examines the radical potential of minor literature. Briefly, Deleuze and Guattari view the "minor" in literature as stemming from a profound linguistic "alienation," a perceived estrangement from the mainstream that gives to minor writing the quality of translation. Paradoxically, their exemplars are Kafka and Joyce, "minor" writers by virtue of their linguistic alienation from the master language—in Kafka's case, Prague German written by a Jew; in Joyce's, English written by an Irishman. Deleuze and Guattari view this use of language as new and revolutionary, an expression of "the people's concern." The "minor," as defined by them, is written in a "major" language; ultimately, it is really a category for the revolutionary conditions within all literature (19). They speak of a kind of "becoming minor," or a "deterritorialization" process by which the writer relinquishes any sense of linguistic security and authority.

There are many reasons one might take issue with this conception of the minor. As Louis Renza points out, by privileging the major "minor" writers who write in a particular mode of anti-Oedipal opposition, this model tends to make neglected and minority writers more minor (35–36). And in her essay in *Cultural Critique,* Caren Kaplan observes that this model is itself based on a notion of a kind of freedom evident in the luxury of the phrase "becoming minor," a freedom that ignores the situation of oppression of most minor and minority texts (despite the origin of the model in the oppression of Kafka and Joyce [191]). "Becoming minor" may come uncomfortably close to a kind of "theoretical tourism on the part of the first world critic, where the margin becomes a linguistic or critical vacation, a new poetics of the exotic" (Kaplan 191).

Despite its curious blindnesses to the special discourses of ethnic, racial, and gender minorities and their relation to the revolutionary potential they applaud, Deleuze and Guattari's emphasis on "deterritorialization" and linguistic alienation nevertheless provides a very useful departure point for a consideration of the relations between "major" and "minor." The disquieting doubleness of language found in "minor" texts fuels postmodernism's assault on the universalized subject of humanism. In a sense, no one is a "native" handler of language; all "use" of language is an appropriation that presupposes estrangement and difference.[8] Lloyd speaks of the possibility that the literature of political minorities can fracture the dominant discourse and "dissolve the canonical form of Man back into the different bodies which he has sought to absorb" ("Genet's Genealogy" 185). And, as Deleuze and Guattari suggest, it is profoundly through a kind of mimicry, or "citation" (to use a term from Derrida), that this fracturing of identity is accomplished.

This idea of mimicry, and the sense of being both inside and alienated from dominant discourses, is a thread that runs through feminist theory, perhaps most suggestively in the works of Luce Irigaray. In "The Blind Spot of an Old Dream of Symmetry," she practices what she preaches, orchestrating her own text in mimicry of Freud's essay on "Femininity" (*Speculum* 13–129). Mimicry serves here as a point of resistance, a means of speaking the language with a difference. To return to Lloyd's phrase, the "bodies" that contemporary feminist theorists seek to recover from absorption in "the hegemonic narratives of identity" are female. A number of the essays in this collection explore the possibilities and dangers of female appropriation of traditionally "male" myths, narratives, genres, and claims to authority. They address the revolutionary potential of such imitation but acknowledge as well its potential traps. They explore the fictional capital as well as the psychic price of "stealing" the language from the altar of patriarchal culture.[9]

The possibilities and specters involved in appropriation or mimicry of dominant discourses are raised as well in relation to the colonial situation. Homi Bhabha has written of the process of "native" mimicry in which the master discourse may be subverted in the citational speech of the colonized. Many recent analyses of resistance literature question how an oppositional literature can be written in the language of the oppressor. In her essay in this collection, Gay Wilentz focuses on the way Caribbean writers, particularly Wilson Harris and Erna Brodber, use the hegemonic language of English as a language of opposition. Wilentz explains the "difficulty" of Caribbean writing to non-Caribbean readers in terms of its attempted political "dismantling" of colonial discourse. And Pat McGee explores the way African writing demystifies the Western master narrative's claim to universal truth and can "transform the dead letters of hegemonic culture into the hope for social revolution."

The question of "resistance," like that of the boundaries between center and margins, is a vexed one in recent deconstructive analyses of colonial discourse. As the burgeoning bibliography of colonial discourse analysis reveals, most recent studies reject a binary, or Manichean, opposition between the literature of the colonial power and that of the colonized. The oppositional terms of major and minor, master and "native" discourse begin to collapse into one another, not only in the strategic conception of the native's mimicry of dominant discourse but in the infiltration of dominant discourse by the discourse of the "other." For example, Spivak contends that colonial discourse depends upon the "othering" of the native and is therefore in a sense constituted by its attempted repression ("Three Women's Texts"). And Bhabha argues that native mimicry leaves its trace in colonial discourse—the sound of the native's mimicry can be heard in the discourse in which the native is supposedly silenced ("The Other Question"). "What is articulated in the doubleness of colonial discourse," Bhabha tells us, "is not simply the violence of one powerful nation writing out another [but] a mode of contradictory utterance that ambivalently reinscribes both colonizer and colonized" ("Sly Civility" 74).[10]

As the essays in this collection show, this overlap of mainstream and marginal discourses is not confined to postcolonial writing. A number of essays explore the way both canonical texts and canon-making criticism bear the traces of what they seek to repress. Both Caserio and Green explore the way the "mainstream" modern British literary tradition represses its own likenesses to more marginalized texts. Caserio contends that the modernists' discrediting of Wells was, in part, a repression of their own ideological tendencies, and Green reads the marginalization of adventure novels as the repression of the Great Tradition's own aggressive impulses. Such theoretical models, which refuse the mutual exclusivity of center and margin, can account for the way aesthetic culture absorbs revolutionary impulses, or, in Lionel Trilling's phrase, legitimizes the subversive (26). It can encompass what Green describes as the process by which the center comes to be made up of previously marginalized texts.

It should be clear from this brief discussion of the issues and attitudes that unite the essays in this collection that to carve them into neat divisions—between feminist and postcolonial analyses, for example—would be to reproduce some of the conceptual and political blindnesses the essays attempt to analyze. However, three general headings seem plausible markers with which to forecast issues raised in the essays as well as connections among them. The first section, "The Politics of Genre," brings together essays that explore the cultural and ideological implications of genre. The book begins with two essays, by Lillian Robinson and Celeste Schenck, that discuss the relation between gender and genre in a wide range of texts. Robinson's "Canon Fathers and Myth Universe" introduces the section with a general discussion of the gendering of literary history and the female appropriation of male myths. She explores the paradigm of the quest, among others, and discusses what myths and narratives in the patriarchal repertoire provide a usable past for the woman writer. Schenck looks at the predicament of the woman writer who inherits a role as object rather than as subject or creator. In " 'Corinna Sings': Women Poets and the Politics of Genre," she explores the repression of the female voice in lyric poetry and the strategies by which female poets have refused, resisted, and reconstructed the "essentially masculine Western lyric inheritance." According to Schenck, the writer's disinheritance occasions both her dilemma and the revolutionary potential of her rewritings. She reads the lyric tradition as a site of conflict rather than an ideal aesthetic type. Focusing on the epithalamium in particular, Schenck discusses the writings of women in "ceremonial" (hence, more public) registers as material for theorizing "a provisional way of thinking about genre that might enfranchise rather than exclude the work of women poets." The essay offers a wide-ranging exploration of the economy of gender in Western literary tradition, ending with readings of twentieth-century women poets who construct new articulations of female subjectivity and erotic relationship.

In the final two essays of this section, Green and Caserio deal with the novels of white male British writers whose noncanonical status, each argues, is related to the cultural implications of the kinds of texts produced. In counterpoint to the feminist surveys of Robinson and Schenck, Green surveys male (and masculinist) adventure novels from 1876 to 1914. His essay, "Adventurers Stake Their Claim: The Adventure Tale's Bid for Status, 1876–1914," highlights some cultural implications of the division between the "serious" and "nonserious" literature of the period, as well as ideological links that bind them and have led to the latter's exclusion from the canon. Expanding on the observations in his important book *Dreams of Adventure, Deeds of Empire,* Green discusses both the ideology of adventure and its repression in the Great Tradition. He argues that the case of adventure exemplifies the way that literary tradition works by struggle rather than either neglect, on the one hand, or passive coexistence, on the other. Green shows how adventure *tested* literature in such a way that literature needed to repress it. In some ways like Fredric Jameson's fascinating analysis of the "fables of aggression" that bind together the work of Wyndham Lewis, Green's essay examines a literature of imperialism that tests our theories of literature from an unexpected angle.

Citing Wells as a writer who did not subscribe to the modernist division between art and politics, Caserio initiates canonical reconsideration in terms of the breakdown of generic boundaries between "literature" and other kinds of writing. In "The Novel as a Novel Experiment in Statement: The Anticanonical Example of H. G. Wells," he describes Wells's attempt to invent and identify "the new essay," a literary form that would allow for an "experiment in statement." Focusing on *Christina Alberta's Father,* Caserio maintains that Wells in a sense anticipated postmodernism's critique of the subject and its insistence on the link between art and ideology. Further, Caserio argues that writers like D. H. Lawrence and Virginia Woolf, who discredited Wells's brand of politics, really share his antinovelistic interests and forms.

In part 2, Rachel Bowlby and Jane Marcus consider two canonical novels, respectively Lawrence's *Lady Chatterley's Lover* and Woolf's *The Waves,* and the processes of their cultural legitimation. Both critics take up the way that social and political norms are implicated in legislating aesthetic value. In " 'But She Would Learn Something from Lady Chatterley': The Obscene Side of the Canon," Bowlby looks at cultural regulation in its material, legal manifestation in the obscenity trial of *Lady Chatterley's Lover.* Through a reading of the discourses of the trial, she shows how aesthetic evaluation was inextricably bound to ideas of social, particularly heterosexual, norms, as much in evidence, perhaps surprisingly, in the rhetoric of the defense as in that of the prosecution. Bowlby goes on to show that even feminist criticism, like Kate Millett's important *Sexual Politics,* has launched its attack on Lawrence's misogyny from the same fairly conservative strategic angle.

Marcus begins "Britannia Rules *The Waves,*" by discussing "nonpolitical" readings of *The Waves* that allowed it to be canonized as a lyrical novel in the tradition of High Modernism. Paradoxically, she contends, this aestheticization has deprived the text of readers who might appreciate its critique of the class and race systems subtending British culture. In Marcus's new reading of the novel as an anti-imperialist and anticanonical text, Bernard, the writer figure, undergoes a revisionary reading. Marcus reverses the traditional identification of Bernard as a figure for Woolf and views him instead as representing the complicity between British literary culture and imperialism.

The links between colonialism and canonicity in Marcus's provocative reading form a bridge to the final section, "Postcolonial Configurations," which reevaluates the literary tradition in relation to the postcolonial condition. The first two essays, Marilyn Reizbaum's and Louise Yelin's, expand and complicate some of the issues in the first section, focusing on the connections and contradictions between feminist and postcolonial analyses. One could say that these essays bear out Robinson's statement that the logic of feminist criticism, by bringing gender into question, "necessarily entails rethinking the entire literary tradition in order to place centrally into it not only an entire excluded sex ... but also excluded classes, races, national groups, sexual minorities, and ideological positions." Reizbaum's essay, "Canonical Double Cross: Scottish and Irish Women's Writing," most explicitly foregrounds the difficult relation between feminist and anticolonial approaches to canonicity. In her discussion of the writing of Irish and Scottish women poets, in particular, she explores the way the concept of subjection, which has been linked historically to feminization in Irish culture, complicates the subject position of the contemporary woman writer. In exploring postcolonial writing in the context of the legacy of the first phase of British imperialism, Reizbaum takes up crucial questions about nationalism and feminism, feminist theory and postcolonial critique, that have often been found only in analyses of non-Western literary contexts.

In "Decolonizing the Novel: Nadine Gordimer's *A Sport of Nature* and British Literary Traditions," Yelin focuses on the conflicting discourses of race, nationality, gender, and ethnicity in Gordimer's novel and reads the sexuality of the white Jewish South African protagonist as politicized in ways that complicate the norms of colonial discourse and female modernism. Thus, she too focuses on the overdetermined discourses that complicate a model of inclusion and exclusion on a single basis like gender or race. Concentrating on the "metissage" of transformed European and indigenous African traditions, Yelin reads Gordimer's novel as a text that thematizes the problem of literary authority and legitimacy and takes an "oppositional" stance toward the canon.

The final three essays in the section further explore the possibilities of oppositional texts generated in colonial or postcolonial cultures in terms of writing produced outside Britain. The first, Derek Attridge's essay on J. M. Coetzee's *Foe,* discusses the possibilities of an oppositional literature composed by a white South African writer. Acknowledging that another rewriting of Daniel Defoe's text-making book *Robinson Crusoe* may seem all too much like a bid for canonical status rather than an interrogation of canons, Attridge argues that the book is an oppositional text that turns intertextuality into a radical and destabilizing technique. In "Oppressive Silence: J. M. Coetzee's *Foe* and the Politics of the Canon," he explores the double bind of such a novel—which, if it succeeds, risks losing its oppositional force; and if it fails to gain readership and legitimacy, risks not being read at all. Finally, Attridge interprets Friday, the silent, maimed black African in Coetzee's narrative, as a figure for the silence upon which cultural formations depend.

Patrick McGee and Gay Wilentz explore the possibilities for resistance literature by black African and Caribbean writers. Both focus on language as the site of potential resistance. McGee, in "Texts between Worlds: African Fiction as Political Allegory," shows that an understanding of postmodernism is not merely augmented by study of the postcolonial situation but is necessarily redefined by it. Drawing on Walter Benjamin's idea of allegory, McGee tries to refine the figure of allegory to describe the relation to language one finds in "third-world" and other oppositional literature. Suggestively relating the political functions of language in English and American oppositional writing and postcolonial African writing, much of it in English, McGee discusses a kind of alienation that is a revolutionary condition of language, all the while acknowledging, as Deleuze and Guattari do not, the particulars of the neocolonial situation. In "English Is a Foreign Anguish: Caribbean Writers and the Disruption of the Colonial Canon," Wilentz also focuses on the revolutionary potential of language in the hands of postcolonials. She explores the way that "standard" English for the Caribbean writer signifies a history of servitude while presenting a revolutionary possibility for dismantling colonial discourse. Wilentz examines the way these writers attempt to "make new" the literary language they inherit, with techniques both similar to and different from those of European modernism.

The essays here do not pretend to cover the field of twentieth-century literature in English, but rather, they suggest ways of remapping the field as well as plotting its ideological components. The essays urge a reading of texts, many of them formerly on the periphery, that critique notions of canonicity and cultural transmission. In reading fiction as theory and critique, these authors demonstrate yet again the breakdown of certain divisions that have sustained our view of modern British literature. But perhaps the greatest "breakdown" they describe is that of the idea of *national* literatures. Instead, they argue for worldwide attention to litera-tures in English. While foregrounding the problems of the linguistic inheritance of British imperialism, the essays in this collection neverthe-less suggest reframing these problems in terms of international literatures in English. As Reed Way Dasenbrock has pointed out forcefully in a number of articles on the cultural assumptions behind our ways of classify-ing literatures, the marginal examples that might seem to threaten the coherence of a nation-based model now seem instead to be central examples in a model based on the expansion of the English language (see, e.g., "What to Teach"). However, one need not merely reverse the terms *center* and *margins,* as Dasenbrock goes on to do in the service of a "new essentialism." Rather, one may argue, as these authors do, for rethinking the opposition between margin and center and redrawing the geometry of inclusion and exclusion. In this context, merely "expanding the canon" is not enough.

Notes

1. See, for example, Lynne Cheney's "Report to the President, the Congress, and the American People." The "profession" has attempted to answer these charges officially, in such publications as *Speaking for the Humanities* and the majority of essays collected in *Profession* 88. In *Literature, Politics, and Culture in Postwar Britain,* Alan Sinfield notes a similar right-wing response in England to what is perceived as "a collapse of cultural authority" in the universities (289). As

a number of essays in this collection make clear, canon reform does not every-where display the same institutional patterns; for example, Marilyn Reizbaum's discussion of Irish and Scottish literature reveals a kind of dual canon formation (national and international) and a more complicated cultural matrix for its production.

2. In a chapter entitled "Cultural Plunder," Sinfield discusses the "slippage" between the terms *English* and *British,* recognizing the nomination as a problem even in books that self-consciously analyze the relationship between politics and aesthetics. This slippage, he claims, "represents confusion and manipulation in respect of the first and last colonies of the English—the more northern and western parts of the British Isles. For the domination of Celtic peoples and cultures has plainly been similar to overseas imperial enterprise. . . . Generally, Britishness is claimed for size and scope, Englishness for core distinctiveness" (117–18). Although the term evokes the earliest phase of England's imperialism, as Sinfield says, I have chosen to use it to signal the general legacy of the colonial past (within England and in its former colonies and territories) and the exclusion of essays on American literature (another colonial legacy) from consideration in the book. I regret that my efforts to solicit essays on the significance of "Black British" writing to canonical reevaluation were unsuccessful.

3. See, for example, the essays in part 1 ("What Do Feminist Critics Want? The Academy and the Canon") of Elaine Showalter's *New Feminist Criticism: Essays on Women, Literature, Theory,* Annette Kolodny's "Integrity of Memory: Creating a New Literary History of the United States," and Christine Froula's "When Eve Reads Milton: Undoing the Canonical Economy." Bell Hooks's *Feminist Theory from Margin to Center* and Hazel Carby's *Reconstructing Womanhood: The Emergence of the Afro-American Novelist* illustrate the importance of race and class as well as gender to the construction of the canon. Carby criticizes feminists for not theorizing the significance of race in the discussion of the role of gender in literary production and reception.

4. Weimann also argues that in modern times—by this he means since the Renaissance—the "social representativeness" of art has diminished, as evidenced in works like Flaubert's *Bouvard et Pécuchet* or Mann's *Tonio Kröger.* He charts the process of the artist becoming more isolated from "the material productions and the social mode of economic appropriation in bourgeois society" (436). Although Weimann narrows too quickly the implications of his thesis to the theme of the alienated artist in fiction, he does have some interesting things to say about the specificity of modernist versions of the erosion of representativeness in its link to an "erosion of representational form" (441). Of course, as Shari Benstock and other feminist critics of modernism have argued, the very homogenizing of modernism is itself an intellectual act of colonization that elides the problem of gender. Benstock believes that tropes of alienation, for example, need to be examined in relation to gender. She also contends that female modernists experience and textualize expatriation and exile differently from male modernists (see "Expatriate Modernism: Writing on the Cultural Rim").

5. For an interesting analysis of social processes and the individual talent from a different point of view, see John Rodden's *The Politics of Literary Reputation: The Making and Claiming of 'St. George' Orwell.*

6. One might add here that the dismantling of communist regimes in Eastern Europe suggests that the Ideological State Apparatus in these countries has been more complicated and less monolithic than Western observers have understood.

7. Gayatri Spivak has theorized the relation between feminism and postcolonial analysis, accusing feminist criticism of reproducing the axioms of imperialism by the exclusion of the native female in the "soul making" of the "first-world" white female (see "Three Women's Texts and a Critique of Imperialism" [245] and "Imperialism and Sexual Difference"). For forceful critiques of Spivak's position, see Benita Parry's "Problems in Current Theories of Colonial Discourse" and Laura E. Donaldson's "The Miranda Complex: Colonialism and the Question of Feminist Reading." See also David Lloyd's *Nationalism and Minor Literature: James Clarence Mangan and the Emergence of Irish Cultural Nationalism* for a discussion of the way the discourse of nationalism may in fact reinscribe the central cultural values of the dominant power that the nationalism seeks to displace. Specifically, Lloyd looks at the way Irish nationalism maintained the discourse of British imperialism (2).

8. Weimann puts it in a more Marxist light when he speaks of the "use" and "exchange" values to be considered in all acts of appropriation and goes on to say: "The process of making certain things one's own becomes inseparable from making other things (and persons) alien, so that the act of appropriation must be seen always to involve not only self-projection and assimilation but also alienation through expropriation" (434). Like Deleuze and Guattari, however, Weimann fails to account for the effect of gender, class, and race on this alienation and on the "crisis of representativeness" that he sees as intensifying in the modern period.

9. See Mary Lynn Broe and Angela Ingram, eds., *Women's Writing in Exile,* and particularly Benstock's essay "Expatriate Modernism," for discussions of women's metaphoric and material cultural exile.

10. This deconstruction, however, engenders other questions about political efficacy and the role of discourse as social praxis. See, for example, Parry's reading of Bhabha and Spivak in "Problems in Current Theories of Colonial Discourse." Parry worries that the deconstruction of the opposition between the discourses of colonized and colonizer is potentially a denial of the "radical force of transgressive appropriations in a reverse discourse that contests the master text on its own terrain" (46).

Works Cited

Batsleer, Janet, with Tony Davies, Rebecca O'Rourke, and Chris Weedon. *Rewriting English: Cultural Politics of Gender and Class.* London and New York: Methuen, 1985.

Benstock, Shari. "Expatriate Modernism: Writing on the Cultural Rim." In Broe and Ingram, 19–40.

Berubé, Michael. *Tolson, Pynchon, and Institutional Criticism.* Ithaca: Cornell University Press, forthcoming.

Bhabha, Homi K. "The Other Question: Difference, Discrimination and the Discourse of Colonialism." In *Literature, Politics and Theory: Papers from the Essex Conference, 1976–84.* Ed. Francis Barker et al. London and New York: Methuen, 1986, 148–72.

——. "Sly Civility." *October* 34 (Fall 1985): 71–80.

Bloom, Allan. *The Closing of the American Mind: How Higher Education Has Failed Democracy and Impoverished the Souls of Today's Students.* New York: Simon and Schuster, 1987.

Bourdieu, Pierre. "Flaubert's Point of View." *Critical Inquiry* 14 (Spring 1988): 539–62.

Broe, Mary Lynn, and Angela Ingram, eds. *Women's Writing in Exile.* Chapel Hill and London: University of North Carolina Press, 1989.

Carby, Hazel. *Reconstructing Womanhood: The Emergence of the Afro-American Novelist.* New York: Oxford University Press, 1987.

Cheney, Lynne. "Humanities in America: Report to the President, the Congress, and the American People." Washington, D.C.: National Endowment for the Humanities, 1988.

Dasenbrock, Reed Way. "What to Teach When the Canon Closes Down: Toward a New Essentialism." In *Reorientations: Critical Theories and Pedagogies.* Ed. Bruce Henricksen and Thaïs E. Morgan. Urbana: University of Illinois Press, 1990, 63–76.

Deleuze, Gilles, and Felix Guattari. "What Is a Minor Literature?" In *Kafka: Toward a Minor Literature.* Trans. Dana Polan. Minneapolis: University of Minnesota Press, 1986, 16–27.

Donaldson, Laura E. "The Miranda Complex: Colonialism and the Question of Feminist Reading." *Diacritics* 18 (Fall 1988): 65–77.

Franklin, Phyllis, ed. *Profession 88.* New York: MLA, 1988.

Froula, Christine. "When Eve Reads Milton: Undoing the Canonical Economy." *Critical Inquiry* 10 (Dec. 1983): 321–48.

Gramsci, Antonio. *Selections from the Prison Notebooks of Antonio Gramsci.* Ed. Quintin Hoare and Geoffrey Nowell Smith. New York: International Publishers, 1971.

Green, Martin. *Dreams of Adventure, Deeds of Empire.* New York: Basic Books, 1979.

Hirsch, E. D., Jr. *Cultural Literacy: What Every American Needs to Know.* Boston: Houghton Mifflin, 1987.

Hooks, Bell. *Feminist Theory from Margin to Center.* Boston: South End Press, 1984.

Irigaray, Luce. *Speculum of the Other Woman.* Trans. Gillian C. Gill. Ithaca: Cornell University Press, 1985.

Jameson, Fredric. *Fables of Aggression: Wyndham Lewis, the Modernist as Fascist.* Berkeley and Los Angeles: University of California Press, 1979.

Kaplan, Caren. "Deterritorializations: The Rewriting of Home and Exile in Western Feminist Discourse." *Cultural Critique* 6 (Spring 1987): 187–98.

Kolodny, Annette. "The Integrity of Memory: Creating a New Literary History of the United States." *American Literature* 57 (1985): 291–307.

Levine, George, et al. *Speaking for the Humanities.* ACLS Occasional Paper No. 7. Washington, D.C.: American Council of Learned Societies, 1989.

Lloyd, David. "Genet's Genealogy: European Minorities and the Ends of the Canon." *Cultural Critique* 6 (Spring 1987): 161–85.

——. *Nationalism and Minor Literature: James Clarence Mangan and the Emergence of Irish Cultural Nationalism.* Berkeley and Los Angeles: University of California Press, 1987.

McGann, Jerome J. *Social Values and Poetic Acts: The Historical Judgment of Literary Work.* Cambridge: Harvard University Press, 1988.

Parry, Benita. "Problems in Current Theories of Colonial Discourse." *Oxford Literary Review* 9, nos. 1–2 (1987): 27–58.

Renza, Louis A. *"A White Heron" and the Question of Minor Literature.* Madison: University of Wisconsin Press, 1984.

Robinson, Lillian S. "Treason Our Text: Feminist Challenges to the Literary Canon." In Showalter, 105–21.

Rodden, John. *The Politics of Literary Reputation: The Making and Claiming of 'St. George' Orwell.* New York: Oxford University Press, 1989.

Showalter, Elaine, ed. *The New Feminist Criticism: Essays on Women, Literature, Theory.* New York: Pantheon Books, 1985.

Sinfield, Alan. *Literature, Politics, and Culture in Postwar Britain.* Berkeley and Los Angeles: University of California Press, 1989.

Spivak, Gayatri Chakravorty. "Imperialism and Sexual Difference." *Oxford Literary Review* 8, nos. 1–2 (1986): 225–40.

——. "Three Women's Texts and a Critique of Imperialism." *Critical Inquiry* 12 (Autumn 1985): 243–61.

——. "Scattered Speculations on the Question of Value." *In Other Worlds: Essays in Cultural Politics.* New York and London: Routledge, 1988, 154–75.

Trilling, Lionel. *Beyond Culture.* New York: Viking, 1965.

Weimann, Robert. "Text, Author-Function, and Appropriation in Modern Narrative: Toward a Sociology of Representation." *Critical Inquiry* 14 (Spring 1988): 431–47.

Zavarzadeh, Mas'ud, and Donald Morton. "Theory Pedagogy Politics: The Crisis of 'The Subject' in the Humanities." *boundary 2* 15, nos. 1–2 (Fall 1986/Winter 1987): 1–22; rpt. *Theory/Pedagogy/Politics: Texts for Change.* Urbana: University of Illinois Press, 1991, 1–32.

PART 1

The Politics of Genre

LILLIAN S. ROBINSON

Canon Fathers and Myth Universe

In the subtext of these remarks are two questions that, together, constitute the pretext for what follows. The first of these questions is that of the reader who asks, *What the hell does that title mean, anyway: Canon Fathers and Myth Universe?* Well, it refers to the generally patriarchal literary canon, the literally patriarchal biblical one that is the source of the canon metaphor, the Fathers of the Church, whose patristic writings include the bases of canon law, the Anglican cathedral clergy, whose title is "canon" and who may be addressed as "Father," and, of course, the military imagination, with its fecund visions of can(n)on fodder. And then there are the notions of a universal myth, the *dominant* myth of a human universal that turns out to be male, and the sexist international competition for Miss Universe. My title is at once the portmanteau that contains all that conceptual baggage and the background upon which the essay itself is projected.

The other question in my sub- and pre-text is one that I have been asking myself with increasing insistence whenever I accept an invitation to give a guest lecture under the aegis of a Department of English or Comparative Literature. Crudely expressed (which is exactly how it *is* expressed in the depths of my consciousness), my question goes: *Shall I choose a subject in feminist criticism or in "regular" criticism?*

This is a genuine question. On the one hand, my reputation and intellectual identity have both been informed by my work as a feminist critic. But the invitation is frequently at the instance of a search committee, as part of the hiring process. As a professional who is not gainfully employed, ought I not show that I can do regular criticism too? So the question is heartfelt and authentic. Yet it horrifies me. For criticism should not be served, like coffee, in "regular" and "variant" versions. In fact, though, depending on the region of this country in which you order it, "regular" coffee is interpreted as meaning that the cream has been added or, conversely, that it has not. (Regular, that is, is the opposite of both black and white—depending on where you stand.) Surely, I have been telling myself, I can construct an argument to show why, at this time, the proper project of "regular" criticism is the one with the feminism *in* it.

In the context in which it originated, my project was clearly something of a peace initiative, an attempt to demonstrate that feminist criticism is not fundamentally different from (and hence in no way a threat to) dominant critical modalities. In its evolution, however, that irenic effort asserted its true identity, coming to resemble a declaration of permanent difference, if not precisely of war, more than the patching-over I intended. For I find that, despite the most pacific intentions, I am still asking to what extent a feminist perspective necessarily challenges all the previous assumptions and conclusions of the critical tradition.

It is on this basis that I inaugurated the Visiting Humanities Chair I occupied at Albright College a few years ago by delivering a lecture entitled "Why Studying Women Means Studying Everything." The anecdotes with which I began that lecture, although they are drawn from other fields, have a special pertinence to the study of literature. Despite that global title, these anecdotes deal modestly enough with my nephew Ian and the elephant seals. They are two distinct stories, but both have their ramifications, and those ramifications turn out to touch each other at a number of points.

When Ian was a teenager, I was invited from Paris to New York for a series of interviews and took advantage of that time for several marathon work sessions with my collaborators on the book *Feminist Scholarship: Kindling in the Groves of Academe.*[1] I was accompanied on my travels by my infant son, who acquired three new teeth in the two weeks we spent in America. As you can imagine, I was much in need of and very grateful for the heroic hours of babysitting provided by Ian and his younger brother. In order to help me in this way, Ian had to refuse requests for his services from his regular clients. He expatiated to me on the relative thickness of blood and water. Then, referring to the neighbor he'd just turned down for the second or third time that week, he added, "Besides, your work is more important than hers. She's just writing some book about women in the French Revolution." Reluctant as I would have been to lose or even share my sitter, I had to know: Why was he so prepared to dismiss this work? "Well," he explained, "it can't be very important. I mean, *I* never heard of any women in the French Revolution!"[2] In the fine tradition of child psychology represented by Ring Lardner's line " 'Shut up,' I explained," *I* explained at the top of my lungs that it was precisely to prevent fourteen-year-old smart asses from being so sure that women were absent from the great events of history that such intellectual work *was* important. This story turns out to have a range of applications to literary study, and I shall discuss some of them shortly.

First, however, the elephant seals. An elephant seal, which I once heard a lecturer describe as looking, in motion, like a cross between a walrus and a waterbed, belongs to a species of belatedly protected wildlife that lives in the Pacific Ocean. Every January, they all come up to Año Nuevo Beach near Santa Cruz, California, and to an island just off its shore, to mate. Each year, thousands of human visitors descend on Año Nuevo in a spirit of learned voyeurism to find out about the elephant seals and their environment. The actual mating takes place on the island, so it is something of an exaggeration to say, as people tend to, "We're going to see (or *watch*) the elephant seals mate." What you do see are seals, asleep, tending their young, or galumphing about, and sometimes interacting with one another. To interpret this set of observations and particularly the interactions, there is an army of volunteer docents, as well as a mass of posters, bulletin boards, and fliers. What emerges from the surfeit of natural history is a picture of male elephant seals fighting it out for dominance over one another in order to be able to control territory and hence to control females. The largest, most aggressive, and dominant males, we are told, win big harems for the mating season; those who are less so get less space and fewer females in the harem; and the adolescents—old enough to mate but not large enough to compete—join the pups and the wimps in hanging out on the beach. Elephant seal behavior that may appear random, playful, or at least neutral to the lay observer is invariably characterized in terms of this rigid lexicon of dominance, hierarchy, territory, and harems.[3]

Now, I have been to see the elephant seals a number of times, and my irritation was at first inflamed by the racist description of the Indians who used to inhabit that section of the coast, a racism presented in the same blandly factual tone as the ecology lecture. (They "disappeared," we were told, but their mysterious evanescence was no great loss, for they were not particularly "interesting" Indians. Lacking a sense of history, it seems, they "had no culture" worth speaking of!) It was this rhetoric that made me compare what was said and written, which is to say *interpreted,* about the elephant seals—as text, if you will—with what could actually be observed. I concluded that all that really can be stated, more humbly but far more honestly, about the elephant seals is that they do come back to Año Nuevo to mate and that not much is really understood about their behavior, their motives, or their community. Perhaps one could add that male elephant seals seem to feel a need for a lot of space around them at mating time and that females prefer to be closer together at that time, as well as at the subsequent birthing of the pups. That is absolutely all we know, and the rest is projecting an oppressive anthropomorphic scenario on those poor creatures just trying to go about the business of reproducing their species.

Within the general framework of canon formation, re-formation, and reformation consequent upon the emergence of feminist criticism, I take the exemplary tale about my nephew and the revolutionary Frenchwomen to embody certain truths about the recovery of women's role in *literary* history. The elephant seals I take as emblematic of the problems—but also the opportunities—encountered when we bring women's reclaimed role into relation with the literary tradition as it has hitherto been perceived.

If you've never heard of any women in the French Revolution, this is a commentary on historical scholarship and even on historians, not on women in the French Revolution. That, of course, is the gist of what I yelled at my nephew. And so, too, in literary studies, where an impressive labor of intellectual reappropriation has begun to document the existence of a continuous tradition of women's writing in English, as well as in a number of other European literatures, a tradition extending well back into the centuries before the Industrial Revolution. Feminist scholarship has also challenged canonical definitions of literature itself by exploring women's private writings—letters, journals, personal memoirs—as literary texts. And it has sought access to mass female experience by considering popular genres produced by women for the female audience as a possible component of the newly acknowledged entity "women's literature." This inclusiveness, where there was once only a brief but oft-rehearsed litany of great names, has also meant a slow opening of the emerging female tradition to the voices of women of color, lesbians who write from and of that experience, and women writing out of the (literal) history of colonization and its aftermath.

But what about "the" canon, the regular canon, so to speak? How, to use my analogy from the study of history, do we *fit* the recently uncovered activities of women into the old story of the French Revolution? There are two quite different approaches to this question. The first is simply to add the new information about what women did to the body of information already in our possession. The second is to raise a more thoroughgoing question: How does what we have learned about the role of women *change* what we know or believe we know about the French Revolution in general? To situate it in the literary context: How does the newly uncovered material by seventeenth-century women affect our previous generalizations about the literature of the seventeenth century? And the answer to that question turns out to depend on essentially aesthetic considerations. As I point out elsewhere, it is really a question about

> the extent to which challenges to the male-dominated canon also entail challenges to the dominant stylistic, thematic, and aesthetic norms. As the archaeological aspect of feminist scholarship is pursued to good purpose, the academic world in general is increasingly likely to admit to us that, yes, after all, there were some women writing in the seventeenth century. But how many of them, we will be asked, we will ask ourselves, were any good? How many of them are good enough to deserve a place in an honest "coed" canon? How many are good enough to deserve to (deep breath) displace some gentleman on "the" syllabus for seventeenth-century literature? These are by no means rhetorical questions; their answers are not obvious. It all depends on what we mean by "good," on how far scholarship alone, simply uncovering the lost or never-heard voices of women of past centuries, suggests or even dictates a new set of aesthetic principles. How do we know that it is as good? Do we leave the definitions untouched and demonstrate, as is clearly possible in some cases, that a given woman meets all the existing criteria for goodness? Or do we implicitly or explicitly modify the aesthetic compact?[4]

These questions, significant as they are for how we think about, say, seventeenth-century poetry, become even more crucial as we consider the various nontraditional *kinds* of texts—the diaries, the sensational or domestic novels—that are part of the women's canon. Does the act of reclamation itself imply a new aesthetic? If so, what is that new aesthetic? What are its new limits?

Similarly, once women's literature includes the writing of women of color, generalizations about "the" female imagination have to be modified accordingly. When this happens, what about "the" canon as it is confronted with the sensibility of the formerly colonized, domestic or foreign? (Here, of course, we are approaching elephant seal territory.) Certainly, one's sense of the present world-historic moment in literature—in English, but also in other national traditions—is quite different depending on the degree to which one is open to this global perspective.

As it happens, moreover, students of women's role in the actual French Revolution have brought to light a most extraordinary series of texts, the *cahiers des plaintes et doléances* written on behalf of women as women. Remarkably modern documents, insofar as they raise issues that we today would label "sexual harassment" or "the right to a career," they are also a remarkable piece of eighteenth-century history, speaking as they do *of* the condition and *in* something very like the voice of the fishwife, the flower seller, the laundress of that period.[5] Unlike the cahiers prepared by males familiar with legal forms and conventions, these documents manage to deal with issues as various as the nature of citizenship, the rights of illegitimate children, and the adulteration of laundry soap, maintaining all the while a clear focus on the connections between and among them in creating the lives of women.[6]

My own impulse would be to admit these documents as women's literature, thus making my French Revolution anecdote part of *my* critical text rather than a metaphor stretched in a number of different directions. But when women's literature starts including the previously inarticulate, the semiliterate, the consumer of popular literature, the literature she consumes, and the writing she does on the basis of that "bad" stylistic model, it offers a challenge to "the" canon. It is a challenge to open its own frontiers not only to excluded social groups but to the widest range of expression of those groups' experience. The result would be to see our whole past, the seventeenth and eighteenth centuries, for starters, as experienced authentically by two sexes and all classes, or our present moment as experienced by all sorts of people with very different relations to the dominant culture and the fact of dominance. And it would be to understand this seeing as a legitimate part of our activity in the world of literary interpretation, not belonging to some other mode of apprehension outside the proper boundaries of criticism.

And here we are right down on the beach with the elephant seals, trying to determine how many of the truths about our culture that we have absorbed can survive such an intellectual upheaval. The confusion starts, of course, with that word *our,* for, as Jane Flax has succinctly put it, "only recently have scholars begun to consider the possibility that there may be at least three histories in every culture—'his,' 'hers,' and 'ours.' 'His' and 'ours' are generally assumed to be equivalents."[7] What I have been doing in questioning that equivalency is to imply the existence of something very like the Outsiders' Society that Virginia Woolf unforgettably creates in *Three Guineas.* My assumption is that the logic of feminist scholarship and criticism, because they invariably bring one social category, that of gender, into relation with traditional critical categories, necessarily entails rethinking the entire literary tradition in order to place centrally into it not only an entire excluded sex—which is an enormous enough task—but also excluded classes, races, national groups, sexual minorities, and ideological positions. (I have also felt free, for the purposes of this ideal system, to ignore the congruences *and the conflicts* between and among the various groups defined by their enforced cultural marginality.) What this means is a more truly comparative literature, one that could, in fact, comfortably be called *our* literature, rather than allowing the universe of cultural expression to remain, in the words of the Nigerian social critic Chinweizu, "the West and the rest of us."[8]

But, as I have indicated, feminist criticism can approach the traditional standards for canonicity, which are supposed to constitute "our" common aesthetic, either by demonstrating how the female tradition conforms to that aesthetic or by challenging the aesthetic itself. Similarly, in speaking of those previously excluded from elite definitions of culture, we ought to recognize where those groups both do and do not partake of "the" tradition. It is this question, both sides of it, that has impelled me to consider the myths that recur in the Western (which is to say, the white Euro-American male, high-cultural) literary tradition. I am principally concerned with them *as* part of literature, that is, not so much as archetypes as *stories* that get told over and over and whose retellings according to the imperatives of different generations depend on the long history of previous tellings.

From this point of view, as you switch perspectives from "insiders" to "outsiders," you note different priorities and preoccupations. Women writers, for instance, do not compulsively retell the history of the Trojan War and its aftermath, not even adapting the myth to fit female conditions. Indeed, in a brilliant paper at the 1984 MLA convention, Carolyn Heilbrun contrasted the literary projects of Joyce and Woolf, citing *Ulysses* as the closing off, in our century's terms, of one myth, while Woolf's work opened new mythopoeic areas for women. In a simpler vein, I find it impossible to imagine *The Odyssey au féminin* because, in the travels of any female, the sexual question looms larger and creates new difficulties of its own. Whom Does She Sleep With? becomes so central as to block out all the other questions such a myth is supposed to answer. It may be that Erica Jong has son ething like *The Odyssey* in mind as she serializes the adventures of Isadora Wing, particularly in *Parachutes and Kisses,* which involves the artist's wanderings and her search for identity through reclamation of the life of the dead artist-patriarch, her grandfather. But Jong's obsessive answering and answering the Whom-Does-She-Sleep-With question obscures the rest for us and makes all her work at least as picaresque as her intentional eighteenth-century pastiche *Fanny*. Meanwhile, for most women writers, the Ulysses myth has proved even less useful, remaining essentially external to any central female project.

However, certain words, forms, and stories from the insiders' tradition *have* been usefully appropriated by the outsiders, and transformed in the process. When the Nigerian novelist Chinua Achebe told us in the very title of his first novel that *Things Fall Apart,* he meant things quite different from what Yeats meant in *his* colony. The use of that title signaled a simultaneous joining of the dominant tradition and an appropriation of it to different needs. The final irony in this deeply ironic novel is that it ends with the colonial district commissioner contemplating *his* eventual text. Speaking of the central character, the last *African* voice in the novel has "ferociously" told him: "That man was one of the greatest men in Umuofia. You drove him to kill himself; and now he will be buried like a dog." Then the speaker's "voice trembled and choked his words." The administrator, by contrast, thinks that the hero's story "would make interesting reading. One could almost write a whole chapter on him. Perhaps not a whole chapter but a reasonable paragraph, at any rate. There was so much else to include, and one must be firm in cutting out details. He had already chosen the title of his book, after much thought: *The Pacification of the Primitive Tribes of the Lower Niger.*"[9] Achebe ends his novel just here, but, in taking his title where and as he does and adapting the novel both to the external conditions and the inner life of a member of one of those "primitive tribes," he shows us who may *really* have "the last word."

To take a more elaborate case, John Gay's *The Beggar's Opera* includes some sharp social commentary. After all, toward the end, the Beggar comments that, "Had the Play remain'd, as I at first intended, it would have carried a most excellent Moral. 'Twould have shown that the lower Sort of People have their Vices in a degree as well as the Rich: And that they are punish'd for them."[10] But Gay's work, for all its intentional reversals, finally remains so securely inside the formal and ideological guidelines of the canon as to be able to play with them. Brecht's *Threepenny Opera* extends these limits considerably in adapting Gay's story to social relations after the Industrial Revolution and by considering those conditions from a perspective that is at once proletarian and experimental. These changes are part of the generational reformulation of a familiar story. To the extent that this story about class, sexuality, power, and reversed expectations claims that status, Brecht's representation re-presents a familiar *myth*. But Brecht is by now securely part of the European canon, too.

The noncanonical stage of the process occurs when Wole Soyinka transports Macheath and Polly to Nigeria in his *Opera Wonyosi*, combining them with traditional African and contemporary political elements to make a searing commentary on neocolonial dictatorships. With "Mack the Knife" playing in the background, Dee-Jay, the narrator, opens the play with a rap on its title:

> One time we called it the Way-Out Opera—for short, Opera Wayo. Call it the Beggar's Opera if you insist—that's what the whole nation is doing—begging for a slice of the action.
> ... You know what, why don't you just make up your own title as we go along because, I tell you brother, I'm yet to decide whether such a way-out opera should be named after the Beggars, the Army, the Bandits, the Police, the Cash-madams, the Students, the Trade-unionists, the Alhajis and Alhajas, the Aladura, the Academicas, the Holy Radicals, Holy Patria[r]chs and Unholy Heresiarchs—I mean man, in this way-out country everyone acts way out. Including the traffic. Maybe we should call it, the Trafficking Opera. Which just complicates things with trafficking in foreign exchange.[11]

As Dee-Jay segues into an Africanized and overtly political version of the familiar lyrics, we are left to realize that the "opera" in fact has none of those proposed titles but rather is named for "the famous Wonyosi," an absurd and absurdly expensive lace version of an African *agbada*, which is to serve as the emperor's (literal) new clothing.

As his play develops, it becomes apparent that Soyinka is simultaneously using and permanently altering the tradition, including the radical tradition, for he openly critiques Brecht's rigid class analysis in order to strengthen a position that is at once fiercely nationalist and what we in the Euro-American world would call liberal humanist. There is a sense in which Brecht, for all his formal iconoclasm and social radicalism, was a good son of his literary father, whereas Soyinka is a rebellious one, asserting a new and radically different reality.

Another example of what I mean might be the quest myth. Women of the metropolis and exotic peoples of both sexes often figure in quests, but as objects, not subjects. It is hard, in our cultural context, to imagine the female, rather than the male, serving as representative of the human spiritual norm, Everyone instead of Everyman, for the female, to us, remains Everywoman, and Everywoman is inevitably sexualized. Thus, in *Surfacing,* Margaret Atwood uses themes as old as the *Gilgamesh* epic, joining them with rituals from native Canadian Indian traditions, in an attempt to ally herself with *that* Outsider community, as well. Her quest as descent into the watery world becomes a metaphor for the fundamental female experience of childbirth—motherhood betrayed and finally accepted—creating a version of the thing that is new in an entirely different *dimension* of newness.

Dante recognized his debt to a long insiders' tradition when he created the special quest that is his *Commedia.* The role of Vergil both embodies and reflects the poet's sense of participation in a tradition. But Dante expands the tradition exemplified by Vergil's own use of the prophetic visit to the underworld by connecting human history and politics simultaneously to the largest spiritual forces in the universe and to the inner life of actual individuals. Those who have used Dante's themes have always built on this enlarged sense of the meaning of a journey to the world of the dead. In the twentieth century, the *Inferno* has spoken more directly to our inner life than either the *Purgatorio* or the *Paradiso.* When "outsider" writers make use of Dante's myth, therefore, it is not to take the tour of *any* part of the afterlife but to show us Hell transplanted to the here and now, the social here and now, and its consequent distortion of individual psyches.

I think, for instance, of the way the American left-wing novelist Sol Yurick gives us a Brooklyn hospital as Inferno in his *Fertig,* in which the indifference, incompetence, and cruelty that kill the protagonist's child are played out and recalled in a setting that is consciously modeled on Dante's imagery, from the symbolic beasts on down to the frozen center.[12] Gloria Naylor's novel *Linden Hills* has been criticized for adapting the "white male Christian myth" of the *Inferno* to her allegory of black bourgeois life. Why not use African or Afro-American symbolic systems, one reviewer asked, instead of that same old high European culture? If there is a flaw in *Linden Hills,* I would not locate it in Naylor's extraordinarily powerful rendering of Dante's hellish vision. These characters are living in Hell, some of them at its very depths, and it is only fitting that the objective image representing their Hell be drawn from the demonic white culture in which they are all so heavily implicated and which constitutes their damnation as surely as Dante's characters experience their sin and their suffering as a single, organically organized concept.[13]

Clearly, there are many ways of appropriating the insiders' charter myths, the ones that were always *supposed* to be universal, as long as one accepts a particular definition of the universal human. For women, as I have indicated, even white, economically privileged Western women, certain of those myths are more readily adapted than others. But it is more problematic to consider whether women writing in the Western tradition may be said to have a characteristic myth of their own. If they have, I believe it is not rooted in the bodily difference between the sexes but rather in the *social* experience of that bodily difference. More specifically, the myth resides in the cultural experience of being forcibly silenced and hence being left without access to language as a source of identity, a means of expression, or a modality of change.

Feminist writers and critics have adapted and retold the myth of Procne and Philomel as a representation of our condition. Jane Marcus's essay "Still Practice" is perhaps the most salient example of feminist critical theory built on this myth of women using the means available to them, speech denied, to tell of the brutal violation visited upon one of their number and on the sex as a whole.[14] Ovid tells us that Philomel, her tongue torn out by her rapist, makes a tapestry and sends it to her sister to show her what has happened. In *Titus Andronicus,* Shakespeare has Lavinia, who has had her hands chopped off as well as her tongue cut out, point with her stumps to the passage in the *Metamorphoses* that describes the rape of Philomel, using the text to explain her plight, and then, with her uncle's staff in her mouth, write the names of her own violators in the sand. To plunge from these sublime heights, another male author, John Irving, in *The World According to Garp,* gives us the actual experience of eleven-year-old Ellen James and the stupid, fanatical self-mutilation of the Ellen Jamesian feminists as complementary propositions in this same dialectic.

From Virginia Woolf's creation of Shakespeare's sister, equally gifted but born in a female body, to Tillie Olsen's discussion of motherhood and female creative incapacity in *Silences,* the emphasis on *not* writing, on being *prevented* from writing, underlies critical discussion of what is and has been written.[15] The next step in the theoretical process is for the female nontext to *become* the text, as in feminist treatments of Freud's *Dora.* As reflected in the lengthy bibliography to Bernheimer and Kahane's *In Dora's Case: Freud—Hysteria—Feminism,*[16] the obsession with this turn-of-the-century text, with its central *agon* between Freud and the hysterical adolescent girl who was his early patient, is not unlike the tradition's recurrent reference to classical myths. *Dora* may be our

Odyssey and our *Metamorphoses* in one. The reason for this recurrence is that the principal symptom of the sexually molested girl Freud called Dora was aphonia. Freud tried hard to put words in her mouth—a proceeding that could be construed as benevolent only by someone entirely unfamiliar with our English idioms. From Hélène Cixous on out, however, feminist creative artists, critics, analysts, and historians have wanted to give the young girl back her own voice—and, in so doing, give one to all of us.

One of the things Alice Walker achieves in *The Color Purple* is to supply a voice to the inarticulate in a more concrete but also more sophisticated way. At the start of the novel, Celie is fourteen years old, barely literate, and with neither the vocabulary nor, seemingly, the capacity to describe her experience of rape by the man she believes to be her father. The rapist's words, which serve as epigraph to the first letter and hence to Celie's beginning to speak—"You better not tell nobody but God. It'd kill your mammy"—constitute the profoundly ironic permission to take the rape and (as in the Philomel myth, *Titus Andronicus,* and the feminist recreations of *Dora*) create a text out of one's own pain and oppression, written in one's own blood, if necessary.[17] The epistolary form, one of the earliest narrative strategies for the novel, is here appropriated as a source of empowerment for a woman who has no access even to the words that properly name violated parts of her own body. Some of us have always had our suspicions of Pamela—or rather of Samuel Richardson, even though he does get the sex and class dynamics right. Celie shows us why our suspicions were justified, as, taking hold of that pen to write first to God, later to her sister in Africa, and finally to "Everything," she becomes the black woman entering a world where telling is an *event* and writing can make something happen.

As the woman whose tongue is ripped out may find an unmutilated sister to tell her story, the woman writer at her best feels her hand guided, like Alice Walker's, by the woman who cannot write her own story because she cannot write at all. As long as, according to UNESCO, 80 percent of the world's illiterates are women, this is not a piece of pretentious rhetoric but a true responsibility. When the woman writer writes within the boundaries of what we already have been taught to recognize as literature, using, even participating in, traditional canonical forms and myths, while asserting the specifically female myth, she surely extends our *common* literary heritage.

It is hard to disagree with Audre Lorde's much-cited dictum that the Master's tools will never dismantle the Master's house.[18] But people have to live in a house, not in a metaphor. Of *course* you use the Master's tools if those are the only ones you can lay your hands on. Perhaps what you can do with them is to take apart that old mansion, using some of its pieces to put up a far better one where there is room for all of us. One where no one asks me and I need not ask myself, as I talk about its fine proportions and human significance, whether I'm engaging in feminist criticism or the real thing.

Notes

1. Ellen Carol DuBois, Gail Paradise Kelly, Elizabeth Lapovsky Kennedy, Carolyn W. Korsmeyer, and Lillian S. Robinson, *Feminist Scholarship: Kindling in the Groves of Academe* (Urbana, Ill., 1985). The intellectual difficulties of collaboration were enhanced and complicated for us by the fact that, at no time after we decided to write a book "together," did all five of us live in the same place. Ellen Messer-Davidow comments on the almost uniquely collective nature of this venture in "The Philosophical Bases of Feminist Literary Criticism," *New Literary History* 19 (1987–88): 102.

2. A version of this anecdote appears, with different applications, in my article "Feminist Criticism: How Do We Know When We've Won?" *Tulsa Studies in Women's Literature* 3, no. 1/2 (Spring/Fall 1984): 143–51; rpt. in *Feminist Issues in Literary Scholarship,* ed. Shari Benstock (Bloomington, 1987), 141–49.

3. The analogous and more destructive generalizations about *and from* the behavior of apes have begun to be roundly challenged by such feminist primatologists as Sarah Blaffer Hrdy. I do not know whether revisionist arguments are also being advanced in the case of the elephant seals.

4. Robinson, "Feminist Criticism," 147.

5. *Cahiers de doléances des femmes en 1789 et autres textes* (Paris, 1981). The best source in English is *Women in Revolutionary Paris, 1789–1795.* Ed. and trans. Darline Gay Levy, Harriet Branson Applewhite, and Mary Durham Johnson (Urbana, Ill., 1979). See also Paule-Marie Duhet, *Les femmes et la révolution: 1789–1794.* Collection Archives (Paris, 1971). Duhet points out here and in her preface to the documents in the *Cahiers de doléances des femmes* collection that there are also a number of (readily distinguishable) "false" cahiers, petitions, and so on, purporting to have female authors, and she comments on the various motives—often satirical, conservative, antifeminist, or anticlerical—behind this widespread assumption of the female persona. One distinction Duhet makes between real women and their impersonators is that: "Les femmes ont trop à dire.... elles ne peuvent pas prendre la distance que suppose le maniement sarcastique de l'écriture. Leurs textes sont toujours marqués par une impatience, une indignation retenues, un souci de dominer les maux présents en y portant remède" ("Women have too much that needs saying.... they can't achieve the

distance presupposed by sarcastic handling of the written word. Their texts are marked by an impatience, a restrained indignation, a concern to surmount present evils by finding a remedy for them" [16, my translation]*).*

6. See, e.g., in *Cahiers:* Anonymous, "Du sort actuel des femmes," 115–23; Madame Grandval, "Pour les droits des enfants naturels," 151–57; and "Doléances des blanchisseuses et lavandières de Marseille," 43–46.

7. Jane Flax, "Postmodernism and Gender Relations in Feminist Theory," *Signs* 12, no. 4 (Summer 1987): 629.

8. Chinweizu, *The West and the Rest of Us: White Predators, Black Slavers, and the African Elite* (New York, 1975).

9. Chinua Achebe, *Things Fall Apart* (New York, 1959), 214, 215.

10. John Gay, *The Beggar's Opera,* 3.16.24–26, in *Dramatic Works.* Ed. John Fuller (Oxford, 1983), II, 64.

11. Wole Soyinka, *Opera Wonyosi* (Bloomington, 1981), 1 (scene 1).

12. Sol Yurick, *Fertig* (New York, 1966).

13. Gloria Naylor, *Linden Hills* (New York, 1985). Naylor herself offers a more dialectical view of the matter. When I mentioned the "white-male-Euro-Christian" critique to her in a public discussion at the University of Pennsylvania in March 1986, she asked, as a former comparative literature graduate student at Yale, who the critics are to say Dante is *not* part of her "own" culture!

14. Jane Marcus, "Still Practice, A/Wrested Alphabet: Toward a Feminist Aesthetic," *Tulsa Studies in Women's Literature* 3, no. 1/2 (Spring/Fall 1984): 79–97; rpt. in *Feminist Issues in Literary Scholarship,* 79–97.

15. Virginia Woolf, *A Room of One's Own* (1929; rpt., New York, 1959); Tillie Olsen, *Silences* (New York, 1978).

16. *In Dora's Case: Freud—Hysteria—Feminism.* Ed. Charles Bernheimer and Claire Kahane (New York and London, 1985), 277–80.

17. Alice Walker, *The Color Purple* (New York, 1982), 11.

18. Audre Lorde, "The Master's Tools Will Never Dismantle the Master's House" (1980), in *This Bridge Called My Back: Writings by Radical Women of Color.* Ed. Cherríe Moraga and Gloria Anzaldúa (Watertown, Mass., 1981), 98–101.

CELESTE M. SCHENCK

"Corinna Sings"
Women Poets and the Politics of Genre

The first half of my title contains a triple allusion, and a polemic. Those who know the original Elizabethan poem by Thomas Campion will remember, the narcissism of all lyric utterance notwithstanding, that Corinna is only ostensibly the subject of that poem. In fact the poem is about the male poet's response to Corinna's lute playing, for which, in the end, her lute playing is at best the accompaniment (*Works* 28). When Adrienne Rich embeds the Campion line in her famous 1960 poem "Snapshots of a Daughter-in-Law," she makes clear what the male poet sees in Corinna's singing (something like, You're so beautiful when you play the lute), and makes explicit the depth of Corinna's exile from her own subjectivity as a singer, from the language and forms of poetic tradition:

> When to her lute Corinna sings
>   neither words nor music are her own;
>   only the long hair dipping
>   over her cheek, only the song
>   of silk against her knees
>   and these
>   adjusted in reflections of an eye.
>   (*Fact* 36–37)

Rich's representation of Corinna characterizes the situation of the woman poet until well into this century. As Ezra Pound put it to his fiancée, the poet H.D., as late as 1915: "You are a poem, though your poem's naught" (quoted by H.D., *End* 12). Corinna, as Rich tellingly repositions her, is not a maker of form but form itself, "adjusted in reflections" of the beholder's determining eye.

I intend my own invocation of the Campion-cum-Rich line to update both of these earlier versions. The "Corinna Sings" of my title is meant to mark a moment beyond both patriarchal objectification and feminist protest. In the work of some contemporary women poets Corinna sings exuberantly, often ironically, occasionally defiantly, not only with a sense of entitlement to "that most assertive, daring, and therefore precarious of modes for women: lyric poetry" (Gilbert and Gubar 582), but also with a marked sense of entitlement to its most exclusive of registers, its most elite of forms. The case of the epithalamium, a genre formally, ideologically, and thematically daunting to the female practitioner precisely because its conventional grammar calls for a bride-object, offers a chronology of the woman poet's gradual access to ceremonial forms: her response to the genre is, in short, the history of her literary "appearance" (Hartman 369), the chronicle of her coming to distinctive poetic voice.

The third allusion in my title is to a poet herself, the fifth-century Corinna, who has haunted me as Judith Shakespeare did Virginia Woolf. Propertius called her "antiqua Corinna" in an elegy in which he conflates her with a woman arousing her lover by her lyre playing, the very poem that seems to have inspired Campion's song (Propertius 2.3.22; in McCullough 63). The Corinna of Rich's poem, invoking both the ancient poet and Campion's siren, thus emblemizes the double exclusion of women from poetic tradition: by omission and (mis)representation (Montefiore 28). In fact we know a meager amount about the classical Corinna, except that she won (some sources say five times) in a poetry contest against Pindar. Pindar apparently called her a "sow" in retribution, blaming "ignorant judges" for the error (quoted in Snyder 7), and Pausanias thought she won because she was "at that time a remarkably good-looking woman" (Pausanias 9.22.2, in Edmonds 9). No more than a few tantalizing fragments of her work survive. I remember her in my title because she was a contender, because her work has not survived to prove that, and, most important for my purposes, because she seems *not* to have written in the contemporary tradition of intimate archaic love poetry. So far as specialists can tell, Corinna was a public poet who wrote choral songs intended for competitive performance at festivals. She may have been, although we will never know for certain, an epic poet; she was certainly a ceremonial poet. The affirmative "Corinna Sings" of my title answers a famous question in one of her few remaining fragments: "Will you sleep forever, Korinna?" (Barnstone 152).

Women poets' exile from the forms high poetry takes at various moments in literary history has been explained variously, "verse genres," in Gilbert and Gubar's words, "hav[ing] been even more thoroughly male than fictional ones" (68). Women writers able to make themselves at home in the house of prose were still exiles when it came to highly codified ceremonial poetry: barred access to forms like the epic, the elegy, the epithalamium, women poets have had necessarily to refuse, resist, and, when possible, reconstruct our essentially masculine Western lyric inheritance.[1] I would suggest that this exile has also to do with the upholding of an exclusionary generic practice, which I have found to be typical *of* and endemic *to* Western literary theory.

That brings me to the second half of my title: "Women Poets and the Politics of Genre."[2] First, literary genres, traditionally viewed as purely aesthetic markers, have been highly politicized (and by that I mean not only gendered but also class biased and racially marked) in the long history of Western literary criticism, a phenomenon that has had enormous implications for the banishment of women writers (among other marginalized groups) from the canon. Genres are not only fairly drenched in ideologies, they may also function as power-conferring agents. My second point follows polemically from the first: conceived of as a politicized space, genre might in fact be occupiable by women writers intent on reclaiming an authority withheld them. This may be what Gwendolyn Brooks intended when she wrote her Pulitzer Prize–winning *Annie Allen* in an elaborate sonnet-ballad, or what Marilyn Hacker reached for, choosing the sonnet sequence for her extended poetic narrative of a lesbian love affair, *Love, Death, and the Changing of the Seasons*. If we assume that women poets have been excluded from access to and participation in the Western canon, then the ways in which women speak in ceremonial registers, when and once they begin to use them, are crucial indices of literary historical, not to mention social and political, change. In short, the work of women poets forces us to address the patriarchal determination of genre theory more generally and to theorize a provisional way of thinking about genre that might enfranchise rather than exclude the work of women poets.

From the first, generic taxonomy—which may be said to be the obsessive and continuing preoccupation of Western genre theory—bore a political undertext: the hierarchical ordering of genres, which preoccupied Plato and Aristotle (and the whole mainstream of literary critics after them), rested upon much more than aesthetic judgment. Given, in fact, that "genres are so clearly implicated in the literary history and formal production they were traditionally supposed to classify and neutrally to describe" (Jameson 107), given that genres are, after all, cultural constructions themselves, they might be more usefully conceived as *loci* of conflict and contention rather than as ideal aesthetic types which transcendentally precede and predetermine the literary work. Although contemporary theory has all but effaced genre as a category of literary interest in favor of a borderless *écriture,* if we are to believe Fredric Jameson, generic perspectives are living something like a "return of the repressed" in current theory nonetheless, probably because they serve the Marxist, or for that matter feminist, critic as a marker of social and historical experience where it intersects with the ideology of form.

But if the history of genre has failed adequately to address its own politics, it has also been blind to its own gender inflection, an elision feminist critics have sought variously to redress. What I hope to question, in addition to the politics of classificatory systems more generally, is the way in which the textual productions of women poets have been misread, or worse, remained unread, because they do not conform to what are upheld as generic norms. In the particular case of epithalamium, because this genre is determined more definingly by its occasion—the celebration of a wedding—than by a specific formal prescription, the experiential component of its production cannot be separated from its formal evaluation. The asymmetries of female and male psychosexual development, and the very different social and political history of marriage as institution for women and men, underwrite and are in turn enforced by the literary representation of that difference. The epithalamium—a minor genre with folk ritual roots, "invented" by Sappho, developed lyrically and dramatically by Catullus, rendered rhetorical and allegorical by medieval poets, canonized by Spenser in the Renaissance, imitated closely by poets from John Donne to W. H. Auden and right up to the poet laureate Ted Hughes[3]—can be read so as to call into question the very issue of canonization it so canonically foregrounds. If, as Jameson suggests, "genre is essentially a socio-symbolic message" and "form is immanently and intrinsically an ideology in its own right," then the subsequent reappropriation of these, genre and form, in different historical contexts by different sexual and racial subjects will functionally reckon them into new forms in ways that necessitate the rethinking of form *and* genre (141).

First I will address the epithalamium's unique suitedness to a consideration of gender's impact on genre. Second, I will describe the almost elegiac response of women poets to the epithalamic genre as a remarkably consistent nuptial poetics of rape, rupture, and loss—the obverse of what this celebratory genre leads us to expect. This group of poems, incidentally, failing to measure up to generic norms, has been excluded from the epithalamic canon. Finally, I will read a group of contemporary poems that engage directly with the epithalamic genre for the ways in which they both articulate a new female subjectivity of the erotic and manifest a sense of entitlement to canonical forms. By way of conclusion, I will address the politics of my own generic choices, my own participation in the politics of canonicity.

Songs for the Bride

The ideological underpinnings of the traditional epithalamium include the following three supports: the genre exalts the patriarchal institution of marriage; it aims at the regulation of heterosexuality and the control of female sexuality by offering the "safety valve" of consummation under the canopy of the marriage bed; and third, as genres go, it is thunderously gendered.[4] To the extent that an epithalamium may be said to have a narrative, its narrative is fully masculine: it bears the impress of male psychosocial experience, traces the arc of masculine desire, celebrates in overtly bellicose terms the capture, conquest, and control of the feminine. The bride, in short, is no more than a marker in an otherwise Oedipal (male) story, and her version of the story—like Penelope's, like Eurydice's, like the Sphinx's—remains untold. A contemporary poem by Louise Glück succinctly captures the genre's ideology and the bride's silencing:

> That is what marriage is.
> I watch the tiny figure
> changing to a man
> as he moves toward her,
> the last light rings in his hair.
> I do not question
> their happiness. And he rushes in
> with his young man's hunger,
> so proud to have taught her that:
> his kiss would have been
> clearly tender—
>
> Of course, of course. Except
> it might as well have been
> his hand over her mouth.
>   (*Descending Figure* 30)

Here is Phyllis Janowitz's bride-centered but equally revealing scenario in a poem called "The Arrangement":

> She dreams a photographer
> comes to shoot her picture,
>   Lulu in her wedding dress,
> holding all those dead daisies
> and afraid to move. She sees
> he has no arms.
> She is
> speechless.

(Visiting Rites 19)

When Teresa de Lauretis finds a sadistic impulse beneath narrative, a battle of will and strength, victory and defeat, the imposition of masculine desire upon its object woman (quoting Mulvey 103, 131–33), and when Roland Barthes pairs Oedipal and marital possession of the female as the dependent causes of narrative, they might be speaking directly of the traditional epithalamium. The Classical wedding poem was traditionally a song sung outside (*epi*) the nuptial chamber (*thalamos*) upon the consummation of the union, in celebration of conquests won: Theocritus speaks of "the mighty spoils thou hast in battle won" (Tufte, *"High Wedlock"* 17); Claudian writes of "triumph's wares" and "conquered wealth" (*HW* 39–40); and later Ben Jonson will call the nuptial dance "Hymen's war" and Giambattista Marino will end his epithalamium with the image of a bloodied cloth, "proof of virginity, emblem of victory" (*HW* 150, 221). Even in Spenser's *Epithalamion*—a Renaissance nuptial ode written upon the occasion of the poet's own marriage, perhaps the most benign and beautiful nuptial poem in the tradition—the paradigmatic arrangement of orphic courtier-bridegroom, master at singing and master in the bridal chamber, and passive, voiceless, decked and wedded bride, inscribes a ceremony with familiar ritual overtones: an initiation ceremony that unself-consciously imprisons the bride ever more firmly in anonymity, a rite that makes of her, in short, a cipher (Spenser 579–84). In Spenser's canonical version, the poem runs the length of the day, includes twenty-four stanzas corresponding to each of the hours of the day, rouses, dresses, and then brings forth a bride virtually definable by her virginity, describes marriage ceremony and participants, evokes the richness and opulence of the bridal chamber, anticipates consummation of the union, pronounces a benediction, and finally ends with impregnation of the bride and projection forth of her issue into eventual sainthood. The genre often bears the overlay of historical allusion, allegorical significance, or cosmological symbolism because the marriage ritual—as the literary tradition continually exploits it—symbolizes in a series of parallel relations the wedding of man to woman, king to subjects, church to state, heaven to earth, even as it seems to deny hierarchy in its transcendental celebration of order and unity.

To localize and historicize the lyric epithalamium at various moments in literary history, we would need to insist upon the different but converging ideologies of marriage that underwrite the genre: the medieval idealization of Christian marriage as a figure for the mystical wedding of Christ and the church; the Renaissance management of social and sexual, not to mention political, tensions by means of the public form of holy matrimony; the late-capitalist fetishizing of bourgeois marriage; the Romantic, particularly Wordsworthian, investment in "spousal bliss" as a figure for what he fantasizes as an equal match between a feminized nature and the imposing mind of man. The entire movement of the epithalamium as genre, however, no matter what the period, is toward conservative resolution and closure. It is to this feature of the genre that Richard Cody refers when he writes that "all pastoral aspires to the condition of epithalamium" (Cody 171).

But how marriage achieves literary representation depends, as thoroughly in poetry as in narrative, upon who is telling the story. While ostensibly singing *for* the bride, male poet-celebrants tend to elide her distinct historical and psychological experience of marriage—at the very least an experience of violation (Chodorow, *Family Structure* 59), but just as often an occasion of separation and mourning which women poets record eloquently and poignantly. For all the seeming harmony of the genre as constituted by the masculine tradition, the story the traditional epithalamium leaves out is a violent one. The genre's social text is basically that of the traffic in women, the way in which women have functioned as objects of exchange under the conditions of the present sex/gender system. Most, including some written in this century, were written to commemorate actual political arrangements about which the brides were less than happy: the reigning peace between England and Holland in the fourteenth century, for example, was secured by the marriage of the Duke of Gloucester and the Countess of Holland, memorialized by John Lydgate (Tufte, *HW* 65).

Equally characteristic of the early epithalamium, and equally gender inflected, are a particular mocking, even sadistic tone, and a profusion of ribald jokes, allusions, and sexual taunts (called fescennine verses), which addressed to the bridegroom may correspond to and even functionally allay the masculine sexual anxiety aroused by the wedding night. But Puttenham, in his Renaissance treatise on genre, maintains that the "tunes of the songs were very loud and shrill, to the intent there might no noise be heard out of the bedchamber by the shrieking and outcry of the young damosell feeling the first forces of her stiff and rigorous young man" (quoted in Tufte, *Poetry of Marriage* 87). Even when the bride's own fears are articulated, as in the rare example of Catullus 62, the bridegroom has the last word, and all the power:

> Your virginity is not all your own—
> In part it belongs to your parents:
> A third part is your father's,
> A third part is given to your mother,
> Only a third part is yours.
> Do not fight with two
> Who have given their rights to son-in-law,
> Together with the dowry.
>
> (Tufte, *HW* 30)

Another gender-inflected convention of the traditional wedding poem is the blazon or catalog of the bride's physical attributes, a poetic figure that mediates fear of female sexuality by verbally dismembering the bride into her scattered, albeit sumptuous, parts. These ideal and unreal comparisons (hair like golden wires, eyes like sapphires, lips like rubies, teeth like pearls, etc.) so disembodied the beloved that Shakespeare was compelled to write a parody in the related genre of the sonnet: "My mistress' eyes are nothing like the sun" (Sonnet #130, 1315). Generally, however, the conventional epithalamium welcomes marriage—from the masculine point of view—as the completion of a compact, the handing over of title, the achievement of efficacy. Its narrative, to reinstate de Lauretis's valuation of that term, is the taking possession of the bride-object upon which the groom's own ascent to stature depends. The project is governed thoroughly by a simultaneous idealization and devaluation of the bride. When, for example, John Donne ends every stanza of his "Epithalamion made at Lincolnes Inne" with the refrain "To day put on perfection and a womans name," he exalts, of course, the virgin's spotlessness, but he also both hints bawdily at the impending male perfection of woman in the act of insemination and suggests the dependence of woman's identity upon a rite of passage into heterosexuality (3–6). His epithalamium ends with a brutal ritual disembowelling of the bride upon the "altar of love." When Richard Crashaw, in his baroque "Epithalamion," speaks of the "rich losse" in exchange of "dying maide" for "dawning wife," he puns brilliantly upon the "little" Elizabethan "death" of orgasm dependent upon the loss of innocence, but he does not do so from the frightened anticipatory vantage point of someone about to lose *hers* (44–49).

"We all know," as Adrienne Rich reminds us in "Writing as Re-Vision," "that there is another story to be told" (*Lies* 33–49). While women poets until recently have not, strictly speaking, written within the genre of the epithalamium (their access to the ceremonial genre having been curtailed by the form's gender inflection and by the restriction of public forms to male practitioners), their poems about marriage do constitute an alternative and important corpus of material. Between Sappho and the twentieth-century formal or mock-formal epithalamia I treat at length in this essay, few epithalamia were written by women poets; indeed, the few anthologies of epithalamia that exist include no women writers between Sappho and the modernists Gertrude Stein and Edith Sitwell, both of whom responded parodically to the form's implicit ideology. We do have, however, an enormously varied body of poetry on marriage that responds thematically, if not formally, to the topos. These poets' experience proves to be in some ways the counterpart of men's, and the contrast provides a useful starting point, although it is neither categorical nor universal. To the extent that psychology can contribute to a theory of genre—and here we must keep in mind Marianne Moore's caveat in "Marriage": "Psychology which explains everything / explains nothing, / and we are still in doubt" (19)—it does offer an explanation of the differences attendant upon gender from the outset of a child's life in a way that bears upon literary forms that attend life's ritual passages: from birth to cradle to grave. As predictably as male writers adopt the shopworn imagery of pen as penis, of writing as ejaculation, women—having experienced themselves as objects of writing—tend to associate with the page and with the experience of being marked upon. In her brilliant analysis of Isak Dinesen's "The Blank Page," Susan Gubar suggests that our metaphors of literary creation coincide with gender-specific experiences of sexuality: thus, as is strikingly evident in the case of the epithalamium, fear of defloration directs the forms of women's self-conception as much as it colors the forms of their writing (Gubar 73–94). The bloodied nuptial sheets *are* the women's texts in Dinesen's story. Arising from an different set of internalized relations, and a social experience of marriage distinct from that of men, women's epithalamia until very recently bespeak a view of marriage as a rite of wounding or violation, as an occasion for mourning broken bonds with female companions and mothers, and, when celebratory at all, as an experience of love more fluid, realistic, and evolving—less symbolic and platonized and transcendental than that manifest in the epithalamia of their male counterparts.

Songs [from] the Bride

Ever since Sappho's poignant wedding poems included an elegy for a lost hymen—"Am I still sad because of my lost maidenhead?" (Barnard 36; her fragment numbers follow in the text)—women poets have written differently of marriage, resisting by an array of strategies the conventional poetic treatment of that ceremony. Sappho's epithalamia—less intimate than her erotic lyrics, seemingly ritualized in their repetitions, and even fully ceremonial in the case of the fragment on the "Marriage of Hektor and Andromache"—have surprisingly survived censorship, probably because wedding poems have not tended to threaten and because the small corpus of poems written for her pupils' and friends' marriages sets the lesbian context of Sappho's corpus in a wider, reassuringly heterosexual context.[5] Additionally, the probable female audience of these poems made possible their idiosyncratically performative and even ceremonial existence.

For women poets after Sappho the audience of the ceremonial genres remained predominantly elite and male. They did, however, write nuptial poetry that paralleled the epithalamic genre, challenging the official story from outside its own exclusive borders. The so-called petticoat authors of the years 1660 to 1720 in England, for example, wrote a number of faintly sardonic poems on the institution of marriage and a range of laments associated with the leaving behind of female companions, alongside "individually appreciative poems to husbands" (Hampsten; in *Women's Studies* 26). Noteworthy among this nuptial poetry are Anne Finch's "The Unequal Fetters" and "A Tale," in which, despite her own happy marriage, she protests the "slender hold" of women in marriage:

> Silently suffering to the Grave
>   Must be our wretched fate.
> Eve when she made herself a slave
>   Determin'd all our fate.
>   (ed. Hampsten; in
>   *Women's Studies* 14)

Lady Mary Chudleigh's ceremonial address "To the Ladies" is similarly antiepithalamic:

> Wife and servant are the same,
> But only differ in the name:
> For when that fatal knot is tied,
> Which nothing, nothing can divide:
> When she the word *obey* has said,
> And man by law supreme has made,

Then all that's kind is laid aside,
And nothing left but state and pride:
Fierce as an Eastern prince he grows,
And all his innate rigor shows:
Then but to look, to laugh, or speak,
Will the nuptial contract break.
Like mutes she signs alone must make,
And never any freedom take:
But still be governed by a nod,
And fear her husband as her God:
Him still must serve, him still obey,
And nothing act, and nothing say,
But what her haughty lord thinks fit
Who with the power, has all the wit.
Then shun, oh! shun that wretched state,
And all the fawning flatt'rers hate:
Value your selves, and men despise,
You must be proud, if you'll be wise.

(Chudleigh 96)

Katherine Philips's reservations about marriage resulted in a similar epistle
to a lady: "An Answer to Another Persuading a Lady to Marriage"
(62). Aphra Behn's personal disappointments may have played a larger
role in her poetic choices than the general prohibition barring women's
access to the ceremonial genres in the seventeenth century. Her parodies
of domestic politics took antiepithalamic form in poems such as "The
Disappointment" and "A Pox of Foolish Politicks in Love." Later, Barrett
Browning's skepticism about marriage as institution took form in Aurora
Leigh's considered refusal of Romney's proposal.[6]

Sappho's epithalamia stand as precursors to this long line of antinuptial
poetry by women because even within her apparently unproblematic
wedding poems, based on humorous folk rituals, are poignantly resistant
fragments: In 27, after being asked to "share in games that the pink-ankled
/ Graces play, and / gold Aphrodite," a young girl proclaims resolutely "O
never! / I shall be a / virgin always." But most poignant are the Sapphic
epithalamia that mourn rather than celebrate the loss of the hymen. When
a bride asks sadly, "Virginity O / my virginity! / Where will you go when I
lose you?" a second voice, probably the hymen itself, responds, "I'm off
to a place I shall never come back from / Dear Bride! I shall never come
back to you" (32). Here is Sappho's elegy for a lost maidenhead: "like a

hyacinth in / the mountains, trampled / by shepherds until / only a purple stain / remains upon the ground" (34). For Sappho, and for the woman poet since Sappho, however, the conflation of death and loss of virginity is more than a poetic conceit. Emily Dickinson would later make the same equation in her poem "Born—Bridalled—Shrouded / In a Day . . . Is *this* —the way?" (#1072).

Rather than lifting the epithalamium into registers other than· the personal and amatory, female epithalamists use the genre to dramatize private rites about which they are infinitely more ambivalent. The Russian poet Bella Akhmadulina in "The Bride" feels both "lucky and poor," knowing her "white gown / Is stained with wine like blood"; both "terror and desire . . . loom in the forward hours" (197). Adrienne Rich finds "a knot of blood" "in the whiteness of the bridal web. / Little wonder the eye, healing, sees / for a long time through the mist of blood" ("The Knot," *Fact* 74). Contemporary Irish poet Nuala Archer describes "The Wedding Day" as a series of stark, pictorial, yet symbolic tableaux: a hunter pursues an albino deer through a white landscape, closing in for the kill—the "bow of stars," the "occult of red fur" against snow, the "paralysis thronging the eye" in the "flurry of leaves" (12–13). Olga Broumas has a poem titled "Bride" in which she rehearses the "old florid story of the blood, repeated wet vow and lament" (*Pastoral Jazz* 17). Sandra Hochman's "The Eyes of Flesh" is a poem of resistance to becoming "a wife": she claims to hate "this place / where we / erase / my childhood"; marriage for her "is where / deep / purposes are / broken / off" (*Masks!* 231–32). In "Bridal Piece," Louise Glück makes the Sapphic point most unequivocally of all: "I want / My innocence" (*Firstborn* 22). As the accretion of examples here is meant to demonstrate, women's poems about marriage are strikingly elegiac: they focus—in a manner fully unanticipated by the traditional epithalamium—on the experience and accommodation of bodily harm and loss.

The *locus classicus* of the marriage-as-death topos, and indispensable to a discussion of women's epithalamia, is the Persephone myth alluded to in the Hochman poem, dating at least as far back in its literary representation as the Homeric Hymn to Demeter (Athanassakis 1–15). What the Persephone story adds to the history of the epithalamium is a female narrative of initiation, albeit even after feminist revision a violent and disappointingly passive one. I will invoke later the counterstory of Psyche's marriage as a sequel and corrective to Persephone's: the contrast represents the two major kinds of poems women poets write about marriage. Roughly contemporary with Sappho's lyrics, the Homeric Hymn to

Demeter provides what is glaringly absent in the central Greek texts on the evolution of human identity, that is, as the writer Edna O'Brien puts it, a record of what Jocasta and Electra talk about when *they* meet at the crossroads ("A Conversation" 40). In this earliest of dramas of female identity, the only story in the Mediterranean to locate itself from the female point of view, marriage not only takes the form of rape, but it is crucially mediated through the maternal relationship. The greater symbiosis between daughter and mother in the ancient Greek world, between daughter and an extended network of female companions and caretakers, lends support to Nancy Chodorow's reflections upon mother-daughter dynamics. The poem begins in an all-female world where Persephone enjoys an innocent virgin state of near-fusion with the mother. The harmony of this pre-Oedipal paradise is shattered by the intrusion of the male in the form of an abductor, because the prerogative to give Persephone in marriage remains paternal: Zeus awards her, an object of exchange, to his brother, the god of the underworld. And Persephone participates in the abduction to the extent that she reaches eagerly for the narcissus/lure, associated with death, phallic power, and sexuality: by this act she is inscribed, as psychoanalytic critics would phrase it, into the Law of the Father, passing from the Imaginary of pre-Oedipal relations to the Symbolic of patriarchal culture. Marriage, then, resonates doubly for Persephone: it facilitates separation from the mother, but it necessitates excruciating loss of a sustaining bond. The poem ends with Persephone's rapturous return to her origin, the mother, by means of an uneasy solution: spending a third of the year with the rapist/lover/husband and two-thirds of the year with the mother/lover in a divided life illuminated by Chodorow's notion of women's suspension in a kind of "bisexual triangle," between mother and father, between homoeroticism and heterosexuality (191–93, 202).

Marriage cannot be greeted other than ambivalently in terms of the female maturational pattern elaborated by Chodorow and emblemized by the Persephone story. The most arresting contemporary poetic treatment of the daughter's division between two loves is that of Enid Dame in a poem called "Persephone." The first part of this poem sets up the daughter's desire to spend her life in her mother's kitchen,

> quietly watching
> her capable fingers
> build fires
> strip corn ears

crack warm eggs
against a blue bowl.

I wanted to be
a part of that room:

She wanted to remain within the contours, as the assonance no doubt
suggests, of that womb. In part two of this poem, at her mother's urging,
Persephone gets married:

I only went
on that blind date to please her.
The man was too old.
His fingers were stained.
Yet he promised
to bring me home safely.

Instead,
he brought me down here.

The only good thing
about this place
is, it's too boggy dark
to see what he looks like.

He says,
"You're my little girl now."
He smells like old clothes.
His body sprouts fingers
fatter than carrots.

They grip me knobbily.
He rocks up and down
like a leaky old boat
rocks on the ocean.

He shipwrecks inside me
every night.

When he kisses me
later,
I call him "Mama."   (60–63)

If, in fact, the girl's first love object, like the boy's, was the mother, then

Helen Deutsch's suggestion that girls, like boys, seek to marry their mothers is borne out by literary evidence. Even when women's poems about marriage do not explicitly name the mother as first lover, as Dame's does, they inevitably mourn the rupture of significant female bonds, focusing on the difference between women's time and marriage, the contrast between the pre-Oedipal and the postnuptial. Even as late in Greek culture as the third century B.C., Erinna's "Distaff" fragment mourns the loss of a friend to marriage by juxtaposing childhood memories with present grief (144–45). Katherine Philips's "To My Excellent Lucasia, on Our Friendship" is a kind of seventeenth-century answer to Erinna, choosing as it does to maintain the perfect "felicity" of female friendship in the face of marriage experienced as conquest: "No bridegroom's nor crown-conqueror's mirth / To mine compared can be: / They have but pieces of this earth, / I've all the world in thee" (61). In a poem called "Marriage," Mary Elizabeth Coleridge invokes the maiden's necessary death and records the lament of "thy merry sisters to-night forsaking," for "never shall we see thee, maiden, again" (215). In Michele Roberts's poem "Persephone Descends to the Underworld," the abducted bride is "crying loudly / for the mother and women lovers I leave behind" (91). And a contemporary "Epithalamion on the Marriage of My Middle Sister," by Megan Macomber, centers on the sadness of the "other two, left behind": "now you turn your white back to us," leaning toward "the one who barely shares your dais, his dark nerves racing toward a smile" (168).

Some epithalamia by women challenge the celebratory register of the genre by a subtle shift in tone alone. In these nuptial lyrics, sorrow, listlessness, yearning, elegiac regret, even boredom replace the hymeneal panegyric conventional to wedding poems. Louise Glück's "Bridal Piece" recalls a honeymoon over which an unnamed *he* presided: "plant[ing] us by / Water, . . . " and "lock[ing] our bedroll / In the trunk for laughs." "He had to have his way," she explains. While "the moon / Lurched like searchlights, like / His murmurings across my brain," she daydreams sadly of her lost "innocence," recalls her "family frozen in the doorway" and "their rice congeal[ing] / Around his car" (22). Her "Epithalamium" has the same airlessness to it, the same fear of violence, the same helpless submission to pattern and despair.

> Then begins
> the terrible charity of marriage,
> husband and wife

> climbing the green hill in gold light
> until there is no hill,
> only a flat plain stopped by the sky.
>
> *Here is my hand,* he said.
> But that was long ago.
> Here is my hand that will not harm you.
>   (*Descending Figure* 17)

In Pamela Stewart's "Prothalamium," the sinister arrival of an interloper brings the wedding night to a sudden end. The poem shades off similarly into danger and despair:

> Behind my eyes
> are yours: pine boards, resin-dark, the white
> quilt bunched in a corner. Like flying,
> our arms rise and fall
> to spread out the bedding. Shoes
> abandoned, your hands press
> at the window as a thrush brings round
> our first evening home. The purple lid
> of sunset dimming behind the ridge.
> I told you it would be like this, once
> at least. And now you look hard into my face
> for the mirror I carry—its infinite
> silver passage that we carefully tend
>
> despite the fat,
> brown-shirted man who taps your shoulder again . . .
>   (*Nightblind* 60)

Other female responses to the marriage topos systematically invert hymeneal imagery, deliberately exchanging nuptial fire for funeral pyre. In poems of this type, bridal veils become shrouds and the marriage torches ominously sputter. A certain amount of play upon Eros's connections with Thanatos is to be expected in the epithalamium, but some women's wedding poems strike chilling notes. H.D. has written a dark, dignified, and solemn masque called *Hymen,* dramatizing by means of an austere procession the inexorable movement from girlhood to wifedom. Until the final stanzas, the entire procession is composed of female figures, girls to matrons, who demonstrate the stages of female development. The only participants to sing happily are the "wood-maidens of Artemis," goddess of chastity. The bridegroom's apparent arrival is not cause for joy: torches go out; flute and trumpet wail; the fringes of the bride's veil are seared by the flare of light. In Phyllis Janowitz's "The Funeral Director's Wedding," the bride is no more than a

> Shy slip
> Who will yield her life to him,
> Wearing the gauze of a reflection?
> All eyes on him, his mien, his perfection.
>   A familiar threnody begins.
>
> Ta Ta Da Dum. Ta Ta Da Doo.
>   The carpeted aisle is not wide
> But leads to an altar where ends reside
> In beginnings.
>
> (*Visiting Rites* 36–37)

A funeral fantasy similarly propels Ann Stanford's ambiguous "Ceremonies." On the marriage day, the bride is as thoroughly removed from the center of the experience as if she were an observer. Point of view here parodies the conventional constellation of the bride as object of the gaze:

> I am inside the box
> I am there in the dark
> And I say to my friends—See
> I am saying goodbye
> Do not be angry
> They do not seem to hear me
>
> The sun is shining
> I am the bride
> Look, I am being kissed
> Jesu, the wedding night
>
> I am too sleepy for love
> I am lost in the stained glass
> Climbing
> I am a gray frog
> Out there in the chorus.
>
> (Tufte, *HW* 284–85)

In the last of my brief examples, in Anne Sexton's "Wallflower," an old woman witnesses a perverse wedding scene, one that leaves the bride laid out in satin on the floor and her hero coolly stirring the fire; with "breasts ... made of straw," with "little stiff legs," with "a back as straight as a book," and with pressed thighs "knotting in their treasure," the old woman's sexless solitude seems preferable to the treacherous nuptial scene laid out before her (76).

Women's nuptial poems, whether allusively, thematically, or formally epithalamic, not only give voice to suppressed evidence of female experience in love and marriage but also sharply critique the ideology of the traditional epithalamium. In their variant use of the genre, women poets often refuse transcendence, and the disembodiment assigned to them in nuptial poetry by catalog or idealization, by writing poems that locate their experience of marriage in the body. The striking shared feature of this representation, from Erinna's third-century B.C. "Distaff" fragment right up to the present, is its different emphasis: in their siting of women's nuptial experience in the material body, women poets mark the genre with the reminder that love *has* a body and, in its vulnerability to assault, that body is female. Canonical epithalamia from the rhetorical poems of the late Middle Ages to some recent poems of state almost always conclude transcendentally, in a gesture replete with significances that women poets, in their appropriation of the genre, pointedly resist. As Pamela Hadas writes in a contemporary parody of Spenser's "Prothalamion":

> We grasp that heaven's no more the sine qua non
> of upthrust—bless bonds—they make us one
> homo-fabric, homo-ludicrous
> and lovely for all that: to bring home the moon-
> lust, dust and impetus
> of passages to us.
>
>   ("Post-thalamion" 8–12)

New Songs [from] the Bride

Women poets do more than resist or subvert a genre that circumscribes them; they also reconstruct uninhabitable forms by imagining new or alternative nuptial scenarios. In contemporary women's poetry, we find not only the challenges and resistances *to* and the inversions and parodies *of* the poetic representation of marriage I have already mentioned; we also find a range of poems that reach after new sexual configurations, sound hitherto unheard erotic melodies, claim a subjectivity for the woman as lover in command of her own songs, engage fully with the genre as a ceremonial form. H.D.'s "Psyche," especially resonant in this context, answers the Persephone poem mentioned above by imagining nuptials other than those imposed upon the violated daughter. If we replace that daughter's tale of a death-wedding, the Freudian narrative of femininity, with Psyche's story of agency, as Carol Gilligan reads it in "The Riddle of Femininity and the Psychology of Love," we celebrate instead Psyche's active negotiation of her bond with Eros. In the Psyche story, ironically lost to psychoanalysis, the woman in love emerges as a perceiver and interpreter of her own experience. Were Persephone to learn from Psyche's marriage to Eros, H.D. suggests in the following poem, even men like Hades might be brought back from the figurative dead:

> If I could sing this god,
> Persephone in Hell
> would lift her quivering lids
> and smile, the mysteries hid,
> escaping all the years
> alike both priest and cynic
> would smilingly prevail;
> dead men would start and move
> toward me to learn of love.
>
> ("Psyche," *Collected Poems* 339–40)

In a different key, the Romanian poet Maria Banus also suggests that brides can teach their grooms to love better. Her poem "Wedding" begins in darkness—"In the nuptial room there was a black, cosmic cold. / / Undress, I told him, make me warm"—but it ends with a vision of the nurturing "sky, a milky streak of cloud" (75). To make the kind of bond this bride seeks in bed, however, the bridegroom has to shed the masculine armor, the violent machinery, of his entire civilization. The bride's undressing of this technological man whose heart, finally, does not "grate" or "clank" or "explode" but instead throbs humanly makes for an odd, but surprisingly warming, epithalamium. To a student of the genre, Banus's solution is a brilliant recasting of a familiar convention: the blazon to the bride, the enumeration of the bride's idealized attributes, is replaced by a different sort of catalog, one that, as it strips this bridegroom naked, frees him to love:

> First he unscrewed his head, it grated like Saturn
> trying to escape the vise of his rings,
> or like the stopper of a bottle

> when it shrieks against the glass throat.
> He unscrewed his right arm
> with its bullet threading.
> He unscrewed his left arm
> like a supple metallic rocket.
> He unscrewed his artificial right leg,
> swearing like a truck driver at a hacking engine.
> He unscrewed his artificial left leg,
> and iron groaned against iron,
> like a boiler room.
>
> ("Wedding," *The Other Voice* 75)

A number of poems by contemporary women writers explore new sexual couplings against the grain of the Western epithalamic mode in a way that not only offers ironic commentary on the heterosexist tyranny of the genre but also insists upon an erotic language for women loving women. Adrienne Rich's "Sibling Mysteries," for example, questions as suspect the compulsory passage to heterosexuality in marriage that amounts to a separation of women from their mothers and from other women: patriarchy itself, for Rich, rests upon the making of "woman's flesh . . . taboo to us" in the course of making women into wives. But Rich's poem is more than a reprisal of daughters' double existences and brides' enslavement in the houses, under the hands, of their husbands. For women to love, to be subjects rather than objects of love, she suggests, women must recover the sensuous mother. Bridal allusions are marshaled here to startlingly different ends:

> The daughters never were
> true brides of the father
>
> the daughters were to begin with
> brides of the mother
>
> then brides of each other
> under a different law
>
> Let me hold and tell you.
>
> (*Dream* 47–52)

That women can be brides to one another suggests a whole new poetry of the erotic, one that in its encouraging contemporary profusion exceeds the limits of this essay. Rich's "Transcendental Etude" and "Twenty-one Love Poems" are magnificent in their erotic lesbianism. Monique Wittig's

The Lesbian Body has been called "an erotic female Song of Songs" (Edna O'Brien, jacket blurb). Olga Broumas too supplants a poetics of love that is heterosexually bound—"A crumpled apron, a headcloth, a veil. / One would keep nothing" (*Beginning with O* 11)—with, first, an act of debriefing—"you are the memory / of each desire that ran, dead-end, into a mind / programmed to misconstrue it" (49)—and, second, a transliteration into a tongue she can recognize. She commits herself to Rich's "whole new poetry beginning here," a poetry of reintegrative femininity in place of the disembodying epithalamium, the tyranny of the blazon.

Three poems in particular actively challenge the politics of the epithalamium by resisting heterosexual pairing, inverting or recasting conventions, insisting upon the bride's right to extend the nuptial invitation herself, and claiming authority for the bride's own heretofore repressed subjectivity in the poetry of marriage. Anne Sexton, for example, in "Consorting with Angels," claims to be weary of contemporary gender arrangements:

> I was tired
> of being a woman,
> tired of the spoons and the pots,
> tired of my mouth and my breasts,
> tired of the cosmetics and silks.
> There were still men who sat at my table,
> circled around the bowl I offered up.
> The bowl was filled with purple grapes
> and the flies hovered in for the scent
> and even my father came with his white bone.
> But I was tired of the gender of things.
>
> (11–12)

In this extraordinary epithalamium, the speaker then finds the "answer" in a dream, deconstructing even the heterosexual coupling of the traditional epithalamium and replacing it with an ungendered bridal hymn (which echoes Song of Songs, that most idiosyncratic yet canonical of epithalamia) for herself: "I lost my common gender and my final aspect / . . . / I was not a woman anymore, / not one thing or the other." Having been passively "opened and undressed" in her sexual life as a woman, she exults now in the intactness of a fish in its single skin. Note the coming to subjectivity marked by the shift in pronouns, the claim of singing her own song, captured in the resolute use of the first person:

> O daughters of Jerusalem,
> . . .
> I am black and I am beautiful.
> I've been opened and undressed.
> I have no arms or legs.
> I'm all one skin like a fish.
> I'm no more a woman
> Than Christ was a man.   (12)

In a long poem called "Why the Bride Kept a Bear," dedicated to Lola Montez, danseuse of the Wild West, Susan Donovan writes in the bride's own richly textured voice. All the conventions of the epithalamium are overthrown or wrested to new purposes in this eccentric bridal monologue, interwoven as they are with the facts of Montez's life (she did keep greyhounds and a pair of bears in her front yard, and she turned them loose on one of her husbands). The poem confidently describes the conquest of several husbands, revels in female sexuality capable of bringing men to their knees, especially the first husband—that "quail in aspic," associates female sexual power with the chained bear in the yard, "my morsel, touchy bear, dear bear, dear, dear bear," finally celebrates the one man who "has outdistanced my longing" (414). Dujarier alone is a match for her, and their emblematic wedding song inverts conventional expectations as to gender: "He the dear door, I the key. / He the famished body, I the appetite. / He the love letter, I the soft and cursive script." The poem is finally a song of bridal greeting sung by the bride herself: "I need to meet you promenading through the / fragrant grass and hear you call me wife" (416).

Subjectivity, the bride's right to articulate her own experience, is mobilized differently in an ironic contemporary poem "A Certain Feminist Sect Gives Itself Premarital Advice," by the Spanish poet Ana Rosetti (36–37). Although the poem echoes the repeated refrain, the conventional imagery of conquest characteristic of the classical epithalamium, it does so with a difference. Rather than giving over to the conquistadors, these virgins determine—almost in answer to Catullus—to take back their dowries and to sack their bodies before surrendering them. The refrain, "And let us kiss each other, beautiful virgins, let us kiss each other [my translation]," heads each of the seven stanzas. The subjectivity reclaimed by this poem is plural since the survival of these brides rests upon their feminist solidarity: the politically composed "we" of the poem occupies the space normally elided in songs for the voiceless, wedded bride.

Finally, even heterosexual marriage has had its new songs, particularly in the ironic contemporary idioms of very new women poets. Descendants of Shakespeare's Rosalind, these new poets disdain idolatry, caution against romance, find symbolism suspect, celebrate the contingent and mortal over the cosmic. There is more humor, more irony, more pleasure, more commitment to process and change in these new epithalamia than in the entire history of women's poetry on marriage. Most important, all three of the poems I will end with are ceremonial epithalamia, written to commemorate actual marriages, and all three, published in the 1980s, occupy the space of epithalamium as genre by manifesting their creators' familiarity with, and sense of entitlement to, this canonical form. As Patricia Storace puts it in her "Wedding Song": "Earth in her mercy permits us to repeat / these acts when consecrate couples meet, / and reap from old sentences like harvest wheat, / the words that fit the only truth we know" (70).

The title of Pamela Hadas's "Post-thalamion" is a double joke. The poem is not only dedicated to Dr. and Mrs. Stephen Post, after whose name it is punningly titled, but Hadas also confronts directly the tradition of ceremonial epithalamia, headed by Spenser, by means of her allusive title. Her "Post-thalamion" rewrites his "Prothalamion," or betrothal hymn, signaling its belated relationship to that earlier poem by the substitution of post- for pro-. "Washed up—the formal poem—the sort of thing / that Spenser did," Hadas's poem begins, establishing its awareness of and superiority to the tradition. But the contrast to and dialogue with that canonical poem only begin there. Her eight-stanza wedding poem closely follows the "Prothalamion" it parodies, celebrating mutability, belatedness, randomness, chance, change in an epithalamium as intent upon rewriting genre as marking a marriage. Spenser's poem included a watery procession down the Thames River; Hadas's is sited alongside the Mississippi:

> Our river is
> not sweet, not visited
> by swans or solitude,
> and the brydale day's not one day after all
> as Old Man River's softly said all fall   (8)

Hadas's refrain echoes Spenser's. The season is late fall rather than the traditional spring or summer, an imagistic shift that tells us something about the timing of this late epithalamium, as well as the age (they have wrinkles) and greater wisdom (they have experience and sex) of its bridal pair. Spenser's attendant daughters of the flood become schoolgirls watching the ceremony wistfully; his "variable flowers" are replaced by "loose-patched purses" stuffed with female paraphernalia; his mythic witnesses by curious loiterers; his pastoral scenery by the famous Saarinen arch of St. Louis; his grave ceremonial registers by the irreverent, posttraditional, yet ever hopeful tone of Hadas's presiding voice:

> The brydale day's post-positive, post hoc
> ergo propter hoc, the poem, the con-
> clusive, unconcluding love: O bedrock-
> anchored bulwark, unabashed design,
> vision-stressed, stressed-skin
> like platinum watered silk, stressed sums
> of past experience made light. Beat, drums.
> Post-bellum, postlude, post-diluvian
> and posturing grace the coupled couple comes
> through the arch, moves on
> or up and comes again,
> as the brydale day's not one day after all
>   as Old Man River's softly said all fall ... (11)

Her witty counterpoint to Spenser's conventions works to deflate the transcendentalizing project of the earlier poem and at the same time to reserve the possibility, symbolized by the arch itself, of making connections, real bridges, between lovers in our late present. What is particularly compelling about this epithalamium is that gender is not its only interest. Hadas explores the poet's relationship to a particular kind of ceremonial poetry, uncovers the ideology both preserved and masked by the genre, and questions the viability of a genre like the epithalamium at the present moment.

Katha Pollitt, in an "Epithalamion" recently published in a special issue of *The Atlantic Monthly* on modern love, knows her sources as well as Hadas does. Like Hadas she pokes fun at the conventions of the traditional epithalamium—bridal innocence, panegyrical hymn, assembled guests, social commentary, benediction, impregnation (her couple is already pregnant)—even as she confidently uses them. The setting is, appropriately enough, Cambridge and the Charles, the politics is post-sixties, the tone nostalgic. This half-ironic, half-serious poem may be characterized as a hippie-become-yuppie epithalamion, an elegy for lost youth, a stubbornly persevering love poem, despite the changed times.

> The boy who scribbled *Smash the State* in icing
> on his wedding cake has two kids and co-op,

reads (although pretends not to) the Living section,
and hopes for tenure.

Everything's changed since we played Capture the Red Flag
between Harvard Yard and the River. Which of us dreamed that
History, who grinds men up like meat, would make us her next meal?

But here we are, in a kind of post-imperial
permanent February, with offices and apartments,
balked latecomers out of a Stendhal novel,
our brave ambitions

run out into the sand: into restaurants and movies,
July at the Cape, where the major source of amusement's
watching middle-aged Freudians snub only just younger Marxist
historians.

And yet if it's true, as I've read, that the starving body
eats itself, it's true too it eats the heart last.
We've lost our moment of grandeur, but come on, admit it:
aren't we happier?

And so let's welcome the child already beginning,
who'll laugh, but not cruelly, I hope, at our comfy nostalgias,
and praise, friends, praise, this marriage of friends and lovers
made in a dark time.   (78)

Patricia Storace has written in "Pamina's Marriage Speech" what I take to be perhaps the most compelling of contemporary epithalamia by women. The poem is both a formal epithalamium in its own right and a rewriting of Pamina's role in Mozart's *The Magic Flute* by assigning to her not aria but speech. Pamina does not have much of a voice in Mozart's opera; throughout, she is gripped by forces that act upon her. "Pamina's Marriage Speech," by contrast, avoids the high notes of aria, presenting an "honest, but agnostic epithalamion" in the level tones of committed human speech. This poem earns the right to reinscribe the "brilliant torches" of the traditional hymeneal hymn at the close, by thoroughly revising nuptial convention: Pamina in her own voice replaces the genre's certainties with conditionals by contracting her own marriage *otherwise* with her husband-to-be. The poem moves from romantic death-marriage to a real-life lasting one, from the "steely certainty of blade" to the "malleable gold of wedding band," from cynicism and despair to a praise of love, conventional but newly coded in a language, in tones, of possibility: love is at best "dubiety, sustained connection, / . . . that questionable reality, / unlikely, but possible, like resurrection." The venture requires vigilance and change on both sides.

> Guard, oh my husband of the literal sex
> against the male bias toward the radiant spasm
> of heroic loss, sad captains gathered
> at the last feast to applaud
> the old lion's shaggy, final roar
> and toss love on the fire, ecstatic holocaust
> suspiciously similar to male orgasm.
> You see the carnal parallel I make;
> so I too for my husband's sake
> will discipline my woman's love
> of endless possibility, the maenad's
> blind absorption in sensation,
> the response, naive, momentous,
> to any cynic's predatory kiss
> by which our love of fresh beginning, generation,
> follows bad directions and misprinted signs
> to that much used freeway, promiscuity.
> Remember, too, that love contains, but is not an emotion;
> is not romance, that color photograph
> of a smiling couple on a short vacation
> whose kisses are purchased, pretty souvenirs,
> in gabled shops with good views of the ocean.
> Love is, in supreme form, concentration.
> Enough of this. Raise the veil, beloved,
> now I've made it dark enough to kiss
> and teach these guests we've rendered skeptical
> love passionate as doubt, as radical.
> By these hands' imperfect light
> receive a resonance of knowledge,
> through flickering palms, lucid embrace,
> read by this uncertain flame,
> achieve description of a face.
> Pray that we withstand the shock of blessing,
> assembled friends, with lowered heads,
> Pray urgently that we may make
> for good the crucial and ecstatic risk
> we take, following brilliant torches to this bed.   (60–61)

This poem invokes and invests with new meaning the time-worn conventions of the traditional epithalamium and their accompanying ideologies—ideas of generation, of bridal innocence and perfection, of monogamy and lifelong commitment, of hymeneal torches signifying social compact and publicity, of reconciling hymns of joy—only after making them, as does Pollitt, "dark enough to kiss." "Pamina's Marriage Speech" names love as a kind of knowledge, an epistemology rather than an ideology; as the "lucid" seeing face to face that freed Psyche to love Eros and him to love her; as a full illumination of what happens in that "uncertain" space between persons; as a humorous recognition of and commitment to change our inheritance of gendered responses in love; and finally, as the "crucial and ecstatic," specific and personal risk we take *now* in following hymen's torches to the marriage bed.

Conclusion

The canonical epithalamium, as this recuperation of women's variant responses has been designed to demonstrate, is incomplete without the record of challenges to its generic borders that women poets have left to us as legacy. I would suggest that the overt prohibition against writing highly codified ceremonial poetry has been less causal in the exile of women poets from the canon than an excessively rigorous definition of poetic genre, along with the elision of experiential and historical differences in the conventional deployment of the genre. As the spectrum of responses indicates, a theory of genre might profitably invite more *telling* of individual stories and less *taxonomy* of generic form. Since those in power are more likely to be invested in generic hierarchies, taxonomy is truthfully a political issue: if women poets are to take their rightful place in the canon, we must use inclusiveness, rather than a gender-biased formal exclusivity, as a criterion of value. We need to ask why female revision of genre has been viewed as a defacement of it, effacing our view of such texts as contributory to generic development. We might also want to explain, in the case of the epithalamium, why the criterion of generic purity has gone hand in hand with an idealization of woman as object of love in the poetry of marriage, as if erotic and aesthetic purity were equivalent and equally crucial to preserve. Also important for genre theory is the refusal of the female epithalamium to make a pure generic statement. Although women's epithalamia share important themes, elements of critical stance, and self-location, they do not set up an alternative reified canon of "ovarian" in place of phallic strategies. Finally, a study of women poets' appropriation of poetic genres hastens the undoing of a Western generic practice based on limit, hierarchy, and taxonomy and exposes the gender specificity of any genre system that pretends to rest completely upon aesthetic criteria. To confront gender with genre in the way that women's epithalamia demand of us is not only to hear the return of the beloved's repressed voice in the poetry of marriage but to problematize the very concept of literary genre. No longer merely a question of language, of aesthetic form, genre itself emerges as an overdetermined site of sexual difference—an experientially determined category as meaningful as a set of formal expectations, even an occupiable political space from which the bride claims at last her right to sing as subject.

That is the first of my endings, and it is tempting to close on this the note of Corinna's triumph. But I do not want to freeze a newly empowered Corinna in an equally imprisoning frame—not this time the frame of the male text that centered her as object of celebration but the feminist text that recenters her as rightful subject of her own poetic discourse. I must, to be fully responsible to my critique of genre theory, end by destabilizing my own too-seductive model. I must ask, in closing, what is wrong with this compelling picture of the female poet as subject, newly enfranchised as an appropriator of genre? What politics underwrites even this well-intentioned restoration of the bride's centrality in her own nuptial scenario, the strategic replacement of Persephone by Psyche? Why may we not rest easy with the restitutive gendering of genre? The clue may lie in my students' impatient reminder that you have to know Greek to know what an epithalamium is. Those women poets empowered by the writing of villanelles and sestinas, sonnets and elegies, albas and odes, those achieving notice and, in some cases, canonization by their alignment with the present neo-formalist vogue of rhyme and meter, stanza form and poetic genre, might be the female counterparts of those male writers—elite, white, privileged, educated—who maintained hegemonic control of lyric poetry for centuries.

Genre, then, might divide women poets as effectively as it joins them. That is—and this is another story—the very accession to form I study here marks no more than the momentary and provisional empowerment of a newly privileged group. This occupation of form will contain its own exclusionary politics, one that silences other subjects, not even all of them female; to use the class-burdened, heterosexist imagery of the epithalamium a final time, not only the bridesmaid who attends Corinna, not only those waiting women of another class or race ritually decking her in jewels and silk, but the pastry chef in the palace kitchen, the footman dreaming of his male lover in nuptial registers we have not yet learned to hear. The force of genre—under the conditions of the literary marketplace and our present sex-gender system—is inevitably conservative, hierarchical, and regularizing. Thus, we will continually need the disruptive energy of new poetry from the margin to occupy the monolithic space of genre, or else the legitimation that genre bestows may corrupt even us as we accede, at last, to its long-withheld power.

Notes

An earlier version of this essay was first published as " 'Songs [from] the Bride': Feminism, Psychoanalysis, Genre," in *Literature and Psychology* 33–34 (Fall 1987): 109–19.

1. Mary Ellen Lamb notes that Renaissance women's learning was confined by influential educators like Juan Vives to church fathers, Scripture, and a few "sad" classical authors. She concludes that since even reading in genres like the sonnet, the romance, and the elegy placed a woman's reputation at risk, writing in them would be fully transgressive (Rose 207).

2. An elaboration of this summarized argument may be found in my article "All of a Piece: Women's Poetry and Autobiography."

3. Standard work on the genre of the epithalamium includes Forster, Greene, Miller, Mulryan, and the two Tufte volumes. Sappho did not, of course, invent nuptial poetry, the origins of which appear to reside in folk rituals and songs. That a tradition of such rituals existed is in part proved by the presence of such images on Achilles' shield in the *Iliad*. But because lyric epithalamia are so rare in classical literature—aside from Theocritus's eighteenth idyll, all of Tufte's examples come from the drama of the period—and because Sappho's small corpus includes so many, historians of the genre assign originary status to her wedding poems.

4. The only male critic to recognize the extent of the genre's phallic imperialism, by my reckoning, is C. S. Lewis, in his "Prelude to Space: An Epithalamium." Turning the genre's conventions back on themselves, he uses the epithalamium as social commentary, indicting the masculine desire to conquer space by means of highly gendered imagery:

> Some now alive expect
> (I am told) to see the large,
> Steel member grow erect,
> Turgid with the fierce charge
> Of our whole planet's skill,
> Courage, wealth, knowledge, concentrated will;

> Shall we, when the grim shape
>   Roars upward, dance and sing?
> Yes if we honor rape,
> If we take pride to fling
>   So bountifully on space
> The sperm of our long woes, our large disgrace.
>
> (Tufte, *HW* 270)

5. Snyder notes, for example, how fragment 39 has been distorted by Ulrich von Wilamowitz-Moellendorff's 1913 recuperation of the poem *as* a wedding poem. The famous fragment has clearly to do with the female speaker's passion for a woman; when the man of the poem is assumed by Wilamowitz to be the beloved's bridegroom, then the speaker's passion becomes "completely honorable," "because she sings of it in the context of a wedding" (19). A more interesting interpretation, according to Snyder, is that of Thomas McEvilley (1978), who finds the poem to be an intentional distortion of the epithalamic genre: beginning with allusions to bridal rites, Sappho upsets her audience's expectations by moving to a description of her own feelings for the bride (20).

6. Needless to say, the brief selection here remains only a sampling of English women's responses to the marriage topos before the twentieth century. Katherine Philips and Mary Elizabeth Coleridge will be cited later in the essay for specific thematic emphasis. A good source for women poets' antinuptial poetry across cultures is the four-volume Feminist Press series *The Defiant Muse* (anthologies of Hispanic, French, German, and Italian feminist poems from the Middle Ages to the present). The overwhelming quantity of such poetry suggests that women poets may have consciously refrained from using the epithalamic genre, so unrepresented were they by its preoccupations and ideologies.

Works Cited

Akmadulina, Bella. "The Bride." In *The Penguin Book of Women Poets.* Ed. Carol Cosman, Joan Keefe, and Kathleen Weaver. New York: Viking Press, 1978.

Archer, Nuala. "The Wedding Day." *Whale on the Line.* Dublin: Gallery Books, 1981.

Athanassakis, Apostolos N., ed. "Homeric Hymn to Demeter." *The Homeric Hymns.* Baltimore and London: Johns Hopkins University Press, 1982.

Banus, Maria. "Wedding." In *The Other Voice: Twentieth-Century Women's Poetry in Translation.* Ed. Joanna Bankier, Carol Cosman, Doris Earnshaw, Joan Keefe, Deirdre Lashgari, and Kathleen Weaver. New York: W. W. Norton, 1976.

Barnard, Mary, trans. *Sappho: A New Translation.* Berkeley and Los Angeles: University of California Press, 1958.

Barnstone, Willis, trans. *Greek Lyric Poetry.* Bloomington: Indiana University Press, 1962.

Broumas, Olga. "Betrothal/The Bride's Lament" and "Snow White." *Beginning with O.* Yale Series of Younger Poets, 72. New Haven: Yale University Press, 1977.

———. "Bride." *Pastoral Jazz.* Port Townsend: Copper Canyon Press, n.d.

Campion, Thomas. "Song VI." *The Works of Thomas Campion.* Ed. Walter Davis. New York: W. W. Norton, 1967.

Chodorow, Nancy. "Family Structure and Feminine Personality." In *Woman, Culture, and Society.* Ed. Michelle Zimbalist Rosaldo and Louise Lamphere. Stanford: Stanford University Press, 1974.

Chudleigh, Lady Mary. "To the Ladies." In *The Norton Anthology of Literature by Women: The Tradition in English.* Ed. Sandra Gilbert and Susan Gubar. New York: W. W. Norton, 1985.

Cody, Richard. *The Landscape of the Mind.* Oxford: Clarendon Press, 1969.

Coleridge, Mary Elizabeth. "Marriage." *The Collected Poems of Mary Elizabeth Coleridge.* London: Rupert Hart-Davis, 1954.

Crashaw, Richard. "Epithalamion." *The Poems of Richard Crashaw.* Ed. L. C. Martin. 1956. Oxford: Clarendon Press, 1966.

Dame, Enid. "Persephone." *The New York Quarterly* 28 (Fall 1985): 60–63.

De Lauretis, Teresa. *Alice Doesn't: Feminism, Semiotics, Cinema.* Bloomington: Indiana University Press, 1982.

Dickinson, Emily. "Title Divine—Is Mine!" *The Complete Poems of Emily Dickinson.* Ed. Thomas Johnson. Boston: Little, Brown & Co., 1980.

Donne, John. "Epithalamion Made at Lincolne's Inne." *John Donne: The Epithalamions, Anniversaries, and Epicedes.* Ed. W. Milgate. Oxford: Clarendon Press, 1978.

Donovan, Susan. "Why the Bride Kept a Bear." *The Massachusetts Review* 24 (Summer 1983): 414–16.

Edmonds, J. M., trans. *Lyra Graeca.* Vol. 3 of the Loeb Classical Library. 1927. London: William Heinemann, 1967.

Erinna. "The Distaff," trans. Marilyn Arthur. In *Women Poets of the World.* Ed. Joanna Bankier and Deirdre Lashgari. New York: Macmillan, 1983.

Forster, Leonard. "Conventional Safety Valves: Alba, Pastourelle and Epithalamium." *Lebende Antike.* Berlin: Erich Schmidt Verlag, 1967.

Gilbert, Sandra, and Susan Gubar. *The Madwoman in the Attic.* New Haven: Yale University Press, 1979.

Gilligan, Carol, and Eve Stern. "The Riddle of Femininity and the Psychology of Love." Ms.

Glück, Louise. "Bridal Piece." *Firstborn.* New York: Ecco Press, 1968.

———. "Epithalamium" and "Dedication to Hunger." *Descending Figure.* New York: Ecco Press, 1976.

Greene, Thomas. "Spenser and Epithalamic Convention." *Comparative Literature* 9 (1957): 215–28.

Gubar, Susan. " 'The Blank Page' and the Issues of Female Creativity." In *Writing and Sexual Difference.* Ed. Elizabeth Abel. Chicago: University of Chicago Press, 1982.

Hacker, Marilyn. *Love, Death, and the Changing of the Seasons.* New York: Arbor House, 1986.

Hadas, Pamela. "Post-thalamion." *Webster Review* 3, no. 2 (Spring 1977): 8–12.

Hartman, Geoffrey. "Toward Literary History." *Beyond Formalism: Literary Essays, 1958–1970.* New Haven: Yale University Press, 1970.

H.D. *End to Torment: A Memoir of Ezra Pound.* Ed. Norman H. Pearson and Michael King. New York: New Directions, 1979.

———. "Hymen" and "Psyche." *Collected Poems, 1912–1944.* Ed. Louis Martz. New York: New Directions, 1983.

Hochman, Sandra. "The Eyes of Flesh." In *No More Masks! An Anthology of Poems by Women.* Ed. Florence Howe and Ellen Bass. Garden City, N.Y.: Doubleday/Anchor, 1973.

Jameson, Fredric. *The Political Unconscious: Narrative as a Socially Symbolic Act.* Ithaca: Cornell University Press, 1981.

Janowitz, Phyllis. "The Arrangement" and "The Funeral Director's Wedding." *Visiting Rites.* Princeton: Princeton University Press, 1982.

Macomber, Megan. "Epithalamion on the Marriage of My Middle Sister." *Helicon Nine* 14/15 (Summer 1986): 168.

McCullough, J. P., trans. *The Poems of Propertius: A Bilingual Edition.* Berkeley and Los Angeles: University of California Press, 1972.

Miller, Paul. "The Decline of the English Epithalamion." *Texas Studies in Literature and Language* 12 (1970): 405–16.

Montefiore, Jan. *Feminism and Poetry: Language, Experience, Identity in Women's Writing.* London and New York: Pandora, 1987.

Moore, Marianne. "Marriage." In *Rising Tides: Twentieth-Century American Women Poets.* Ed. Laura Chester and Sharon Barba. New York: Washington Square Press, 1973.

Mulryan, John. "The Function of Ritual in the Marriage Poems of Catullus, Spenser and Ronsard." *Illinois Quarterly* 35 (1972): 50–64.

O'Brien, Edna. "A Conversation with Edna O'Brien: 'The Body Contains the Life Story,' " ed. Philip Roth. *New York Times Book Review,* Nov. 18, 1984.

Philips, Katherine. "An Answer to Another Persuading a Lady to Marriage" and "To My Excellent Lucasia on Our Friendship." In *The World Split Open: Four Centuries of Women Poets in England and America, 1552–1950.* Ed. Louise Bernikow. New York: Random House, 1974.

Pollitt, Katha. "Epithalamion." *Atlantic Monthly,* Sept. 1986.

Rich, Adrienne. *The Fact of a Doorframe: Poems Selected and New, 1950–1984.* New York: W. W. Norton, 1984.

———. *On Lies, Secrets, and Silence: Selected Prose, 1966–1978.* New York: W. W. Norton, 1979.

——. *"Sibling Mysteries." The Dream of a Common Language: Poems,* 1974–1977. New York: W. W. Norton, 1978.

Roberts, Michele. "Persephone Descends to the Underworld." *The Mirror of the Mother: Selected Poems,* 1975–1985. London: Methuen, 1986.

Rose, Mary Beth, ed. *Women in the Middle Ages and the Renaissance: Literary and Historical Perspectives.* New York: Syracuse University Press, 1986.

Rosetti, Ana. "A Certain Feminist Sect Gives Itself Premarital Advice." *Indicios vehementes,* 1979–1984. Madrid: Hiperion, 1985.

Schenck, Celeste. "All of a Piece: Women's Poetry and Autobiography." In *Life/Lines: Theorizing Women's Autobiography.* Ed. Bella Brodzki and Celeste Schenck. Ithaca: Cornell University Press, 1988.

——. "Songs [from] the Bride: Feminism, Psychoanalysis, Genre." *Literature and Psychology* 33–34 (Fall 1987): 109–19.

Sexton, Anne. "Wallflower" and "Consorting with Angels." *The Complete Poems.* Boston: Houghton Mifflin, 1981.

Shakespeare, William. Sonnet 130. *The Complete Works.* Ed. Charles Jasper Sisson. New York: Harper & Row, 1953.

Snyder, Jane McIntosh. *The Woman and the Lyre: Women Writers in Classical Greece and Rome.* Carbondale: Southern Illinois University Press, 1989.

Spenser, Edmund. "Epithalamion." *Poetical Works.* Ed. J. C. Smith and E. De Selincourt. London and New York: Oxford University Press, 1970.

Stewart, Pamela. "Prothalamion." *Nightblind.* Memphis: St. Luke's Press, 1985.

Storace, Patricia. "Wedding" and "Pamina's Marriage Speech." *Heredity.* Barnard New Women Poets Series, 1. Boston: Beacon Press, 1987.

Tufte, Virginia. *The Poetry of Marriage: The Epithalamium in Europe and Its Development in English.* Los Angeles: Tinnon-Brown, 1970.

——. *"High Wedlock Then Be Honoured": Wedding Poems from Nineteen Countries and Twenty-five Centuries.* New York: Viking Press, 1970.

Women's Studies: An Interdisciplinary Journal 7, nos. 1/2 (1980). (Special issue, ed. Sandra Gilbert and Susan Gubar.)

MARTIN GREEN

Adventurers Stake Their Claim
The Adventure Tale's Bid for Status, 1876–1914

I want to begin by defining my own position on the subject of this volume. I think that canon formation is a fact of literary life (the part of that life oriented toward the scholarly/critical/pedagogical pole) and I do not believe in attempts to stop it. The related idea I do believe in, and want to see built into the teaching of literature, is a dialectical reading of literary history. This can be defined in three steps.

First, canon formation is a thetic activity within a dialectic. It provokes its antithesis, in the work of individual writers and in the popularity of genres. (In this antithetical activity, critics and scholars lose the initiative to readers and writers.) Thus, a D. H. Lawrence will see his work as a kind of opposite to that of a canonical author like George Eliot. Then an F. R. Leavis will perform a synthesis, showing that Lawrence is nevertheless *like* Eliot; and other writers hitherto associated with Eliot will drop out of consideration. This becomes the new thesis, and a later writer will set out to be unlike both Eliot and Lawrence. And at the level of genre, gifted and ambitious writers like Graham Greene, Raymond Chandler, and Kingsley Amis will write thrillers even though (or because) that genre is not literature, and so is free of certain constraining forms of self-consciousness. Then ingenious critics will recuperate their thrillers too for the canon.

Second, the canons we treat as traditional have been white, male, and middle class. It is now possible and desirable to change them, by introducing writers of color, and female and proletarian writers, of the past as well as of the present. To do so will exact a certain price of literature understood as a scholarly/pedagogical activity, because it will make the maintenance of critical standards, the idea of such standards, much vaguer. Leavis could present English literature as an intellectual discipline partly because all his texts were white and middle class, and he treated his women and men writers alike. He even restricted his attention to British writers. If we abandon his categories for these others, and value them for being different from each other, we shall not be able to apply the same methods of interpretation and evaluation to all of our texts. We shall in effect cultivate our yea-saying faculties and let our nay-saying grow feeble; and there can be no real method or discipline without the latter. Nevertheless, it is probably right to make that sacrifice. Of course, compromises and combinations are always possible; but it is easy to foresee the reproaches of the next generation.

Third, literature itself (including the whole dialectic described in my first point) is a partly antithetical activity. It represents (not always, but usually) forces in society that resist or protest or contradict establishment values. Leavis is again a good example; a man critic, a "manly" critic, making his great tradition out of novelists who were either women or wrote about women. And though he presented himself as an exception, that claim was true only in that he was more *vigorous* than his colleagues. In their beliefs, most of them were just as liberal as he.

Thus we should not identify the traditional canon with the social establishment: with the policies of the business world, or the civil service, or the armed services. It is much more plausibly designated as liberal, and quite often radical, in its behavior as well as its sympathies. Women writers have always been widely read and discussed; colored writers like V. S. Naipaul were quickly welcomed and awarded; the literary establishment is a cultural opposition. (It is true that the curricula of many schools and colleges remain conservative, and there are many reasons for that, some of which I have suggested above; but they are the most conservative aspect of a whole that is in other ways liberal.)

That is why it is important to study adventure as the test case of canon formation—a case in which what was excluded was masculinism, imperialism, political reaction. This should remind us of how beneficent the canon process often is. It was by canonical means that the Kipling ethos was largely kept out of English Literature from 1910 on, and Conrad was so misread as to seem anti-imperialist. Even more important for our present purposes, this case shows us where to seek the vested interest at the motive core of canon formation.

The adventure tale has nearly always been the poor relation of fiction, from the point of view of literary critics and scholars—and in the view of the women of letters even more than that of the men. At the level of popular reading, it is men and not women who buy from the paperback racks marked "Adventure." For this reason I am going to use "man of letters" throughout this essay, because the writers and readers of adventure are predominantly men.

There is and always was a strong affinity between adventure and "men," or manliness, while the world of letters is androgynous by aspiration. It has, of course, a gender bias in favor of men that is in some ways very strong, but a male-biased androgyny is very different from the rank masculinism frequent or usual in adventure. That is at least one, if not the main, reason why critics and scholars have rarely recommended the latter form to readers or to writers with literary aspirations, or even discussed it seriously.

Insofar as adventure is part of literature, the latter becomes alien territory to feminists. If women writers feel, as their theorists claim, that they trespass in a masculine preserve just by the act of wielding a pen, then that feeling must derive mostly from adventure books and adventure lovers. If literary critics and historians sometimes employ a male-clubman rhetoric, tainted with a whiff of the locker room, that is often because they are laying claim to a (rather implausible) fraternity with those writers and readers. The critics who have no truck with adventure, like Leavis, are likely to select women novelists for their great tradition. This is the idea of literature in which I—and many others—grew up.

There are some indications, however, that we are now ready to pay adventure some attention. Among writers in English this attention seems to be partly a function of the new interest in the literary history of the British Empire and partly a result of the feminist interest in men and masculinism. But at the level of literary theory, the most interesting work is being done in Germany.

In such an essay as this, I can do no more than drop names, obviously. Michael Nerlich's two-volume *Ideology of Adventure* was published in English translation by the University of Minnesota Press in 1987, and Nerlich has long been at work on the idea of adventure in both literature and history—an idea that he shows to have been of major importance in the history of the modern mind. In an earlier generation, Ernst Bloch developed theories of the cultural function of adventure tales which have been taken up by a number of contemporary scholars: for instance, Gert Ueding, Volker Klotz, Rolf-Peter Maertin. One of Bloch's exemplary adventure writers was Karl May, most famous in English-speaking countries for his Westerns; and there is now a whole branch of German literary studies, quite independent of Bloch, devoted to May's work.

Perhaps the biggest single idea behind the work of Bloch and his followers is that some kinds of popular culture, and notably adventure tales, do not dissipate the reader's intellectual and moral force but generate and concentrate that force. Bloch set himself in opposition to the culturally pessimistic Frankfurt school of cultural theory (Theodor Adorno and Herbert Marcuse) and in tendency, therefore, in opposition to all the philosophers of rootedness, from Karl Mannheim and Martin Heidegger to F. R. Leavis and T. S. Eliot. The titles of Bloch's collections of essays show the value he set on popular adventure books as resources for and allies to the regenerative and revolutionary forces in society: *Erbschaft dieser Zeit* (Heritage of these times), *Das Prinzip Hoffnung* (The principle of hope), and *A Philosophy of the Future.*

These German scholars have directed their attention primarily to German and French authors, but their ideas and methods would apply very profitably to English-language adventures and would root that literature in political history and theory in a new and valuable way. It may be time for Anglo-American scholars to turn from France to Germany as a source of literary ideas and to recapture that connection between literature and history that has recently been largely lost. (For instance, Rolf-Peter Maertin's *Wunschpotentiale* is the tenth in a series entitled "Literatur in der Geschichte, Geschichte in der Literatur" [Literature in history, history in literature].)

It seems that English and American scholars may need help from outside to recapture that connection. The literatures in English are notable equally for their large number of brilliant adventures—they have led the world in this field—and for their small number of ideas *about* adventure. Anyone who has tried to use research tools like the MLA's annual bibliography or the bibliographic index in order to study adventure can testify to that paucity. Fantasy, on the other hand, is a genre well provided for by our scholarship; indeed, many scholars want to stuff all of adventure into that category—but that must be called a barefaced attempt to kill the concept. Adventure has been exiled from the canon with a more severe sentence than seemingly comparable genres.

Adventure's twofold significance for literature as a system derives from that fact. First, adventure stories constitute an outlying province, far outside the canon, the capital city of literature, but a province that deserves to be visited because these stories are the reflection of the experience, and the dreams, of our men of action and of power. If you want your interest in history to benefit from your study of literature, you cannot afford to leave that province of the imagination out of account; to do so is to reduce literature to a preserve of the Brahmin caste. Second, the adventure tale has a more radical significance: as that which is not and cannot be literature; as the literary expression of imaginative sympathies and loyalties to which the man of letters must be hostile. In this usage, of course, "man of letters" refers primarily to critics and scholars; it is a common usage, determined by the concept of literature itself. Taken in this sense, adventure is the antithesis in a dialectic that continually brings into literary studies revolutionary and regenerative material. (A commonsense example is the fondness of many gifted writers for the form, and the valiant efforts of admiring critics to suppress this fact or explain it away.)

My subject is therefore very large, but I want to restrict my attention here to the period 1876–1914 and the attempt by British and French writers to give literary dignity to adventure. The earlier date reminds us of Disraeli's installation of Queen Victoria as empress of India and the celebration of the empire that inaugurated, while the later date, of course, announces the outbreak of the Great War, which resulted in such a revulsion of feeling against imperialism. The empire was always (not just in this period) the locus of written and unwritten adventure. And other events of this period were also signs of this imperialism, which was not just a British phenomenon: the 1887 Congress of Berlin, which regulated the scramble for Africa of various European powers; the 1898 Spanish-American War, which announced the epoch of American imperialism (and evoked Kipling's poem "The White Man's Burden"); and the Boer War in the first years of the twentieth century.

In this period of conscious imperialism, a great deal of adventure writing was produced, and some of it was by writers of talent and literary ambition. Even the critics wavered in their prejudice against adventure. There was an attempt (most obvious in the early reception of Kipling) to make adventure a major literary genre and to build a cultural alliance between literature and the rulers of the empire. If this attempt ever had a chance of success, it was wounded by the Boer War, which revived the anti-imperialist feelings of men and women of letters, and killed by the Great War. The new novelists like E. M. Forster and D. H. Lawrence were opposite in every tendency to Kipling; and so were Bloomsbury and the left-wing writers of the 1930s, on the surface. But if the Kipling phenomenon gave this period its special character, adventure writing by no means began or ended with these dates, any more than imperialism did. Both date back to Elizabethan times and continue today, but they are most obvious and can be studied most easily in this period.

Among the prominent literary figures who wrote adventures were Robert Louis Stevenson, Rider Haggard, and John Buchan. The greatest man of letters of their group was, of course, Kipling, but he was neither a writer of adventure tales nor a theorist of adventure. His genius expressed itself in oblique and ironic ways (I compare his literary psychology with Bertolt Brecht's in *The English Novel in the Twentieth Century*) partly because he felt such a tension of opposition between himself and the mainstream of letters. One can pick up some very interesting ideas about adventure writing from his essays, and from his novel, *The Light That Failed,* but they usually declare themselves by implication. Thus his work certainly can be read as bearing upon the subject of this essay, but his case is so complex that it needs separate discussion.

The writers who did most toward making a theoretical case for adventure were Robert Louis Stevenson and his friend Andrew Lang. The latter is now a largely forgotten figure, but he was prominent in the English aesthetic movement (in its earlier phases) and remained influential up to the time of his death in 1912. Stevenson's crucial essays on the subject were collected in *Memories and Portraits*. He also wrote some essays in practical criticism, like his prefaces to the English edition of Victor Hugo's work, which applied those ideas.

There is a moral dimension to Stevenson's taste that gets expressed in his essay on *Le Vicomte de Bragelonne,* the sequel to *Les Trois Mousquetaires* (the essay is entitled "A Gossip on a Novel of Dumas's" and is published in *Memories and Portraits*). He says this book belongs to the innermost circle of those that have influenced him morally, and that he feels himself at all times under the scrutiny of its hero, d'Artagnan, "a man so witty, rough, kind and upright, that he takes the heart by storm" (144).

In the opening scenes of *Le Vicomte de Bragelonne,* d'Artagnan teaches the young Louis XIV how to be a man; and it is clear that it is the masculinism of d'Artagnan's and Dumas's morality that attracts Stevenson—the *natural* (as opposed to pious) morality of *men* (as opposed to other human groups): "There is nothing of the copy-book about his virtues, nothing of the drawing room in his fine, natural civility; he will sail near the wind; he is no district visitor—no Wesley or Robespierre; his conscience is void of all refinement, whether for good or evil; but the whole man rings true like a good sovereign. . . . if I am to choose virtues for myself or my friends, let me choose the virtues of d'Artagnan" (Stevenson 144). Lang, following Stevenson, says the young should learn from Dumas frankness, kindness, and generosity (*Essays in Little*).

There is also a political dimension implicit in Stevenson's work, which becomes clear as one examines the ideology of his admirers. The Stevenson enthusiasts of the 1880s, men like Leslie Stephen, were often former liberals who had gone over to the Conservative party because of their new awareness of the British Empire and of the guilts and powers it brought with it. Indeed, Stevenson himself, in his last years on Samoa, played a small part in the Great Powers politics of the South Seas.

Stevenson's argument, however, was basically aesthetic. He drew a contrast between the novel of character and the novel of incident, and he protested against the literary world's bias in favor of the former. The adventure, he said, absorbs the reader into a completely actualized world, wholly other than the writer's self-consciousness, his self-discourse, and offers the reader the chance for a much freer and fuller response. He made less of the nonaesthetic implications of that preference, in politics, for instance, than the German critics I have cited.

Stevenson's ideas evoked a burst of interest among French intellectuals that lasted some thirty years or more. *Le Roman d'Aventures,* by Jean-Yves Tadié, sums up the controversy, which involved Marcel Schwob, André Gide, Jacques Rivière, and the *Nouvelle Revue Française* (Kevin O'Neill's *André Gide and the Roman d'Aventures* also provides a useful introduction). The excitement began in Paris when essays and fiction by Stevenson caught the attention of Marcel Schwob, in the 1880s. The Frenchman was impressed by these essays, and by Stevenson's fiction, and he began to call for French writers to try to tell tales of adventure. He was joined by Camille Mauclair, in an article in the *Revue du Palais,* in calling for a new kind of novel-hero: instead of the wraith of *Symboliste* stories, or the primitive of Naturalist stories, an adventurer—"un conquérant du monde extrême-orientale, capitaine, pirate, dictateur d'anarchie." (Mauclair, quoted in O'Neill, 16). French literature had become overintellectualized, Mauclair insisted, and unless French writers and readers found new heroes in their stories, and thrilled to heroic adventures, their imaginations would be killed by the spirit of criticism.

Both Schwob and Mauclair were friends of André Gide, who was already a powerful figure on the French literary scene. By 1898, in fact, Gide was writing *Les Caves du Vatican* (which he then thought of precisely as an adventure tale) in a bold attempt to radically alter the character of his fiction. They all liked Stevenson's rebellion against detailed realism of description, especially of the Zola variety. Gide and his friends, like Stevenson, preferred a bare, stripped narrative of action.

In 1913 Jacques Rivière cited Stevenson as a model, in a three-part essay in *Nouvelle Revue Française* that amplified and clarified much that had gone before. Part 1 was on symbolism, the art and art doctrine to be displaced: "un art d'extrême conscience, l'art de gens qui savent terriblement ce qu'ils veulent, ce qu'ils font" (an art of extreme consciousness, the art of people who are terribly aware of what they want, of what they are doing). The subject of Symbolist writing was always an emotion, not an object or an event; all of the subject's anecdotal origin and interest was removed. It had been a very French kind of art—Mallarmé, for instance, could have belonged to no other nation but France (244).

But now even Frenchmen had new souls and wanted new pleasures: "Les symbolistes ne connaissaient que des plaisirs de gens fatigués" (The symbolists knew only the pleasures of the tired) (244). Rivière continues: "Nous connaissons aujourd'hui des plaisirs plus violents et plus allègres. Tous ils sont contenus dans le plaisir de vivre. . . . C'est le matin encore une fois. Tout recommence. Plaisir d'être au milieu des hommes! Les symbolistes avaient perdu le goût de l'homme; ils n'avaient plus aucun désir à le voir" (We today know more violent and lively pleasures. All of them are contained within the pleasure of living. . . . It is again morning. Everything begins again. Pleasure of being amongst men! The Symbolists had lost the taste for man; they had no desire to see him any more) (247). This has the true Renaissance and masculinist lustiness, and so far it seems as if the English adventure tale, with its imperialist associations, is indeed what Rivière wants. *Robinson Crusoe* is often cited as exemplary.

In part 3, however, "Le Roman d'Aventures," Rivière tells us that this new fiction, "tout entière en actes," will be "classical" (253). Moreover, Cubism is mentioned as an equivalent in the visual arts, as is a turn away from Wagner toward Bach, in music; and in philosophy, Descartes is a prime example and sponsor of this classicism. All of this clearly suggests something quite different and more intellectual—in fact, another in the literary world's series of attempts to throw off the oppressive yoke of Romanticism. And this mood and motive became stronger as time went by, especially with the experience of the Great War, which disillusioned literary people with imperialism and even with "the taste for man." When, in 1919, Rivière became editor of the *Nouvelle Revue Française,* he again wrote, in introducing the first issue, that his interest was in everything that seemed to foretell a classical revival (Roskill 90). This cue was taken up in many places, for instance, by T. S. Eliot, and in England, where it signaled a taste for almost anything but the traditional adventure tale.

Whatever else they *came* to mean by "classical," Rivière and his friends had begun by identifying it with the actual English adventure. For instance, Rivière said that Defoe was an example of the perfect actualization he wanted in fiction; there was a seventy-six-page article on Defoe in the *Nouvelle Revue Française* in 1912, and Gide's hero in *Les Caves du Vatican* reads only *Aladdin, Robinson Crusoe,* and *Moll Flanders.* Camus's fic-

tional use of Defoe in *La Peste* is perhaps an example of the classicism
they wanted; or better still—since it was closer in time, and since it
included more adventurous action—Hemingway's fiction. (When Rivière
reminded his readers that Stevenson told Schwob to stop singing and tell
us what happened, he seemed to be giving Hemingway his cue [264].)

What concerns us is the intense attention these theories led readers to
give to adventure writers. This was true even of the opposition. Albert
Thibaudet replied to Rivière in 1919 with a defense of the French tradition in novel writing: "un roman, en français, c'est où il y a de l'amour"
("A novel, in French, is where there is love") (73). When he, as a preco-
cious child, asked for a Jules Verne novel at his parochial library, he was
allowed it because, as the librarian said, Verne's books were not novels;
because they contained nothing about love, they were adventure stories,
and so were morally safe.

But in France, Thibaudet admitted, the adventure was poorly developed,
while in England it was a genre "vivace, puissant, enraciné en pleine
humanité" ("lively, powerful, rooted in full humanity"). At its foundation
stood one of the capital books of the Anglo-Saxon race and of all Western
literature—*Robinson Crusoe* (74). (Within French literature, equivalent
books—mutatis mutandis—would be Madame de Lafayette's *La Princesse
de Clèves,* exemplifying the *roman d'analyse,* and Corneille's *Le Cid,*
exemplifying the heroic classical drama.) Thibaudet compared *Robinson
Crusoe* with the *Odyssey,* both of them stories "de l'énergie, de l'intelligence
utile, et de l'action" (of energy, of useful intelligence, and of action);
books written "pour une race, pas pour un public" ("for a race, not for a
public") (75). These are suggestive distinctions and allot a high destiny to
the English adventure novel, even though Thibaudet's own allegiance
goes to the French novel.

Finally, it is appropriate to mention Pierre Mac Orlan, a writer of
adventures, who brought out in 1920 a *Petit Manuel du Parfait Aventurier*—
no doubt in response to all this critical interest in the genre. However, his
remarks, though shrewd and interesting, do not move on the same level of
theoretical interest as those of Rivière and Thibaudet—or even those
of Stevenson. He dwells, instead, on the difference between those who
like to read or write about adventure and those who enjoy it when it
happens.

For Mac Orlan, as for most of the critics, Verne was a bad writer, one
who betrayed adventure values as well as those of traditional literature.
Apart from Stevenson and Defoe, the name these critics most often cite is
Conrad; Rivière was general editor of a big translation of Conrad into

French. But, as Tadié says, they were not really interested in the adventure character of Conrad's novels, for his way of inviting the adventure tale inside the city of literature was highly intellectual and made its adventure content largely symbolic. It ignored not only the minute-by-minute excitement and plausibility of the tale but its cultural context; for instance, in Conrad's case, the myth of the English merchant marine. Stevenson and Lang, though feebler than the French critics in their theoretical interest, kept hold of an important clue or orientation the others let slip.

It is worth reflecting on the fact that Stevenson and Lang were both Scotsmen, and so were their spiritual father, Walter Scott, and their son and heir, John Buchan. The British tradition of adventure writing would be a poor thing if all the Scottish writers were eliminated. (There are other Scottish names that deserve mention in this context, such as R. M. Ballantyne, Neil Munro, and James Barrie.) Fully to discuss why this is so would take us too far afield, but one can say summarily that the function of Scottish writers in British literature strictly parallels the function of Scottish soldiers, engineers, and missionaries in the British Empire. In exchange for her submission to England, Scotland was granted a junior partnership in the empire—more than junior, in some ways. Scotsmen were the younger sons of Britain; they went abroad to seek their fortunes while Englishmen, the elder sons, stayed at home to inherit the ancestral lands. The metaphor has factual and institutional referents. There were, for instance, long-lasting and close links between Scotland and the East India Company (and later the Indian Civil Service) and the Hudson's Bay Company in Canada; indeed, generations of young Scotsmen regularly found jobs in those companies, and there were other such machineries of emigration. The Scottish adventure writers, therefore—while addressing, of course, English readers as much as their own countrymen—inherited with a special directness the imagination of enterprise, seamanship, emigration, and colonialism. And in their writing they fed that imagination again with equal directness.

The genial reception or acceptance by English men of letters of Scottish writers' adventure work probably owed something to literary geopolitics. The distance of Edinburgh from London, both geographically and politically, probably made it easier to swallow the books' implicit imperialism or expansionism—just as the historical distance of their subjects did. All these factors took the curse off Scottish adventure. An English author's account of the 1745 rebellion, describing it from a Hanoverian point of view and with a Hanoverian enthusiasm, would have been far less palatable than *Waverley.*

The kind of adventure these Scottish novelists wrote and Scottish critics praised, the kind originated by Scott and developed most notably by Dumas in France, was of course only one of many. The first kind of specifically modern adventure, as judged by most criteria, was the Robinson Crusoe story, which was retold in every European language and with an almost infinite set of variations on its theme and mood. (In a forthcoming book I propose a scheme of seven such types of adventure tale that tries to identify the types predominant in Western adventure writing in the period from 1719 to the present; of these seven, the Robinson Crusoe story and the historical novel are the first two.) In the short space of history discussed here, in fact, a different, more savage, and more atavistic kind of adventure was claiming the attention of adventure writers. We can call this the saga or Viking adventure; it was written by American and German writers most notably, but in England by, for instance, Rider Haggard.

The writers of these stories justified their work by the way it continued or re-created—and certainly imitated—the Icelandic sagas of the thirteenth century. But this adventure type had a close connection also to the imperialism of the late nineteenth century. For instance, one of the theorists of the interest in the Vikings was Paul du Chaillu (1831–1903), whose first books were about European colonials in Africa. He wrote a two-volume historical work, *The Viking Age,* in which he claimed to give scholarly proof for the popular theory that the English descended from the North Teutons, and a historical novel, *Ivar the Viking.*

Du Chaillu was famous in his day first of all as "the gorilla hunter," because of the books in which he aroused late nineteenth-century Europe's fascination with the big apes. In that capacity, he was one of the precursors of Edgar Rice Burroughs and the Tarzan story. But then his attention turned, in America, to the Vikings. His biographer tells us: "In America he had seen immigrants from the north countries and had been impressed by their physical perfection and almost epic qualities of appearance and character" (Vaucaire 220).

Du Chaillu himself explains: "While studying the progress made in the colonization of different parts of the world by European nations, I have often asked myself the following questions:—How is it that over every region of the globe the spread of the English-speaking people and of their language far exceeds that of all the other European nations combined? Why is it that, wherever the English-speaking people have settled, or are at this day found, even in small numbers, they are far more energetic, daring, adventurous, and prosperous, and understand the art of self-government and of ruling alien people far better than other colonizing nations?" These questions led him to study the Vikings, and to believe that contemporary England and America drew their strength from that heritage. Because "all the nations which have risen to high power and widespread dominion have been founded by men endowed with great, I may say terrible, energy; extreme bravery and the love of conquest being the most prominent traits of their character. The mighty sword with all its evils has thus far always proved a great engine of civilization" (du Chaillu, vii–viii).

Britain gradually became the most powerful colony of those northern tribes, du Chaillu explained, and then waxed more powerful than the Vikings' mother country, just as England saw America taking over world leadership. "The impartial mind which rises above the prejudice of nationality must acknowledge that no country will leave a more glorious impress upon the history of the world than England. Her work cannot be undone; should she today sink beneath the seas which bathe her shores, her record will forever stand brilliantly illuminated on the page of history" (viii). Thus du Chaillu's interest in the Viking sagas, and his writing of a modern Viking adventure story, is closely linked with the world triumph of the Anglo-Saxons.

Such interest was quite international. Germany and Scandinavia are special cases, because of their closeness to the historical source. But some of the writers and thinkers of the United States were also strongly influenced—and not merely the complacent ones, as the case of Thorstein Veblen shows. The idea of the society of the sagas was an important criterion and analytic tool for Veblen in devising his sociology of contemporary America and Europe.

There was also a link to the theories of racism that became popular at the end of the nineteenth century. For instance, the Comte Arthur de Gobineau, whose theories were received with enthusiasm by Wagner and his circle, claimed Viking ancestry for his class, and for himself in particular, in purely narrative form. In 1879 he wrote *L'Histoire d'Ottar-Jarl, pirate norvégien, conquérant du pays de Bray en Normandie* (The story of Ottar-Jarl, Norwegian pirate, conquerer of the land of Bray in Normandy), in which he claimed to descend from this Ottar-Jarl, who was—like du Chaillu's Ivar the Viking, a semidivine son of Odin. (This strain of imagination was, of course, hard to combine with Christianity and was more or less openly pagan.) The contemporary French scholar Ernest Seillière, whose lifework it was to trace the imperialist passion in the politics, but also the aesthetics and general philosophy, of the European nations of this period, called his readers' attention to these modern saga-stories.

The theory behind or around the saga adventure was therefore more cultural than literary. These stories were understood (implicitly) to answer to the political needs of imperialist nations and their ruling classes. They were written, often, in protest *against* the literary climate of their times; their claim to resemble the epics of the past only emphasized their difference from the literary fiction of their own and recent generations. Kipling and Haggard had obviously very little in common with George Eliot and Henry James—as they themselves acutely felt.

But adventure as a whole nevertheless came to be understood as a crucial component of the idea of literature. Around the turn of the century, stories by Kipling, Wells, and others featured characters (male characters) who think they are, or want to be, adventurers; who ludicrously fail to measure up to that idea and yet who *are* adventurers, finally, by grace of their idealism. And thus do they win their place in the world of literature. One such figure is the Cockney clerk who reads about adventure; for instance, Wells's Mr. Polly. "Mr. Polly had been drinking at the poisoned fountains of English literature, fountains so unsuited to the needs of a decent clerk or shopman" (80).

Many writers, then and later, thought of themselves, or wanted to think of themselves, as adventurers. Let me cite D. H. Lawrence and George Orwell, whom I select as rather surprising cases. In his early years, Lawrence made Stevenson his life model, and he always played with the idea of being one who "rode away" or "sailed away." Orwell's stance, even in his most responsible social criticism, was that of a man standing on the edge of society, moving tangentially to it. An essential element in their angle of vision was this claim to a risky and peripheral life.

The same idea of literature and adventure can be found in autobiographical writings by James Barrie and Leonard Woolf, and in the figure of Leonard Bast in E. M. Forster's novel *Howard's End.* Literature is seen as the province of life's wanderers—of "adventurers," in the loose sense; and adventure proper is seen as the province of the aristo-military caste. Other classes, such as the middle class and the proletariat, do not own these ideas by natural right. (By the time of the Great War, however, the triumph of the Schlegel sisters over the Wilcoxes in *Howards End,* and the triumph of the Brangwen sisters over Skrebensky and Crich in *The Rainbow* and *Women in Love,* announced the defeat of adventure and masculinism, as far as the most talented writers were concerned.)

But temporarily even the Viking saga was, as an adventure, a part of literature.

R. B. Allen, in *Old Icelandic Sources in the English Novel,* lists some fifty-seven novels of some note that were directly modeled on the sagas, most of them from the last quarter of the nineteenth century or the first quarter of the twentieth. (He does not pay as much attention to writers of stories for boys, like J. F. Hodgetts, a professor of literature, who wrote *The Champion of Odin* [1885] and other stories with similar titles for *The Boys' Own Paper.* Hodgetts said English boys were too straightforward to like the Greek gods, while the Norse ones would appeal directly to their natural "Teutonic" impulses.) Two of Allen's fifty-seven novels were by R. M. Ballantyne (who wrote one of the famous Robinson stories, *The Coral Island*), one by John Buchan, one by Rider Haggard, one by Scott, and one by Charles Kingsley (*Hereward the Wake,* 1866). I distinguish these titles from the rest because their authors are, in other ways, notable figures in the history of adventure. Kingsley, for instance, wrote a book about the rise of the Teutonic race, called *Heroes;* he inherited from the Carlyle of *Heroes and Hero-Worship* the calling to give Victorian England contact with the saga world and its fierce masculine virtues. His Hereward defines himself as a Viking and a Berserker, though at other times he is just a boisterous English lad. At the end, he is said to have been the last of the old English, while the first of the new English is an "agricultural squire" whose like Kingsley's readers can see around them in their own day. (This way of linking the bloody past to the peaceful present was taken further by Kipling, in *Puck of Pook's Hill.*) Others among Allen's titles, in some way or other remarkable in themselves, are Allen French's *The Story of Rolf and the Viking's Bow,* E. R. Eddison's *Styrbiorn the Strong,* and above all Julian Corbett's bloodthirsty but powerful *The Fall of Asgard.*

The ideology of these stories is usually very plain. The preface to French's *The Story of Rolf,* for instance, declares: "The sagas reveal the characteristics of our branch of the Aryan race, especially the personal courage which is so superior to that of the Greek and Latin races, and which makes the Teutonic epics (whether the Niebelungen Lied, the Morte d'Arthur, or the Njala) much more inspiring than the *Iliad,* the *Odyssey,* or the *Aeneid.*" He associates this personal courage with "the prominence of law in almost every one of the Icelandic sagas" (ix).

Their meaning for the readers of the day lay in their reference to various kinds of contemporary experience, as well as to history and myth. *Guy Livingstone,* G. A. Lawrence's novel of 1857, suggests the connections between these stories and the experience of public school life. Lawrence's novel is largely a document of Regency dandyism, but it uses the imagery of Vikings and Berserkers to define its hero, and it delights in his atavistic reversions to primitive fury. The narrator, a weak boy at school who there received Guy Livingstone's protection, adores him for the rest of his life and reflects that no one in adult civilized life receives such undivided admiration as a school hero. He connects this with premodern modes of feeling and relationship. "The prestige of the Liberator [Daniel O'Connell] among the Irish peasantry comes nearest to it, I think; or the feeling of a clan, a hundred years ago, towards their chief" (21). This expresses, in concentrated form, the atavistic attraction of leadership and, implicitly, of violence. Many historical novels were written for children in the nineteenth century, and many of them were adventures about saga heroes; for instance, the Keary sisters' *The Heroes of Asgard* (1857) and George Dasent's *Tales from the North*.

These stories, like J. F. Hodgetts's, appealed to and rationalized the experience of male adolescence, especially as it was experienced in the English and American boarding schools that prepared future rulers of the Anglo-Saxon empire. We saw one example of this in *Guy Livingstone;* another is *Tom Brown's Schooldays,* especially as it was understood at the time.

When Thomas Hughes's novel was published in 1857, it was welcomed by, among others, Fitzjames Stephen, who wrote an appreciative essay, published in *The Edinburgh Review,* in January 1858. He treated the story as a documentary representation of public school life and brushed aside its Christian pietism to point to a pagan or Viking ideology underneath, which rationalized a brutal training in "manliness," "leadership," and power. Stephen described the Rugby boys' celebration after winning a house match as being like a carouse in Valhalla; the effect of the comparison is primarily to enhance the reader's feeling for that ethos. (J. R. Mangan, mentioning this in his essay "Social Darwinism and Upper Class Education in England," agrees that a Social Darwinist ethos was what the public schools taught.)

It seems clear that one of the attractions of this kind of adventure was its image of passions and actions simpler and stronger than educated white men at the end of the nineteenth century felt themselves capable of—passions and actions they thought came more easily to their national and class enemies. We can see an early example of this in one of the versions of the Robinson Crusoe story, R. M. Ballantyne's *Coral Island,* when the boy Jack is intoxicated with battle and reverts to a primitive fierceness. Other striking examples come in Rider Haggard's novels; for instance, in *King Solomon's Mines,* where mild Sir Henry, when forced to fight, turns into a Berserk Viking and then is an equal and comrade to the Zulu warrior-giant Umbopa.

Both Winston Churchill and Graham Greene have mentioned the importance of Haggard's Umslopogaas in their fantasy life as boys, and Haggard said that his African stories owed their popularity to the Zulu's presence within them (Fisher 207). In *Nada the Lily,* the most impressive and bloodthirsty of those stories, Umslopogaas runs with a wolf pack, an atavistic fantasy that Kipling took over in *The Jungle Book.* Haggard apparently drew Umslopogaas from a real axe-wielding Zulu warrior he knew when he was in Africa in 1876 and 1877, and Umslopogaas lived long enough to hear of the novels in which he figured and to declare that Haggard ought to pay him half the takings. (The relation between the two was like that between Tolstoy and the Cossack Epishka, from whom Tolstoy drew the Eroshka of *The Cossacks.* Tolstoy was a writer of adventures—perhaps the most striking case of a writer equally powerful in literature and that other imaginative world.) There is a complementary relationship between the Zulu warrior and Allan Quatermaine, the white hunter, that extends the contrast between the two sides of Sir Henry and energizes many of these tales. Quatermaine is physically unimpressive and emotionally inexpressive; dry and prudent, he does not belong in the company of heroes that includes Umslopogaas. But he is, of course, the master of the situation in the stories in which they both appear, just as the white man is the master in his dealings with all savage and heroic races.

Haggard develops a theory of this atavism, and of how much the denizens of England have forgotten—sheltered as they have been—of the fierceness of nature, including their own deeper nature; his characters who have lived adventurous lives abroad feel themselves very much out of place in England. (Cecil Rhodes and Kipling felt this; it was a widespread feeling in the imperialist epoch.) And this theory becomes a premise of adventure writing from this point on—you find it in Kipling and John Buchan and Edgar Rice Burroughs, for instance. Kipling offered his readers subtler versions of the reassurance Haggard offered, and Burroughs (in his Tarzan stories) much cruder ones.

John Buchan's adventure tales belong to yet another type, one I call the Hunted Man story, which has a political implication significantly different from that of the other two. But all these kinds of adventures are at the same time closely related, just as all forms of real-life adventure are closely related. There is a tradition of adventure quite as strong and intricate as the tradition of canonical literature. Buchan was a great admirer of Stevenson and Scott (as Scott was of Defoe, and Dumas and Cooper were of Scott, and so on).

To discuss Buchan's work as a whole would take us out of our period, but it is worth pointing out—as a suggestion of this subject's importance—that his tales were favorite reading for at least three English prime ministers (A. J. Balfour, Stanley Baldwin, and Clement Attlee), and his more serious works were read by, for instance, the Kennedys. Jacqueline Kennedy Onassis has told us that Buchan's autobiography was one of her husband's favorite books.

Buchan often used the word *adventure* in his fiction titles (chapter and collection titles, like *Adventurers All* [1942], rather than book titles). He also discussed the idea historically and exhortatively in speeches and essays, just as he discussed the idea of empire. (He was one of the chief spokesmen for the British Empire in its post-1918 phase.) Needless to say, such ideas have not been taken seriously by major modern critics, who have excluded adventure from the canon quite as rigorously as the Victorian humanists did, though on quite different aesthetic grounds. Nor can Buchan's books be called neglected masterpieces of literature or thought. But there is enough substance to them (and to the ideas of the German and French critics cited before) to make us at least ask what hidden drives lie behind the Anglo-American determination not to take adventure stories seriously. (Approving their political or moral message is, of course, another matter, which demands another essay, but I should make it clear that I do not share the implicit faith of most critics that we can discharge our cultural responsibility by turning our backs on such books.)

The measure of literary merit—that is, the declaration that these are simply not "good books"—cannot, I think, be taken to settle the question of why we dismiss adventures. First of all, because the talents and achievements of men like Defoe and Scott are by general agreement great enough to win full attention from scholars of literature. Second, because the literary merits of a genre are as much consequence as cause of the esteem in which it is held. The literary establishment has given writers the clear message that adventures are not books to be written carefully—with literary sensibility and literary passion—and that no artistic prizes are in prospect for their writers.

No doubt, one of those hidden drives, and a perfectly honorable one, is to discountenance empire and masculinism (and related chauvinisms) by means of discountenancing adventure. But—as I need hardly say—none of those ideas are limited to or ruled by literature, or are to be repressed as social forces by a consensus of literary critics. There have been, and will be, adventure and empire, whatever we scholars say. All we can do is keep them out of literature—out of the canon. To do so has certainly not been meaningless. Such acts of censorship belong to the social function of literature in this sense. But if we want literary sensibility to be the agent of the most serious kind of knowledge, to bring it to bear on the experience and, even more, the dreams of society's heroes—our captains, explorers, engineers, missionaries—those who have determined, and most probably will continue to determine, the main lines of historical development, then we must study adventure.

Works Cited

Allen, R. B. *Old Icelandic Sources in the English Novel.* Philadelphia: University of Pennsylvania Press, 1933.

De Gobineau, Arthur de. *L'Histoire d'Ottar-Jarl, pirate norvégien, conquérant du pays de Bray en Normandie.* Paris: Didier, 1879.

Du Chaillu, Paul. *The Viking Age,* 2 vols. London: John Murray, 1889–90.

Eddison, E. R. *Styrbiorn the Strong.* New York: A. and C. Boni, 1926.

Fisher, Margery. *The Bright Face of Danger.* London: Hodder and Stoughton, 1986.

French, Allen. *The Story of Rolf and the Viking's Bow.* 1904. Boston: Little, Brown, 1924.

Green, Martin. *The Robinson Crusoe Story.* University Park: Pennsylvania University Press, 1991.

Lang, Andrew. *Essays in Little.* London: Henry, 1891.

Lawrence, George A. *Guy Livingstone.* 1857. New York: F. A. Stokes, 1928.

Mangan, J. R. "Social Darwinism and Upper Class Education in England." In *Manhood and Morality.* Ed. J. R. Mangan and J. Walvin. Manchester: Manchester University Press, 1987.

O'Neill, Kevin. *André Gide and the Roman d'Aventures.* Sydney: Sydney University Press, 1969.

Rivière, Jacques. *Nouvelles Etudes.* Paris: Gallimard, 1947.

Roskill, Mark. *The Interpretation of Cubism.* Philadelphia: Art Alliance Press, 1985.

Stevenson, Robert Louis. *Memories and Portraits.* London: Pentland, 1907.

Tadié, Jean-Yves. *Le Roman d'Aventures.* Paris: P.U.F., 1982.

Thibaudet, Albert. *Reflexions sur la Littérature.* Paris: Gallimard, 1938.

Vaucaire, M. *Paul du Chaillu, Gorilla Hunter.* New York: Harpers, 1930.

Wells, H. G. *The History of Mr Polly.* London: Nelson, 1910.

The Novel as a
Novel Experiment in Statement
The Anticanonical Example of H. G. Wells

Our limited awareness of H. G. Wells's fiction (it has no live presence in American literary study), and our exclusion of Wells from the modernist canon, is a liability for any theory of the novel and a potential embarrassment for literary history. We need to reevaluate the range and purport of Wells's work—to talk in terms suitable for appreciation and theory about more than *Tono-Bungay* (1909). What if the Wells of *The Undying Fire* (1919) or of *Christina Alberta's Father* (1925) or of *The Bulpington of Blup* (1932) has a significance for us, in spite of the accumulations of critical contempt for his ideas and for his alleged lack of literary quality? It might be that the ideas have been misconstrued or merely caricatured; or that Wells's treatment of the ideas has been underestimated. And now that critics are less bent on distinguishing great books and ideas from just plain good ones—that is, from the sort of books and ideas Wells characteristically produced—we are in at least the right frame of mind for reopening his case. Happily, the later novels are being reissued; and an intelligent new biography has been written by David C. Smith. There also appears to be a promising match between two of Wells's convictions and the beliefs of younger literary scholars. Wells preceded them in the distrust of aesthetic value judgments and of the ritualized canonization of this or that writer or work. *Boon* (1915), the often-mentioned but mostly unread attack on Henry James (on Conrad too), questions evaluation and canon formation in a way that is as up-to-date as *Critical Inquiry*. And Wells's idea that "art" is a bourgeois invention that masks political and economic realities we cannot afford to leave covered up complements the latest analysis of "literature" as a history-bound, class-bound ideological artifact. These are promising signs for a revival.

But if a Wells revival is to be long lived, it will have to shake off two strong, interrelated influences—one modernist and literary, one postmodern and literary-critical. In excluding Wells from our attention, we repeat mechanically the exclusion of Wells handed down to us by James, Ford, Lawrence, and Woolf. We thereby underwrite their self-canonizing efforts and accept the version of literary history—especially of what modernism and the novel are or ought to be—involved in the canonization. We also abet these modernists' theoretical distinction between "literature"—what James, Ford, Lawrence, and Woolf produced—and some other kind of writing—that is, Wells's. Three years before *Boon,* in 1912, James declared to Edmund Gosse that Wells "has cut loose from literature clearly—practically altogether; he will still do a lot of writing probably—but it won't be *that*" (611). The same judgment is repeated in Woolf's review of *Joan and Peter* in 1918 and in her "Mr. Bennett and Mrs. Brown" in 1924, in Lawrence's review of *The World of William Clissold* in 1926, and in Ford's last discussion of Wells in *Portraits from Life* in 1937. These four writers, submerging considerable differences among themselves, for twenty-five years maintained an agreement on this one thing: that Wells sacrificed literature and the novel to essay writing, to outright discussions of ideas; but that literature and the novel could be no such thing.

What the novel can be, the canonized figures say, is various: a realistic picture of life, a character study or an impression; a set of formal experiments; even a fantasia of ideas—*as long as,* and only insofar as, the novel appears as a picture of a whole world, in the mode, that is to say, of "experience." For there to be "the novel," apparently, a statement or overt ideology must be neutralized, must be *rendered* as nonstatement or as a transcendence of statement and ideology. Our narratologies abet this assumption, which underlies most canonized narrative fictions. Analysis of a narrative might be a recovery of the statement or the ideology displaced by the narrative. But analysis of this "recovering" kind still presumes that narrative does not speak itself as statement so much as it speaks itself as experience.

There is a postmodern, literary-critical influence that abets this novel-istic and narratological assumption. The phrases I use about picturing a world and about rendering statements derive from reading the Marxist critic Terry Eagleton. Like Eagleton, Wells attacks aesthetic value judgments and canons; and like Eagleton, Wells believes the novel is a bourgeois invention masking realities that should not be covered up. It seems that Eagleton and Wells make a good match. Yet Eagleton is not a match for Wells when Eagleton *claims* that a literary text, no matter how embedded in ideology, still is "the most revealing mode of experiential access to ideology that we possess," and that in literature the elaboration of "categories and protocols is not carried to the point of producing *concepts*" (101). Eagleton tells us, of course, that "the function of criticism is to refuse the spontaneous presence of the work," yet arguably the spontaneous presence in fiction of "the textures of lived experience" (101) remains the central focus even of the refusal. What Eagleton gives us is another version of the difference between ideology or statement and experience or real history, in which difference the traditional novel—and modernism, and the story-plot distinction of narratology, and even ideological criticism—always locates itself. In contrast, Wells insists on negating this difference that seeks to neutralize, to displace, or to see as displaced fiction's relation to statement. For Wells, fiction came to be important insofar as it made passé the cultivation of "experience." Wells's fiction explicitly refuses its own spontaneous presence.

Wells accepted his fellow writers' characterization of his work—and his exclusion from them—without protest; and he stubbornly wrote on. This stubborn acceptance must not be taken as a sign of Wells's consent to the marginalization of his fiction. Such a response, suiting our prejudices, would leave our sense of the literary landscape unchanged. But I suggest that Wells's chosen form of fiction, to the modernists apparently unique and aberrant, has been far more in literary play than his critics have assumed; and his form might be more genuinely prophetic of the shape of fictive things to come—to *have* come—than any of his historical predictions. What, then, was Wells writing, and what widespread transformation of the novelistic endeavor does it grasp?

In *Experiment in Autobiography,* Wells calls his novels "experiments and essays in statement . . . outside any established formula for the novel." According to Wells, "it required some years and a number of such experiments" before he got clear what he was doing. He realized that his ideal reader "cared no more for finish and fundamental veracity about the secondary things of behavior than I. I did not want to sweep under the mat for crumbs of characterization, nor did [the reader]. . . . What we wanted was . . . ventilation of the point at issue" (418). Now this thing outside established formula, which Wells got clear some time after *Tono-Bungay,* is not entirely unique. Partly it is a version of Menippean satire, of what Northrop Frye calls "anatomy"; and as Frye said long ago, "a clearer understanding of the form and traditions of the anatomy would make a good many elements in the history of literature come into focus" (312). A number of Wells's books—*Boon,* especially—have affinities with Burton, Swift, and Carlyle, and can be read as samples of the anatomical genre.

But Wells, I think, is more outside established formulas than that. He is combining the anatomy with a revival of the traditions of the essay; and this hybrid of anatomy and essay, the Wellsian New Essay (if I may call it so), is connected with an attempt to put the experiment in statement *in the place of* the novel, not to maintain the novel, along with the anatomy and the essay, as *separate* literary kinds. The New Essay is intended to execute a revolution in generic history. The science fiction component of Wells's output might be seen as part of this revolution—as a means of forcing the novel out of the mode of "experiential access" and into an essayistic, purely or predominantly conceptual realm, as a sign of the novel's turn from "life" to ideology.

It is not only Wells who has practiced this conceptual form and who thereby—so to speak—invades the novel's sphere and takes it over. The New Essay's nineteenth-century forebears include Carlyle, much of Hawthorne and Melville, *Marius the Epicurean,* Mallock, Butler, Bellamy, and Howells. But in Wells's era we especially see the rise of fictions that move outside the established novelistic formulas—and, as they move, compete for the place the novel holds in literary history and in our attention. We could group with Wells's work an ever-increasing quantity of twentieth-century essays in statement, from Gissing's *Henry Ryecroft* to Aldous Huxley's and Djuna Barnes's discursive fictions; to James Branch Cabell's work, Cummings's *The Enormous Room,* Robert Coates's *Yesterday's Burdens,* Kenneth Burke's *Towards a Better Life* (this text from 1931 is especially important, as we shall see), and Santayana's *The Last Puritan;* to most of Gertrude Stein's and Wyndham Lewis's fictions; to *Finnegans Wake,* which is arguably an essay on language; to Beckett's and Nabokov's experiments in statement—say, *The Unnamable* and *Ada;* and to fictions like Paul Goodman's, Christine Brooke-Rose's, and Raymond Federman's—indeed, to most of what we think of from the 1950s on as experimental writing. In the latter, the New Essay turns out to be primarily about the concept of fiction itself, rather than—as in Wells—about political or socioeconomic or psychosocial matters. But the tie of such experiment to Wells lies in a common link with his attempt to subvert the novel and to replace it with a new mode. There are even stronger likenesses to what Wells was doing outside Anglo-American tradition: Nietzsche in *Thus Spake Zarathustra,* Proust, Mann, Genet and Sartre, even Bataille and Blanchot are among writers who seem to be rethinking the novel along essayistic lines. And in the kind of criticism represented by Eagleton—in spite of his attachment to the novel as a form of "experience"—there is a growing tendency to treat all fictions as just the essaylike ideological experiments Wells intended to produce.

My list of authors to be grouped with Wells appeals to readers' intuitions of affiliation. But argumentation, not intuition, is needed. In pursuit of the former, two considerations can best expound the New Essay. One can point out in Wells's opponents a practice of the very kind of writing they castigate in Wells "the non-artist." Such an active internal contradiction is symptomatic of the forcefully growing influence of the object of censure. Is it not striking that Lawrence *and* Woolf join hands in condemning Wells's aesthetic practice? Woolf—the writer of such stories as "The Mark on the Wall," "Monday or Tuesday," and "An Unwritten Novel"; the writer of *The Waves* and the producer of *The Pargiters*—creates work of her own that is difficult to distinguish from abstract assertion and discussion. Might Woolf represent a Wellsian revolution against "novel" writing from which she only self-deceptively dissociates herself? And Lawrence, who in *Fantasia of the Unconscious* calls his novels and poems "pure passionate experience" (57) and defines his abstract analytic assertions as mere secondary derivatives of the former, filled the last decade of his life with texts that critics say have broken down into mere experiments in statement. In the name of Woolf's and Lawrence's shared idea that the novel must be "pure passionate experience," we turn away from *Aaron's Rod, The Lost Girl, Kangaroo,* and *The Plumed Serpent.* But the Lawrence we reject has the look of Wells; and this look is that of the New Essay, of what novels generally have perhaps already become. When I later discuss *Christina Alberta's Father* as a response to both "Mr. Bennett and Mrs. Brown" and the *Fantasia,* I shall be educing Wells's idea that the modernists' essays are indistinguishable from their own novels—and from his.

Before we can see the cogency of this idea, however, a second consideration has priority. The hypothetical or theoretical genre of the New Essay can be kept in sight if I propose for it a set of identifying formal characteristics. Trying to put a different fictional discourse in the novel's place, Wells (I hypothesize) uses form to fight form—but for the sake of making it all the more possible for form to carry a writer's statements. In the light of the New Essay's formal characteristics, insofar as I can extract them from Wells's practice, we can better measure whether or not Woolf, Lawrence, and other modern or postmodern proponents of novels are writing what they say they are. To begin with, then, in spite of the relation of the New Essay to an older essay form, which in the past emphasized first subjectivity and then objectivity, Wells's practice is to explore a statement—an overtly ideological position—without attaching the statement to a personal subject. Or if such a subject is there, it is present in order to be (at best) a heuristic persona or (at worst) to be discredited and subverted. A Wellsian essay expresses an aspect of what Wells called the mind of the race and what our era would call—to borrow a phrase from Catherine Belsey—"subjectless discursive knowledge" (139). Yet even though it is not subjectively personal, the New Essay is not in contrast objective or matter-of-fact. This is because its focus is not objective fact but speculative ideology—or fact only in the light of speculation. The mind of the race, and the mind that unfolds itself in a text by Wells, ought to be described not as knowledge but as subjectless discursive speculation. For Wells, speculation is a compromise between fact or knowledge, on the one hand, and idea and theory, possibility, fantasy, even nonsense, on the other. Hence, even Wells's life appears to him as a persistent tentative speculation, as an *experiment* in autobiography, in which he exhibits himself as a provisional persona who knows experience primarily as a set of theoretical probabilities and possibilities. He and the race are not what they have been but what they are becoming—what in terms of speculation and probability they *might* be. The New Essay accordingly foregrounds not the raw truth or falsity of persons, things, and ideas but an ideology of their possibilities and probabilities.

A third characteristic especially distinguishes the Wellsian experiment from traditional novel narrative. The latter is constituted by elemental differences and contrasts, all of which undergo change; even their repetition is touched by transformation. In contrast, the essay in statement is unified by insistent repetition of its overt thematic and ideological burden—of the point at issue's being ventilated. Whereas we can construe the transformations of novelistic narrative as a dialogue or dialectic, it is more difficult to do this with Wells. Eagleton, saturated in dialogics and dialectics, says, "The [aesthetic] text is . . . never at one with itself, for if it were it would have . . . nothing to say" (89). But a text—even a novelistic one—can say the same thing in a variety of ways and so still be "at one with itself." In the New Essay "characters" and "plot" are modes of intoning the experiment's overtly presented ideas. They are equivalent to what Kenneth Burke, eschewing narrative, names as the Six Pivotals out of which he builds *his* New Essay of 1931, *Towards a Better Life.* Burke's statements undergoing experiment are expressed in a series of rhetorical variations, which Burke names "lamentation," "rejoicing," "beseeching," "admonition," "aphorism," and "threat." Wells's mature works, starting with the "prig" novels of 1912–14, look like narrative but are really his themes given a performance upon Burke's rhetorical pivots. Thus, to James's complaint that Mary Justin, the heroine in *The Passionate Friends,* does not have a voice or a presence in sufficient live contrast to the hero-narrator Stephen, one might respond that she and the narrator are to be read as a single ideological discourse on jealousy, inflected by Stephen as admonition, inflected by Mary as threat. The New Essay arguably redraws novelistic character as a mode of rhetoricity—thus interpreting or reading "the novel" and "character" in a way that forecasts structuralist narratology's way of reading them.

The last characteristic of the New Essay is an innovative relation of its speculative discourse to time. Like conventional fiction, the form unfolds its thematic repetitions as a species of time traveling; the statements that constitute the text traverse a past, present, and future that belong to the text and to the actual time of the world. But in the conventional novel, this traversal represents an attempt by the novelist (and an invitation to the reader) to reconstitute time by reversing the text's diachronic sequence of tenses. The traditional novel and its reader collect—or re-collect—the novel's diachronic sequence as a unity of the narrative and of its significance. Even in the modernist novel's attempts to disperse the unity of traditional novelistic form and to cultivate disjunctions of time and meaning, coincidence inherent in the disjunct parts turns modernist narrative back toward unity. In Woolf's *Mrs. Dalloway,* for example, the similar personal quality and the similar personal relation to time of the heroine and of Septimus Smith amount to a unifying bridge built over the text's formal and temporal disjunctions. In contrast to both traditional and classically modernist work, in the New Essay unity has a different source and a different correlation to time.

To begin with, the New Essay's unity derives not from a surmounting of time's production of differences but from the obvious ventilated point—the ideological statement—at issue. This unity is differentiated or varied (but is also preserved) by the writer's experimentation with the Six Pivotals. But then, even as this unified statement traverses the Pivotals and the tenses conjugated by any discourse, the New Essay's statement has an idiosyncratic relation to the future. A remark of Burke's hints at this relation: "What is right for a day," he says, "is wrong for an hour, what is wrong for an hour is right for a moment—so not knowing how *often* or how *long* one should believe in the . . . aphorisms of [*Towards a Better Life*], I should say there is more sincerity in their manner than in their content" (xvi). Experiments in statement, Burke realizes, whatever their unity of content, are curiously vulnerable to transformations of their speculative ideological power by time's intrusions upon them. Hence, the New Essay's speculative manner is as much its matter as any other content. It is especially in the light of future developments that the New Essayist's statements will undergo changes of relevance and value. Thus, in comparison to traditional and modernist narratives, the New Essay's relation to time is more "toward" a time not of or in the text and not yet of or in the world. Whereas the novel, whether premodern or modernist, ultimately makes present a coinciding of the temporal and meaningful elements within itself, the New Essay is coincident with a future outside itself and beyond the world's current time. The speculative nature of the New Essay is underwritten by this orientation toward the intrusive shadow of what is ahead of us, which is already cast back on our present. Clearly, Wells's *The Time Machine,* a novel named after an engine that might be said to figure narrative, predicts in its story the turn toward the future given by Wells to the form of his "thing outside any established formula for the novel."

The characteristics I have just sketched need to be filled out, so I turn to Wells's *Christina Alberta's Father* (1925). The speculation ventilated here concerns a collapse of the reality of the self. Wells points out that Freudian psychology and feminism engender this collapse, because they argue the illusive and conservative nature of the ego, which the text represents as a product of patriarchy. The undermining of selfhood is proposed by *Christina Alberta's Father* as a great expansion of awareness and political possibility. But the expansion is perplexed. Wells shows women, even the most liberated feminists, and men embedded—stuck—in Oedipal structure. Indeed, Wells argues, Freudianism is embedded in the patriarchy its insight promises to dissolve. Christina Alberta and her father suffer the pathos of being both helped and victimized by Freudian ideas and their political possibilities. Yet the pathos and victimization, the Essay argues, is the necessary first step into a better future state in which the self will give way to identities that are no longer restrictively fixed.

This New Essay is interesting not just in its own right but as a response to two old-style essays by those conventional novelists Woolf and Lawrence. "Mr. Bennett and Mrs. Brown" appeared a year before Wells's book; and the "character" or "hero" named Albert Edward Preemby in Wells's experiment is said in the text to have discovered and been influenced by a "nice deep confusing" (85) book of 1922 called *Fantasia of the Unconscious.* To see how Wells uses these essays as both complements and foils for his own practice, and as indirect interpretations of his critics, we can remind ourselves first of the argument of "Mr. Bennett and Mrs. Brown." "All novels . . . deal with character," Woolf says, "to express character—not to preach doctrines" (117). In the light of this belief, the historical specificity invoked by the essay's assertion that in 1910 human character changed is considerably qualified. With the passing of the Edwardian era, Woolf says, the novelistic *conventions* (whereby character was expressed) changed; but character itself is "eternal, . . . is human . . . , [and] . . . changes only on the surface" (122). The essentialism of Woolf's critique of the Edwardians, which bases her own experiments in the novel in an antagonism to history, is marked. "The Edwardians were never interested in character in itself, or the book in itself" (119); they were interested in the world outside the book, in history and ideology.

Ironically, critics have used Woolf's feminist essays to inspire a recovery of the novel's relation to history and to ideology; but in doing this they have made Woolf the Edwardian she did not want to be in 1924. For to be an Edwardian was, as she saw it, to be not a novelist—it was to be like Wells. Of him Woolf says that "in his passion to make [Mrs. Brown] what she ought to be [he] would [not] waste a thought upon her as she is" (119). This misreading, which presumes that Wells is interested in maintaining character at all (no matter in what changed conditions) and which is blind to the New Essay's special sense of futurity, underwrites Woolf's insistence that *novelists* "feel . . . there is something permanently interesting in character itself" (114). The role of the novel for Woolf is to maintain this interest even if it requires art to avoid the appearance of being art. Unlike Wells, Woolf allows "Mrs. Brown" to escape description and ideation alike, because any formulation of her—even an aesthetic one—would force the character to be one thing rather than another. To be sure, this final emphasis is not coherent, since by the end of Woolf's essay "character in itself" escapes both itself and the book "in itself." But we might surmise that Woolf willingly subordinates her ideas to incoherence in the name of the novel's alleged access to experience, which is not carried to the point of producing concepts—or conceptual coherence. As Woolf says in her 1918 review of Wells's *Joan and Peter,* "being talked at" (coherently or not) by a text about ideas is "unfortunate for art" (*Contemporary Writers* 90).

Twenty years later, the Woolf of *Three Guineas* might not have cared as much about art. As I shall point out in my conclusion, *Three Guineas* brings to fruition what *A Room of One's Own* begins—an even greater approximation of Woolf's ideological practice of writing to Wells's. But in 1924 the idea of character, or—by extension—of self, exhibited by Woolf is that it is a substance existing beyond any of the conventions or ideas whereby it is expressed. The idea of character or self exhibited by *Christina Alberta's Father* is that character is a speculative convention, no more factive or fictive than any other. Hence, the title *Christina Alberta's Father* (which makes us wonder to begin with just who this story is to be about—the daughter or the father) names a character who cannot be identified and a kinship of dubious character. Albert Preemby appears to be the titular hero, but he is only Christina Alberta Preemby's unwitting adoptive parent. The daughter's biological father is the psychoanalyst Wilfred Devizes. As a young man, Devizes impregnates his girlfriend, Christina Alberta's mother, then palms her off on Preemby, so that Devizes can pursue a medical career. In turn, the mother deceives Preemby into thinking the child is his own. Twenty years later, Devizes reappears and becomes the man with whom his biological daughter falls in love (and who falls in love with her), while he is treating her other father, Preemby. Devizes reappears because he is called in to treat Preemby on account of Preemby's having developed the conviction that he is not Preemby but Sargon, a Sumerian king of the twenty-eighth century B.C. Preemby's conviction is not treated by Wells as a psychosis but as the effect of a plausible way to reconstruct our conventional ideas of character and of individuation. The book's sympathy with Preemby is not the result of wry compassion for a utopian who has lost his grip on ineluctable reality; it is a sympathy with Preemby's groping toward the possibility, even the probability, that our usual ways of determining and fixing identity are wrong. Preemby/Sargon predicts a probable future state in which the ideology of individuation has ceased to matter and in which even historical epochs are no longer distinctive.

In Preemby, Wells is writing about a character who undermines the narratological possibility of talking about character or individual agency. The whole of the discourse, instead of character, remains the only agency in the New Essay. But what of the heroine's identity? She is caught—as my adumbration of the novel's story has suggested—in an unsettling transference and countertransference. Christina Alberta desperately needs to overcome her unconsciously precipitated romance with her father, who of course needs equally to overcome his romance with his daughter. The father rushes defensively into marriage with another woman—repeating, by the way, his evasive conduct toward Christina Alberta's mother. But the heroine, smarter than the father/psychoanalyst, defends herself against family romance by eschewing marriage altogether. Apparently, she also turns her back on the book's idea "that our race has reached, and is now receding from, a maximum of individuation . . . [that] it will swallow up individual egotistical men in its common aims" (393). She protests thinking in terms of the mind of the race. "I am Christina Alberta; I am not Woman or Mankind. As Christina Alberta, I want and I want and I want. . . . I hate the idea of self-sacrifice. . . . I am an egoist pure and simple. . . . I refuse altogether to mix with that promiscuous anybody-nobody" (399–400).

Christina Alberta's protest seems to turn statement into a conflict that narrativizes and neutralizes Wells's ideology. Yet Wells's discourse does not use the heroine's protest to open itself to "experience" or to contradict Preemby/Sargon's undermining of the self. Even Christina Alberta admits her protest is provisional: "I am giving in—what can I do but give in?—and soon I will be a Sargonite. . . . But not this summer. Not now" (401). Not now, but in the future. Her plea for the natural difference of her ego from all others is a passing phase of her rhetoric—and of the rhetoric of the text. This does not mean that Wells shrinks from making readers feel the impact of the self and even the necessity for relying upon its construction and for invoking its agency, even in the teeth of the self's demise. Christina Alberta's sense of self is centered in "a pitiless conscience . . . with no foundations and no relationships; it just floated by itself in her being" (59), because it has no external supports. The heroine "did not believe in respectability, Christian morality, the institution of the family, the capitalist system or the British Empire"; she has a mind "entirely swept and void of restraining convictions" (60). But the "entirely" is qualified, after all; one conviction remains, perhaps because all the rest are absent. "Christina Alberta had to be Christina Alberta, clear and sound, or the court of conscience made things plain and hard for her" (61).

But this self, a form of conscience that is generated by the collapsing authenticity of everything outside it, is presented by the book as temporary, as a passing phase corresponding to a Christian and imperialist phase of culture that is passing away. Which is to say that the anti-individualist statement of Wells's text is at times, first early in the book, in the description of the heroine's conscience, and then again in the finale, voiced as the statement's rhetorical inversion. The collapse of self is voiced as *lamentation* for the collapse of self, or as *threat* against the collapse ("I am giving in—what can I do but give in? . . . But not . . . now"). This variety of voicings only furthers the text's anti-individualist statement. To paraphrase Burke, the intonation of identity is here more sincere as a manner of expression than as a content. Such intonation, however, is not a statement rendered as nonstatement or as transcendence of statement, for it does not escape the book's collectivist ideology.

Just as the heroine's assertion of identity cannot escape Wells's statement against self, so it cannot escape the universal Oedipal network. Christina Alberta's individuation as a character, especially at the final moment of her supreme appeal to its own distinctiveness, is exhibited as a psychic and erotic defense, a temporary construction and idealization whereby she can renounce her father. True to Freud, Wells discloses the ego as an Oedipal precipitate. The ego is exhibited at the same time as an accession of superego, in spite of the ego's desire to defend itself against the superego. The latter, however, is not just the father but also the collective being of women, which collective Christina Alberta invokes ("We don't think of children. We don't want to think about them. There it is! And anyway children do not take a woman out of her egotism; they only extend and intensify it" [399–400]), even as she is proclaiming the supreme value of her unique self. It is Wells's assertion here that the new collective female superego, a female Sargonism, is the growing point of consciousness and social order, the advance against patriarchy. But we see the heroine torn between individualism, between what she "really" is (albeit what she really is, is a defense against Devizes, hence still an expression of him), and the anti-individualist existence to which she *will* bow ("soon I will be a Sargonite"). In this conflict Christina Alberta shows Wells's grasp of the division within Freud's thought, which reveals the ego to be not a single self but a multiplicity of selves, yet which refers this multiplicity back to patriarchy rather than forward to a new, anti-Oedipal order.

Characteristically, this New Essay ends by claiming its significant correspondence to be not with a present to which it refers but with a future state, one that will reduce the narrative to a prefatory symptom of the future's antiegoistic, antipatriarchal social being. Indeed, Wells uses a play on form in *Christina Alberta's Father*—a self-reflexive erasure of the text's presence as a novel and even as the reader's object of reading—to show the relation between his ideological statement and what he implies is our era's peculiar forward-looking temporality. The source of this temporality is explained in the *Experiment in Autobiography,* where he tells us that he believes political analysis in terms of class war and class division is out of date, is "a real obstacle to the onward planning of world order" (616). This is because "existing political structures"—whether constituted or described as divisible, distinct persons, classes, or nations—"have fallen behind the great world-order foreshadowed by scientific and industrial progress" (556). What is foreshadowed, however, is already in existence: science and industry have created a global unity with which any consciousness focused on divisions must catch up. That is to say, the world already has the monologic unity that the New Essay cultivates and that utopians assign only to the future; but there seems to be in us a continually insufficient understanding of the future order we have foreshadowed and even produced. Like Christina Alberta and her father/psychoanalyst, we tend to lean backward in consciousness rather than forward—even as we foresee future life. The temporal dilemma of this state is expressed in *Christina Alberta's Father* when the text introduces a new Pivot (or character), Bobby Roothing, who discovers "that there is not, and there never has been, a world that is; there is only a world that has been and a world that is to be" (409).

Wells's treatment of Bobby bears on the formal and especially on the political "moral" of the New Essay. Bobby is an aspiring novelist who pursues Sargon and Christina Alberta as the perfect material for his novel, even though the heroine reminds him of "the people in some horrid Utopia by Wells" (361). But as Bobby starts to write, Wells gives us the end of *Christina Alberta's Father*. The sudden death of Preemby/Sargon affects Bobby "as though all [the] concluding chapters [of an interesting story] had been torn out rudely and unreasonably" (373). Bobby carries on, nevertheless, and a reproduction of the first page of his *Ups and Downs: A Pedestrian Novel* dominates the sixth-but-last page of Wells's text. The same first page then reappears on Wells's last, where it is overlooked by Bobby as a chance wind blows it into a fireplace. What Wells does here is make the reader attend to the last third of *Christina Alberta's Father* as to the abortion of a pedestrian novel, hence to the text as not itself a novel in Bobby's common understanding of the term. Wells is also making the reader think of the end of his text as no more than the start of a future whose power is a capacity to intrude itself on everything present, including his "story." After all, it is the *future* possibility of women in relation to the Oedipal past that has incited this experiment in statement. It is future possibility in general that blows away the novel's first-last page. The experiment is dwarfed, even erased, by what it foreshadows—and by the forward time that foreshadows *it*. Christina Alberta figures this intrusive future; the text tells us that "intrusion was in [the heroine's] nature. . . . she has got herself hatched into this story very much like a young cuckoo . . . and it is impossible to ignore her" (59). Like the psychoanalyst, the heroine remains an intrusive force; unlike him, she figures futurity. And the engagement of the text with this futurity (which the text enwombs, as if it were Christina Alberta's *mother*) is a political one. Wells suggests that the necessity as well as the possibility of politics is underwritten not just by our immediate struggles for power but by our ability to engage anticipations. No less than a pragmatic conflict of interests, politics is an experiment in ideological speculation and is anchored in the shape of things to come.

The relation between Lawrence and Wells named by *Christina Alberta's Father* is represented as Lawrence's intrusion upon Preemby's awareness. But Wells offers us the possibility of seeing himself intrude upon *Fantasia of the Unconscious* in a funny sort of reversal of the chronological influence of (for example) *Ann Veronica* on *The Rainbow.* Put side by side, the 1922 and the 1925 works make us see more of the formal and political bearing of the New Essay and suggest that Lawrence cannot practice the novel as he preaches it—or, rather, that he can only practice it *as* he preaches, that is to say, as he writes his own version of Wells's overtly ideological form. Of course, there is no gainsaying Lawrence's explicit insistence that the *Fantasia* is not a novel, that "this pseudo-philosophy of mine is deduced from the novels and the poems, [which]...come unwatched.... [*they*] are pure passionate experience," whereas the *Fantasia* is composed of "inferences made afterwards, from experience." In jokey derogation, Lawrence calls these "inferences" not just "pseudo-philosophy" but "pollyanalytics" (57). Yet *Christina Alberta's Father,* by its reference to Lawrence, seems to ask two questions: *What* is the *Fantasia* if not a novel, in spite of its author's disclaimer? And—most importantly—what is the *Fantasia,* even if it *is* a novel, but an unavowed revelation of the absence of a difference between novelistically represented "experience" and "analytics" (of any sort)—indeed, of the absence of a difference between novel and fantastic essay or essayistic fantasia? The earnest formal and poetical role played by nonsense in such fantasy, moreover, comes especially into relief when we juxtapose the two texts.

What is first demonstrated by the juxtaposition is that Lawrence's text is more than the uniquely personal or individualized text we remember. Lawrence appears to be affirming *the* self—*his* self—while he maps the bodily unconscious. But as the charmingly cantankerous voicing of the text proceeds, the voicing agent becomes an object of discussion rather than a subject producing a discussion. The self that produces the discourse is anatomized—and dismembered. The discussion—an experiment in statement—and not the self doing the discussing, rules our attention; we become engaged by the rhetorical pivots whereby the discussion is continually varied. *Pace* the alleged priority of experience and life in relation to analytics, the analysis here seems indistinguishable from vitality. Whenever the unique voice—or the immediate experience—of Lawrence emerges in the text, it takes on the pathos of Christina Alberta's "I want" speech: we are struck by the way his individuation shows itself as an apparent defense against an inescapable, anti-individuating, nonimmediate network of relations. And this is because Lawrence's anatomy of life reveals a subjectless discursive weave in which every unique center turns out to be decentered, one of a pair or a match whose reference is to a center somewhere else, in an unlocated "beyond."

The *Fantasia of the Unconscious* locates the self in the solar plexus, but it also makes clear that the self travels. The solar plexus is inextricable from the lumbar ganglion, with which it forms a center of sensual comprehension. But this center refers to another—to a center of dynamic cognition, this time—composed of the cardiac plexus and the thoracic ganglion. In turn, these two pairs (four "centers" now) refer themselves to two others that relocate the self—or disseminate its location—at puberty. These other pairs are the hypogastric plexus and the sacral ganglion, and the cervical plexus and the cervical ganglion. Conscious and unconscious in Lawrence are this series of differentiations within differentiations; not surprisingly, only midway through his discourse, Lawrence says, "So now we see we can never know ourselves" (112). And even though he says that after puberty individuality results from a dynamic relation of the solar and hypogastric plexuses, even though he says that puberty is "the first hour of true individuality" and that "sex is always individual" (144), what is most important in the *Fantasia* is not a song of my (hypogastric) self. The text is weighted, rather, toward this key assertion: "We have got to get back to . . . a passionate unison in actively making a world. This is a real commingling of many. And in such a commingling we forfeit the individual. In the commingling of sex we are alone with *one* partner. It is an individual affair. . . . But in the commingling of a passionate purpose, each individual sacredly abandons his individuality" (144). Such a Wellsian passage—it takes us back to *The Passionate Friends*—no doubt inspired Preemby. It suggests that Lawrence, even when he is writing with his eye on "I" and "experience," is giving an analytic privilege to a comprehensive unity that complements both Wells's idea of the division-transcending world state and the New Essay's emphasis on a monologically unified discourse.

Set beside Wells's experimental practice (and beside the insight we can get from Burke into the structures of that practice), Lawrence, it can be argued, writes about his own rhetorical organization all the time he writes about "experiences" that transcend rhetoric. It is possible to see his meditation on plexuses and ganglia as a meditation on his intonations of his content—on his use of rhetorical pivots that not only represent "the body" but *are* the body of his work. The pleasure of reading the *Fantasia* is that of attending to a monologic rhetorical tour de force. The experiment in statement here takes the form of a repertory of invented attitudes, largely comic, addressed now to the text's ideology, now to the reader, now to the world in general, and ranging emotionally from cockiness to diffidence, from silliness to great earnestness. But in spite of the text's look of impromptu variety, which again suggests (to quote Lawrence's review of Wells's *Clissold*) "passionate and emotional reactions which are at the root of all thought, and which must be conveyed in a novel" (*Phoenix* 350), the "reactions" here, even the "spontaneous" digression on trees in the fourth chapter ("It's nice just to look round, anywhere" [85]), are perfectly seamed into the text's ideological unity. The trees come back later ("the whole tree of our idea of life and living is dead" [119]) in a way that shows how planted a rhetorical device is the trees' initial "spontaneous" intrusion. Perhaps the moment where Lawrence comes closest to admitting the rhetorical nature of this work's body is when he immediately follows the assertion, "For me there is only one law: *I am I*" with the comment, "And that isn't a law, it's just a remark" (66). The body of the *Fantasia,* even though it is dressed up as scientific (or counterscientific) law is just a chain of remarks upon one insistent ideological assertion concerning the Oedipus. Wells's interest in this assertion must have been complemented by his interest in the rhetorical vehicle of the assertion. When under the reader's eyes *Christina Alberta's Father* erases itself as a conventional novel, it draws closer to its inspiration in the *Fantasia*—and thereby mocks Lawrence's privileging of "experience" over the devices of argument.

The single assertion or argument of the *Fantasia,* duplicated in *Christina Alberta's Father,* is that Freudianism is embedded in the patriarchy Freud's insight promises to dissolve—that Freudianism cannot picture the human future as anything but the Oedipus's eternal return. Since futurity is the favorite reference point of the New Essay, it is as if Lawrence is quarreling with a Freudian challenge to the form (inferior to the novel, of course) of his own New Essayistic text. But what is at stake is far more than formal. The key assertion about turning one's back on individuality, about "commingling" for the sake of making a new world, depends upon an idea of development that Lawrence sees as antagonistic to the solar and hypogastric plexuses. The "great sex goal . . . is no goal, but always cries for . . . something beyond, . . . futurity, that which [man's] purpose stands for, the future" (220). This purpose is communal, anti-individualist.

Freudianism troubles Lawrence because it forecasts an obstruction of futurity, an inevitable intrusion upon the psyche, but not of the fruitful kind either Wells's or Lawrence's essays enwomb.

The communal, commingled future Wells and Lawrence write toward is figured as a blessedly intrusive stranger or group of strangers whose communal endeavor has left Oedipal structure behind—even though they have benefited from the discovery of the structure. But as Lawrence interprets Freud, in the latter the future is a repetition of one's past relation to one's parents. And when the Oedipus is coupled with modern ideas about child-rearing, in which a kind of equality and friendly intimacy is offered as the model relation of parent and child, then Lawrence believes a kind of universal psychological incest becomes the fate of modern culture. The future appears as only an intrusion of a bitter kind—as the parent's premature stimulation of the postpubescent plexuses and ganglia. "And this is fatal. It is a sort of . . . dynamic spiritual incest, more dangerous than sensual incest, because . . . more intangible and less instinctively repugnant" (152–53). Lawrence credits psychoanalysis for "this great service of proving . . . that the intense upper sympathy between parent and child . . . inevitably involves us in . . . incest" (153); but then he discredits it for not helping us "to strive for the living future" (160). Thus, Lawrence believes that the Freudian model of mind forecasts as impossible the future realization of anti-individualizing, communal desire because, according to this model, the incestuous origins of desire foreclose development and satisfaction beyond what is individual. "They say it is better to travel than to arrive," Lawrence says ruefully about the yet unsatisfied journey of his communal desire. "It's not been my experience at least. . . . The best thing I have known is the stillness of accomplished marriage." He admits, "I know a great deal more about the craving and raving . . . than about the accomplishment." But at the same time he asserts that the accomplishment of "fulfilled being" in marriage is "only a preparation for new responsibilities ahead, new union . . . , the effort to make . . . a little new way into the future" (169).

What is the intellectual creditability of Lawrence's argument with Freud? " 'I don't believe in this,' said Christina Alberta out of the depths of her chair" (395), while she listens to Devizes's Wellsian analysis of Sargon and the future. Perhaps this exclamation is in order here. Wells transforms the Lawrence of the *Fantasia* into his heroine, who lives the dilemma between futurity and the Oedipus, and then exclaims that she does not believe in the dilemma or in its explanation. Like the unbelieving Christina Alberta, Lawrence turns against his text's ideological speculation. Having referred in his foreword to his own book as "the whole wordy mass of revolting nonsense" (54), Lawrence returns in his conclusion to the same description. This time he puts it into the mouth of Columbia's "Liberty statue," whom he asks to judge his experiment in statement. Accordingly, he imagines *her* protest against "this wordy mass of rather revolting nonsense" (223). Yet, while he uses this refrain to suggest that he does not believe in his experiment, he also hangs onto the nonsense. And is Lawrence here not more senseless and madder than Preemby? Lawrence subjects Freud to outrageous question, and he also asserts that our bodies produce the sun and the moon, and that the latter are governed by our solar plexuses and lumbar ganglia. "I do not believe one-fifth of what science can tell me about the sun. . . . I have believed it for twenty years, because it seemed . . . ideally plausible. Now I don't accept any ideal plausibilities" (181, 182)—just, it appears, fantastic ones.

Nevertheless, Lawrence lends himself to such fantasy apparently to remind us that even Freud—who in American literary study has become as canonical a figure as any, and whom we have come to see as a secure ground of our intellectual lives in a way that forgets Freud's root-and-branch speculativeness—is a fantasist. Lawrence ends the *Fantasia* with a return to his ideas about the moon via mention of an announcement by a Harvard professor "that it's almost a dead cert that there's life on our satellite" (224). He asks Liberty to judge which is the more "high-falutin' Nonsense" (225)—his own or the professor's lunar theories. "I'll bet my moon against the Professor's anyhow," he concludes, careless of the judgment. Of course, Lawrence is not just betting against the Harvard astronomer; he is betting his picture of the unconscious, or his criticism of Freud's picture, against Freud. And he does so in a manner that underscores the way he and Freud both, by virtue of their inflexible commitment to ideological speculation, are lunatic. But this lunacy, because it strains against the limits (from solar plexus to social order) of here and now and against the separation of fact from fantasy, sense from nonsense, promises a liberty that Lawrence and Wells assign to the future because their experiments in statement are already producing it. As Bobby thinks to himself, "The new age dawned anywhere in the social order where people could get free enough to work out new ideas" (359).

The nonsense Lawrence hangs onto in the *Fantasia* turns out to be a political matter as well as another sign of his practice of the New Essay. The new experimental form inevitably involves (Preemby-like) a transgression of common sense, a violation of reason's sobriety. It is the political aspect of futurity that justifies Lawrence's transgression of sense. Because the New Essay presents speculation as a compromise between knowledge or fact, on the one hand, and idea, theory, possibility, even nonsense, on the other, it mixes the knowable and the unknowable in a way that is a likeness of our relation to the future. That relation is a fantasia, a compromise of what is predictable, sensible, and intelligible with what is unaccountable and (for now) senseless and impossible. The way nonsense works in Lawrence's New Essay figures the futurity toward which he wants an opening—in the name of a finer communal order. So there is a serious and not nonsensical logic in his involvement of Freud, the future, and nonsense in the *Fantasia*. The involvement is an expression of political hope; and to condescend to the text the way Liberty does is to reject not just silliness but the *Fantasia*'s political dimension.

If we call Bobby's thought about new ideas and futurity idealist, we will be sharing in the division between experience and analytics, between solid reality and nonsense, that Lawrence tried consciously to underwrite. Here is a case, however, of our needing to trust not the teller but the New Essay. The homage paid Lawrence by *Christina Alberta's Father* suggests the interchangeable nature of Lawrentian novel and Wellsian experiment. They are interchangeable, Wells seems to say, because the *Fantasia* shows the commingling of ideology and rhetorical variation, on the border of sense and fantasia, that characterizes all of Lawrence's work in spite of Lawrence's working literary-critical distinctions. Lawrence is essentially a writer of the argumentation that he and his proponents have been embarrassed by and have tried to submerge in their (and his) notions of how "the novel" subordinates ideology to the drama of experience. The splitting off of Wells from "the novel" and from the modernist canon suppresses the likeness between Lawrence and Wells and covers up Lawrence's place in novelistic form's supersession by the New Essay.

I have tried to show how recovering an uncanonical writer can change our theorizing of literary form and our construction of literary history. With Wells more in mind, we might no longer regard the *Fantasia* as a minor moment in its author's career. Instead, it would become a central Lawrentian text, and also a takeoff point for a revisionary look not just at Wells and Lawrence but at the structures and configurations of modern British fiction and literary history. The professed anti-Wellsian Virginia Woolf might become a notable object of this revisionary look. Thus, I want to end with a suggestion about Woolf as a New Essayist.

Three Guineas is the product of conflict within Woolf's process of composing *The Years*. *The Pargiters,* the manuscript that is called "the novel-essay portion" of *The Years,* might be construed as evidence of Woolf's toying with the Wellsian form. Of course, the "essay" chapters of *The Pargiters* are really more blocks of narrative than they are experiments in statement; but clearly Woolf was interested in not dividing up what issued as *The Years,* a novel that neutralizes ideological statement, and as *Three Guineas,* a non-neutral non-novel. However, the Wellsian question that hangs over Woolf's enactment of the division is: By what logic or for what purpose must the art of the novel and the ideological speculativeness—not to speak of the overt politics—of the New Essay be kept apart? From the moment of her production of *A Room of One's Own,* Woolf had answered the question: There need be no such division. Was the answer unconscious, and the unconsciousness motivated by the neutralizing of statement on behalf of art in Woolf's hostile response to Wells in her early reviews and essays? "Let us look again at the opening pages of *A Room of One's Own,*" Jane Marcus writes. "Woolf identifies herself as a writer of fiction, a 'liar'; she invents Oxbridge and Fernham, rejects 'I' as unreal, and claims anonymity through the three Marys [Beton, Seton, Carmichael] rather than identity as the descendant of . . . Austen and . . . Eliot" (170). By pointing to these things, in effect Marcus is asking us to look at the New Essay components of Woolf's text.

A Room of One's Own unsettles the generic distinctions Wells unsettled. It is a report on the facts and an ideological speculation, but it is a fantasia too. It is neither subjective nor objective; and it is full of devices—the Marys, and Shakespeare's sister—that enable Woolf's deployment of the Six Pivotals to intone her feminism. Moreover, her book is what she complained about in Wells's picture of Mrs. Brown: a picture of woman as she ought to be. Everything in *A Room of One's Own* and in *Three Guineas* has an anchor in the futurity of *ought to be* and *might be.* This anchor gives both texts a borderline relation to fact: "Fiction here is likely to contain more truth than fact" (4), *A Room of One's Own* begins. But now the blurring of fiction and fact, the utopianizing speculation about what Mrs. Brown ought to be, has become an earnest political "nonsense" that empowers Woolf to fight off the high-falutin' nonsense of patriarchy. Although *Three Guineas* seems more factual than *A Room,* the fiction of the guineas is a discourse-originating foolery or play, a ploy whereby the author becomes an anonymous rhetorician whose addresses are all conditioned by future possibilities. *Three Guineas* recirculates *Fantasia of the Unconscious* and *Christina Alberta's Father.* It identifies patriarchal Oedipal fixation as the principal cause of women's oppression and of war, and as the great obstacle to futurity.

If we take Wells to heart, we must consider *Three Guineas* to be as canonical a fiction by Woolf as any. *Three Guineas,* from Wells's standpoint, is the non-neutral thing the state of the world, no less than the state of art, makes it right that the novel should become. Did Woolf not take Wells to heart (however unconsciously) in her last novel experiment? In *Between the Acts,* Wells's *The Outline of History,* which Mrs. Swithin is reading, figures as a model for Woolf's argument that history so far is only an outline—prehistory and not history proper. Miss La Trobe's pageant, and Isa and Giles's marriage are only outlines too, equivalents of the first page of Bobby Roothing's pedestrian novel. Accordingly, the end of *Between the Acts* is represented as a mere beginning. As present objects of the reader's attention, the literary-historical pageant and the marriage are erased under the reader's eyes. What happens is a pointing to the future, whose shadowing forth (at dusk) is the only sign of political hope.

The progress of Woolf's career toward the essays of 1929 and 1938, and her last novel, might represent a remarkable Wellsian turn—and might testify that our ideological criticism, our narratology, and our literary history are not seeing what, if seen, could change them. Uncanonized or anticanonical figures like Wells take revenge for their exclusion. Their exclusion traps us in repetition, so that we see always the same things, make always the same distinctions—say, between novel and essay, or character and convention, or art and life—and thereby see and make nothing new.

Works Cited

Belsey, Catherine. *Critical Practice.* London and New York: Methuen, 1980.

Burke, Kenneth. *Towards a Better Life.* Berkeley and Los Angeles: University of California Press, 1966.

Eagleton, Terry. *Criticism and Ideology.* Thetford, Norfolk: Thetford Press, 1978.

Frye, Northrop. *Anatomy of Criticism.* New York: Atheneum, 1969.

James, Henry. *Letters.* Vol. 4: 1895–1916. Ed. Leon Edel. Cambridge, Mass: Belknap Press, 1984.

Lawrence, D. H. *Psychoanalysis and the Unconscious* and *Fantasia of the Unconscious.* New York: Viking Press, 1960.

———. "*The World of William Clissold,* by H. G. Wells." In *Phoenix.* Ed. Edward D. McDonald. London: William Heinemann, 1936.

Marcus, Jane. *Virginia Woolf and the Languages of Patriarchy.* Bloomington: Indiana University Press, 1987.

Wells, H. G. *Christina Alberta's Father.* London: Jonathan Cape, 1925.

———. *Experiment in Autobiography.* Philadelphia: J. B. Lippincott, 1934.

Woolf, Virginia. *A Room of One's Own.* New York: Harcourt Brace Jovanovich, 1957.

———. *Contemporary Writers.* New York: Harcourt Brace Jovanovich, 1965.

———. "Mr. Bennett and Mrs. Brown." In *The English Modernist Reader, 1910–1930.* Ed. Peter Faulkner. Iowa City: University of Iowa Press, 1986.

———. *Three Guineas.* New York: Harcourt Brace Jovanovich, 1966.

PART 2

Cultural Legitimation: The Cases
of *Lady Chatterley's Lover*
and *The Waves*

"But She Would Learn Something from Lady Chatterley"

The Obscene Side of the Canon

Modern British Literature, the final volume of *The Oxford Anthology of English Literature,* includes a long extract—nine pages, almost the whole essay—from D. H. Lawrence's "Pornography and Obscenity." This could be cited as one of many pieces of evidence for the contemporary stature of Lawrence, the kind of writer whose auxiliary publications are considered canonical; and the essay's subject matter might be seen as an allusion to the particularly violent curbs Lawrence's works faced (among others, *The Rainbow* and *Lady Chatterley's Lover* were banned following their publication) and overcame before he attained his deserved place. The anthology's editors, John Hollander and Frank Kermode, draw attention to this latter aspect in their introduction to the piece: They begin with the statement that "Lawrence had first-hand experience of those he called 'the censor-morons'" and then provide a brief history of the fortunes of *Lady Chatterley*. [1] In light of the triumphant ending, Lawrence's struggle seems all the more heroic, retrospectively a story of popular philistinism prior to the due assignment of his deserved literary status.

It would be possible to proceed from this point to the common allegation that the merit of works in the canon is largely a function of their inclusion, rather than the other way around. But the exaltation of "Pornography and Obscenity" suggests a somewhat more forceful possibility: that the establishment of literary value might be dependent on a corresponding exclusion, not just of a great remainder of works classified as merely indifferent, unexceptional and unexceptionable, but of a category of the obscene, with the recommended values of literature functioning only so far as they can be defined as the obverse of the vilified values of obscenity. It is not that Lawrence happened to write a good piece on a subject he had all too much reason to have thought about long and hard but that the very formation of this canon involves its active differentiation from what is defined as pornographic or obscene. From this point of view, the inclusion within the canon itself of a piece that is expressly concerned with the distinguishing of literary values from pornography and obscenity has a perverse and revealing logic. This may be related to the fact that precisely 2 of 679 pages of text in the Oxford anthology, published in 1973, contain writing by women (Edith Sitwell and Stevie Smith, a poem apiece).

"Wragg Is in Custody"

Before turning to Lawrence and *Lady Chatterley,* a piece of preliminary evidence to set the scene for the preoccupations of that trial:

> "A shocking child murder has just been committed at Nottingham. A girl named Wragg left the workhouse there on Saturday morning with her young illegitimate child. The child was soon afterwards found dead on Mapperly Hills, having been strangled. Wragg is in custody."

This extract from Arnold's "Function of Criticism at the Present Time" (1864) is a "paragraph on which I stumbled in a newspaper," quoted verbatim.[2] In its new context it serves him as a graphic illustration of what is wrong with England, following the scornful citation of speeches by two men who represent the "exuberant self-satisfaction" of the English. Arnold comments upon the newspaper report:

> Nothing but that; but, in juxtaposition with the absolute eulogies of Sir Charles Adderley and Mr Roebuck, how eloquent, how suggestive are those few lines! "Our old Anglo-Saxon breed, the best in the whole world!"—how much that is harsh and ill-favoured there is in the best! *Wragg!* If we are to talk of ideal perfection, of "the best in the whole world," has any one reflected what a touch of grossness in our race, what an original shortcoming in the more delicate spiritual perceptions, is shown by the natural growth among us of such hideous names,—Higginbottom, Stiggins, Bugg! In Ionia and Attica they were luckier in this respect than "the best race in the world"; by the Ilissus there was no Wragg, poor thing![3]

By the Ilissus, there were reputedly quite a few abandoned children; but it is not this which preoccupies Arnold. His citation seems at first as if it may be going to lead to a reflection on the particular moral condition of nineteenth-century England and its fallen women. But England suffers from "an original shortcoming," not a contingent one, manifest in the irrefutably patent evidence of its "hideous names." Wragg's tragedy is in her name, in its blatant exhibition of a peculiarly English combination of a "grossness" at once linguistic and natural. Something has been lost, and irretrievably, constitutively: the sound of the words of ancient Greece is Arnold's standard of comparison for Victorian England, which could never, by definition, be remedied (its shortcomings are its nature).

"Wragg is in custody" thus takes on the function of a kind of antipoetic touchstone or refrain, to be muttered as a token of the otherwise unspeakable qualities of the modern English:

> And "our unrivalled happiness";—what an element of grimness, bareness, and hideousness mixes with it and blurs it; the workhouse, the dismal Mapperly Hills,—how dismal those who have seen them will remember; the gloom, the smoke, the cold, the strangled illegitimate child! . . . And the final touch,—short, bleak and inhuman: *Wragg is in custody.* The sex lost in the confusion of our unrivalled happiness; or (shall I say?) the superfluous Christian name lopped off by the straightforward vigour of our old Anglo-Saxon breed! There is profit for the spirit in such contrasts as this; criticism serves the cause of perfection by establishing them. . . . Mr Roebuck will have a poor opinion of an adversary who replies to his defiant songs of triumph only by murmuring under his breath, *Wragg is in custody;* but no other way will these songs of triumph be induced gradually to moderate themselves, to get rid of what in them is excessive and offensive, and to fall into a softer and truer key.[4]

The very economy of the phrase "Wragg is in custody," which might have been taken as an abstention from superfluous commentary, becomes "the final touch,—short, bleak, and inhuman," "bleak" picking up on the "gloom" of the hills outside Nottingham, which seem already to have determined the atmosphere of the events of which they are doomed to be the setting. The lack of Wragg's first name is taken as a violation ("lopped off"), denying her the dignity of the marker of a fragile femininity that might have mitigated her unredeemable contemporary crudeness. It is the very unacceptability of the phrase "Wragg is in custody" that makes it, for Arnold's purposes, repeatable, endowed with a function of negative education symmetrically opposite to that of the consoling "touchstone" lines of good poetry he later evokes in "The Study of Poetry."[5]

The Woman on Trial

The sensationalistic potential of the newspaper report—a murder, a trial, and behind them a story of poverty and sexual shame—serves Arnold indirectly as a contrast with genuine literary values, and the place of Wragg in Arnold's canonical essay may stand as an emblem for the peculiar association between degraded woman, degraded language, and degraded England that manifests itself time and again in the history of literary trials. When the first proposal in the English parliament for a law on obscene publications was made in 1857, a few years before Arnold's essay, its advocate, Lord Campbell, was at pains to ward off the fear that his proposed legislation might apply to anything published as serious literature. At one point during the debates on the bill, Campbell produced a copy of Dumas' novel *La Dame aux Camélias* in the English translation, declaring that although he disapproved of it himself, "it was only from the force of public opinion and improved taste that the circulation of such works could be put a stop to."[6] The subsequent history of obscenity trials and legislation was to prove him wrong: in future years both literature and the lady were to be pursued by the "force" of law. For it is as though the ambivalent status of those books hovering uncertainly on a crucial boundary between "literature" and "obscenity" was derived in some in-dissociable way from the dubious figure of a woman and her sexual character. Situated on the verge between two equally untenable verdicts, depravity or respectability, she stands in for the book, a surrogate object of attack or defense. This concern in turn seems inseparable from the wider issues of cultural value that the book and the trial are called upon to represent and to adjudicate.

Arnold's essay was written almost a century before the trial in 1960 of *Lady Chatterley's Lover,* the novel by Lawrence that had been banned in England since its first publication (from Italy) in 1928 (and only just freed in the United States, in two trials in 1959). Despite their geographical and nominal affinities, the case involving the Nottinghamshire writer and the Chatterley seat in Wragby seems a far cry from the Victorian gloom of "Wragg is in custody," representing a victory for literary and sexual enlightenment of a kind unthinkable in relation to Arnold's concerns for the moderation of the "excessive and offensive" and the inculcation in its place of "a softer and truer key."[7] If the crime of the unmarried and unnatural, murdering mother stands as a cause for outraged lament against the condition of England and its language, Lady Chatterley seems to represent a moral victory for modern literature and modern attitudes to sex. Against the obviousness or the evidence of this story, I want rather to suggest that the 1960 trial and the understanding of Lawrence's work that surrounds it reveal some surprising continuities in the harnessing together of issues of language, sexuality, and morality in English cultural criticism.

The Trial of Lady Chatterley

The 1960 trial was a test case following the passing of new legislation. The Obscene Publications Act of 1959 added a supplementary criterion for cases considering whether a book (or some other publication) should be banned on the grounds of its obscene content. Henceforth the verdict of obscenity—defined, in a phrase that dates back to Sir Alexander Cockburn's 1868 interpretation of the Campbell Act, as the "tendency to deprave and corrupt"—might be overridden by the consideration of "public good." The official formulation in the 1959 act is as follows:

> A person shall not be convicted of an offence against Section 2 [the section referring to obscenity] if it is proved that publication of the article in question is justified as being for the public good on the ground that it is in the interests of science, literature, art, or learning, or of other objects of general concern.[8]

What this meant in the case of *Lady Chatterley's Lover* was that if the defense could show that the book was of intrinsic literary merit, then it would not matter if it was obscene or not, literary merit being considered "for the public good." This the defense did with astonishing success. It brought on a devastating array of experts, professional people ranging from literary critics like Raymond Williams and Graham Hough to teachers, social workers, a Church of England bishop, and well-known writers such as C. Day Lewis and E. M. Forster. In all there were thirty-five witnesses and thirty-six more who were not called upon.

This parade of respectable people speaking on behalf of a notoriously "dirty" book provided a rare media spectacle such that the newspapers could tantalize or shock the public with reported citations or interpretations from the work that no one was yet authorized to buy. In this context it is significant that one of the most persistent side issues to emerge was the question of its likely readership. The trial had been instigated when Penguin Books, in light of the new act, declared their intention to publish the banned book at the low price of three shillings and sixpence. This was consistent with Penguin's declared policy at the time of its founding in the 1930s: a low cover price to reach a working-class readership. The defense lawyer made explicit reference to this in his opening speech: "The next year he [Allen Lane] formed this company, Penguin Book Limited, to publish good books at the price of ten cigarettes."[9] The concern of the prosecution was not just that the book might be published but that it might be both cheap and accessible; and here it was not only workers, the presumed purchasers of packets of ten cigarettes, but also women who were seen as either dangerous or endangered potential readers.

Near the beginning the chief prosecution lawyer, Mr. Griffith-Jones, asked: "Is it a book that you would even wish your wife or your servants to read?"[10] Far from being taken as the rhetorical question for which it was presumably intended, this question provoked laughter from the jury and, C. H. Rolph remarks, "may have been the first nail in the prosecution's coffin." The question took on a synecdochic status in cultural mythology for the significance of the trial as a whole, standing for the way that it seemed to mark a turning point in British culture that had already taken place. Mr. Griffith-Jones had appealed to a world no longer there—the world of a homogeneous "we" consisting of middle- or upper-class Englishmen with servants and wives, from whom all dangerous reading matter should rightfully be kept. Griffith-Jones's question backfired because it was taken to reveal the anachronism of his case against *Lady Chatterley*. Postwar Britain no longer appeared to contain even a significant proportion of middle-class households with living-in servants; and although many middle-class men no doubt had wives, it was not self-evident, as the question required, that their reading should be vetted by their husbands.

In a fascinating way these specifications by age, sex, and class reenact variations and hesitations in the history of legal definitions of obscenity in relation to readers' susceptibilities. Campbell's formulation in 1857 wavered between, on the one hand, an echo of Socrates' accusers in the mention of a particular vulnerable group and, on the other, an appeal to a general concept of mental discipline:

> The measure was intended to apply exclusively to works written for the single purpose of corrupting the morals of youth, and of a nature calculated to shock the common feelings of decency in any well-regulated mind.[11]

Cockburn's modification of this in 1868 omitted the youth and made a number of other significant changes:

> I think the test of obscenity is this, whether the tendency of the matter charged with obscenity is to deprave and corrupt those whose minds are open to such immoral influences and into whose hands a publication of this sort may fall.[12]

The tone is now more ominous, "deprave and corrupt" implying more serious and long-term consequences than a transient upset to ordinary "feelings of decency." Cockburn has shifted the emphasis from exclusive intention to likely effect and restated the general psychological formulation in terms not of personal and transient shock to the average individual but of immoral influence to a group marked off as especially susceptible. And crucially, he has added a clause that draws in the conditions of distribution. The combination supplies the first legitimation for discriminations in terms of price that could clearly bear a relation to class. In *To the Pure...,* published in 1929, Morris Ernst and William Seagle called the effects of this structure "the aristocracy of 'smut,'" in other words, the relative invulnerability to prosecution of books with high prices and discreet marketing methods: "ordinarily the publisher, if he confines his advertising to 'Physicians, Clergymen, and Lawyers,' has not much to fear."[13]

The wording of the 1959 act recapitulates Cockburn with the same distinctive yoking of gothic psychology and the sociology of consumption:

> An article shall be deemed obscene if its effect or (where the article comprises two or more distinct items) the effect of any one of its items is, if taken as a whole, such as to tend to deprave and corrupt persons who are likely, having regard to all relevant circumstances, to read, see or hear the matter contained or embodied in it.[14]

There is thus a legal basis not only to the reference in the *Lady Chatterley* trial to particular vulnerable groups but also to the concern about mass readership, never openly named. And, interestingly, interrogating lawyers hark back to Campbell's preoccupation with juvenile welfare: to Griffith-Jones's wives and servants are added the differently used category of children, or at least adolescents. Witnesses are habitually asked whether they have children and whether they would mind them coming across the book, the implication being that the book must be all right (or all wrong) if these experts feel happy about their own offspring reading it. Whereas with the wives and servants there is a joke in the idea that gentlemen would take it upon themselves to determine their reading matter, with children the point seems to be taken as reasonable that any responsible parent would withhold literature that was liable to do them harm.

The "wives and servants" conjunction is particularly telling in regard to this novel, whose story concerns the romance of a lady with a man of a lower social class: her husband's gamekeeper. There is thus a strange repetition in this worry about who might read the book, as if it were implicitly being acknowledged that it might be taken as a kind of recipe or invitation for women and servants, ladies and gamekeepers, not to keep their social and sexual places. Against this the defense argues for the validity and worth of "human relationships" between the sexes and between different social classes, not excluding a sexuality in relation to which the woman, too, is now to be regarded as having needs and desires. The defense takes the line that, far from being pornographic or obscene, *Lady Chatterley* is in fact highly moral, not least because it implicitly advocates ideals whose validity has now come to be acknowledged in the mid-twentieth century, the age of social and sexual enlightenment. One of the witnesses, an educational psychologist named James Hemming, puts it like this: "It is now well recognised that for young people to grow up and marry with a prudish and ashamed attitude towards sex is positively harmful. *Lady Chatterley's Lover* presents sex as it should be presented."[15] At the same time (and here literature is serving the same social function as it does for Matthew Arnold), because the generality of culture is debased, it is all the more crucial for the true values the novel teaches to be made available. Hemming uses the language of scientific medicine when he describes *Lady Chatterley* as a potential "antidote" to the prevailing "shallow and corrupting values with regard to sex and the relationships between the sexes."[16]

In this regard, it is interesting that the defense witnesses in fact tend to make their case by picking up exactly the same terms as those used to damn *Lady Chatterley's Lover.* The prosecution rests its case on the idea that this is a dirty book, liable to "deprave and corrupt" the minds of those who read it. The defense does not say that that is an inappropriate way of putting the matter, that it might be difficult or futile to determine the difference between a dirty book and a non-dirty book. Instead, it claims that *Lady Chatterley's Lover* is an exceptionally clean or wholesome book. Where the prosecution is saying that it will have a deleterious effect on public and private morality, the defence says not only that it won't but that it will have an effect that is positively salutary. In other words, the defense, too, adopts the categories of clean and dirty, wholesome and unwholesome, moral and immoral.

Such moves emerge in relation to two particular features of the novel, the aspects with which the trial seems to be most preoccupied. The first is the question of what are euphemistically referred to throughout as "the four-letter words," generally to be located in "purple passages" and in the context of "bouts." The words that particularly concern the prosecution are "fuck" and "cunt"; some of the funniest moments in the trial occur when the prosecution lawyer tries reading passages that contain these words, written in Lawrence's transcription of the Nottinghamshire dialect that Mellors, the gamekeeper, would have spoken. The intention of the lawyer here is to demonstrate—it is supposed to need no further argument than the mere showing—how filthy the book quite clearly is. The defense's response is not simply to disagree with the "touchstone" criterion (to hear or to see is enough to damn). Instead, a definite case is made in relation to the positive virtues of these words: Lawrence was trying to purify, to clean up, the language by getting back to the original unsullied significance of these words which modern culture has debased.

Richard Hoggart, for instance, argues as follows when he is in the witness box:

> Fifty yards from this Court this morning I heard a man say "fuck" three times as he passed me. He was speaking to himself and he said "fuck it, fuck it, fuck it" as he went past. If you have worked on a building site, as I have, you will find they recur over and over again. The man I heard this morning and the men on building sites use the words as words of contempt, and one of the things Lawrence found most worrying was that the word for this important relationship had become a word of vile abuse. So one would say "fuck you" to a man, although the thing has totally lost its meaning; it has become simply derision, and in this sense he wanted to re-establish the meaning of it, the proper use of it.[17]

An entire theory of linguistic history and sexuality is contained in this. Like Arnold, Hoggart sets some store by the repetition of an obnoxious phrase as a kind of negative incantation, overhearing this thrice-muttered curse. But the word "fuck" is not, for Hoggart, "vile" or abusive in itself: it has become so by being severed from its original sexual meaning. The problem is not that the word names sex but that it does not: and "this important relationship" has suffered too, by implication, since the word for it has been turned to other ends, to the point that "the thing has totally lost its meaning." Sexual and linguistic faults and proprieties are inseparable;

the "proper" employment of the one has to be matched by that of the other.

It is significant too that what Hoggart says here is entirely consonant with pronouncements that Lawrence made himself. More than most novelists, Lawrence was given to expressing his opinions on matters of art, sex, society, morality, and language—all the matters that are supposed to be under consideration in the trial of *Lady Chatterley*. In "Pornography and Obscenity," for instance, written in 1929 after the thwarted publication of *Lady Chatterley's Lover,* he states:

> Pornography is the attempt to insult sex, to do dirt on it. This is unpardonable. Take the very lowest instance, the picture post-card sold under hand, by the underworld, in most cities. What I have seen of them has been of an ugliness to make you cry. The insult to the human body, the insult to a vital human relationship! Ugly and cheap they make the human nudity, ugly and degraded they make the sexual act, trivial and cheap and nasty. . . .
>
> It is the same with the dirty limericks that people tell after dinner, or the dirty stories one hears commercial travellers telling each other in a smoke-room. Occasionally there is a really funny one, that redeems a great deal. But usually they are just ugly and repellent, and the so-called "humour" is just a trick of doing dirt on sex.[18]

As in Hoggart's statement, and, in a different way, as with Arnold's desperate contrast between Attic Greece and the smoke of the Mapperly Hills, an original purity of language has been sullied. Sex itself, "a vital human relationship," has been subject to "insult," and the "cheap and nasty" urban commodity epitomizes "the very lowest instance" of degradation that is indicated by its exclamatory opposition to what it is not.

In Arnold's commentary on Wragg, the girl's sins or misfortunes are displaced onto the offensiveness of her name, which is found guilty in its own right of the crimes and abuses perpetrated by or on its bearer. In the case of the *Lady Chatterley* trial, however, it is the morality of the woman herself, fictional in this instance, that comes to stand in for the whole question of the book's merits or crimes. Lady Chatterley, like Wragg, is herself in custody. This second feature of the prosecution's attack is closely related to the focus on linguistic propriety: Was she or was she not justified in her adultery with the gamekeeper? As with the question of dirty language, the defense witnesses do not refuse the relevance of this issue. Instead, they provide the symmetrically opposite case, arguing that

Constance Chatterley's conduct was not only not immoral, but as moral as could be. And there are several grounds for them for saying this.

In the terms of the novel itself, Constance Chatterley is rather an unusual adulteress, since her husband is incapable physically of sex (he was mutilated in the war) and has suggested at various times that she might like to have a child, which would clearly not be his biologically.[19] The defense's argument is made sometimes in terms of "a woman's natural desires," as when C. Day Lewis replies to Griffith-Jones's interrogation by saying, in the normative language of sexology, "I think it is in her nature because she is an averagely sexed woman."[20] But there is no suggestion that indiscriminate or noncommittal sexual involvements might be acceptable. Hoggart, for instance, is moved to revive by negation the specter of Victorian sexual grime: "If it had simply been a [*sic*] case that her husband was impotent and she wanted sex, she could have, and would have, had sex in every hedge and ditch round Wragby."[21] The case is also made on the grounds of the sanctity of marriage and the indispensability to this of a sexual relationship. According to this argument, Constance's marriage to Lord Chatterley is effectively null and void, not an issue, because it cannot include sex. The real marital relationship of the novel is that of Constance and Oliver, who are working their way toward the complete union that is marriage in the proper, spiritual sense. In the words this time of no less qualified a judge in matters theological than the Bishop of Woolwich, "what Lawrence is trying to do is to portray the sex relationship as something essentially sacred."[22]

Here again, this defense in fact accords with Lawrence's own published view of the matter. In 1930, following what was already a complicated story of the vicissitudes of the novel's publications and piratings, he wrote a piece called "A Propos of *Lady Chatterley's Lover*" in which—among many other things—he declared that the greatest contribution of Christianity to Western civilization had been the invention of matrimony. Defense witnesses have a gift in being able to refer to this, which sounds so unlike the image of Lawrence the sex-obsessed pornographer which they are at pains to contradict. Lawrence also states here, as though giving Arnold's strictures about Wragg's sexless English name a more virile revision, "An England that has lost its sex seems to me nothing to feel very hopeful about."[23] (A later passage in the essay goes on to stress the virtues of "the phallic religion," and it is fortunate for the defense that Mr. Griffith-Jones does not pick this up.)

There is thus an unexpected complicity in the cases brought by the two sides of the trial. Both are against dirt, against what they are calling obscenity. Lawrence can be defended on the grounds that his writing is not dirty at all—neither in the words he uses nor in the forms of life that he advocates. He is in fact more wholesome than his detractors, who make of sex a "dirty secret," whereas modern society recognizes that it does not have to be, and indeed should not be. The respectable qualifications of the defense indicate to all the world that this is a matter not of gutter literature but rather of purity itself, a higher form of art precisely because it is restoring the importance of sexuality in marriage, as the highest form of human "communion" (another word that, like "sacred," brings together sexual and religious experience).

"A Woman's Love"

The way in which the *Lady Chatterley* trial was regarded as an indicator of changes in social attitudes to sex at the beginning of the 1960s was linked, as we have seen, to ideas of progressive cultural enlightenment. In this connection, it makes perfect sense that the test-case novelist should have been Lawrence, whose advocates in less manifestly legal spheres had presented his work as central to that understanding of the problems of modern English culture that a literary education might play a useful part in disseminating. In particular, F. R. Leavis chose Lawrence as the sole twentieth-century writer deserving to be tacked on to the "great tradition" of English novels combining literary merit with social criticism: in 1955, he had written a lengthy study called, laconically, *D. H. Lawrence: Novelist.* This text is instructive in that it shows the solidarity between those values the experts, both literary and nonliterary by profession, saw in *Lady Chatterley* and those that were being claimed for Lawrence more generally as the representative of literature and its social value.

Leavis himself pointedly refused to stand as a witness for the defense in the *Lady Chatterley* trial. His reasons were made evident in a piece called "The New Orthodoxy," which he wrote for *The Spectator,* on the publication of Rolph's transcript of the trial shortly after it as a Penguin Special. For one thing, the novel was not one he considered representative of Lawrence's art (he had barely mentioned it in his book): "*Lady Chatterley's Lover,* then—it is important that this obvious enough truth should be asserted—is a bad novel."[24] More generally, he distrusted the facile switch of allegiances on the part of some who had never been eager to come forward as Lawrence's defenders when Leavis was attempting to make the case for him in criticism, and saw their case as a transposition of his own to the wrong object: "Reading the testimonies now printed in the Penguin Special, I couldn't help feeling that I had a heavy degree of responsibility. It gave me a sense of guilt when I saw those formulations, which were so familiar to me, applied to *Lady Chatterley's Lover,* to which I (explicitly) did not apply them."[25] Leavis thus belatedly enters the litigation, protesting guilt by multiple proxy and therefore also making himself responsible for the defense's success. And, ironically, the absence of Leavis in person from the trial does highlight the degree to which the defense of Lawrence as a great writer was conducted in terms compatible with, if not directly derived from, his own.

We have observed the extent to which the defenders of *Lady Chatterley* take up the terms of cleanliness and social wholesomeness that are simply the reverse side of the prosecution's accusations of dirt and social damage, and how they maintain the distinction of good from pornographic writing by insisting on the literary distinction of the novel on trial. The same structure of thought can be seen to operate in Leavis's approach. The following quotation from the book on Lawrence gives the characteristic tone: "Any great creative writer who has not had his due is a power for life wasted. But the insight, the wisdom, the revived and re-educated feeling for health, that Lawrence brings are what, as our civilization goes, we desperately need."[26] In "revived" and "re-educated," the "re" draws on that sense of a return to something formerly existing but now lost in modern civilization, which appeared in Hoggart's statement. The two words combine life—"revived"—and education. In Lawrence, and perhaps even more in Lawrence's advocates, Life is a value whose potency has been covered over or distorted under modern social conditions; and which (great) literature has the vocation of bringing back to us, or bringing us back to. Literature is then by the same token educative, didactic: it will teach us what we have forgotten. The urgency, even emergency, in Leavis's emphatic final clause continues the Arnoldian tradition of seeing literature as a desperate remedy (stronger here in its dose than Hoggart's bland "antidote") for a social situation identified as mechanistic and devalued. Criticism annexes itself here to a function taken to be inherent in the literature, one whose life-restoring powers it points out.[27]

This linking of literature and life, so forceful in Leavis's appeal on Lawrence's behalf, is reinforced by a strain in Lawrence's own writing, in his novels and elsewhere. It is not only that his novels can be said to offer an image of a different "civilization"; but they also offer outright criticism of a negatively represented modernity. In *Lady Chatterley's Lover,* there are several points at which Lawrence's narrator lashes out against the state of contemporary culture:

> The car ploughed uphill through the long squalid straggle of Tevershall, the blackened brick dwellings, the black slate roofs glistening their sharp edges, the mud black with coal-dust, the pavements wet and black. It was as if dismalness had soaked through and through everything. The utter negation of natural beauty, the utter negation of the gladness of life, the utter absence of the instinct for shapely beauty which every bird and beast has, the utter death of the human intuitive faculty was appalling. The stack of soap in the grocers' shops, the rhubarb and lemons in the greengrocers! the awful hats in the milliners! all went by ugly, ugly, ugly, followed by the plaster-and-gilt horror of the cinema with its wet-picture announcements, "A Woman's Love!"[28]

Here, with "dismalness . . . soaked through and through everything," we are back on Arnold's "dismal Mapperly Hills" with a vengeance. Instead of a crime and a dead baby, there is "the utter death of the human intuitive faculty"; instead of Wragg denied her femininity by the newspaper, there is the sequence of crude commodities and the headlined "wet-picture" title of "A Woman's Love!," its declarative force sufficient to indicate its unnaturalness when set against "the instinct for shapely beauty which every bird and beast has."

The passage works partly by repetition—"utter . . . utter . . . utter . . . utter," "ugly . . . ugly . . . ugly"—and by loaded words like "squalid," "blackened," "horror," "awful," "dismalness," all taken as self-evident evaluative terms and contrasted with their polar opposites: "the gladness of life," "the instinct for shapely beauty," "the human intuitive faculty." It is fascinating that here, as regularly in Lawrence, the cinema epitomizes what is wrong with modern culture—"horror," no less (along with the scorn for commerce in general in the form of a random assortment of shops)—but that the view of the town is from inside another thoroughly modern cultural artifact of the 1920s, the car. The cinema stands for counterfeit feminine emotion and for a cheap veneer (the "plaster-and-gilt" exterior), yet the car is the place from which the observer with the genuine critical eye can see it for what it is. The reader's view is aligned with that of the speedy narrating traveler who knows with an unquestionable assurance that a film called "A Woman's Love!" is superficial, whereas a novel about the love of a woman called Lady Chatterley is not. And in the same way, Leavis can refer in relation to Lawrence to "the major orders of value-judgement, those depending on the critic's sense for the difference between what, in his time, makes for health and what makes against it."[29]

Lady Chatterley's Lover itself partakes of that dismal dismissal of mass culture with which Lawrence's and Leavis's followers became associated. One of the ways in which the unfortunate Chatterley is shown to be thoroughly feeble is by the fact that he is always "listening in" to the radio. Constance herself calls it "the emotional idiocy of the radio";[30] it is expressly represented as a poor imitation of earlier sounds of life:

> "Will you have Mrs Bolton play something with you?"
> "No! I think I'll listen in."
> She heard the curious satisfaction in his voice. She went upstairs to her bedroom. There she heard the loudspeaker begin to bellow, in an idiotically velveteen-genteel sort of voice, something about a series of street-cries, the very cream of genteel affectation imitating old criers.[31]

Lawrence is against all these mechanical things that he opposes to the "life" values; against the "velveteen-genteel" veneer, Mellors will set his peculiar version of pastoral, involving a return to a nature of colorful masculinity: "An' I'd get my men to wear different clothes: appen close red trousers, bright red, an' little short white jackets. Why, if men had red, fine legs, that alone would change them in a month. They'd begin to be men again, to be men! An' the women could dress as they liked Because if once the men walked with legs close bright scarlet, and buttocks nice and showing scarlet under a little white jacket: then the women 'ud begin to be women."[32] The restoration of a preindustrial ideal community crucially depends upon a call for a return to a natural difference of the sexes.

It is revealing that the targets chosen by Lawrence should now seem so inappropriate. The radio and the cinema are two of his favorites; another is the gramophone. The first two at least now have wonderfully authentic-sounding, almost old-fashioned overtones: in the age of television and home videos, there is no great concern with the potentially damaging effects of radio or film, and certainly not in relation to silent movies or the crackling wireless voices of the twenties. Where previously they could serve as a symbol of mechanization and commercialization, these two now carry a connotation nearer to that of a lost social harmony.[33] These shifts in the rhetoric should indicate how difficult it is to maintain the kinds of clear-cut demarcation that Lawrence (and later Leavis) wanted to assert.

The Trial Continues

In the passage from the novel cited above, the intertwining of sexual and social views of health is once again apparent. As we have seen, the vindication of the novel at its trial rested heavily on the claim that its version of sexual relationships was not only permissible but positively beneficial (with this mode of argument partly determined by the need to prove not only that the book was not harmful but that it was "for the public good"). Even though the trial was seen as a watershed for the liberalization of sexual values associated with the 1960s, the case is actually made in quite traditional terms: Lawrence is promoting a monogamous, heterosexual form of love. Promiscuity is explicitly rejected, homosexual love is not mentioned, and the scene of anal sex—highly euphemistic in the novel itself—is strategically ignored by the defenders of the novel.

I want finally to move to one side and look briefly at a different issue raised in relation to Lawrence's representation of sexuality in the years since the trial. In 1970 the American Kate Millett published *Sexual Politics,* an inaugural work in what has subsequently become the well-established field of feminist literary criticism. Millett proceeded by analyses of texts by male writers as manifestations of the workings of patriarchy. First among these culprits of phallocracy was D. H. Lawrence. What Millett saw in Lawrence was not dirt exactly, nor wholesomeness either, but maleness of a particularly extreme, misogynistic, and offensive kind. Where others would have attributed Lawrence's success to his articulation of commonly held twentieth-century feelings and opinions about human life and values, Millett took it quite simply as a function of his all-too-clear articulation of the violent, megalomaniacal tendencies of masculinity.

Without entering into the details of Millett's criticisms, I would like simply to note two things. First, her critique represents one of the first examples of a quite different tendency, developing over the past twenty years, in arguments about pornography and obscenity. In 1960 the question was about the lifting of taboos, a new enlightenment in which there would be no need to shrink away shamefully from a sexuality now seen as part of the fullness of healthy human life. For Millett, and for a host of feminists since then (by no means all feminists, but a significant proportion), the question is about how pornography misrepresents women and their sexuality, how it does violence to them in ways that may or may not be materially different from actual physical violence and that may directly encourage it. The pornography-literature relationship has shifted: the *Lady Chatterley* trial marked very strongly the difference between them, and maintained a clear demarcation between good healthy sex and bad vulgar sex, with literature figuring as precisely what transcended common, street pornography; but now literature is taken as potentially tainted with the same brush and all the more insidious for being privileged as exempt. Millett's targets have to be "great literature" for her polemic to have some effect. For all the respectable people already agreed that what is called pornography was unpleasant and violent (though they might not have worried about its being misogynistic). The scandal was to declare that what they thought absolutely different from that run-of-the-press trash was in fact not so at all.

The second point I want to note in relation to Millett's criticism of Lawrence is that in many ways she does not depart from the criteria of her own opponents, just as the defenders of *Lady Chatterley* share common ground with the novel's attackers. Millett too has a notion of healthy, wholesome sex between mature people, which—in spite of herself, in a way—is thoroughly Lawrentian. For example: "Though his prose can be as loving a caress to the male body as any of Genet's, it is never as honest. Moreover, the projected masculine alliance, the Blutbruderschaft, is so plainly motivated by the rather sordid political purpose of clubbing together against women, that this too gives it a perverse rather than a healthy and disinterested character, either as sexuality or as friendship."[34] "Rather sordid," "healthy and disinterested," "honest": the terms are exactly Lawrence's—or Leavis's, for that matter. Once again, there is a firm standard of what is to be thought genuine—honest, disinterested, healthy— and what is not, and this standard is taken as read. It can only be pointed to by the gesture of "of course"—"*so plainly* motivated," she says—which implies that the writer assumes the reader will agree with her. In this light Millett is a worthy successor to the English tradition of cultural criticism that operates in the declarative mode, assuming clearly separated catego- ries through which the absolutely good (or honest or healthy) is set up unproblematically against its opposite. There is an arbitrary assertion whereby one term being taken as natural and good, the other is a fake or distorted or mechanical substitution for it.

This appeal to common standards is related to the prescribed question decided at the trial of *Lady Chatterley*. Before the issue of "public good" was considered, the jury had first to determine whether or not the work was obscene, with obscenity defined, as noted above, in this way: "The book is to be deemed to be obscene if its effect... if taken as a whole, [is] such as to tend to deprave and corrupt persons who are likely, having regard to all relevant circumstances, to read... the matter contained . . . in it."[35] There is a wonderful contradiction built in here. The jury is supposed to decide, on behalf of the populace at large, whether or not the book has this "tendency to deprave and corrupt." (In the case of the Lawrence trial, the jury was not permitted to take *Lady Chatterley* home, but sat reading it in a room next to the court for three full days.) If it then *had* been depraved or corrupted, presumably, by the terms of the trial, it would no longer be in a position to judge the book: it had become depraved and corrupt. But the jury would not know this because a depraved person is no judge of depravity. Thus there could never, in these terms, be such a thing as a fair trial for obscenity. Either it does not corrupt you, which proves it was not obscene in the first place since obscenity corrupts; or it does, but then you are corrupt, no longer a sane, reasonable person, and hence in no position to judge. In either case, you cannot be supposed to know your own state of mind.[36]

This impasse applies in some version to all forms of delegated censorship or cultural gatekeeping (not to be confused with gamekeeping). Someone or some group of people has to take upon itself the position of superior immunity to whatever is supposed to be potentially harmful in the film or book under consideration. It is the same structure as with the insinuation that three and sixpence is rather a dangerously low price for a high book that might thus risk looking like a low book (or for a purely, or impurely, low book, quite simply, depending on which side you're on): some people know better than others what is good for "us." (There is an additional contradiction, built into the 1959 act, that the saving attribution of "public good" cancels out the legal but not the alleged psychological effects of an obscene publication: the book would still, presumably, be getting on with its depraving and corrupting even while it was compensating for this by its public benefits.)

The same problem, then, that occurs in the distinctions drawn between healthy and unhealthy sexuality, and between genuine and artificial social forms, is built into the very form of the demand that a book be tried for obscenity defined in this way as what tends "to deprave and corrupt." The addition of the incompatible escape clause referring to public good only serves to make evident the complicity of this banning of the obscene with the process by which works are legitimated as positively valuable—as tending to revive and reeducate, for instance.

In the case of *Lady Chatterley's Lover* itself, there is a particularly eccentric illustration of this in the form of an opinion delivered by George Bernard Shaw not long after its first appearance:

If I had a marriageable daughter, what could I give her to read to prepare her? Dickens? Thackeray? George Eliot? Walter Scott? Trollope? or even any of the clever modern women who take such a fiendish delight in writing able novels that leave you hopeless and miserable? They would teach her a lot about life and society and human nature. But they would leave her absolutely in the dark as to marriage. Even Fielding and Joyce and George Moore would be no use: instead of telling her nothing they would tell her worse than nothing. But she would learn something from Lady Chatterley. I shouldn't let her engage herself if I could help it until she had read that book. Lawrence had delicacy enough to tell the best, and brutality enough to rub in the worst. *Lady Chatterley* should be on the shelves of every college for budding girls. They should be forced to read it on pain of being refused a marriage licence.[37]

The mixture of the ludicrous and the tyrannical here adds a new piquancy to Leavis's "force" for life, in this enumeration of the extraordinary controls to be exercised by the well-meaning fatherly dictator, lasciviously or sadistically imagining a college full of "budding girls" for whom the forced reading of a novel prompted by "brutality enough to rub in the worst" is their only ("on pain of") escape into the brutality of which it has just given them a foretaste. Truly, the wives and servants never had it so good: whether or not the exaggeration is meant as a joke, it is revealing. Shaw presents in an extreme form the argument of many of the novel's later defenders, asserting not merely that *Lady Chatterley* does not corrupt but that it should be (literally) required reading.

Thirty years after the event to which the title of the transcript refers quite simply as *The Trial of Lady Chatterley,* the issues it raises are again to the fore in many areas of cultural representation in Britain. The oppositional language of "sick" or "depraved" as opposed to "sane" or "healthy" individuals or social groups continues to structure debate on issues of pornography, censorship, and illegitimate sexualities (the ambiguous "Clause 28" ban on the "promotion" of homosexuality). In many ways, as the vaunted return to "Victorian" values would suggest, some of the categories and concerns are thoroughly recognizable in the terms of the first legislators against obscene publications and the first advocates of the restorative powers of the literary canon. There is still a constant attempt to establish or police the boundaries between what is thereby decreed either dangerous or permissible material. Lady

Chatterley may have been vindicated in 1960, but Wragg is still in custody.

Notes

The first version of this essay was written as an informal lecture for the 1988 Scottish Universities International Summer School at Edinburgh University, organized by Patrick Williams.

1. Frank Kermode and John Hollander, eds., *The Oxford Anthology of English Literature,* vol. 6: *Modern British Literature* (New York: Oxford University Press, 1973), 449.

2. Matthew Arnold, "The Function of Criticism at the Present Time" (1864), in *Selected Prose,* ed. P. J. Keating (Harmondsworth: Penguin, 1970), 145.

3. Ibid., 145–46.

4. Ibid., 146.

5. "The Study of Poetry" (1880) is described in the *Norton Anthology of English Literature,* vol. 2, ed. M. H. Abrams (New York: W. W. Norton, 1986, p. 1441) as having been "extraordinarily potent in shaping literary tastes in England and in America." For a full analysis of Arnold's place in the history of English criticism, see Chris Baldick, *The Social Mission of English Criticism* (Oxford: Oxford University Press, 1983).

6. Morris L. Ernst and William Seagle, *To the Pure . . . : A Study of Obscenity and the Censor* (London: Jonathan Cape, 1929), 136.

7. Lest this connection seem farfetched, the reader is referred to the fifth edition of *The Norton Anthology of English Literature.* This includes all but the beginning of Arnold's essay; among the helpful footnotes is one explaining the reference to the Mapperly Hills: "Adjacent to the coal-mining and industrial area of Nottingham (later associated with the writings of D. H. Lawrence)" (1420).

8. C. H. Rolph, ed., *The Trial of Lady Chatterley: Regina* v. *Penguin Books Limited* (Harmondsworth: Penguin, 1961), 11.

9. Ibid., 25. Cigarettes would at the time connote a working-class purchase, a cheap, everyday luxury. For more on the implications of the trial from the point of view of both social and publishing history, see John Sutherland, *Offensive Literature: Decensorship in Britain* 1960–1982 (London: Junction Books, 1982), chap. 1, "November 1960: Lady Chatterley's Lover," 10–31.

10. Rolph, 17.

11. Quoted in Alec Craig, *The Banned Books of England* (London: George Allen and Unwin, 1937), 23.

12. Ibid., 24.

13. Ernst and Seagle, 75–76.

14. Quoted in Alec Craig, *The Banned Books of England and Other Countries:*

A Study of the Conception of Literary Obscenity (London: George Allen and Unwin, 1962), 123.

15. Rolph, 119.

16. Ibid., 118. In the next sentence, these values are exemplified in the terms of feminist cultural criticism: "For example, the picture is put before the young girl that if she has the right proportions, wears the right clothes, uses the right cosmetics, she will become irresistible to men and that that is the supreme achievement of a woman."

17. Ibid., 98.

18. "Pornography and Obscenity," in D. H. Lawrence, *A Selection from Phoenix,* ed. A. A. H. Inglis (Harmondsworth: Penguin, 1971), 312.

19. In "A Propos of *Lady Chatterley's Lover,*" Lawrence responds to whether Lord Chatterley's paralysis was meant to be symbolic: "When I read the first version, I recognized that the lameness of Clifford was symbolic of the paralysis, the deeper emotional or passional paralysis, of most men of his sort and class today. I realized that it was perhaps taking an unfair advantage of Connie, to paralyse him technically. It made it so much more vulgar of her to leave him" (359–60). Yet in "Pornography and Obscenity," Lawrence takes a special exception to *Jane Eyre,* which is singled out as pornographic partly because of the physical state of Rochester at the end: "Mr. Rochester's sex passion is not 'respectable' till Mr. Rochester is burned, blinded, disfigured, and reduced to helpless dependence" (314). In some sense, Clifford might then be understood as a properly defunct and incapacitated version of Rochester, representing by caricature the "counterfeit" impotence of the type of sexuality which the later novel rejects.

20. Rolph, 153.

21. Ibid., 101. The description of Wragby near the start of the novel has many points of correspondence with Arnold's description of the setting of Wragg's misadventure:

> Wragby was a long low old house in brown stone, begun about the middle of the eighteenth century, and added on to, till it was a warren of a place without much distinction. It stood on an eminence in a rather fine old park of oak trees, but alas, one could see in the near distance the chimney of Te017tershall pit, with its clouds of steam and smoke, and on the damp, hazy distance of the hill the raw straggle of Te018tershall village, a village which began almost at the park gates, and trailed in utter hopeless ugliness for a long and gruesome mile: houses, rows of wretched, small, begrimed, brick houses, with black slate roofs for lids, sharp angles and wilful, blank dreariness. (14)

22. Rolph, 70.

23. Lawrence, "A Propos of *Lady Chatterley's Lover,*" 352.

24. F. R. Leavis, "The New Orthodoxy," *The Spectator,* Feb. 17, 1961, 229. The following week (p. 255), the paper published a letter from Martin Turnell that

gleefully quotes Leavis's opinion of the novel in 1933. In *For Continuity,* he had written: "There is no redundancy in *Lady Chatterley's Lover,* no loose prophecy and passional exegesis, and no mechanical use of the specialised vocabulary. He returns here to the scenes of his earlier work, and the book has all the old sensuous concreteness without the fevered adolescent overcharge: ripe experience is in control." Touché. Nonetheless, Leavis comes back unchastened, referring (Mar. 3, 1961, 291) to "that obscure pioneer essay" and continuing: "What was important at the time—and for long afterwards—was to insist that he had a major claim on our attention, and above all, that he was not a pornographer or anything of the kind. Now, thirty years later, things are very different. Work of critical advocacy has been carried on with some pertinacity—at the cost (I speak from painful experience) of obloquy, slander and worldly disadvantage." "Not a pornographer," "what was important at the time": here Leavis defends himself against the charge of inconsistency by claiming to have used precisely the strategic approach he abhors in the case of the defense witnesses at the 1960 trial.

25. Ibid., 230.

26. F. R. Leavis, *D. H. Lawrence: Novelist* (1955; rpt. Harmondsworth: Penguin, 1973), 16.

27. On the insistence upon the relationship between Literature and Life in Leavis and the group of critics around him, see Francis Mulhern, *The Moment of "Scrutiny"* (1979; rpt. London: Verso, 1981).

28. D. H. Lawrence, *Lady Chatterley's Lover* (1928; rpt. Harmondsworth: Penguin, 1961), 158.

29. Leavis, *D. H. Lawrence,* 28–29.

30. Lawrence, *Lady Chatterley's Lover,* 144.

31. Ibid., 128.

32. Ibid., 228–29.

33. Not, however, for F. R. Leavis, objecting in 1966 to a journalist's allusion to "a familiar resentment and envy, often seen in Britain, that working people should be going to Florence and Majorca, and buying Beethoven long-playing records" (quoted in F. R. Leavis and Q. D. Leavis, *Lectures in America* [London: Chatto and Windus, 1969], 4). Leavis resents her premises: "I myself, after an unaffluent and very much 'engaged' academic life, am not familiar with Majorca or Florence, but in those once very quiet places very much nearer Cambridge to which my wife and I used to take our children the working-class people now everywhere to be met with in profusion carry transistors around with them almost invariably" (5). The rebuttal is curious in its logic. The sense seems to be that since he hasn't been able to get to Spain or Italy to test the hypotheses on the ground, then at least he can speak from firsthand experience of the mob ("now everywhere to be met with in profusion") that has invaded the local retreats for overworked and underpaid dons. The foreign locations and domestic music somehow get conflated. First, if these people are trailing their trannies round East Anglia, then evidently they do not have any classical LPs. And second, the working class's

experience is oddly put into relation to the Leavises': if *he* can't afford to go abroad, they might at least not blast out the former decent pastoral havens with their vulgar noise.

34. Kate Millett, *Sexual Politics* (1970; rpt. London: Virago, 1977), 267–68.

35. Rolph, 10 (the passage from the Act is here quoted in abbreviated form, as it applied to the particular publication the jury was to consider).

36. On one occasion, however, a witness did announce his own corruption. At the 1967 trial of Selby's *Last Exit to Brooklyn,* David Sheppard, former England cricket captain and now Church of England bishop, declared himself "not unscathed" by reading the book. At this trial, the remarkable decision was taken to have an all-male jury, as though paternalism of the "wives and daughters" were a foregone conclusion in matters of literary judgment. Recalling this recently, an article in *The Guardian* (Jan. 4, 1990, 26) came up with a sentence that, if taken at face value, would seem to have altered the course of Western history at a stroke: "This was in keeping with the Establishment spirit of the times and the idea that men rather than women needed protection from sexual candour."

37. Quoted in Craig, *The Banned Books of England,* 31–32, from Frank Harris's *Bernard Shaw* (London: Victor Gollancz, 1931), 232–33, where one further sentence, italicized, concluded the quotation—*"But it is not as readable as 'Ivanhoe' or 'A Tale of Two Cities'"*—which is followed by three italicized exclamation marks. In *Bernard Shaw: A Reassessment* (New York: Atheneum, 1969), Colin Wilson supplies an anecdote that seems to clarify this: "He was incapable of grasping this [postwar] poetry of spiritual bankruptcy, or D. H. Lawrence's attempt to find true values again in sex. (Although he told General Smuts [*sic*] at a luncheon party that every schoolgirl of sixteen should read Lady Chatterley's Lover, he later admitted to [Stephen] Winsten that he had never succeeded in reading Lawrence" (267). Barbara Bellow Watson, author of *A Shavian Guide to the Intelligent Woman* (London: Chatto and Windus, 1964), who also (p. 130) gives the quotation from Harris, makes no remark about its language, taking it straight as an illustration of Shaw's liberal views on sex education: his endorsement of the novel's uses "becomes even more emphatic when we realize how strongly Shaw disapproved of Lawrence's language."

JANE MARCUS

Britannia Rules *The Waves*

What has made it impossible for us to live in time like fish in water, like birds in air, like children? It is the fault of Empire! Empire has created the time of history. Empire has located its existence not in the smooth recurrent spinning time of the cycle of the seasons but in the jagged time of rise and fall, of beginning and end, of catastrophe. Empire dooms itself to live in history and plot against history. One thought alone preoccupies the submerged mind of Empire: how not to end, how not to die, how to prolong its era. By day it pursues its enemies. . . . By night it feeds on images of disaster.

J. M. Coetzee, *Waiting for the Barbarians*

The waves drummed on the shore, like turbaned warriors, like turbaned men with poisoned assegais who, whirling their arms on high, advance upon the feeding flocks, the white sheep.

Virginia Woolf, *The Waves*

Rise and Fall

Canon building is Empire building. Canon defense is national defense. Canon debate, whatever the terrain, nature and range (of criticism, of history, of the history of knowledge, of the definition of language, the universality of aesthetic principles, the sociology of art, the humanist imagination), is the clash of cultures. And *all* of the interests are vested.

Toni Morrison, "Unspeakable Things Unspoken"

Virginia Woolf's novel *The Waves* (1931) has consistently been read critically as a work of High Modernism, a novel of the thirties that is not a thirties novel. Its canonical status has been based on a series of misreadings of this poetic text and of Woolf herself as synonymous with and celebratory of upper-class genteel British culture. My reading claims that *The Waves* is the story of "the submerged mind of empire." Woolf has, to use Coetzee's terms (133), set her experimental antinovel in "the jagged time of rise and fall," explicitly repeating the words "rise and fall and and rise again" throughout the text. But this text (roman in typeface as opposed to the italics recording the rise and setting of the sun) of humans making their life history (plotting against history?) is surrounded by an italicized text of "spinning time" in the cycle of the seasons. These italicized interludes take the form of a set of Hindu prayers to the sun, called Gayatri, marking its course during a single day. These (Eastern) episodes surround a (Western) narrative of the fall of British imperialism. Imperialist history is divided into chapters called "the rise of . . . " or "the fall of. . . ." *The Waves* explores the way in which the cultural narrative "England" is created by an Eton/Cambridge elite who (re)produce the national epic (the rise of . . .) and elegy (the fall of . . .) in praise of the hero. The poetic language and experimental structure of this modernist classic are vehicles for a radical politics that is both anti-imperialist and anticanonical.[1]

Woolf dramatizes the death of the white male Western author, Bernard, his fixation with "how not to die," while exposing the writer's collusion in keeping alive the myth of individualism and selfhood that fuels English patriotism and nationalism. This violent homosocial narrative of English national identity, in its simple-minded racism (and sexism) and nostalgia for class bias, which Woolf mercilessly parodies in an infantilized fictional focalization of "he said" and "she said," is nevertheless so powerful in its intertextuality with hundreds of lines from familiar Romantic poems that readers for five decades have been taught to read Percival and Bernard as Hero and Poet, without recognizing Woolf's fictional prophecy of fascist characters. *The Waves* quotes (and misquotes) Shelley, not to praise him but to bury him. Woolf is infusing her discourse about Orientalism in England at the beginning of the postcolonial period with Shelley's Orientalism, exposing the implications of race and gender in the still-living English Romantic quest for a self and definition of the (white male) self against the racial or sexual Other. There has been so much critical resistance to Woolf's politics that her anti-imperialist effort of enclosing a Western narrative in an Eastern narrative in order to critique Western philosophy and politics in *The Waves* may have seemed too radical for a descendant of Anglo-Indian policymakers. But as a socialist, feminist, and pacifist, Woolf had far more reason to explore Indian history and religion than T. S. Eliot did, for example, whose references to the great Indian texts are taken seriously. It is my contention that Woolf uses Shelley's poems, specifically "The Indian Girl's Song," to create a discourse for an alienated Western woman like Rhoda to have a "heroic death," like Indian widows in sati.

In creating Rhoda's internal speech out of the texts of Shelley's poems, Woolf participates in and exposes at least two historical Orientalisms that force us to look at race and gender in relation to colonialism. Shelley's visions of Indian love/death come from his readings of Sydney Owenson's (Lady Morgan's) novel *The Missionary* (1811), as hers came from reading Sir William Jones, an early English "Orientalist." The abjection of Rhoda's suicide is politicized by mirroring the acts of Shelley's Indian maidens, though her Western sati is death by water, not by fire. Rhoda's silence invokes the silence of the Indian woman (Gramsci and Spivak's "subaltern"?), so verbal and intellectual a figure in Owenson but transformed in Shelley into a Romantic suicide, thereafter speechless, absent, or dead in Western texts. Shelley's Romanticization of sati recalls British colonial chivalry, arguing that colonialism would free Indian women from such "barbaric" practices, as one patriarchy invokes its superiority to another patriarchy, in the same way that the overturned bullock cart, righted by Percival, recalls the throngs of worshipers run over and killed by Krishna's cart at religious celebrations, another excuse for English intervention.

The history of the reception of the text, particularly its rejection by those leftist critics whose ideology it presumably shares, exposes an awkward gender and class bias, a certain paternalism in British Left criticism from Leavis to Williams, which cannot come to terms with a marxist novel that is not realist, an anti-imperialist novel that is not (I am sorry to say) written by a man.[2] The failure of the text to reach its contemporary intended audience, and its subsequent status as "difficult" or only available to an elite, has ensured its relegation to the unread, except in formalist or philosophical terms, and has operated as a cultural imperative that continues to deprive Virginia Woolf of readers of color or of the working class. Left-wing guardians of English culture steered such readers to Lawrence and Orwell for their moral and political heritage, rather than to the radicalism of Woolf. What a different narrative of modernism might have emerged if Jameson had read *The Waves* with Conrad's *Lord Jim* as exposing the ideology of the British ruling class. Perhaps he would have been forced to question his privileging of *Lord Jim*.

Said's praise of *Kim* and Jameson's exploration of fascist modernism are moves that seem deliberately to avoid reading or acknowledgment of the profound critique of imperialism and the class system in Virginia Woolf's work. Some very astute critics are unable to accept Woolf's irony about an author figure so like herself in the portrait of Bernard; they ignore the antipatriotic and anti-imperialist outbursts in the text because they are inconsistent with these critics' notion of the author's politics, based on her gender and class. The interpretive history of *The Waves* for a socialist feminist critic, then, is largely a negative burden, for *The Waves* simply does not exist as a cultural icon of the 1930s, as part of the discourse about (the rise of . . .) fascism, war, and imperialism in which it participated. The critical act of re-placing it in this discourse is an aggressive cultural move made possible now, I would argue, by the legitimation of cultural studies and the combined methodologies of feminism, marxism, revisionist Orientalism, and the recognition of certain postmodern characteristics in some modernist texts.

The rescue of the text, which I here attempt, is addressed to those deeply indoctrinated by the Leavisite legacy of a mythical "Virginia Woolf," created to stand for that elite, effete English culture against which the democratic Great Tradition strenuously struggled. Adena Rosmarin has theorized the cultural process of recuperative reading: "the argument that best accounts for the work is coincident with the argument that best accounts for the manifold histories of its reworkings" (21), an idea that moves me to say it is the project of cultural studies that now allows one to read *The Waves* as a narrative about culture making. Exploring the relations between race, class, and gender in the text *and* in the history of its production allows us to see those forces at work in criticism as well. Bernard in *The Waves* authorizes his role as inheritor of civilization by summoning a recurring vision of a "lady at a table writing, the gardeners with their great brooms sweeping" (192). This is a vision in which English culture is represented as an aristocratic female figure in a grand country house called Elvedon, leisure for creativity provided by the security of the fixed class position of servants. Bernard insists that the two figures are inseparable, that you cannot have one without the other. As inheritor of culture, he will always have a Mrs. Moffat to "sweep it all up." The figure of the lady represents the gentleman artist; once the reader pries apart Bernard's pairing of the writing classes and the sweeping classes and questions the inevitability of Elvedon as a figure for art, it is possible to read the novel as a critique of the culture-making process, and especially as Woolf's feminist exploration of the patriarchal representation of Woman as Culture, a representation that nevertheless silences and intimidates women like Rhoda. Bernard's fetishized Portrait of the Artist as a Lady has more to do with his own image as a ruling-class writer than with the possibility of women's producing culture. (Desmond MacCarthy, the model for Bernard, would never concede that there were any great women writers.)

Marina Warner, in *Monuments and Maidens: The Allegory of the Female Form,* discusses the allegorical use of female figures for national and imperial projects. She wittily points out the irony in the history of the symbolism of Britannia, in recent years portentously figuring official state power in cartoons of Mrs. Thatcher as the armed warrior woman when, in fact, Britannia was originally a figure on coins struck by the Roman emperors Hadrian and Antoninus Pius to celebrate the colonization of Britain. In the seventeenth century Britannia was mythologized as the British constitution and the triumphant naval nation, and engraved with Neptune yielding his scepter to her. In 1740 James Thomson's poem "Rule, Britannia!" with music by Thomas Arne, was sung as the finale of his masque *Alfred;* it did not become a popular unofficial national anthem until the next century. Thomson's text reflects the tension between free democracy and the dread ruler of subject nations: Britannia is commanded to rule as if in fearful memory of Roman subjection; other nations are joyfully given over to tyrants while Britons shout their determination never, never to be slaves. This is a fitting anthem for imperialists.

As nineteenth-century figures of Britannia began to impersonate Athena, the democratic persona gave way to the figure of might and power. Warner writes: "It is noteworthy that Britannia appears more frequently on the stamps of subject nations than on the stamps of Great Britain herself, revealing her shift from personification of a free people to symbol of the authority which endorses it" (49). My calling upon the figure of Britannia in the title of this essay is meant to convey the national anxiety of the former colony about the colonizing process itself, as if there were no other role but colonizer or colonized. The Lady at a Table Writing serves as a "Britannia" figure and an allegory for Bernard. But in order to read it this way, one has to be open to irony in Woolf's voice, particularly toward Bernard, the writer figure, and be aware of and open to Woolf's critique of class and empire. Bernard is a parody of authorship; his words are a postmodern pastiche of quotation from the master texts of English literature.

Woolf's "biographeme," her model for the character of Bernard, is Desmond MacCarthy, the man of letters, editor of *Life and Letters,* prominent reviewer and arbiter of taste, writing as "Affable Hawk" a series of judgments of literary value in which he claims that there is no such thing as a "great" woman artist (Woolf argued the point with him in "The Intellectual Status of Women," but he never wavered). This process by which the actual Desmond and the fictional Bernard figure Woman as

Culture while denying either women or the working class the possibility of creating culture, to follow Rosmarin again, can be plotted both in formalist and materialist readings of *The Waves* and in the problematic scapegoating of Virginia Woolf herself. She may represent culture, but she may not create it. Insofar as Elvedon *is* Bloomsbury in the novel and Bloomsbury/Virginia Woolf is an enormous inflated straw woman against whom both the Left and Right may fulminate (and did; and still do?) from the 1930s to the present, we notice that the figure of Woman as Culture in *The Waves* is constructed as demanding the continued oppression of the working class, a move that allows certain marxists to continue their misreading. Such interpretations of the author's class and gender as "lady" denied feminism a founding place in modernism or in English Left criticism by insisting on its inability to ally itself with the working class. This deprived socialist women of a model critic and founding mother and foreclosed the possibility of inserting, at an earlier historical date, gender (and race) into a predominantly class-centered oppositional narrative.

Other cultural narratives about Virginia Woolf were invented and circulated around this master narrative of the lady: Quentin Bell's biography was constructed backward from the suicide and produced versions of madwoman and victim; feminist narratives of the survivor of child abuse were fashioned; American feminists revived *A Room of One's Own* as a founding text for women's studies as a field, a practice that sometimes ignored the class narrative in the text. Also problematic was the explicit rejection of Woolf as the origin of modern socialist feminist critical practice by American empiricist feminists, responding, it appears, to the demand of English Left cultural authority. Woolf alienated a contemporary leftist audience in "The Leaning Tower" by exposing the way leftist intellectuals romanticized the working class and neglected the political education of their own class. (Their heroizing of Lawrence is as problematic as the demonizing of Woolf.) Her fiction relentlessly connects imperialism to patriarchy; *Three Guineas,* for example, insists that the origin of fascism is in the patriarchal family, not in Italian or German nationalism, a politics recuperated by certain 1970s feminisms but certainly not by the British Left.

It is not my purpose to claim subaltern status for Woolf or for *The Waves,* or even to claim that my reading of its politics is a restoration of a lost original text. But what becomes apparent in reading *The Waves* with the benefit of recent cultural methodologies is that the text itself provides strategies for readers excluded from the cultural inheritance it represents.

Woolf provides such strategies through Bernard's demand as an artist for an audience of "other people's eyes" (I's, ayes). Bernard's is an act of literary hegemony; he absorbs the voices of his marginalized peers into his own voice—he needs "other people's eyes" to read him and other people's I's, their lives and selves, to make his stories. As Bernard's audience, however, we are made to see this act of appropriation. The text as a whole thus invokes a reader who can read as a barbarian or outsider, not just as a Greek or inheritor of the tradition. As readers, prying open the difference between the two positions allows us to enter into the racial/colonial narrative in the way that opening the lady/sweeper pairing assists in the interrogation of class.

I argue here that *The Waves* is a thirties novel and that it is concerned with race, class, colonialism, and the cultural politics of canonicity itself. In *The Waves* Woolf interrogates the color problem, setting a metropolitan "whiteness" against the colored colonial world as a vast desert against which an intellectual elite like the Bloomsbury Group creates itself as culture. *The Waves* might have been called *Waiting for the Barbarians* because of its emotional evocation of white fear and guilt for colonial and class oppression, the national dream of being assailed by the assegais of the savage enemy as "white sheep." But fifty years of readings are difficult to displace—just as readers of Edith Sitwell's *Façade* have been prevented from hearing its profound critique of British naval power because of a narrow notion that the political is foreign to a performative aesthetic emphasizing sound, dance, and nonsense children's rhymes. Postmodern performance art may allow us to recuperate Sitwell's text, music, and megaphone, as well as the mockery of English maritime power she shared with Woolf. We might think of Woolf's rehearsal for *The Waves* in her youthful participation in the "Dreadnought Hoax" in 1910, a prank in which she and her friends, posing as the emperor of Abyssinia and his court, successfully boarded a formidable secret man-of-war of which her cousin, William Fisher, was flag commander.

Consistent with the socialist politics and antifascist ethics of *The Years* and *Three Guineas,* which explore the relation of the patriarchal family and state institutions to fascism, *The Waves* investigates the origin of cultural power in the generation or group formed by the British public school and in its values. Woolf mocks snobbish, eternally adolescent male bonding around the ethos of "the playing fields of Eton" and she exposes the cult of the hero and the complicity of the poet in the making of culture as he exudes cultural glue (in the form of an elegy for the dead hero) as a source of social cohesion, the grounding for nationalism, war, and eventually fascism. I claim here that in 1931, despite her personal privilege in class terms, Woolf prophesied the doom of the insular civilization that produced her by specifically problematizing whiteness as an issue. If, as I have argued, *A Room of One's Own* is an elegy for all the lives of women left out of history, then *The Waves* deconstructs the politics of the elegy as an instrument of social control. In the process of inventing a new name for her fictions, Woolf thought "elegy" might do. But in exploring its function, she revealed the ethical problems to be faced in using this patriarchal genre. Bernard's production of culture is authorized by the politics of the elegy in the history of poetry; his writing mourns the death of Percival in India: "He was thrown, riding in a race, and when I came along Shaftesbury Avenue tonight, those insignificant and scarcely formulated faces that bubble up out of the doors of the Tube, and many obscure Indians, and people dying of famine and disease, and women who have been cheated, and whipped dogs and crying children—all these seemed to me bereft. He would have done justice. He would have protected. . . . No lullaby has ever occurred to me capable of singing him to rest" (243).

The Waves insists that the modernist epic-elegy is a melodrama for beset imperialists. (*The Waste Land, Ulysses,* etc., might be read in the same way.) It marks the end of empire, but to read it this way, as part of what I call the "postcolonial carnivalesque," one must be willing to read the comic and ironic and perhaps even regard with relief the death of the author which it enacts. The study of the silenced colonial other and the search for the subaltern voice, while not articulated in Woolf's text, do lead us to recognize the power of the white woman's critique of herself and her social system, and of the complicity of English literature with imperialism and class oppression, especially when such a critique is not to be found in the writing of modernist men. The gardeners and the natives do not speak in *The Waves;* they are pictures taken under Bernard's imaginary Western eyes. But their presence, and that of Mrs. Moffat, the charwoman, and Bernard's nanny-muse, suggests that we ask whose interest was served by marking this text apolitical for five decades.

Virginia Woolf self-consciously creates here a literature of color, and that color is white, a literature written under the protection of the "white arm" of imperialism and defining itself by the brown and black of colonized peoples, ideologically asserting itself even in the unconscious of oppressed and silenced women in Rhoda's fantasy of her white flower fleet. The Haule-Smith concordance reports 117 instances of "white" or "whiteness" in this very short text, evidence of Woolf's effort to interrogate the color problem of whiteness as ideology. A barbarian reading notices *The Waves* as a white book, as Toni Morrison's provocative reading of Melville recalls the moment in American history "when whiteness became ideology. . . . And if the white whale is the ideology of race, what Ahab has lost to it is personal dismemberment and family and society and his own place as a human in the world. The trauma of racism is, for the racist and the victim, the severe fragmentation of self" (15–16). Bernard's "world without a self" is the white postcolonial world. The fragmented selves of the "civilized" characters in *The Waves* are directly related to the politics of British imperialism. If Bernard is an Ahab figure, then the vision of a "fin in a waste of waters" may belong to his own white whale, his obsession with Percival and India. (We know that Woolf read *Moby Dick* on February 14, 1922, and again on September 10, 1928; her centenary article on Melville, for which she read all his works, appeared in *TLS* on August 7, 1919. Her diary mentions *Moby Dick* in connection with Desmond MacCarthy [Diary III, 195], and she also jokes about Moby Dick's whiteness.)

This Occidental tribe of alienated characters, so often read as figures in a roman à clef of Bloomsbury intellectuals, collectively inscribe their class and race superiority only by imagining a world of the Savage Other in India and Africa, where their representative, Percival (a Siegfried, a Superman, the strong silent bully who will by the end of the decade be a fascist idol), secures their privilege by violent exertions of brute force. As *Orlando* writes the history of English literature based on a founding gesture of violence and conquest, Orlando slicing at the shrunken head of a Moor, the trophy of a violent British adventure against African blacks, *The Waves* reveals that the primal narrative of British culture is the (imperialist) quest. Bernard and his friends idolize Percival, the violent last of the British imperialists, as his (imagined) life and death in India become the story of their generation. Percival embodies their history, and Bernard, the man of letters, ensures by his elegies to Percival that this tale, the romance of the dead brother/lover in India, is inscribed as *the story* of modern Britain. My reading of the novel goes against the grain of its reception as ahistorical and abstract by insisting that it records a precise historical moment—the postcolonial carnivalesque—in Percival's quixotic ride on a fleabitten mare and his fall from a donkey, of England's fall from imperial glory and the upper-class angst of the intellectuals, their primal terror in imagining the assegais of subject peoples turned against them, their agony at contact with the masses and the classes at home, who threaten the order of their whiteness with blood and dirt. The success of Woolf's postmodern practice is evident in her ambivalence about the "fall," unless she was joking when she wrote to Quentin Bell in 1935 that she shed a tear at the film *Bengal Lancers* ("that's what comes of being one generation nearer to Uncle Fitzy" [*Letters* 5, 383]).

The Waves is about the ideology of white British colonialism and the Romantic literature that sustains it. Its parody and irony mock the complicity of the hero and the poet in the creation of a collective national subject through an elegy for imperialism. In its loving misquotation and textual appropriation of Romantic poetry, *The Waves* may participate more fully in postmodernism as Linda Hutcheon defines it than it does in that modernism where its tenuous canonical place is earned by praise for technical difficulty and apparent antirealism as a representation of consciousness. *The Waves* undermines humanistic faith in the individual coherent subject while exposing the role writing plays in shoring up *national* subjectivity; it challenges the idea of the artist's integrity. In its allusions to Romantic poetry, and, specifically, to Shelley's earlier Orientalism, Woolf's text recalls another historical moment of English fetishization of selfhood and individualism as the struggle against death. It questions the white man's anxiety about identity as universal. Woolf mocks the Western valorization of individual selfhood in her exhaustion of the form of soliloquy, and she disposes of the notion of individual literary genius by an overdetermined intertextuality with Romantic poetry, which simultaneously pokes fun at Romantic diction and ideology and demonstrates how powerful certain phrases and images are in the invocation of patriotism and nationalist claims for English genius. Harold Bloom completely misses this aspect of Woolf's cultural critique when he interprets *The Waves* as belated Romanticism and calls Bernard's last speech a "feminization of the Paterian aesthetic stance" (5). This canonical move denies the politics of Woolf's parody of the English culture-making machinery in which one genius succeeds another. *The Waves* is the swan song of the white Western male author with his Romantic notions of individual genius, and his Cartesian confidence in the unitary self. Byronic man, the Romantic artist-hero, sings his last aria against death.[3]

The waves that interest me in this essay are the waves called up in the English national anthem, "Britannia Rules the . . . ," waves that surround an island imperialist culture defining itself as civilization against the perceived savagery of those whom it has conquered across the seas, specifically, in this text, India. The children of empire, the British ruling class of the 1930s, six characters lacking patronymics and fixed forever in their first names by an absent authority, fixate on the seventh, Percival, the hero, the man of action, the figure whose body they all identify with England. (Since they address only themselves and not each other, and the women don't even call themselves by name, Woolf enacts a discursive infantilization that she emphasizes by the use of the pure present—"I come; I go.") Her authorial hand has torn these characters from the bosoms of their families as if to isolate for scientific study the peer group as carrier of ideology. While *To the Lighthouse* and *The Years* provide acute social critiques of marriage and the family, *The Waves* examines the role of childhood friendships and schooling in the formation of individual, group, and national identity, and the group's production of the figures of hero and poet in the consolidation of cultural hegemony. The school scenes are in fact an indictment of the British public school system, exposing the barbarism and cruelty by which upper-class boys learn to be "Greeks," inheritors of culture, what Woolf's cousin J. K. Stephen first called "the intellectual aristocracy."

Woolf exposes as well the way that white women are implicated in, rather than exempt from, this imperialistic project. Correctly, I think, she reveals the way each of the white women in their Foucauldian roles as sexualized social beings—Rhoda the hysteric, Ginny the prostitute, and Susan the mother—collaborates in Bernard's plot to canonize the physical and verbal brutality, class arrogance, and racial intolerance of Percival. Feminist readings often argue that Bernard's fluency depends upon the suppression of Rhoda, that her silence is necessary for his speech. But in their roles as victims, silenced subjects, the women still participate in imperialist practice.

In representing the relation between women and imperialism, particularly in the context of India, *The Waves* develops and extends an anti-imperialist critique found in Woolf's previous novels. Peter Walsh, in the mode of Brantlinger's "Imperial Gothic," sees himself as "an adventurer, reckless, he thought, swift, daring, indeed (landed as he was last night from India) a romantic buccaneer" (*Mrs. Dalloway* 80), as opposed to the crowds of returned Anglo-Indians "in the Oriental Club biliously summing up the ruin of the world" (246). "Fresh from the centre"—in this case India, not London—Peter is sought out by Lady Bruton at the party where the prime minister discusses what the government means to do about the crisis in India (244, 274). Even though Peter "disliked India, and empire, and army" (82), he admires the statue of Gordon and imagines a mythical Grey Nurse, a sinister matriarchal figure combining Mrs. Dalloway and Queen Victoria as England, fantasy representations of female figures in whose name he acts. Mrs. Dalloway serves as symbolic Mother Country for the colonials and as a figure of the Home Front, willingly accepting the belated war death of Septimus Smith as her due. The patriarchal mythologizing of woman as a figure to mask or take the blame for imperialism explodes in the description of Conversion "even now engaged—in the heat and sands of India, the mud and swamp of Africa, the purlieus of London . . . even now engaged in dashing down shrines, smashing idols, and setting up in their place her own stern countenance" (151). Mrs. Dalloway herself, and the novel bearing her name, becomes Britannia.

Woolf figures colonialism as radical-liberal womanizing in her portrait of Peter Walsh. Peter's role as failed colonial administrator is figured in fantasy inventions of the conquest of strange women he follows and seduces. The empire is run by this marginal, daydreaming, anxious ladies' man with the assistance of women like old Miss Parry, one of the seemingly harmless amateur anthropologists and naturalists who catalog exotic orchids (to establish difference even among the animals and plants?) so that the sins of the spinster aunts and the lady travelers are on the heads of the nieces and daughters of the empire. White women are complicit in colonialism. Miss Parry is one of the army of surveillance experts in information retrieval, satisfying the imperialist urge to know, the lust to set eyes on everything under the sun. Only the indifferent listener to Bernard's tale—the unnamed someone, met before on a ship going to Africa, who is collared on Shaftesbury Avenue as captive audience for Bernard's autobiography, the story of a man of letters and his coterie, a belated defense of Western culture and its obsession with death—is innocent of complicity, offering the reader a model of refusal and resistance.

India and the Makers of Ideology

In writing *The Waves,* Woolf critiqued the system from within, acknowledging her own role as inheritor of class privilege and Stephen family history, her concern for the sins of the fathers as makers of imperialism and patriarchy. As I have argued in "Liberty, Sorority, Misogyny," Stephen family members in the nineteenth century were the great professionalizers who consolidated the power of the rising middle class in British institutions. They were also great reformers. The Stephen dynasty escaped its poor Scottish origins and began with the first James Stephen writing his way out of debtors' prison by claiming that such imprisonment was against the Magna Carta. James's son was educated courtesy of money earned by his uncle in the West Indies, and the second James Stephen was made into an abolitionist by witnessing a slave auction on St. Kitts in 1783 and joined Wilberforce and the Clapham Sect on his return from the West Indies. Beginning with Woolf's great-grandfather, who wrote the Anti-Slavery Bill (though it was her paternal grandfather, James Stephen, permanent undersecretary for the Colonies, who got it passed), the Stephen family shaped British ideology, especially in relation to colonial policy in India. A patriarchal tyrant at home, Mr. Mother-Country-Stephen, as he was called by the press, brilliantly invented the family metaphors that locked colonial subjects into the roles of infantilized bad children in relation to a benevolent "Mother Country."

All the Stephens were conscious makers of ideology, but the mother-country metaphor made an impact in shaping colonialism British style in behind-the-scenes bureaucracy by creating the colonial subject as a child and displacing the patriarchal power that fueled colonialism onto a less-threatening female figure. It ensured that any revolt of the colonized could be constituted as a crime against the sacred institution of motherhood. Queen Victoria grew into the role of imperial mother as the century progressed. My argument is that the Stephens invested the philosophy of imperialism with the theology of the patriarchal family, rewarding their complicitous women with power over servants in a replication of the master-servant relationship that James Fitzjames Stephen argued as a political philosophy was the model for a man's relation to his wife and children. James Stephen implemented a policy of making the conquered colonies British, members of a family. His son Fitzjames was one of the chief codifiers of Indian law, a major feat of cultural hegemony, for it was through the rigorous application of law and a system of courts and judges that the British were able to govern and to create a native governing class. This classification and centralizing of disparate systems of law served as a rehearsal for similar work in England, a centralizing and professionalizing activity that standardized the law according to an Old Testament evangelical obsession with punishment. Often the colonies served as practice grounds for policies later implemented at home. It is clear that this codification of disparate practices into a single system laid the groundwork for certain narratives of nationalism in both India and England. Leslie Stephen, in his monumental *Dictionary of National Biography,* created a master cultural narrative of

England as a history of the lives of Great Men, and in her youth his sister Caroline wrote a history of sisterhoods, nuns, and nurses that argued all such separate organizations of women were a threat to the patriarchal family.

Fitzjames's daughter Katherine was principal of Newnham College, and her sister Dorothea spent many years in India studying Indian religions, publishing *Studies in Early Indian Thought* in 1918. This work done by the Stephen family was all cultural anthropology—classifying information. Katherine and Dorothea's brother J. K. Stephen, the model for Percival in *The Waves,* "bard of Eton and of boyhood," misogynist poet and parodist, studied law and edited a journal called *The Reflector* before his strange death at age thirty-three related to a fall from his horse (the origin of the tragic and culturally unifying scene in *The Waves*). Julia Stephen, Woolf's mother, wrote on two subjects, the power of the nurse over her patient and the responsibility of upper-class women to discipline and control their servants. Woolf's insistence in her work on the relation of patriarchy to imperialism and of both to class and fascism comes from careful study of her family's legacy and her guilty refusal to be the inheritor of the class privilege and power over servants with which such women were bribed to serve the interests of patriarchal state institutions and colonialism.

Imperialism in India and the exploitation of servants in England thus fused in Woolf's imagination with her own revolt as a feminist; and, as I argue elsewhere, the charwoman appears as a major figure in each novel, marking Woolf's concern with class, along with barbed references to India and other colonies, marking her concern with race. Middle-class white women in England traded their own freedom for power over servants (or natives in the colonies) which replicated the master/slave relationship of husbands and wives. That these markers in Woolf's writing have generally been ignored or misread by critics does not diminish their signifying power. Even that classic text of feminist emancipatory literature, *A Room of One's Own,* clearly indicates that literary freedom for the white middle-class English woman writer is bought at the expense of complicity in colonialism. The narrator dissociates herself from the racism of her family and class by announcing that she could pass even a "very fine Negress" without wanting to "make an Englishwoman of her." She will not participate in the social mission of "civilizing" the natives in the manner of her family. Yet the word "fine" suggests that she is not wholly free, for it is a word used to describe an object, not a fellow subject, as if the Negress were an exotic work of art displayed for a collector. (Here, of course, one may see Woolf's part in the Orientalism of modernism, from Picasso's appropriation of African sculpture for his painting to the cult of black American jazz and dance in Paris and other European capitals.) Woolf had a double legacy regarding race. While her great-grandfather had devoted his life to the emancipation of slaves (in recognition that his own rise in status had been paid for by exploitation of the colonies), her grandfather had introduced a different system of exploitation by creating the bureaucracy that governed the Empire.

The narrator of *A Room of One's Own* owes her freedom and £500 a year to a legacy from an aunt who died in Bombay from a fall from her horse. This fall recurs in Woolf's writing as the sign of the sins of the fathers. It anticipates Percival's carnivalized fall from a donkey while racing in India (obviously also a reference to Forster's *Passage to India*), the move from horse to donkey signifying the decline of the raj in the comic end of British colonialism. Woolf's cousin's quixotic fall from a horse and his early death, the various versions of this event that circulated as family mythology, and Desmond MacCarthy's elegy for this ferocious figure in *Portraits,* invest this fall with literary and political resonance in Woolf's work. She often uses figures of horses and donkeys to describe her own work as an artist. Neville, in *The Waves,* constructs his whole worldview around the opposition between the rider and the reader, the hero and the poet, marking again the complicity between culture and colonialism. In *The Waves* Woolf criticizes the twentieth-century colonial and postcolonial discourse that replaced her grandfather's nineteenth-century myth of the Mother Country and her childish colonies as Imperial Family Romance. The new myth for twentieth-century colonialism was an imperialist Boy's Own Story, the Adventure of Brotherly Love, a homoerotic adoration of the strong, silent, violent hero conquering the desert alone. All the characters in *The Waves* participate in this drama of Percival's riding against the spears of the enemy, and they gain a national identity by mythologizing the hero. Reflecting on their common feeling, one may begin to understand the rise of fascism.

Leonard Woolf, Virginia Woolf's husband, veteran of seven years in the Ceylon Civil Service, and author of *The Village in the Jungle* (1913), reprinted by the Hogarth Press in 1931, the year of publication of *The Waves*, always associated his years in Hambantota with the image of himself on horseback among natives on foot. In his letters to Lytton Strachey (housed in the Harry Ransome Humanities Research Center at the University of Texas) he reveals his desire on coming down from

Cambridge to teach in a British public school. When he found that Jews were never hired for these positions, he chose the civil service but agonized at length to Strachey about his difficulties learning to ride, a necessity for such a post. His memoirs trace the "innocent, unconscious imperialist" to his rejection of the role of "imperial pro-consul." Accused by a native lawyer of whipping him in the street, Woolf rejected the accusation as false on the literal level though sym-bolically true, for he realized that the people of Jaffna were "right in feeling that my sitting on a horse arrogantly in the main street of their town was as good as a slap in the face" (*Growing* 113–14). Later, as secretary of the Labour party's Advisory Committee on Imperial Affairs, he advocated self-government for India, espousing advanced but not revolutionary views. His novel is bold in its narrative rejection of the notion of the possibility of justice in the application of British law in Ceylon, but its diction participates in the portrayal of the jungle and its people as savage, cruel, and sinister by the repetition of the words "evil" and "obscene."

In *The Waves* the scene of the hero's fall from his donkey is myth-ologized by Bernard as the death of the Christian knight in pursuit of the Holy Grail, as part of Bernard's vision of the "rise and fall and fall and rise again" of the narrative of colonialism. Neville opposes the rider to the reader, sees Percival as Alcibiades, Ajax, and Hector. His fall from a donkey while racing becomes History. Critics have re-marked here on Virginia Woolf's memorial to her dead brother, Thoby. But the mention of Ajax and the ignominious nature of his fall reminds me of Woolf's cousin J. K. Stephen, whom she compares to Ajax, and the strange and contradictory reports of his fall, which led to madness and early death. Leslie Stephen and Quentin Bell tell of a stone thrown from a train that hit J. K. Stephen's head and knocked him off his horse, and again of his riding into a windmill. The stuff of legends, J. K. Stephen was a violent man made into a hero by all the Cambridge men who wrote about him.

Indeed, Woolf's cousin, whose violent, misogynistic poetry and strange early death play a part in some contemporary claims that he was Jack the Ripper, either alone or with the Duke of Clarence, whose tutor he was at Cambridge, makes an interesting source, not only for Percival, but for the whole hero-poet narrative that is British culture. As I show elsewhere, Woolf read Wortham's 1927 biography of Oscar Browning, which describes her cousin as a hero, and, more important, Desmond MacCarthy's sketch of him in *Portraits*. Woolf saw, I believe, the Bernard-Percival relationship acted out in Desmond's memoir of J. K. Stephen in *Portraits* as "our real laureate," mooning, as Neville and Bernard do about Percival, over the giant who was "violently masculine, a lover of law and abstract argument," the "Philistine," the "Bard of Eton and of boyhood." MacCarthy praises the "prowess of that wild-looking man with rolling but abstracted eye and path-clearing gait, whom I can just remember, hatless and slovenly, mouching round the Playing Fields" (249). This is the origin of Woolf's Eton scenes in *The Waves,* where Percival mouches around the same playing fields. Much of Browning's obituary for Stephen is concerned with Stephen's Eton poems, but MacCarthy remembers his parodies best (and they are still praised and collected in volumes of satire). In the parody of Byron (recall Bernard's obsession with Byron, an obsession shared by MacCarthy), Stephen writes:

> Whoever will may write a nation's songs
> As long as I'm allowed to right its wrongs. (252)

and the parody of Wordsworth reads:

> Two voices are there: one is of the deep;
> It learns the storm-cloud's thunderous melody,
> Now roars, now murmurs with the changing sea,
> Now bird-like pipes, now closes soft in sleep;
> And one is of an old half-witted sheep
> Which bleats articulate monotony,
> And indicates that two and one are three,
> That grass is green, lakes damp and mountains steep;
> And Wordsworth, both are thine: at certain times
> Forth from the heart of thy melodious rhymes,
> The form and pressure of high thoughts will burst:
> At other times—good Lord! I'd rather be
> Quite unacquainted with the A B C
> Than write such hopeless rubbish as thy worst. (252)

While MacCarthy calls Stephen a "Hallam without a Tennyson" he may have had too many Tennysons for Woolf's taste—her father in his biography of Fitzjames Stephen, Oscar Browning and Browning's biographer, and Desmond MacCarthy. All these apostrophes to the dead hero add up to "culture," what Bernard does to re-create England by memorializing Percival. MacCarthy moans about being a failure and overpraises his male peers while ignoring or despising women artists. He does create J. K. Stephen as Percival. His book of portraits, dedicated to himself at age twenty-two, is the tidal wave that never breaks, which Woolf parodies in *The Waves*.[4] "It is curious," MacCarthy writes, "how nearly every group of young men, some of whom afterwards became famous, has had its inconspicuous hero to whom, while the world was looking up at them, they looked up to." Bernard is Desmond and Percival is J. K. Stephen, the patriarchal imperialist makers of British culture.

Bernard's memories of Percival repeat the figure of oscillation ("rise and fall and fall and rise again") of the force of cultural inheritance as a wave that drowns alternative voices. The story of Percival's fall is countered by the story of how he raised the bullock cart and imposed his Western values on the lazy and incompetent natives. ("I see India. . . . I see a pair of bullocks who drag a low cart along the sun-baked road. The cart sways incompetently from side to side" [*The Waves* 135].) For Woolf this recurring fall is a primal scene of the Fall, England's fall from heroic history, her family's fall from ethical purity, her culture's fall into colonialism and its angst. In *The Waves* Woolf uses the case of her cousin (conflated with her dead brother, Thoby, who was said to look like Jem) to explain the deadlock embrace of violence and poetry in the English male cultural script. Her version of the fall and the poet's mythologizing of violence is a critique of family history as well as cultural history.

Mrs. Moffat Will Sweep It All Up

The most powerful undertow in *The Waves* is class. The ruling-class characters define themselves as clean, free, and dominant against the dirt and ugly squalor of the masses. Bernard is bound to the big house by strong narrative ties. Elvedon and its *lady at a table writing, its gardeners with their great brooms sweeping,* the haunting memory that fuels his sense of himself as a writer, is *not* a fixed and eternal figure for writing. Not only do the characters imagine their racial superiority by conjuring up Asia and Africa as the enemy whose assegais are poised against them, but they build their class superiority by hating and despising the working class.[5] Rhoda is afraid of the "squalid" people in the Tube; Neville "cannot endure" that shopgirls should exist next to beautiful buildings; Susan sees country folk living like animals on a dungheap; and even Bernard composes little stories that betray his class and gender bias. He plots the greengrocer's Saturday night dream as an oscillation between thoughts of having posted his letter to the lottery and killing a rabbit, a projection of his own obsessions with chance and violent death onto

Mrs. Thatcher's parents' class. This story makes life "tolerable" for him. The lady/gardener aesthetic is surely being mocked by the author of "The Leaning Tower," who urged the thirties poets to convert members of their own class to divest themselves of privilege, rather than become missionaries to the lower classes. This aesthetic, which figures English culture as a lady, not a woman, and insists on the unalterable relationship between the gardener and the lady, the working class and the writing class, is historically specific to Bernard in England in the early 1930s and certainly not in any way an aesthetic Woolf endorses. If those readers who despise Woolf for her supposed class loyalty and snobby membership in the Bloomsbury Group were to read the novel without its critical history as a canonical text, they might see that it deconstructs the idea of the cultural elite, showing that their power is derived from sex, class, and racial privilege.

The Corpse of the Canon

The boundaries between self and other, between classes and sexes, between the colonizers and the colonized that Woolf maps here are perhaps best expressed in Neville's appalling vision of "death among the apple trees," the doom of the "unintelligible obstacle," his version of the "immitigable" Wordsworthian tree (24), which literally stops him in his tracks and figures the dilemma of the postwar intellectual dealing with the pastoral myth of England's green and pleasant land. The origin of the "story" for which Bernard and his friends search is in the burbling of blood from a cut throat, the wars and imperialist adventures on which their power was built. The violence of Woolf's subject, the dominance of monologic male voices over culture, is clear in the language of blood which she uses in discussing revisions in her diary—"And I am getting my blood up." She wants to avoid chapters and run all her scenes together "so as to make the blood run like a torrent from end to end." She views her achievement as if she had created in the novel a living body "done without spilling a drop" (343). The body of her text, *The Waves*, is the corpse of the literary canon, the mausoleum of white male English culture.

Bernard figures himself as the "continuer" of a dead tradition with a "devastating sense of grey ashes in a burnt-out grate" (80). In this modernist wasteland the poet, like T. S. Eliot, "is he who now takes the poker and rattles the cinders so that they fall in showers through the grate" (81). The ashes and cinders that haunt this novel as aftermath of World War I and as prophecy of the Holocaust for the modern reader invoke dirt and disorder as the artist's inspiration, marking his own urban civilized dependence on the slum. The ash-grey dawn of the opening prelude pictures the canvas of sea and sky as a wrinkled grey blanket, a smoky woolen cloth over a bonfire, a kind of blank page "barred with thick strokes moving" (7) where birds sing "their blank melody." Like Bernard's "dead fire" in a burnt-out grate, this ominous opening scene suggests the end of writing and the end of a certain kind of culture—Bernard's dependence on servants like Mrs. Moffat to reinforce his image of himself as "chosen."

In this opening scene the arm of the lady with the lamp clarifies the light until "the dark stripes were almost wiped out" (7), recalling the traditional representation of Britannia ruling the waves. It seems to me that this opening passage as a hymn to Dawn also invokes the Indian text, the *Rig Veda,* as Virginia Woolf's cousin Dorothea Stephen explained it in *Studies in Early Indian Thought,* to call up Indian philosophy and its emphasis on astronomy and the randomness of the universe, a major subject of *The Waves,* which incorporates relativity theory and the new physics into fiction.[6] Stephen argues that Indian thought emphasizes that personal character is not important in the scheme of the universe: "In early Indian thought we have the boldest and the most consistent effort that the human mind has ever made to show that it is nothing" (172). Is it too much to suppose that Woolf used an Indian religious text to write the death of a particular form of white Western culture? When she called *The Waves* "mystical," did she mean Eastern mysticism? (The Vedas are in fact mentioned on page 186 as texts Bernard will never read, though Louis, the T. S. Eliot figure and the white colonial returned to the mother country, is familiar with them.) The specific uncanniness of the poetic language of *The Waves,* its ecstasies of apostrophe, are common both to the Romantic lyric of Shelley and Keats and to prayer—in this case, the mode of Hindu religious texts. While popular sentiment might declare that the sun never sets on the British Empire, *The Waves* emphatically dramatizes the very historical moment in which the sun does set. By making the sun set on the British Empire in her novel Woolf enacts the possibility of writing as liberation rather than collaboration. If we read the opening sections, the interludes, as a Western imitation or homage to the Hindu Gayatri, or as prayers on the course of the sun, we may see that Woolf surrounds the text of the decline and fall of the West (the transcendental self striving and struggling against death) with the text of the East, random natural recurrence.

But the narrative of violent struggle bleeds into the interludes; they are not entirely passive and innocent—assegais appear even here (though the text is not sure how to spell these African interlopers in Woolf's Indian novel). While no native of the subcontinent actually speaks in *The Waves,* Hindu philosophy embracing death is invoked at the ending in an ironic reading of Bernard's famous ride against Death as "the enemy." Bernard sees himself "with . . . spear couched and . . . hair flying back like a young man's, like Percival's" (297), galloping in India. In fact Percival was riding a donkey, not galloping, and this long-haired rider seems to be not Percival but a reincarnation of Shiva, in what may be read as a new dawn "kindling" in the East, as Western "civilization is burnt out" (296). (This Eastern dawn also ends *The Years.*) W. B. Yeats recognized Woolf's incorporation of Eastern philosophy into her text, linking it with *Ulysses* and Pound's *Cantos,* which "suggest a philosophy like that of the Samkara school of ancient India, mental and physical objects alike material, a deluge of experience breaking over us and within us, melting limits whether of line or tint; man no hard bright mirror dawdling by the dry sticks of a hedge, but a swimmer, or rather the waves themselves" (Yeats 64–65).

"Our English past—one inch of light" (*The Waves* 227), Bernard's vision, is more pessimistically viewed by Louis, the Australian T. S. Eliot figure who thinks "the lighted strip of history is past and our Kings and Queens; we are gone; our civilization; the Nile; and all life . . . we are extinct" (225). As a former colonial subject, Louis is most afraid of the dissolution of empire. He hears the great beast of revolution stamping on the shore. He commutes between a garret room, where he can observe sordid sights of poverty and degradation, and a mahogany desk in a posh office, where he plans for swimming pools on luxury liners: "I pick my way over broken glass, among blistered tiles, and see only vile and famished faces" (202). (Doubtless, it is on one of his company's ships going to Africa and ruling the waves that Bernard met the unnamed person to whom he tells his life story in the last section of the book, the only "dialogue," such as it is, when the Other is a reluctant listener, in this deliberately monologic text.) In Louis's soliloquy, Woolf connects the British businessman, spreading commerce and colonialism, militarism and patriarchy, with Napoleon, Plato, and Sir Robert Peel: "I like to hear . . . the heavy male tread of responsible feet down the corridors. . . . The weight of the world is on our shoulders" (169). Louis's identity is so insecure that he needs continual reinforcement of his class position from walking the slums. He participates in what Stallybrass and White call the nineteenth-century "construction of subjectivity through totally ambivalent internalizations of the city slum" (21).

Bernard constructs his subjectivity by internalizing the second of the figures pointed out by Stallybrass and White—the nurse or the nanny. Using the work of Jim Swan and Jane Gallop, Stallybrass and White look at Freud's obsession with his own and his patients' nurses or nannies during the time that he was working on the theory of the Oedipus complex. The critical role of the nurse in initiating the child sexually while engaged in hygiene (by bathing children of the middle and upper classes) is displaced when Freud claims this role for the mother of the male child. Both mothers and fathers are absent in *The Waves,* but Bernard remembers his nurse, Mrs. Constable, for his whole life. She is his muse, and the primal scene of writing is for him the memory of her turning over the pages of a picture book and naming the objects. But his recurrent dream of her squeezing the sponge over his naked body, releasing "arrows of sensation" (239), is so fearful a moment that he wishes to save other newborns from the experience. Are we to see that his rigid Tory politics, imperialistic hero-worship, and barely repressed homosexuality are all derived from this childhood experience? He does have an image of his appetitive self as a "hairy ape" who lives inside his body, a self he despises and also projects onto the "savages" Percival is taming in India. One could say that his life is circumscribed by his nurse and his charwoman, Mrs. Constable and Mrs. Moffat. Woolf is laying out a psychological trail to explain Bernard's origin as the self-appointed arbiter of British culture.

The clearest exposition of the politics of the novel is in the scene at an expensive restaurant, where the six young white inheritors, sleek and well fed, eat roast duck and think of themselves as the center of civilization. They create themselves as civilized only by imagining Britain's colonies as savage. The Greeks define themselves against the barbarians. (There are nineteen direct references to India in the novel and several indirect ones.) And they each fantasize India as dark, dirty, disordered, and directly threatening their own deaths. The language of their dreams of Percival in India is thoroughly racist and colonialist—"incompetent," "natives in loincloths," "strange sour smells," "remote provinces are fetched out of darkness," "muddy roads," "twisted jungle," "the vulture that feeds on some bloated carcass," "the dancing and drumming of naked men with assegais," "ruthless," "flapping bladders," "painted faces," "bleeding limbs which they have torn from the living body" (136, 137, 140). India silently becomes Africa; the "Oriental problem" becomes the "African problem."

Woolf's white British characters see the colonized as cannibals. Neville says, "We are walled in here. But India lies outside" (135). The following passage, with its mythologizing of Percival as a hero in his righting of the bullock cart (a rewriting of the classic scene with a bullock cart in Kipling's *Kim*), exposes Bernard's complicity with imperialism—how necessary his myth-making capacity is to the maintenance of domination and submission, master and slave:

> "I see India," said Bernard. "I see the low, long shore; I see the tortuous lanes of stamped mud that lead in and out among ramshackle pagodas; I see the gilt and crenellated buildings which have an air of fragility and decay as if they were temporarily run up buildings in some Oriental exhibition. I see a pair of bullocks who drag a low cart along the sun-baked road. The cart sways incompetently from side to side. Now one wheel sticks in the rut, and at once innumerable natives in loin-cloths swarm round it, chattering excitedly. But they do nothing. Time seems endless, ambition vain. Over all broods a sense of the uselessness of human exertion. There are strange sour smells. An old man in a ditch continues to chew betel and to contemplate his navel. But now, behold, Percival advances; Percival rides a flea-bitten mare, and wears a sun-helmet. By applying the standards of the West, by using the violent language that is natural to him, the bullock-cart is righted in less than five minutes. The Oriental problem is solved. He rides on; the multitude cluster round him, regarding him as if he were—what indeed he is—a God." (135–36)

This scene is a carnivalization of racism's master plot, a scene created again in film and fiction—the white man brings order and reason to the natives and is made a god. Woolf's grammar is strangely off-kilter here—the incompetent cart, the absent Percival as the subject of the bullock-cart-righting—why is there a passive construction? Bernard's colonialist fantasy contains all the elements of a textbook study of the operations of racism, imperialism, and colonialism—and yet there is something comic in the flea-bitten mare, the sun-helmet. (This resembles a scene from a colonial exhibition or a film like *The African Queen*. There was in fact a Colonial Exhibition in Paris in 1931, and Josephine Baker, the black exotic dancer, was chosen queen until it was pointed out that she was in fact an American.) It seems possible also that Woolf's image of the overturned cart invokes in some readers the figure of the juggernaut, Krishna's cart under whose wheels the faithful would throw themselves—to the British, along with sati, evidence of the savagery of India. Rhoda sees "beyond India," imagining "pilgrimages" from her peers into a landscape where a "white arm" "makes no sign, it does not beckon, it does not see us" (139). One could imagine that Rhoda alone sees the white arm of the mysterious woman with a lamp who brings the dawn, a Britannia in endless surveillance of conquerable lands. But it seems important that the arm is white and that it forms a triangle when resting upon the figure's knee, then a column, then a fountain. The mighty white arm of empire and civilization.

Andreas Huyssen argues that the mark of modernism is fear of contamination. This is Bernard's fear (Mrs. Moffat will sweep it all up). Rhoda fears the puddle and all human beings; Neville fears the recurrence of murder; Louis fears the "great Beast stamping" in the East; Susan hates Ginny all her life for having kissed Louis. The contamination of kisses and classes, the fear of dirt, disorder, and dying, the fear of Africa and India, is the recurring theme of the speakers' monologues. Neville says, "We must oppose the waste and deformity of the world, its crowds eddying round and round disgorged and trampling. One must slip paper-knives, even, exactly through the pages of novels, and tie up packets of letters neatly with green silk, and brush up the cinders with a hearth broom. Everything must be done to rebuke the horror of deformity" (180). If the speakers in *The Waves* are waiting apprehensively for the barbarians, the postcolonial reader may be the barbarian Woolf's text has awaited.

Notes

My thanks to Louise Yelin, Mary Mathis, Patricia Laurence, and Mary Ann Caws for their comments on an early draft; to Karen Lawrence for her rigorous critique and her editorial skills in shaping this essay; to James Haule and his *Concordance;* to Regina Barreca's seminar at the University of Connecticut; and to Ruth Perry for pointing out the connection between my argument about white ideology and Toni Morrison's essay, when I read an earlier version of this essay at Harvard in 1988. Thanks also to audiences at CUNY Graduate Center, SUNY Purchase, the University of Hawaii, Texas A & M, SUNY Stony Brook, and Emory University. My deepest debt is to my student Mary Mathis, who inspired this essay by asking if *The Waves* could be recuperated for feminism and by discussing questions about the death of the author and the influence of Shelley. My thanks also to the M.A. students at City College in fall 1987, where this reading of *The Waves* was first worked out.

1. It is ironic that *The Waves,* a novel that critiques the canon-making process itself, should have been among the first four volumes in the Cambridge University Press Landmarks of World Literature series, begun in 1986 with *The Iliad, The Divine Comedy,* and *Faust.*

2. See the appendix in Raymond Williams's *Politics of Modernism* for the responses of Said and Williams to the question of gender. Williams's well-known attacks on Bloomsbury reveal a need to maintain a muscular macho modernism of the working class. As late as 1965 Leonard Woolf answered Queenie Leavis's claim that Virginia Woolf's novels were not *popular* with sales figures to show that they were (*TLS,* Mar. 2–8, 1990, 211).

3. The classic essay on Romanticism and *The Waves* is McConnell's " 'Death among the Apple Trees.' " Also relevant is J. H. McGavran, "Alone Seeking the Visible World," and J. W. Graham, "MSS Revision and the Heroic Theme of *The Waves.*"

4. Woolf writes of MacCarthy as "a wave that never breaks, but lollops one this way & that way & the sail hangs on one's mast & the sun beats down" (Diary 3, 27).

5. Louise De Salvo points out that the drafts of *The Waves* originally mentioned working-class children who were "washing up plates" as the upper-class children sat at their desks, and "Florrie" who went out as a kitchenmaid when the others went off to school in Switzerland (183).

6. Throughout December 1930, when she was revising *The Waves,* Woolf was reading and discussing Sir James Jeans's books and listening to his lectures on the radio (Diary 3, 337–40). Readers can find some of these brilliant and readable essays in Jeans's *Mysterious Universe* (1933), Alfred North Whitehead's *Science and the Modern World* (1925), and Sir Arthur Eddington's *Stars and Atoms* (1927). Imagine Woolf listening to the broadcasts that aided her in recording the atoms as they fell and fictionally mirroring nature as flux, the randomness of a universe without cause and effect, the intersections of time and space. The monologues are full of waves and loops, literary versions of the new science of her time, as she heard it on the radio. Woolf wrote in her diary: "Talk about the riddle of the universe (Jeans's book) whether it will be known; not by us; found out suddenly about rhythm in prose" [Diary 3, Dec. 18, 1930, 337]. The connection between *The Waves* and relativity and wave mechanics was first suggested to me several years ago in an unpublished paper by Carol Donley (Hiram College) in which she graphed the spatial and temporal movements of the characters alone and together as wave patterns.

Works Cited

Bakhtin, M. M. *Rabelais and His World.* Trans. H. Iswolsky. Bloomington: Indiana University Press, 1984.

Bloom, Harold. *Modern Critical Views of Virginia Woolf.* New York: Chelsea House, 1986.

Coetzee, J. M. *Waiting for the Barbarians.* New York: Penguin Books, 1982.

De Salvo, Louise. *Virginia Woolf: The Impact of Childhood Sexual Abuse on Her Life and Work.* Boston: Beacon Press, 1989.

Eddington, Sir Arthur. *Stars and Atoms.* New Haven: Yale University Press, 1927.

———. *The Philosophy of Physical Science.* New York: Macmillan, 1939.

Graham, J. W. "MSS Revision and the Heroic Theme of *The Waves.*" *Twentieth Century Literature* 29 (1983): 312–32.

Haule, James M., and Philip H. Smith. *A Concordance to The Waves.* Ann Arbor: University Microfilms, 1986.

Hutcheon, Linda. *A Poetics of Postmodernism: History, Theory, Fiction.* New York: Routledge, 1988.

Huyssen, Andreas. *After the Great Divide: Modernism, Mass Culture, Postmodernism.* Bloomington: Indiana University Press, 1986.

Jeans, Sir James. *The Mysterious Universe.* Cambridge: Cambridge University Press, 1930.

MacCarthy, Desmond. *Portraits.* New York: Macmillan, 1932.

McConnell, Frank. " 'Death among the Apple Trees': *The Waves* and the World of Things." *Bucknell Review* 16 (1968): 23–29.

McGavran, J. H. "Alone Seeking the Visible World." *MLQ* 42 (1981): 265–91.

Marcus, Jane. *Virginia Woolf and the Languages of Patriarchy.* Bloomington: Indiana University Press, 1986.

———. "Liberty, Sorority, Misogyny." In *The Representation of Women in Fiction.* Ed. Carolyn Heilbrun and Margaret Higonnet. Baltimore: Johns Hopkins University Press, 1983.

Morrison, Toni. "Unspeakable Things Unspoken: The Afro–American Presence in American Literature." *Michigan Quarterly Review* 27, no. 1 (1989): 1–34.

Rosmarin, Adena. "The Narrativity of Interpretive History." In *Reading Narrative: Form, Ethics, Ideology.* Ed. James Phelan. Columbus: Ohio State University Press, 1989, 12–26.

Said, Edward. "*Kim,* the Pleasures of Imperialism." *Raritan* 7 (1987): 27–64.

———. *Orientalism.* New York: Pantheon, 1978.

Schlack, Beverly. *Continuing Presences: Virginia Woolf's Use of Literary Allusion.* University Park: Pennsylvania State University Press, 1979.

Stallybrass, Peter, and Allon White. *The Politics and Poetics of Transgression.* Ithaca: Cornell University Press, 1986.

Stephen, Dorothea Jane. *Studies in Early Indian Thought.* Cambridge: Cambridge University Press, 1918.

Stephen, James Fitzjames. *Liberty, Equality, Fraternity*. Ed. J. R. White. 1873. Cambridge: Cambridge University Press, 1967.

Stephen, J. K. *The Living Languages: A Defense of the Compulsory Study of Greek at Cambridge*. Cambridge: Macmillan and Bowes, 1891.

Warner, Marina. *Monuments and Maidens: The Allegory of the Female Form*. London: Picador, 1985.

Whitehead, Alfred North. *Science and the Modern World*. New York: Macmillan, 1925.

Williams, Raymond. *The Politics of Modernism: Against the New Conformists*. New York: Verso, 1989.

Woolf, Leonard. *Growing*. New York: Harcourt Brace, 1961.

——. *The Village in the Jungle*. 1913. New York: Oxford University Press, 1981.

Woolf, Virginia. *The Waves*. 1931. New York: Harcourt Brace Jovanovich, 1959.

——. *The Waves*. New York: Cambridge University Press, 1986.

——. *The Diary of Virginia Woolf*. Vol. 3. Ed. Anne Olivier Bell and Andrew McNeillie. New York: Harcourt Brace Jovanovich, 1980.

Yeats, William Butler. Introduction to "Fighting the Waves," *Wheels and Butterflies*. (New York: Macmillan, 1935), 64–65.

PART 3

Postcolonial Configurations

MARILYN REIZBAUM

Canonical Double Cross
Scottish and Irish Women's Writing

The two major critical challenges to the established canon of
literature—indeed, to the idea of a canon—have come from feminists
and (other) "cultural critics." Although the two groups are arguably
indistinguishable, until recently the concerns of one have not necessarily
been accounted for by the other, so that the two groups have gone their
separate, sometimes antagonistic ways. The unhappy distance that marks
the exchange between them was evident at a November 1987 lecture by
Edward Said at Harvard University on the hegemony of empire in culture
and in literature. Said charged that the bulk of contemporary criticism
ignores the effects of the ideology of empire (what he describes as the
hybridization of culture, which I take to mean that neither the colony nor
the "imperial city" returns to a "pure" state of culture after colonization);
and he particularly pointed to feminism as insensitive and oblivious to the
manifestations of imperialism. Susan Suleiman rose from the audience to
countercharge that the kind of criticism Said proffered typically omitted
women's issues, literature, or a feminist perspective (almost all of the
writers to whom Said referred were male). In other words, some arbitrary
line had been drawn between the study of gender and the study of culture,
when, as Suleiman argued, they are interdependent and inseparable.

In what follows, I wish not only to suggest ways in which the gap
might be and is being bridged but to address the issues that seem to me to
account for the gap. In doing so, I will describe the phenomenon of
"double exclusion" suffered by women writing in marginalized cultures,
in this case Scotland and Ireland, where the struggle to assert a nationalist
identity obscures or doubly marginalizes the assertion of gender (the
woman's voice). Even critics who combine the concerns of gender and
culture (or nationalism) in their work, most notably Gayatri Chakravorty
Spivak, address such a relationship in a third-world context. In "The

Politics of Interpretation," included in her collection *In Other Worlds: Essays in Cultural Politics,* Spivak foregrounds the "gap" and the debate when she takes on Donald Davie's claim that the vocabulary of feminism does not allow for a relationship between feminism and national identity: "The heterogeneity of international feminisms and women's situations across race and class lines is one of the chief concerns of feminist practice and theory today. To document this claim would be to compile a volume of bibliographical data. And no feminist denies that women's as well as men's consciousness can be raised with reference to such notions as patriotism or total womanhood" (131). In a note Spivak does catalog a selection of works that address this connection, and all but one make the connection in the Third World. It is a significant omission, I think, that women writers in (postcolonial) cultures that may be seen as dominant (white, Christian), despite the way in which those cultures have been marginalized by hegemonic ideologies, have not been included for consideration in these terms.[1]

The feminist call in Scotland and Ireland for the reformulation of the canon of Scottish and Irish works parallels the challenge to the mainstream Anglo-American establishment presented by Scotland, Ireland, and other countries or cultures like them—former colonies who retain a marginalized standing in relation to the former colonizer. For example, while British anthologies often ignore Scottish and Irish authors, anthologies and critical works of Scottish and Irish writing typically treat women writers with the same disregard. This parallel clarifies the ideological debate between critics like Said and Suleiman and adds a dimension to it that does not readily obtain when the debate takes place within the larger mainstream establishment. It explains why, when we speak about opening the canon to literature from marginalized cultures, the issue of gender is subsumed by the cultural imperative, and why the response of feminists from within and from without may be to lump all cultures under the rubric of patriarchy. The incentive to create a dialogue between "culture" and feminism is more likely to come from countries where there can be little complacency about cultural identity. By decompartmentalizing the question of canon formation, we may re-create and broaden the spectrum of contexts—historiopolitical, social, literary, institutional—in which the discussion takes place and perhaps move beyond what has become the impasse of canonicity.[2] The more fluid the contexts for discussion, the less static the canon becomes.

It seems appropriate to mention here the problematic of nationalism in a postmodern context. At a time when there is a call for pan- or transnationalism, a recognition of the heterogeneity of nation-states, nationalist movements such as those in Scotland and Ireland are often implicated as retrogressive, even dangerous. Nationalism and feminism encounter many of the same vexing questions: that is, does an assertion of positive identity necessarily move toward unanimity, homogeneity, essentialism, fixity, to an ironic betrayal of the principles by which the movement is guided? Certainly, nationalist movements fall into these traps and are often encouraged to do so by those whom they seek to challenge. In both Scotland and Ireland, for example, certain writers serve up caricatures of national types that have to some degree been created cooperatively through imposition and internalization by the colonizer and the colony (dubbed "green prose" in Ireland and "kailyard" in Scotland). We are familiar with the "stage Irishman," the "Paddy," whose counterpart in Scotland is the "gentle Highlander." We recognize the atrocities and hopelessness engendered by sectarianism and the insidious tendency toward nostalgia for a sealed mythic past, a symptom of the historical assault on cultural expression. This latter was, for instance, Joyce's complaint against the Celtic Twilight. In his-four part series, "Postmodern Ireland," published in the *Irish Times* (1987), Richard Kearney, a professor of philosophy at University College, Dublin, addresses the problematic of Irish nationalism:

> What is certain is that one must *discriminate* between different kinds of political nationalism—those that emancipate and those that incarcerate, those that nourish and those that oppress, those that affirm a people's cultural identity in dialogue with other peoples and those that degenerate into ideological closure—into xenophobic racism and bigotry. . . .
>
> To roundly condemn Irish nationalism, refusing to distinguish between its constitutional and non-constitutional expressions, without also adverting to the historical sins of British colonialism and Unionism, amounts to a tacit *apologia* of the latter. (8)

In his provocative study *Nationalism and Minor Literature,* David Lloyd identifies this distinction between "emancipation" and "incarceration" within the same Irish nationalist movement, arguing that despite its possible origins in a resistance to imperialist power, the movement is vulnerable to or actually reproduces the imperialist ideology, namely, "that Irish nationalism itself becomes the means of maintaining British cultural hegemony" (3): "The larger argument of this book is that while nationalism is a progressive and even necessary political movement at one stage in its history, it tends at a later stage to become entirely reactionary, both by virtue of its obsession with a deliberately exclusive concept of racial identity and, more importantly, by virtue of its *formal* identity with imperial ideology. Ultimately, both imperialism and nationalism seek to occlude troublesome and inassimilable manifestations of difference by posing a transcendent realm of essential identity" (x).[3]

As I will show, women in the cultural field (what Lloyd calls the "primary site of struggle") in Scotland and Ireland have sought to alter this dynamic, seeing on the one hand the paternalistic nature of cultural marginalization (their identification with the nationalist cause) and, on the other, the patriarchal dimension of their own cultures' nationalist movements (their exclusion from it). As feminists they do not wish to be susceptible to the same claim of essentialism, and they suggest that the call for a dynamic relation of movements, in this instance, nationalism and feminism, is more "revolutionary" in its resistance to a reductive and/or idealized type. As a rule, in this regard even the more alert and astute commentators on Irish culture have failed to consider seriously the position of women or women's writing (e.g., Kearney, in his most recent work, *Transitions: Narratives in Modern Irish Culture*).

Why Scotland and Ireland? What is marginal, one might ask, about cultures that have produced writers like Burns, Boswell, Stevenson, and Scott, on the one hand, and Wilde, Shaw, Yeats, and Joyce, on the other? In fact, one might argue, the literature of these countries makes a significant canonical display. To begin with, all the Scottish writers mentioned here—except for Boswell, who has been anglicized and remembered only through his association with Johnson—retain a marginal position within the established canon: Burns is sentimentalized, remembered as little more than the author of "Auld Lang Syne" and "quaint" verse in dialect; Stevenson is genericized—he is the creator of adventure novels, a marginalized genre (see Martin Green's essay in this collection for a treatment of this subject), and his *Dr. Jekyll and Mr. Hyde* has suffered a fate similar to that of Mary Shelley's *Frankenstein* by becoming, at least in the United States, an *unread* classic Hollywood horror film; Scott is regionalized, disinherited from his place in literary history as one of the originators of the historical novel (the *Waverley* novels) by virtue of the local(e) (his ambivalent treatment of that locale might account for the position he does hold). I did not list but will mention Hugh MacDiarmid here, the modernist poet who is hardly known though thought to be vaguely canonical.

Of the Irish writers mentioned, all are *Anglo*-Irish except Joyce, and Joyce has been internationalized, his Irishness often seen as primarily a rhetorical, or almost incidental, dimension of his work.[4] In fact, I would argue that Joyce's Irishness is a significant part of what makes his work "minor," in the contemporary critical sense of that term. Critics of minor literature such as Louis Renza, in line with the theories of Deleuze and Guattari, identify Joyce as a "minor" writer, suggesting that he has been misread, ushered into the canon by what is tantamount to a denial of (in Lloyd's terms) the work's "oppositional relationship" to the canon and its operations. This means that Joyce's "revolution of the word" is an act of "deterritorialization," since Joyce is writing in a (m)other tongue (his colonial language from birth); it is through his treatment of both language and subject that his work remains revolutionary: critically self-reflexive and resistant to the "idealism of identity thinking" of which Lloyd speaks (although this has been interpreted as lack of political and national interest), which thereby registers the "radical non-identity of the colonized subject" (Lloyd xi). (In *Ulysses,* the Jew or Jewishness becomes the cultural analogue or field of such nonidentity.) As to the historical canonicity of Joyce, Deleuze and Guattari suggest that it is worldwide reterritorialization—an appropriation to the mainstream "high culture" aesthetic—that is accountable (19).[5]

There is, of course, an obvious absence of women from any of the lists one might draw up, and there is a significant absence of "canonical" writers from these cultures after the early part of the twentieth century. After Beckett, the only writer from Ireland to emerge on a major international scale since the establishment of the Republic in 1949 is Seamus Heaney, a poet from the North who, while he considers himself an Irish writer and is considered as such by readers, is more often than not included in anthologies of British poetry. Unless one lives in Scotland, or takes particular care to keep in touch with the Scottish literary milieu, one will be at a loss to name many modern or contemporary Scottish writers. Or one might name them without knowing that they are Scottish since they have been publicized through and often appropriated by British, specifically English, sources—writers like Douglas Dunn, Edwin Muir, and Kathleen Jamie.

I feel I can talk about Scotland and Ireland together in this context, without homogenizing them and thereby further marginalizing them (all Celts are alike), because they have comparable "colonial" histories with respect to England (unlike Wales) and because their status as minority cultures, which has more or less continued in psychic and/or political ways, has had a similar impact not only on the dissemination of their respective literatures but on the nature and means of the writing. Of course, there are significant differences, and my discussion of individual writers should serve to illuminate these as well as their commonalities. Both countries have experienced cultural isolation from Britain while being politically tied to it; both are perceived as "other" cultures, despite Britain's claim to them, past or present, as homogeneous parts of the nation. A distinction should be made here between Northern Ireland and the Republic, although there are varying responses to any kind of designated separation. There is the obvious political distinction as regards possession and national boundaries, in contradistinction to which persists a dominant historical and political vision of Ireland as the united "32 counties," a vision that has demonstrable manifestations within both countries (e.g., the Arts Council of the Republic funds citizens from the "32 counties"). Perhaps more in the North than in the Republic, partition has had a divisive effect, to some degree, on all aspects of the culture. Nevertheless, most writers in the North consider themselves Irish writers, even if some of them at the same time see themselves as part of a British culture.

A history of cultural isolation produces a dynamic of inside/outside which must be taken into consideration in any discussion of canonicity in relation to the literatures of such cultures. Our view must be two-dimensional. When we speak about "the canon," we mean a fixed pantheon to which all literature in English aspires. We perhaps do not realize that those countries falling outside the domain of canonical authority (in short, England and the United States) establish their own canons, vehicles for placement and publicity within. Such canons take on the formal features of canonicity, while only in part complying, through inclusion (or by excluding indigenous literature), with the "authoritative" canon from without. In effect, two canons coexist: one that is for the most part contained by geographical and cultural boundaries; and one that is presented as universal, its "universality" responsible by omission for the creation of the "inside" canon. Through the nationalist imperative in both Scotland and Ireland, efforts have been made to influence the "mainstream" canon, if not outside the countries, then within, in school and university curricula, for example; however, to the degree that these cultures see themselves bound in social and intellectual relations with the mainstream establishments, they are forced to adhere to what in canonicity becomes a universal language, a charged issue in countries where domination has meant the near extinction of native languages (Irish, Scots, and Gaelic).

The complexities produced by this dynamic of inside/outside are dizzying. There are, as a result, serious repercussions for almost every

aspect of cultural life. Overwhelmingly, most publication and performance of indigenous work occurs locally, stigmatized by the sense that
local recognition is contained and therefore less significant. Those who
are picked up by outside (mainly English) publishers or who regularly
perform or work outside the country are often tokenized, culturally
neutralized, and, at the same time, for these reasons, and through what
appears to be a feeling of abandonment or betrayal, devalued by the native
literary establishment. School and university curricula have historically
omitted the work of native writers, except for those who have mainstream
canonical status. And where changes have been and are being made,
problems of legitimacy still exist. At the University of Edinburgh, for
example, where the study of Scottish literature has until recently been
reserved for the Scottish studies department, those few courses that are
taught within the Department of English Literature are attended almost
entirely by Scottish students, producing a kind of "ghettoization" of
Scottish literature even in a Scottish context. Furthermore, since much
of the literature is not taught, the academy has very little impact on the
making of the "inside" canon, unlike in the United States and England
where the canon-makers are, for the most part, literary critics working
inside the educational system. In Ireland there is a fierce division between
the academy and the writing establishment, the latter perceiving the
former as the protector of a tradition that is exclusive and imposed from
without.[6] Reviews of new writing in many journals and in almost all
newspapers are done by writers. The writing establishment, then, has
primary control over the generation of the "inside" canon, in dynamic
relation, as they see it, with the reading public. One can see, on the one
hand, the historical and cultural force behind this process, the desire to be
self-determining and a suspicion of a critical heritage that employs an
exclusive, "universal" language; on the other hand, it seems that the
absence of a productive working relationship between a critical community and the writing establishment contributes, as do all of the manifestations of the inside/outside dynamic, to a kind of cultural divisiveness, at
the same time that the nationalist imperative seeks to empower.

It is less my intention to bemoan the fate of Scottish and Irish writing
and its absence from the canon—or, indeed, to argue for its inclusion in
the canon that is extant—than to demonstrate that the problems these
literary establishments face illuminate the debate between feminists and
cultural critics in their approach to canonicity. When a culture has been
marginalized, its impulses toward national legitimization tend to dominate in all spheres and forms of cultural realization. What women writers

in Scotland and Ireland are now addressing within their struggle to emerge is the relationship between their national and sexual identities, and in doing so they are redressing the terms by which the mainstream in their own countries establishes itself—the very terms of literary production. Ironically, while feminism and the recognition of women's writing in Scotland and Ireland have progressed at a much slower rate than within the dominant cultures—England and America have different nationalistic aims—the advances in establishing at least a literary if not a theoretical dialogue between culture and gender are, perforce, greater. And, interestingly, the reasons for both the retardation of the former and the success of the latter are substantially the same.

Women have been traditionally excluded by the mainstream literary establishments in Scotland and Ireland in historical consonance with the exclusion of women's writing elsewhere; and these establishments have further, with a righteous sense of justification fueled by the political imperative of nationalism, neutralized the claim of women to a place in the tradition. Women have found themselves in a peculiar predicament, compelled to resist or challenge the demands of the nationalist imperative in order to clarify the terms of their own oppression, and consequently disregarded on the basis that their concerns do not embrace the *more* significant issues of national self-determination. This means that the nationalist struggle has been defined in patriarchal terms and has effectively excluded many women not only from a tradition of writing but from any identification with nationalist aims, while for men the two have often been essentially linked.

The need to define nationalism in patriarchal terms in countries that have struggled against a colonizing "father" is perhaps a response to the historical figuration of cultural "inferiority" in stereotypes of the feminine; where the disempowerment of a culture becomes an emasculation, subjugation is gender-inflected.[7] In "Poésie des Races Celtiques" (1860), Ernest Renan described the Celtic "race" as "emotional and melancholic" and "essentially feminine," a necessary complement to the barbaric, "masculine" Teutons. While the "feminine character" of the Celts was often presented in a positive light, as having this capacity to civilize or sensitize, its subtext of servility and instability gave place to a justification for hegemony, as in Matthew Arnold's *On the Study of Celtic Literature* (1866).[8] This image took hold and formed the basis for much evaluative analysis of the culture—its literature, its language, its ability to govern. Gregory Smith's *Scottish Literature: Character and Influence* (1919), for example, proposed national habits of expression that were evident in Scottish literature over the centuries—a combination of attention to domestic detail and wild emotional flights of fancy.[9] In *Writing Ireland: Colonialism, Nationalism, and Culture* (1988), David Cairns and Shaun Richards examine this issue in a chapter entitled "An Essentially Feminine Race":

> In Ireland, the implications of linking femininity as a racial trait with subservience were sufficiently recognized for nationalist writers to respond by emphasizing the manly and masculine aspects of the Irish character and by locating the metropolis as the source of the "effeminate follies" and "masher habits" that were creeping into Irish life (Croke, 1884). In some writers, however, awareness of the negative connotations of femininity was so well developed that they employed it themselves to castigate the political and organizational ineffectualness of their audiences. As the journalist D. P. Moran wrote in 1899: "On all sides one sees only too much evidence that the people are secretly content to be a conquered race, though they have not the honesty to admit it. . . . There is nothing masculine in the character, and when the men do fall into line with green banners and shout themselves hoarse, is it not rather a feminine screech, a delirious burst of defiance on a background of sluggishness and despair?" (Moran, 1905, p. 6)[10]

This historical motive for the nationalist movement's dissociation of itself from the "feminine" may explain not only the alienation of women from nationalist rhetoric and activity but their exclusion from a literature that often takes as its subject the national. It is ironic, particularly in this context, that the subject of the national, except in its most sentimentalized or sensational form, has contributed to the exclusion of this literature from the mainstream canon.

In acts of reclamation, feminists in Scotland and in both Northern Ireland and the Republic have set out to reinterpret nationalism and to establish a role for themselves as feminists within it; but they are by no means univocal on this issue. Scottish women, who are not faced with the immediacy of "the Troubles," have until recently been hardly vocal, as attested by Liz Lochhead, one of Scotland's leading woman writers, in an interview she gave in 1987: "So far, I've not explored [*sic*] Scottishness, because until now I've felt that my country was woman. I feel that my country might be Scotland as well. . . . I do; it is mine, and it's part of my problem" (Nicholson 3–4). Margaret Ward, author of *Unmanageable Revolutionaries: Women and Irish Nationalism* (1983), puts it this way:

> Feminists were not a united group with an agreed manifesto, but what we had in common was a determination to have women's needs listened to. In the absence of any defined role for women within political groups, or indeed any political programme for women at all, theory and practice had to be developed from first principles, out of our own perceptions of the situation. And so some argued for parity of rights with women in Britain; some attempted to influence republicanism, to make a rigidly masculine tradition more receptive to women's needs; others argued for the integration of revolutionary socialism with feminism; while still others concentrated their energies upon single-issue campaigns. (61)[11]

Pat Murphy, a filmmaker who lives and works in Dublin, makes this reclamation and reinterpretation the subjects of her film *Maeve,* set in modern war-torn Ulster. The film pieces together the life of the titular character, an invocation of the mythological woman warrior (Medbh), and thereby sets out to demonstrate that there is more than one struggle for freedom going on in Ireland.[12] Maeve's modern-day incarnation seeks to rewrite history by refusing to be appropriated by the struggle, to be subservient to the cause; she struggles to imagine a legitimate place for herself as a woman in a nationalist movement. To prevent what easily happens with films about "the Troubles" in the North, Murphy ensures that the viewer does not get sidetracked from the subject of her film by including several somewhat allegorical exchanges between Maeve and her former boyfriend, Liam, a committed republican who views Maeve's withdrawal from Belfast to London as a betrayal of the cause. The following is an excerpt from their final exchange:

MAEVE. When women put themselves behind male politics, the result has not been a recognition of our rights, but a moderation of our aims. When you're denied power, or when it's continually co-opted, the only form of protest is through your body. Our struggle is for autonomy, for the control of our bodies.

LIAM. You can't claim that as a form of protest. What about the blanket men? Their only form of protest is through their bodies.

MAEVE. Well, instead of claiming it back, couldn't you see a similarity?

LIAM. (*really amused*) No, I couldn't. It amazes me that you would even think of that. Those are men ready to give their lives for their country. (*pause*) I understand what you're saying but what you're proposing sounds like some kind of women's nationalism. You behave as if you're part of a different culture; a nation within a nation.

MAEVE. Maybe that's a way for you to understand what I'm talking about. Nationalism is a reaction to attack, to imperialism. We *are* like a nation within a nation. Men's relationship to women is like England's relationship to Ireland. You are in possession of us. You occupy us like an army.

LIAM. What you're doing is reactionary. You're splintering us. Bringing us down. You become one more faction for us to contend with. Women are like anarchists. When it comes down to it you don't want to win. You maintain yourselves in your defeat so you can continue to feel world weary and superior. You don't want to win, but by defining your struggle as separate you weaken us.

MAEVE. Win what? What is there to win? Tell me that! When this war's over how will it be different for me? Will I be free? Will I be able to live the way I want? Can I have children if and when I want, an abortion if I need one?

LIAM. Your revolution is obviously not mine.

MAEVE. And your national liberation won't work while you exclude half of us. I belong to a class that's oppressed whatever happens.

LIAM. See you! "I want! I need!" You don't represent the women here. In fact you don't represent anyone here. You rejected it long ago. Remember? You left. Well you can leave again. You don't have to deal with this shit if you don't want to.

MAEVE. Being a woman is a nationality I carry around with me. If you are closer to the women here it's because they're fighting for freedom like you. They are demanding that the aims of the revolution include them. And if when this war is over, they are still oppressed, they will identify you as the next stage in their struggle.

LIAM. It's a great pity you don't find something more useful to do with your anger.

In an interview about the film, Murphy explained that "whatever way you look at it, the language of republicanism is patriarchal," but one could easily substitute "nationalism" for "republicanism" (in *Iris,* June 1984, 30).[13] Murphy believes and hopes her films demonstrate "that it is crucial that feminism and republicanism confront each other in a useful way." In its struggle to achieve cultural autonomy, the movement's adoption of a patriarchal discourse will only reinscribe the historical privileging of one culture over another.

The predicament of women's writing in Scotland and Ireland provides an analogy, then, with the fate of Scottish and Irish literature on the whole, which has been trapped by its cultural identity, excluded from the canon from without because of it, or included at the expense of or through a distortion of it. Eavan Boland, a poet from the Republic of Ireland, has written about this predicament:

> Early on as a poet, certainly in my twenties, I realized that the Irish nation, as an existing construct in Irish poetry, was not available to me. It was not a comfortable realization. There was nothing clear-cut about my feelings. From the first they were composed of tribal ambivalences and doubts. Nevertheless, even then, I had a fairly clear perception of the conflict which awaited me: as a poet I could not easily do without the idea of a nation. Poetry in every country draws on that reserve. On the other hand, as a woman I could not accept the nation formulated for me by Irish poetry and its traditions. Therefore, it looked as if I must remain outside that poetry and that tradition, cut off from its energy, at a distance from its archive, unless in some sense, and by some means I could repossess it. ("National Tradition," 148–49)

When Boland refers to "the Ireland formulated for me by Irish poetry and its traditions," she refers, in part, to the convention of female personification of Ireland in Irish writing, to "the fusion of the national and the feminine, and the interpretation of one by the other" (152). "Romantic Ireland" is imaged through such idealized female figures as Cathleen Ni Houlihan, figures tinged with darkness and drawn with distortions (Dark Rosaleen, Deirdre, Maeve), the tragedy of Irish experience somehow best represented through female travail. It seems that a tradition historically characterized as feminine has at once adopted and withdrawn from that image through its objectification of the woman. For while Ireland has traditionally been figured as female, the modern image is toughened: she is the sacrificial mother whose sons must die for the motherland, a brutalized version of the Christian martyr, the "degraded pastoral," as Boland calls it. This image has been inherited and variously exploited by the early Yeats, and such writers as Padraig Pearse, Patrick Kavanagh, Richard Murphy, and John Montague. As Boland remarks in her reading of Kavanagh's "Pygmalion": "the woman in this poem is one-dimensional because, under the texture and surprise of the language, she is fused with the idea of Ireland. . . . she ceases to be a vital poetic image and becomes a passive cipher" (153–54). Recall Joyce's manipulation of this tradition, which underscores the degradation of these figures—the "exposed" harp in "Two Gallants"—or the emblem of self-destruction that they offer—the old sow who eats her young. Boland sees such emblems or muses as simplifications of womanhood, "reflexive feminizations of the national experience; those static, passive, ornamental figures do no credit to a poetic tradition which has been, in other ways, radical and innovative, capable of both latitude and compassion" (156).

Boland laments that the Irish poetic tradition is devoid of women writers, another source for her sense of alienation (152). This happens, she says, "because national traditions have the power to edit out human complexities which do not suit its programme." (As Barbara Johnson points out in her study of Zora Neale Hurston, "Unification and simplification are fantasies of domination, not understanding" [170].) Boland goes on to say that her consciousness of her invisibility as a woman provided her with a way into an identification with her culture that had not been realized or tapped; in other words, there was an analogy between the invisibility of culture and of gender—they were "metaphors for one another."

> A society, a nation, a literary tradition is always in danger of making up its communicable heritage from its visible elements. Women, as it happens, are not especially visible in Ireland. They are very indistinct indeed in its literary canon. Years ago I came to realize when I published a poem that what was seen of me, what drew approval, if it was forthcoming at all, was the poet. The woman, by and large, was invisible. It was a unsettling discovery. Yet I came to believe that my invisibility as a woman was a disguised grace. It had the power to draw me, I sensed, towards a greater invisibility; towards the suffering which lay below the surface of Irish history and out of reach of its tribalism.
>
> Marginality within a tradition, however painful, confers certain advantages. It allows the writer clear eyes and a quick critical sense. That critical perspective, in turn, may allow him to re-locate himself within a tradition which alienated him in the first place. I wanted to re-locate myself within the Irish poetic tradition. I felt the need to do so. A woman poet is rarely regarded as an automatic part of a national poetic tradition. There has been a growing tendency, in the past few years, for academics and critics to discuss women's poetry as a sub-culture within a larger tradition, thereby depriving both of possible enrichment. I felt it vital that

women poets such as myself should establish a discourse with the idea of a nation, should bring to it a sense of the emblematic relationship between the feminine experience and a national past.

The truths of womanhood and the defeats of a nation. An improbable intersection? At first sight perhaps. Yet the more I thought of it, the more it seemed to me that if I could find the poetic truth of the first then, by virtue of that alone, I would re-possess the second. If so, then Irishness and womanhood, those tormenting fragments of my youth, would at last become metaphors for one another. (156–57)

Eavan Boland, roughly a contemporary of Seamus Heaney, is one of Ireland's best-known poets, yet *The Journey and Other Poems* was only the first of five books to have been made readily available in the United States and to have received a major review.[14] Some might attribute this to her insistence on publishing with an Irish women's press, Arlen House, which, before it folded in 1988, established double publishing rights with Carcanet Press, a maverick among English publishing houses. This insistence is a testimony to Boland's commitment to the twin concerns for women's writing in Ireland and Irish writing that she outlines above and elsewhere. Amid difficulty and some controversy generated within the male-dominated and the feminist writing establishments (dismissed by one for her commitment, perceived by factions in the other as a moderate),[15] she has become an important and outspoken voice for women's writing. While she, along with others, like Evelyn Conlon, a prose writer, Ailbhe Smyth, a lecturer in French at University College Dublin, and Pat Murphy, has forged the way for the development of a discourse between Irish nationalism and feminism, many in the male establishment continue to bicker over the degree to which poets from the North in particular, such as Paul Muldoon, Tom Paulin, and even Seamus Heaney, have achieved fame outside Ireland through their subjectification of the national. To put it another way, Boland's efforts have opened the door, not to an established canon (although those doors have begun to open), but to a dialogue from without and from within about the nature of canonicity; those who are committed to the "inside" canon are generally wedded to traditional ideas of canonicity and, despite their resentments, are preoccupied with acceptance from without in traditionally canonical terms—a rigidifying and often self-defeating approach.

In such essays as "The Woman Poet in a National Tradition," Boland charts the progress of her poetry from what she describes as "forms explored and sealed by English men hundreds of years before" (151), through an Irish poetic tradition, and finally to a "subversion of preexisting structures" (quoted in Reizbaum, 2). I include here, in its entirety, one of her more recent poems that speaks to and realizes this development in her work.[16]

The Achill Woman

She came up the hill carrying water.
She wore a half-buttoned, wool cardigan,
a tea-towel round her waist.

She pushed the hair out of her eyes with
her free hand and put the bucket down.

The zinc-music of the handle on the rim
tuned the evening. An Easter moon rose.
In the next-door field a stream was
a fluid sunset; and then, stars.

I remember the cold rosiness of her hands.
She bent down and blew on them like broth.
And round her waist, on a white background,
in coarse, woven letters, the words "glass cloth."

She was nearly finished for the day.
And I was all talk, raw from college—
week-ending at a friend's cottage
with one suitcase and the set text
of the Court poets of the Silver Age.

We stayed putting down time until
the evening turned cold without warning.
She said goodnight and started down the hill.

The grass changed from lavender to black.
The trees turned back to cold outlines.
You could taste frost

but nothing now can change the way I went
indoors, chilled by the wind
and made a fire
and took down my book
and opened it
and failed to comprehend

the harmonies of servitude,
the grace music gives to flattery
and language borrows from ambition—

and how I fell asleep
oblivious to

the planets clouding over in the skies,
the slow decline of the Spring moon,
the songs crying out their ironies.

We see in this poem the speaker's relationship to an image that combines past and present, country and gender, myth and palpable presence, forms that are at once as breakable and durable as the words on the woman's apron indicate—"glass cloth." Achill is a large island off the west coast of the Irish Republic in County Mayo, a barren and beautiful area whose resort industry belies the history of difficulty in subsistence for its inhabitants. It is the kind of place that has lent itself to the metaphorical romanticization of Ireland, supplying the woman of archetypal proportion. The poem is like a catalog of the materials romantic images are made of—the Easter moon, the fluid sunset, the cottage in which the speaker studies the Court poets of the Silver Age—but they are tourists, like the speaker, to a setting that provides the poet with a re-vision of her relationship to country, gender, and poetry. They are resonant but reconstituted in the "harmonies of servitude" and "songs crying out their ironies." What is oddly harmonious here is the woman as subject, the woman as poet, and a tradition from which these have been excluded. It is ironic that the speaker is oblivious to the way in which the landscape realizes the poetic conventions she studies in a book. Boland avoids the co-optation of her subjects by tradition through her variation of the poetic line and language. A more conventional meter frames the appearance of the Achill woman, while the language that is used to describe her is prosaic; the line breaks and becomes irregular, and the language bursts into metaphor as soon as the Achill woman disappears and the speaker is alone with her task—the study of a poetry that imposed upon itself a classical metrical tradition unsuited to its own language. By disturbing the poetic conventions, the poet forges a relationship among elements whose traditional disparateness she at once wishes to reveal. The Achill woman (as poem and as palpable presence) is not a distanced emblem but stands in direct relation to Boland; the subject(s) and the poet are irreducible parts of a poetic line that may be broken, in both a canonical and formal sense of such poetic inheritance, commanding an audience that will not be oblivious to the movement between resurrection and insurrection.

This is not the only poem in Boland's work that speaks to the interaction among gender, nation, and poetry, and it by no means demonstrates her range of treatment. "The Journey," which Anthony Libby calls "a poem for the ages" (*New York Times Book Review,* March 22, 1987), takes up the issue of literary authority and classical convention—indeed, the very idea of a poetry of the ages—when it dedicates itself to an antibiotic in a refashioned Homeric descent into a women's underworld, guided by Sappho:

> And then the dark fell and "there has never"
> I said "been a poem to an antibiotic:
> never a word to compare with the odes on
> the flower of the raw sloe for fever
>
> "or the devious Africa-seeking tern
> or the protein treasures of the sea-bed.
> Depend on it, somewhere a poet is wasting
> his sweet uncluttered metres on the obvious
>
> "emblem instead of the real thing. . . .
>   (*The Journey and Other Poems,* 39)

Sappho here becomes more than a "scholiast's nightingale," as the poet refers to her; she is a woman's guide to the suffering of women, here expressed through the loss of children whom disease overtook before the discovery of the antibiotic. In "The Journey," such suffering and such language are given "epic" proportions in contrast to the poetic tradition: "Instead of sulpha we shall have hyssop dipped / in the wild blood of the unblemished lamb, / so every day the language gets less / 'for the task and we are less with the language.' " The "real thing" in Boland's work does not represent a hierarchical departure from the subjects of an inherited tradition but a valorization of that which by exclusion has been decreed poetically undignified.

Liz Lochhead, a Scottish poet and playwright, also has contributed greatly to the creation of a discourse between culture and gender, a contribution that has been significant, I believe, to the revitalization of theater and writing in Scotland. As I already suggested, the discourses have developed at different paces in these countries because of the difference in apparency and immediacy of the national conflict. While in Ireland, "the Troubles" in the North enact on a regular basis the history of strife and make the potential for obscuration of other issues that much greater, the absence of physical struggle in Scotland produces a subtler nationalist imperative, a primarily psychic and internalized sense of struggle and marginalization that has obscured the connection between nationalism and feminism. As we have seen, discussions among women about loyalties within the exchange of feminist and nationalist ideologies are regular and visible occurrences in the North and in the Republic of Ireland; in Scotland these are not as visible, not heated by the same fire. Lochhead, however, has made the connection. She has identified her society as "repressed, violent and colonized" and also her need to become "more assertively feminist" in response to the manifestations of these elements (quoted in *Twelve More Modern Scottish Poets* 140). One such manifestation is, in her words, "the exclusion from either BBC or STV (Scottish Television) of plays which are about any other element of Scottishness than sentimentalized, violent, self-perpetuating Glasgow and West of Scotland male machismo" ("Staging a Revival" 30). What she sees in the reductive presentation of her culture by the British and even the Scottish media is the historical interaction between the marginalization of culture and sexism.

Of Lochhead's recent work, the piece that best illustrates this interaction is *Mary Queen of Scots Got Her Head Chopped Off,* a play that brings the issue of religion into dialogue. The Reformation in Scotland coincided with the reign of Mary, a Catholic, and ostensibly the last sovereign of an independent Scotland. As in Ireland, national identity was linked with religious affiliation and union with England meant the adoption of Protestantism as a national faith (although it should be noted here that Scottish Presbyterianism dissented from English Anglicanism). The play revives and reinterprets what has been submerged, making Mary a symbol of marginality in the interlocking terms of gender, culture, and religion. The dramatic focus of the play is the historical relationship between Mary and her cousin, Elizabeth I, by whose decree Mary was beheaded for treason in 1587. Although the two women never met, Lochhead positions them in relation to one another as women whose gender becomes a factor in their acquisition and manipulation of power.

Lochhead's point that women and political power have been traditionally viewed as incompatible is not new. Mary and Elizabeth are presented as personally and historically trapped: the former is remembered for her sexual exploits and her infamous death—her quatercentenary marked the anniversary of her beheading—the latter as a powerful ruler, albeit a sexual curiosity. What is new here is Lochhead's dramatic proposition that these figures are united, not by political defeat and conquest and not by gender alone, but by a re-vision of the interplay among their roles as women, heads of state, and defenders of the faith. Lochhead invokes the historical linkage of cultural marginalization, gender, and religion, but she disrupts the essentialist fiction by suggesting it is loss of autonomy that joins them. The respective fates of these queens and their kingdoms have been attributed to "woman's frailty" or the resistance to that; the play tells us that Mary's insistence on the expression of her gender and Elizabeth's denial have been coterminous with Scotland's cultural imperative and England's cultural hegemony. Both women refused to give men the power of their kingdoms—Elizabeth did not marry and Mary would not give her husband the "crown matrimonial," the conveyance of power of the kingdom during her lifetime and after. Yet in Lochhead's reading of these historical facts both women are inescapably subject(s) to (of) the patriarchy: any expression of Mary's sexuality was exploited and even her son did not secure her position, while Elizabeth's guise of virginity enabled her to maintain and wield power. Furthermore, it is not Mary's insistence on Catholicism (she was purportedly tolerant of the Reformation) but Knox's insistence on Protestantism—any prescription of religion—that is aligned with sexual denial and cultural hegemony.

Lochhead's dramaturgy here and elsewhere achieves the effect of defamiliarization. This play is highly stylized, using a mélange of musical and dramatic forms, including a kind of chorus in the form of an "ambiguous" personification of a crow (identified as the Scottish national bird), a fiddler who plays the music of many cultures, both traditional and modern, an Elizabeth who appears in a petticoated prom dress and dark sunglasses—all refashioned or re-dressed stock symbols. The title of the play comes from a children's rhyme and a game popular in the west of Scotland, enacted at the conclusion of the play, in which the characters appear as twentieth-century children with the same names as their historical counterparts—they call up history through a pantomime of the same roles. The play is self-conscious about history as dramatic fiction and responds by presenting what Lochhead calls "new clichés," an examination and reconstitution of commonplaces about women and culture and the forms these take.

Lochhead's poetry, collected in a volume entitled *Dreaming Frankenstein and Collected Poems,* for the most part has eschewed the subject of nationalism in favor of "my country of gender." Increasingly, as her interest in the relationship between these two "countries" has grown, Lochhead has used Scots in her work, a hybrid of Old English and

Anglo-Danish, identified against Gaelic as the language of lowland Scotland and at one time the official language of all Scotland. It is historically accurate as well as politically compelling that Mary and her court speak in Scots in Lochhead's play. Other writers in Scotland have used and are more and more using Scots, despite the example of writers like Hugh MacDiarmid whose use of Scots has made his work seem inaccessible to or unworthy of an English-speaking audience. But when writers like Lochhead or Agnes West or Jessie Kesson employ Scots, they help to prevent, at least in this respect, a language of nationalism from becoming the domain of the male "inside" establishment.

In Scotland and Ireland there are still very few recognized women writers, although it is recognized that many women are writing. And although writers like Lochhead and Boland have prominence at home and are gaining it abroad, they too continue to be marginalized by the inside literary establishments. In 1988, for example, Trinity College, Dublin offered a course on contemporary Irish poetry that did not include Boland or any other woman writer. And a radio program on contemporary Scottish poetry highlighted five poets, none of whom are women; when I asked why this was so, I was offered the argument of tokenism as a reply, an insidious rationale that ensures tokenization through exclusion. In the north of Ireland, a writer like Medbh McGuckian has suffered from the kind of tokenism that conspicuously includes and promotes the exclusion of others. In the cases of Boland and Lochhead, at least, the examination of the issue of women's writing in their cultures has forged the way for a reconsideration of the relationship between culture and gender and is beginning to make a dent in what I term the "double exclusion" of Scottish and Irish women's writing. They are to some extent bypassing the restraints of their own establishments while working within them. Even though their autonomy and recognition may come from an outside that continues to be invested in canonicity, the dialogue they establish between themselves and the outside—that is, between consideration of the question engendered by a collection like this and their own contribution— works not only to enrich the dialogue but redounds to the recognition and perhaps even the production of the literatures of which they are a part. Boland has said that she believed she would go forward because of the historical force behind her work. By this I think she meant not only the force produced by the feminist movement and not only the consider- able force exerted by critics of culture in this century to overturn the hegemonic legacy but a *concert* of these forces.

Notes

1. A work like Kumari Jayawardena's *Feminism and Nationalism in the Third World* points to the significance of the history of Irish colonization as a model for nationalist movements in many third-world countries, without acknowledging that Ireland may have produced a comparable feminist response, even if differently (historically) conceived. In part, this may be because Jayawardena wishes to critique the role of Western feminism in the development of a feminism outside the West that is unsuited to the cultural needs of the women in these countries. (She brings the class dimension into her discussion of the mirroring effect produced by the local bourgeoisie's desire to resist through conformity the imperialist power, and the way in which this kind of co-optation extended to women who were to become "civilized housewives." (David Lloyd identifies a similar "effect" in Irish nationalism.) Within the Western feminist establishment such a critique has come primarily from African-Americanists (and, again, from critics like Spivak) who, like Barbara Smith in "Toward a Black Feminist Criticism," speak to what has historically been the invisibility of gender in a consideration of African-American literature. In the effort to establish feminisms and to recognize that there are power differentials that obtain among women of different classes, races, and sexual preferences, women from what Benedict Anderson calls "white" colonies (89) should not be assigned an oppositional role. For example, I will show that women from these Celtic countries would have been included in the general indictment of their culture as racially inferior, an inferiority couched in "feminine" terms.

2. In "Canonical and Non-canonical: A Critique of the Current Debate," John Guillory suggests that it is urgent "to theorize in a new way the question of the canon" (484). One reason for this is that the "pragmatic struggle" between canonical and noncanonical "moves to an impasse that takes the form of an unreflective annexation of non-canonical works to a hegemonic tradition—a phenomenon of cooptation" (483). In his conclusions Guillory offers the following: "The fact that social groups defined by gender, race, ethnicity, or national status are permitted to represent themselves within a hegemonic sociolect is a complication of the system of social reproduction that cannot be resolved simply by equalizing the status of canonical authors, without reference to the conditions of literary production" (519–20). And Liam O'Dowd, who has written on the relationship of culture and ideology in Ireland, speaks to the issue of broadening the spectrum of contexts in the discussion of national identity. While he faults what he calls cultural intellectuals for "neglecting the material dimension," he himself neglects to mention gender as a legitimate concern of cultural and national identity (8).

3. While many reasons are adduced, both economic and political, for the rise of nationalism in Scotland and Ireland, it is generally agreed that the consistent threat to the loss of nationhood is at the base of the modern nationalist movements in both countries, movements that in their current organized forms are

relatively recent (see, for example, Lloyd and also D. N. MacIver). In his effort to detach nationalism from racism and, perhaps as Kearney does, to identify different kinds of nationalisms, Benedict Anderson seems to succumb momentarily to a romanticized idea of nationalism as yielding "cultural products that show love—poetry, prose fiction, music, plastic arts" (128). Lloyd insists that for Ireland such cultural products may "replicate the very aesthetic history that legitimates the subordination of the Celtic races" (76) by recurring to and creating an unified vision of the people which seeks to capture the "spirit of the nation."

4. In emphasizing the "Anglo," I refer to the distinction that has been drawn between those Irish who come from "English stock," most of them descendants of the Anglo-Irish Ascendancy that began in the eighteenth century, and the indigenous Irish. The Anglo-Irish were Protestant and during the Ascendancy passed a series of penal statutes against Catholics in Ireland. For this reason, as many have pointed out, Irish nationalism has been associated with Catholicism, despite efforts by various groups in the last two centuries to dissociate them and to establish a nonsectarian nationalist movement. It is generally believed that after partition in 1922 the Catholic church worked to fortify the association in order to maintain control. Therefore, the Anglo-Irish tradition of writing, of which Yeats is perhaps the most notable of representatives, emerged as distinct and was legitimated by the English literary establishment (see Lloyd, for example, on Yeats as Irish modernist [23]).

5. All the critics of minor literature mentioned here provide criteria by which Joyce becomes a minor writer, but they seem to account differently, either implicitly or explicitly, for his canonical status. Louis Renza is the most polemical. He wonders whether the fact that Kafka (like Joyce) is canonically honorific points to a privileging on the part of Deleuze and Guattari of minor writers whose work "the major language or canonical critical codes can misrecognize according to their own standards" (34). In other words, the minor in these terms "requires the preexistence of a major literature or language it can deconstruct" (34) and/or an Oedipal structure it can overthrow: these always figure by virtue of the work's oppositional relation to them. Lloyd, on the other hand, faults Renza for not emphasizing "the historical determinants of the institution of criticism, according to which the distinction between the major and minor work is posited" (4). This ahistorical treatment "therefore also blurs the distinction that continually haunts [Renza's] work, that between a radically minor literature and one that is still seeking to 'fill a major function' " (5). So that while a radically minor text might bring into play a consciousness of the mainstream aesthetic, its oppositional relation would not be binary or transcendental. And since, as we know and as Lloyd makes clear, the nationality of writers like Joyce, Burns, or Stevenson alone does not have absolute import for their "exceptional" status, either as canonical or marginal, an understanding of the historical conditions for canonicity is crucial in the effort to explain that status. While I have argued elsewhere in somewhat different terms that Joyce's work is "minor," it will be the subject of another study

to examine the reasons for its susceptibility to appropriation by the "high culture" aesthetic.

6. There is some difference between Northern Ireland and the Republic of Ireland in this respect. Many in the Northern Irish establishment see themselves as entitled by their place in the union and as protectors of their rightful place in a tradition to which they belong. Disagreement about this in the North is often drawn down sectarian lines.

7. See, for example, Sander Gilman's *Difference and Pathology: Stereotypes of Sexuality, Race and Madness* for a discussion of such historical figuration in relation to blacks and Jews, in particular. One might also consider, as does Lloyd, for example, the related context provided by the Oedipal paradigm, where the son's rebellion against the father becomes a necessary response to the "failures" of the forefathers (to establish/reclaim a homeland) and an internalization of the paternalistic role ascribed to a "transcendental principle of paternity" (Lloyd 160). Lloyd argues that "nationalist propaganda mobilizes all the figures of a familial romance" (161). Deleuze and Guattari, as well as Lloyd, identify in various ways the "radical refusal to subscribe to the paternal metaphor" (Lloyd, 189) as a characteristic of the minor.

8. David Cairns and Shaun Richards discuss Renan and Arnold at some length in *Writing Ireland: Colonialism, Nationalism, and Culture:* "Arnold produced a Celt whose foremost characteristic was emotion, where 'the Celtic genius, sentiment as its main basis, with the love of beauty, charm, spirituality for its excellence, [had] ineffectualness and self-will for its deficit.' Throughout 'On the Study of Celtic Literature' this theme allowed the ingress of those judgements which, having established the Celt as '*always ready to react against despotism of fact* (sic),' 'ineffectual in politics,' and 'sensual,' concluded, like Renan, that 'no doubt the sensibility of the Celtic nature, its nervous exaltation, have something feminine in them, and the Celt is peculiarly disposed to feel the spell of the feminine idiosyncrasy; he has an affinity to it; he is not far from its secret.' Hence, in mapping the strategic formation which underpinned Celticism, to the positivism of philology, ethnology and anthropology must be added the positivism of that science of sexuality which produced a femininity for the nineteenth-century bourgeois woman which underwrote her ineffectualness, whether by medicalization and the reduction of woman to the status of a womb, or through the celebration of her disabling femininity, itself arising from the same source" (48–49).

9. Cited in Watson (Introduction, 3). Watson devotes five pages to contemporary Scottish literature, and two lines to Liz Lochhead's work.

10. This idea of the metropolis as a source of "effeminate follies" may allude to Oscar Wilde but nevertheless reminds us that Dublin was the seat of Anglo-Irish power until independence. This characterization represents an inversion of roles. Cairns and Richards's study further suggests a simultaneous process of internalization, through which the Irish took on an image of themselves that was imposed from without, a process characteristic of a marginalized people (42–57).

11. This excerpt is from a "Critical Forum on Feminism in Ireland", which appeared in *The Honest Ulsterman* (Summer 1987), a quarterly published in Belfast. The North and the Republic were represented in separate pieces. Ward is summarizing here the proceedings of a 1986 symposium devoted to Northern feminism. The piece representing the Republic is in the form of a discussion by four women who are active in the feminist movement—Alibhe Smyth, lecturer in French at University College, Dublin and author of *Women's Rights in Ireland* (Dublin: Arlen House, 1983); Pauline Jackson, a social scientist who lectures and writes extensively on issues relating to women and work; Caroline McCramley, at the time chairperson of the governmental Council for the Status of Women and active in the Trade Union Woman's Forum; and Ann Speed, a republican socialist and trades unionist.

12. Murphy often speaks about the difficulty of working in a medium for which there has been little national support and the added difficulty of being one of the few women in such a fledgling industry. *Maeve* was released in 1981, *Anne Devlin* in 1985. Just as *Maeve* reinterprets the myth of its namesake, *Anne Devlin* rewrites or fills in the role that Robert Emmet's maid played in the 1803 uprising. The myth of Anne Devlin as the girl who committed herself to the cause for the idealized love of the hero Emmet is at odds with her own prison journals upon which Murphy bases the portrayal. I am grateful to Pat Murphy for allowing me to quote from the script of *Maeve*.

13. Richard Kearney addresses this film and these issues in relation to it in *Transitions: Narratives in Modern Irish Culture* (183–90).

14. Boland's second volume of poetry, *The War Horse* (1975), was published by Victor Gollancz, Ltd., in London as well as by Arlen House; *Introducing Eavan Boland* (1981), collected from *The War Horse* and *In Her Own Image* (1980), was published by the Ontario Review Press. The review to which I refer is Anthony Libby's in the *New York Times Book Review* (March 22, 1987). A review of Boland's work among the work of other Irish women poets appeared in James McElroy's "Night Feed: An Overview of Ireland's Women Poets," in *American Poetry Review* (Jan./Feb. 1985); her work is also appearing with greater regularity in various American journals and publications—*The New Yorker, Partisan Review, Seneca Review*. Boland has had a somewhat greater visibility in English journals and media. Her most recent collection—*Outside History: Selected Poems* 1980–1990 — was published by Norton & Co. (1990).

15. In "The Woman Poet: Her Dilemma" and in my interview with her, Boland discusses her views on the subject of separatism in the feminist movement. Radical elements in Irish feminism have regarded her practice of "subversion of pre-existing structures" as susceptible of co-optation by the male-dominated literary tradition. At the same time, works like *In Her Own Image* and *Nightfeed* were criticized by that very establishment for their focus on women, motherhood, and domestica, suggesting, as Boland has pointed out, that these subjects are poetically undignified.

16. "The Achill Woman" appeared for the first time in the *Atlantic Monthly* (August 1988). It appears in her most recent collection, *Outside History*. I wish to thank Ms. Boland for her permission to use the poem in this essay.

Works Cited

Anderson, Benedict. *Imagined Communities: Reflections on the Origin and Spread of Nationalism.* London: Verso, 1983.

Arnold, Matthew. *On the Study of Celtic Literature.* New York: Macmillan, 1909.

Boland, Eavan. "The Woman Poet in a National Tradition." *Studies* 6, no. 302 (1987): 148–58.

——. "The Woman Poet: Her Dilemma." *American Poetry Review,* Jan./Feb. 1987, 17–20.

——. "The Journey." *The Journey and Other Poems.* Manchester and Dublin: Carcanet and Arlen House, 1987, 39–42.

——. "The Achill Woman." *Outside History: Selected Poems, 1980–1990.* New York: W. W. Norton, 1990, 35.

——. *The War Horse.* London: Victor Gollancz, 1975.

Cairns, David, and Shaun Richards. *Writing Ireland: Colonialism, Nationalism, and Culture.* Manchester: Manchester University Press, 1988.

Deleuze, Gilles, and Felix Guattari. *Kafka: Toward a Minor Literature.* Trans. Dana Polan. Minneapolis: University of Minnesota Press, 1986.

Foster, John Wilson, ed. "The *Honest Ulsterman* Critical Forum." *The Honest Ulsterman* 83 (1987): 39–70.

Fox, Trisha. "Culture and Struggle: An Interview with Rita Donagh and Pat Murphy." *Iris,* June 1984, 30.

Gilman, Sander. *Difference and Pathology: Stereotypes of Sexuality, Race, and Madness.* Ithaca: Cornell University Press, 1985.

Guillory, John. "Canonical and Non-canonical: A Critique of the Current Debate." *ELH* 54, no. 3 (1987): 483–527.

Jayawardena, Kumari. *Feminism and Nationalism in the Third World.* London: Zed Books, 1989.

Johnson, Barbara. *A World of Difference.* Baltimore: Johns Hopkins University Press, 1987.

Kearney, Richard. *Transitions: Narratives in Modern Irish Culture.* Dublin: Wolfhound Press, 1988.

——. "Creatively Rethinking the Break-up of the Nation State." *Irish Times,* December 28, 1987, 8.

Libby, Anthony. "Fathers and Daughters and Mothers and Poets." *New York Times Book Review,* March 22, 1987, 23.

Lloyd, David. *Nationalism and Minor Literature: James Clarence Mangan and the Emergence of Irish Cultural Nationalism.* Berkeley: University of California Press, 1987.

Lochhead, Liz. *Dreaming Frankenstein and Collected Poems.* Edinburgh: Polygon Books, 1984.
———. "Staging a Revival: Playwrighting in Scotland Today." In *Radical Scotland,* April/May 1988, 30.
———. *Twelve More Modern Scottish Poets.* Ed. Charles King and Iain Crichton Smith. London: Hodder and Stoughton, 1986, 140.
MacIver, D. N. "The Paradox of Nationalism in Scotland." In *National Separatism.* Ed. Colin H. Williams. Vancouver: University of British Columbia Press, 1982.
Murphy, Pat. *Maeve.* Film typescript.
Nicholson, Colin. "An Interview with Liz Lochhead." *Inter Arts* 1, no. 6 (1988): 3–4.
O'Dowd, Liam. "Neglecting the Material Dimension: Irish Intellectuals and the Problem of Identity." *Irish Review* 3 (1988): 8–17.
Reizbaum, Marilyn. "An Interview with Eavan Boland." *Contemporary Literature* 30, no. 4 (Winter 1989): 471–79.
———. "James Joyce's Judaic 'Other': Text and Contexts." Ph.D. diss. University of Wisconsin–Madison, 1985.
———. "A 'Modernism of Marginality': The Link between James Joyce and Djuna Barnes." In *New Alliances in Joyce Studies: "When It's Aped to Foul a Delfian."* Ed. Bonnie Kime Scott. Newark: University of Delaware Press, 1988, 179–89.
Renan, Ernest. "La Poésie des Races Celtiques." In *Essais de Morale et de Critique.* Paris: Calmann-Lévy, 1859, 374–456.
Renza, Louis A. *A White Heron and the Question of Minor Literature.* Madison: University of Wisconsin Press, 1984.
Smith, Barbara. "Toward a Black Feminist Criticism." In *Feminist Criticism: Essays on Women, Literature, and Theory.* Ed. Elaine Showalter. New York: Pantheon Books, 1985, 168–85.
Smith, G. Gregory. *Scottish Literature, Character, Influence.* London: Macmillan, 1919.
Spivak, Gayatri Chakravorty. *In Other Worlds: Essays in Cultural Politics.* New York: Methuen, 1987.
Ward, Margaret. *Unmanageable Revolutionaries: Women and Irish Nationalism.* Dublin: Brandon Books, 1983.
Watson, Roderick. *The Literature of Scotland.* New York: Schocken Books, 1985.

LOUISE YELIN

Decolonizing the Novel
Nadine Gordimer's A Sport of Nature
and British Literary Traditions

A Sport of Nature, Nadine Gordimer's 1987 novel, begins with its protagonist shedding one name and taking another. Traveling by train from Salisbury, where she goes to school, to Johannesburg, where she spends her vacations, the girl "threw Kim up to the rack with her school panama and took on Hillela" (3). Much later in the novel, Hillela, now married to the president of an unnamed West African country, is given the name Chiemeka by her husband. If, in the opening scene, Gordimer asks us to consider whether a name can be shed like a hat, or whether in shedding name or hat a character can undergo a change of identity, the renaming of Hillela as Chiemeka asks us to consider whether in marrying an African Hillela becomes an African. In the protagonist's transmutation from Kim to Hillela to Chiemeka, Gordimer raises the related questions[1] of whether or how Jewish, English-speaking whites in South Africa can become Africans and whether or how English-speaking white writers in South Africa can become African writers. At the same time, since the protagonist reclaims the name Hillela—she is originally named for her immigrant great-grandfather Hillel, namesake of the leader of the Sanhedrin, who is known for his activism and liberal interpretation of Jewish law[2]—by discarding the name of Rudyard Kipling's picaresque hero, Gordimer invites us to consider the relationship of white, English-speaking South African writers to the canonical texts and traditions of British literature and, specifically, to consider her own relationship to the literary traditions— English, European, modern, colonial—in which she had her genesis ("A Writer in South Africa" 24–25).

In this essay I approach these questions by examining the ways that *A Sport of Nature* confronts some of the canonical traditions of British and European fiction. First, I look at the way that the novel represents its protagonist from the outside, as a vantage point, rather than as the subjectivity or consciousness that comprises the dominant mode of representing female protagonists in English novels. Next, I discuss *A Sport of Nature* as a rewriting of *Kim* which dismantles the colonialist ideology that structures Kipling's novel. Finally, I examine the novel as a generic hybrid that grafts the picaresque narrative of Hillela onto the more conventional story of her cousin Sasha. As a revision of narrative, ideological, and generic norms and strategies, I suggest, *A Sport of Nature* at once exposes and subverts the patriarchal and colonialist assumptions that underlie the canon of British literature and raises the question of whether it is, like its main character, a spontaneous mutation (sport of nature) or a harbinger of a new literary-political order.

The dominant version of the British woman's novel is the novel of consciousness or sensibility. Whether in Elizabeth Bennet's recognition that she has been "blind, partial, prejudiced, absurd," Esther Summerson's ruminations on Mrs. Jellyby's stays and Mrs. Woodcourt's snobbery, or Lily Briscoe's reflections on Mrs. Ramsay's chivalry and Mr. Ramsay's boots, British novels generally give us the perspectives, points of view, thoughts, and feelings—interior lives—of their female protagonists. On the one hand, the identification of women and subjectivity inscribes women's powerlessness in the bourgeois society the novel describes. As Myra Jehlen points out, "an impotent feminine sensibility is a basic structure of the novel, representing one of the important ways that the novel embodies the basic structures of this society" (600). On the other hand, the identification of women and subjectivity "balances" women's consciousness and men's power, inviting us to believe, for example, that Elizabeth can hold her own against the power with which class and gender endow Mr. Darcy.

Colonial and postcolonial women's writing extends Jehlen's analysis of the gendering of genre, for it destabilizes the identification of women and consciousness that, Jehlen argues, is central to the novel of sensibility and to the bourgeois-patriarchal ideology the novel of sensibility exemplifies, reproduces, and reinforces. In addition, colonial and postcolonial women's writing makes us see the female consciousness that occupies the foreground of English or European novels as the consciousness of white, middle-class females and as a product of a specific colonial (racial) and patriarchal (sexual) ensemble in which the consciousness of white women and the power of white men are dependent on the exploitation of women and men of color.[3] For example, Jean Rhys's *Wide Sargasso Sea* enacts its critique of "female subjectivity" by displacing Jane Eyre, the quintessential heroine-as-subject, and putting in the foreground what *Jane Eyre* relegates to the attic or puts in the background: not only Bertha Mason but the laws that denied married women the right to own property, the exploitation of black slaves, the colonial political economy of the Caribbean.[4] Gordimer's *Burger's Daughter* exposes the colonialist assumptions that structure the novel of consciousness by playing off the first-person narrative of the intensely self-conscious protagonist, Rosa Burger, and the third-person narratives that represent Rosa as subjectivity, treat her as an object of surveillance, or, as Stephen Clingman points out (190), exclude her altogether. In *A Sport of Nature,* as in *Burger's Daughter,* the decentering of (white) female subjectivity is associated with the dismantling of apartheid society: in both novels, Gordimer juxtaposes the personal or "private" life—read: romance—of the protagonist and events in the public history of South Africa.

In *A Sport of Nature* Gordimer also adopts a different narrative strategy for revising the novel of consciousness: she represents Hillela not as subjectivity—consciousness or self-consciousness—but almost exclusively from the outside, as a kind of cinematic vantage point. In the opening scene, for example, Hillela is presented at once from the point of view of an unidentified narrator and as a perspective, like a moving camera eye, on a world she traverses but to which she does not quite belong:

> Somewhere along the journey the girl shed one name and emerged under the other. As she chewed gum and let slide by the conveyor belt of balancing rocks, the wayside halts where black children waved, the grazing buck sloping away to the horizon in a blast of fear set in motion by the passing train, she threw Kim up to the rack with her school panama and took on Hillela. The brown stockings collapsed down her legs, making fine hairs prickle pleasurably. She would dig sandals and a dress out of her suitcase and change without concern for the presence of other women in the compartment. She was going, each time, to her aunt, one of her mother's sisters, in whose home she was given every advantage. She was coming from the Rhodesian girls' school to which, she would say when asked why she didn't go to school in South Africa, she was sent because her father had grown up in Salisbury. (3)

In this opening scene, Gordimer revises both the dominant mode of conceiving female identity in British novels and the dominant mode of representing female character, for she treats identity as a function of name and costume as well as race and gender: Kim is a boy's name at the turn of the nineteenth century when Kipling writes, but by the mid-1950s, when this episode takes place, it is a name for girls, specifically for Christian girls. Here and throughout the novel, we rarely encounter Hillela as interiority. The narrator's observation (or conjecture) that "the brown stockings collapsed down her legs, making fine hairs prickle pleasurably" is about as close to Hillela as we get. We accompany Hillela as she moves from one man to another and from one place to another, but we have no access to the thoughts and feelings that would seem to authenticate her as a novelistic character.

A number of the novel's readers have been troubled by the absence in the portrayal of Hillela of a realized inner life. These readers approach the novel expecting to find a canonical woman's story, one in which the heroine's subjectivity occupies the foreground of her narrative and serves as an index of her (moral) power and as a mode of opposition to the ideological hegemony of patriarchy. In *Villette,* for example, Lucy Snowe's subjectivity literally constitutes the narrative, which is predicated on and in turn suppresses a colonial plot in the shape of the West Indian fortune with which M. Paul endows Lucy's school. Colonial and postcolonial writers like Rhys revise the novels of Brontë and others by focusing on the racial exploitation that makes possible both bourgeois patriarchy and (English) female subjectivity. Gordimer, in contrast, deemphasizes the (white) female consciousness that looms so large in British women's novels by representing Hillela from the outside. This strategy should be seen as part of Gordimer's project of destabilizing the colonial(ist) assumptions reproduced, often uncritically, in the English woman's novel and in the consciousness it canonizes.

> "Are there any more like you in India?" said Father Victor, "or are you by way o' being a *lusus naturae?*" (*Kim*)

If, in the opening scene, Gordimer "throws up to the rack" the British traditions in which she had her literary genesis and especially the women's tradition that presents women as subjectivity, she also opens up a space in which *A Sport of Nature* takes shape—paradoxically, under the sign of *Kim,* the name its protagonist sheds with her hat. Gordimer borrows more from *Kim* than just a name and a label for her main character. She takes also an angle of vision on the protagonist, or a way of representing the protagonist as an angle of vision: in other words, she borrows from Kipling, or through her appropriation of Kipling (re)invents, a picaresque tradition for the "serious" modern novel in English.[5] At the same time,

Gordimer repudiates the colonialist ideology that shapes Kipling's depiction of spying, subverts the narrative authority he assumes, and disrupts his representation of race and gender.[6] In rewriting Kipling's imperial picaresque, Gordimer adapts the anticolonial critique of Aimé Césaire's *Discourse on Colonialism* and Frantz Fanon's *The Wretched of the Earth* and the antipatriarchal narrative and political strategies of British women's novels: that is, she turns her irony on Europeans who, blinded by colonial (racist) misconceptions, misread Africa and Africans and misconstrue their own experiences, and on men who misread Hillela as a free spirit, a femme fatale, or an instance of the eternal feminine.

Gordimer reworks Kipling's treatment of spying as a "great game" and rewrites the plot that conscripts Kim as an agent—at once master and subject—of the secret service. Surveillance is represented in both novels as a set of discursive practices that organize knowledge and power. But while the violence that sustains the imperial order in *Kim* is occluded by the novel's sense of fun,[7] the violence that sustains apartheid and its regime in *A Sport of Nature* is palpable. Like Kim and picaresque protagonists generally, Hillela offers us a perspective, like that of a spy, on the world she travels through: South Africa, especially white, English-speaking, middle-class South Africa, under apartheid; the communities of South African political exiles in Tanzania, Ghana, and England; Eastern Europe; the United States in the 1970s; postcolonial West Africa; and, finally, the liberated South Africa celebrated in the novel's last scene. But even though Hillela may do intelligence work of some sort, she works not for imperialism—the British secret service or its South African epigones—but for African liberation. Thus, Gordimer rewrites not only *Kim* but also one of the master plots of colonial discourse from the sixteenth century onward. In this plot, a class of "masterless men," the "ungoverned and unsupervised [men] without the restraining resources of social organisation" (Brown 52), furnishes the Stephanos and Trinculos and, later, the Kims who literally become the agents of colonialism.

Brown notes that the discourse of colonialism in the sixteenth and seventeenth centuries operates in three main areas: masterlessness (class), savagism (race), and sexuality. According to Brown: "Masterlessness analyzes wandering or unfixed or unsupervised elements located in the internal margins of civil society. . . . Savagism probes and categorizes alien cultures on the external margins of expanding civil power" (50). Although he writes about England, a similar case might be made for the Spanish picaresque, around 1600, for the rogues and delinquents who populate these novels closely resemble Brown's masterless men.[8] Gordimer writes against the grain of colonial discourse, in part because her masterless man is a woman. She destabilizes colonial discourse by giving Hillela two once-distinct lines of filiation: she makes Hillela a hybrid descended, on the one hand, from the figure of Miranda and, on the other, from the masterless men whose desire Miranda symbolizes.[9]

Hillela, moreover, is as much an object as a subject of observation or surveillance. Much of what we learn about her takes the form of conjectures based on surveillance reports compiled by the South African government from its own intelligence or from other sources: "Everything is known about her movements. Americans are such industrious documenters: the proof of her presence among them, like that of their own existence, is ensured by reports of symposia and conferences, prospectuses of institutes and foundations, *curricula vitae,* group photographs, videos, tapes, transcripts of television interviews. She and her child came to the United States under the auspices (that's the vocabulary) of a new kind of white hunter" (237). This passage presents Hillela not as an individual subject—the typical protagonist of women's novels in English—but as the object of a surveillance dossier: here, she is less like Kim than like the objects counted and cataloged by the curator of the Lahore Wonder House and the agents of the British secret service. But the irony of the last sentence, and especially of the parenthetical aside—"(that's the vocabulary)"—subverts the authority of surveillance and thus the portrait of Hillela that surveillance constructs.

In rescripting Kipling's great game, Gordimer also calls into question the authority of his narrative stance and the idea of narrative authority in general. Kipling's omniscient narrator recounts Kim's career in an authoritative voice that makes the narrative appear as unproblematic as the empire for which it speaks.[10] *A Sport of Nature,* however, is composed of several narratives that present conflicting accounts of many of the events of the novel, and it has no master narrative that takes precedence over the others. Gordimer undermines not only the authority and authenticity of any particular account but also narrative authority and the narrative ideology of authenticity in general. For example, Hillela ignores her childhood in describing her own life, presumably for journalists reporting on African politics:

> Hillela herself, as they knew her, disappears in the version of a marriage that has a line in the *curriculum vitae* devoted to Whaila Kgomani in a *Who's Who* of black 20th-century political figures. *In 1965 he married in Ghana, and had a daughter.* From this

accident of geography reports assume he married a Ghanaian; a suitable alliance with a citizen of the first country in modern Africa to gain independence, . . . a citizen of Nkrumah's capital. . . .

The girl is mother to the woman, of course; she has been acknowledged. In fact, the woman has generally chosen to begin her existence there, when asked about her early life:—I was very young, working at an embassy in Accra when I met Whaila at a reception given by the late Kwame Nkrumah.—

Well, it's not impossible. (170)

In this passage, Gordimer subverts the authority and authenticity of first-person narration and of official political discourse alike. As the ironic allusion to Wordsworth's Intimations Ode and a more indirect echo of *David Copperfield* suggest, Hillela's choosing to "begin her existence" with her marriage is an act of narrative bad faith that obscures her childhood and her family—the parents who abandoned her and the aunts and uncles who brought her up.[11] At the same time, although Hillela's beginning her existence with her marriage is meant to signify the political commitment that marks for her a second birth, it conflates the political commitment to ending apartheid with the personal (marriage). The idea of political commitment is undercut, moreover, by the unidentified ironic voice that says, "Well, it's not impossible." Thus, Gordimer privileges neither the personal nor the political and destabilizes the narrative ideology of authenticity that makes one more authoritative than the other.

In much the same way as *A Sport of Nature* dialogizes *Kim*'s imperial monologue, Gordimer alters Kipling's depiction of race. As Abdul R. JanMohamed suggests, *Kim* interrogates the idea of race as either a biological or a cultural absolute ("Economy" 97–100), but the oscillation in *Kim* between race as an absolute category and race as a relative category is eventually dissipated by the plot that normalizes race by bringing it within the colonial system and establishes Kim's identity not only as an English agent but also as an Englishman. Like *Kim, A Sport of Nature* undermines the idea that racial identity is fixed, but Gordimer's text does not reach closure through the kind of racial sorting that *Kim* enacts. Rather, *A Sport of Nature* presents race as an assemblage of contradictory or incongruous political, economic, cultural, and ethnic attributes. On the one hand, race is a matter of political allegiance, economic position, or cultural affiliation.[12] On the other hand, race designates ethnicity, although this designation is neither immutable nor absolute but historically specific. Thus, the daughter of Hillela and Whaila—

Hillela names her Nomzamo after Nomzamo Winnie Mandela—is at once "our color" and, as Hillela tells the maternity nurse, black like her father (177–79). (This child of the future becomes a famous fashion model, valued, ironically, for her "exotic" looks.) In short, *A Sport of Nature* treats race as a category of ascribed, significant difference, and as a category in which difference appears insignificant.[13]

Gordimer also unravels the colonialist articulation of race and gender that Kipling uncritically reproduces, and she rewrites the colonial family romance that Kipling borrows from *The Tempest* and transforms. As numerous critics and theorists have suggested,[14] colonial discourses effect a slippage or conflation of race and gender by ascribing feminine traits to the colonized "other" or by colonizing the female body. This slippage of race and gender is reproduced in what I call the colonial family romance. In *The Tempest*, for example, Sycorax stands for the absent mother of all the characters, while Prospero is the father whose patriarchal authority is eventually subsumed under that of the king. Thus, Mother is identified with lost or forgotten origins, while Father appropriates the authority of the colonizer.

Kipling elaborates on this articulation of race and gender in *Kim*. Kim consolidates his identity as a British subject through his relationships with a series of surrogate mothers and fathers. Some of the fathers—Creighton and Lurgan, Father Victor and Mr. Bennett—are English, while others are Indian,[15] but even the Indian fathers are identified with England, for Mahbub Ali and Hurree Babu work for the secret service and the Teshoo Lama provides the money for Kim's imperial education at St. Xavier's school. In contrast, the mothers—Huneefa (the blind prostitute who paints Kim black), the woman of Shamlegh, the Kulu woman who nurses him back to health, and the Mother Earth at whose breast he is revived (278)—are all identified with India, which becomes in effect his mother. As in *The Tempest*, Oedipal-patriarchal and colonial themes (gender and race) reinforce each other, for Kim moves toward a fixed identity by acquiring mothers, fathers, language, and culture.

I do not mean to posit a universal or transhistorical colonial family romance but rather to suggest that colonial family romances refigure specific colonial situations. For example, the absent mother, like the fact that no one in *The Tempest* with the exception of Caliban and possibly Ariel is born on "Prospero's" island, is a trope for the colonial situation of the Caribbean, while the plenitude of nurturing mothers in *Kim* is one aspect of the imperial strategy of domesticating—feminizing, pacifying, or in Said's terms, Orientalizing—India. But underlying these differences (variations) is a common identification of father/colonizer and mother/

colonized. *A Sport of Nature* dissolves this identification and consequently unbalances the patriarchal and colonial equilibrium of both *The
Tempest* and *Kim,* for Hillela achieves her identity by sleeping with
political mentors or father figures who are also lovers and by leaving
behind the mothers who symbolize not the colonized "other" but the
culture of colonialism.[16] Thus, *A Sport of Nature* alters the dominant
articulation of race and gender in colonial discourse. It accomplishes this,
I suggest, by politicizing Hillela's sexuality in ways that rewrite the norms
of (Anglo-American) feminism or female modernism.

> When we write of a woman, everything is out of place; the accent never
> falls where it does with a man. (*Orlando*)

One of the features that differentiates the *picara* from her male counterpart is the sexual character of her adventures (Monteser 4). But whether
the *picara* actually trades on her sexuality or whether she is simply
rumored to do so, she affronts the hypocritical sexual morality that
exemplifies the disintegration of the society on whose margins she moves.
Like the classical *picara,* Hillela appears to be an opportunist who uses
sex as a strategy for survival, yet she also enjoys her sexuality. In one of
the early episodes in *A Sport of Nature,* Hillela is expelled from her
Salisbury boarding school because she goes out with a "colored" boy
whom she meets in a movie theater. Even though Hillela's relationship
with the boy is sexually and racially innocent—she does not recognize
when she meets him that he is "colored"—it violates the color bar and
transgresses the laws that regulate race and gender. This episode sets the
plot in motion, for it marks Hillela's expulsion from the questionable
Eden of sheltered colonial adolescence. (Actually, Hillela's innocence
ends when, in telling her father what happened, she hides behind racist
platitudes and describes "the advances of that boy, that face, those unnatural eyes that shouldn't have belonged to one of his kind at all, like that hair,
the almost real blond hair" [13].) In addition, this episode points to
Hillela's subsequent history, for the same picaresque conjunction of innocence and transgression characterizes her later sexual involvements with
men (father figures) married and/or black and with her cousin Sasha.
Finally, this episode raises for the first time one of the central questions of
the novel: it asks us to consider whether Hillela is, as the schoolmistress
and apartheid society would characterize her, a freak of nature or whether
her innocent transgressions prefigure a new sexual economy.

Hillela's sexuality is a harbinger of a new articulation of race and gender and also serves as her mode of inscription into postcolonial African politics. She has numerous lovers and two black African husbands, the African National Congress leader Kgomani, who is assassinated soon after the marriage, and the General, head of state of an unnamed West African country, to whom she is still married at the end of the novel. (The General gives her the name Chiemeka, but "between the couple, she remained Hillela, . . . the name of intimacy" [303–4].) In both marriages, Hillela's self-realization is identified with or subordinated to her husband's political program. Or more precisely, in both marriages Hillela's self-realization is identified with the political program of the ANC, since she may have married the General to advance the cause of the ANC.

In Hillela's career, then, Gordimer appears to be giving us a version of both the heroine's submission to a powerful and erotically idealized man[17] and the subordination or conscription of women's desire in a male-identified, male-dominated politics. Unlike *Burger's Daughter,* which focuses explicitly on the conflict between the personal (sexual) liberation of the (white) female protagonist and the project of ending apartheid, *A Sport of Nature* elides this conflict or places it in the background.[18] But underlying this difference of emphasis is a more important similarity, for the situation of Hillela takes shape in the same colonial political matrix as that of Rosa Burger and plays out the same contradiction between the struggle against apartheid in South Africa and the ideals—privileged (canonized) in female modernist texts and (Anglo-American) feminist theory generally—of women's, specifically white women's, autonomy, self-realization, and sexual fulfillment. On the one hand, the picaresque irony that governs Gordimer's treatment of Hillela deemphasizes the conflict between politics and personal liberation. On the other hand, *A Sport of Nature* subsumes the personal (sexual) under the political by identifying Hillela's sexual fulfillment with her marriages to black African political leaders and with her affairs with other political men as well. But if the description of Hillela's intense and erotic feelings about Whaila, rendered in large measure without irony, ruptures Gordimer's control of the narrative,[19] Hillela's marriage to the General, depicted as a mutually convenient political arrangement, marks a return to the cool idiom so prevalent in the rest of the novel. In fact, a critical perspective that deidealizes or delegitimates the plots and heroes of romance is a common feature of the picaresque and (Anglo-American) female modernism:[20] in grafting a critique of romance onto an explicitly anticolonial politics, Gordimer produces a text unevenly inflected by place and gender and constructs a kind of generic hybrid or sport of nature.

Although Gordimer's irony distances us from the political and sexual conflicts implied in Hillela's situation, Gordimer offers us a political understanding of Hillela's sexuality—and of sexuality in general—by contrasting her with her mother, Ruthie. In an attempt to escape from a banal, lower middle-class colonial existence, Ruthie abandons husband and daughter and elopes to Mozambique with a Portuguese lover, but her life with her lover virtually replicates her experience in marriage. Ruthie's career suggests that sexuality is an arena in which political contradictions are contested or displaced but evokes, too, the limits of a purely sexual politics. Like Ruthie, Hillela leaves behind the claustrophobic family—specifically the families of her mother's sisters, the fashionable Olga and the politically committed if self-righteous Pauline—but unlike Ruthie, Hillela makes a life that cannot be reduced to the symptomatology of the colonial family romance.

In addition to contrasting Hillela and Ruthie, *A Sport of Nature* contrasts Hillela and her "sibling cousin" (314) Sasha, Pauline's son. Like such sister-brother pairs as Maggie and Tom Tulliver and Lily Briscoe and James Ramsay, Hillela and Sasha represent complementary possibilities: for example, he chafes against family constraints from which she is largely free. As sibling cousins, they are a version of the nonromantic couple or group protagonist that, DuPlessis argues, displaces the romantic couple in female modernist texts (*Writing Beyond the Ending* 57, 162). But Hillela and Sasha also briefly make up a romantic couple when, as teenagers, they have a passionate, yet innocent, love affair that, like all of Hillela's erotic adventures, offends the prevailing sexual morality. At once a romantic and a nonromantic couple, Hillela and Sasha elaborate the both/and strategy that, DuPlessis notes in "For the Etruscans," characterizes female modernism.

Hillela and Sasha also belong to different generic traditions and reflect complementary possibilities for The Novel. While she exemplifies the picaresque, he is the sort of character one might expect to encounter in "serious" political fiction. Representing the Dostoyevskian hero M. M. Bakhtin classifies as an ideologue or man of ideas (*Problems* 78), Sasha reads *The Brothers Karamazov* during his romantic idyll with Hillela.[21] He is imprisoned for his part in the liberation struggle. In the letters that he addresses to Hillela and tries unsuccessfully to smuggle out of prison, he reflects on South African history, politics, and society, and on his own personal (family) situation.[22] Sasha appears in his writings as thoughts and feelings—as a subject of consciousness—while Hillela is seen as a subject of action. Thus, Gordimer destabilizes the generic distinctions between the domestic novel in which women, as/and consciousness, and the family romance occupy center stage, the adventure novel dominated by men of action, and the political or philosophical novel, which encompasses consciousness and action alike.

The trajectories of Hillela and Sasha also reflect their complementary relationships to postcolonial African politics. Sasha typifies white opponents of apartheid from the 1960s through the 1980s. As he explains in his letters to Hillela (300–302, 314–23), he is initially a participant in protest movements led by whites like his parents. Forced by the Black Consciousness Movement of the 1970s to assess his position and that of whites in the antiapartheid struggle generally, he subsequently becomes an organizer for a black trade union that affiliates with the United Democratic Front.[23] Sasha inherits his fierce political passion from both his parents and especially his mother, but except when Pauline follows his lead and works with the detainees' parents group, he feels her as a constantly constraining presence. After his release from prison, he bombs a police station and goes into exile. In one of the novel's most poignant ironies, Sasha speaks for the utopian future he will see only from a distance, addressing the thoughts he jots down to Pauline: "Don't you see? It's all got to come down, mother. Without utopia—the idea of utopia—there's a failure of the imagination—and that's a failure to know how to go on living. It will take another kind of being to stay on, here. A new white person. Not us. The chance is a wild chance—like falling in love" (187). When the novel ends, the narrator tells us, "Sasha has not yet come back home" (340).

Hillela, by contrast, drifts from one man to another, but the end of the novel finds her attending the celebration of a liberated South Africa with the General, now head of the Organization of African Unity. The novel asks whether Hillela is the "new white person" able to stay on, although, strictly speaking, she does not stay on but rather visits as an honored guest in "Whaila's country" (341). Gordimer seems to suggest here that "spontaneous mutations" ("another kind of being") are most at home in the postcolonial future, for Hillela is unencumbered by the constraints of family, class, and culture that weigh Sasha down. As a sport of nature, Hillela recalls Jane Eyre, who is called a *lusus naturae* by the conventionally feminine Rosamond Oliver (chap. 32): both Jane and Hillela are unconventional women whose marriages prefigure new social orders—for Jane, the English bourgeois patriarchy made possible by colonial exploitation; for Hillela, the postcolonial African future. (In contrast, Maggie Tulliver, the "spontaneous mutation" of *The Mill on the Floss,* becomes extinct in the apocalyptic flood that ends the novel.) Thus, *A Sport of Nature* seems to reach closure by inscribing Hillela in a new order whose founding is celebrated in the moving and utopian final episode: "Whaila's country" are the novel's last words. But the ending sustains rather than resolves the tensions the novel puts into play. Although we see the celebration in large part from Hillela's perspective, the narrative bars access to her (as) consciousness, since she is rendered from the outside, as "the public face assumed, along with appropriate dress for exposure." Yet the narrator calls her not Chiemeka, the public, ceremonial name, but Hillela, "the name of intimacy."

In juxtaposing Sasha's utopian passion with Hillela's picaresque detachment and making Hillela's sexuality her mode of inscription in the postcolonial future that Sasha, ironically, observes from the distance of exile in Europe, Gordimer produces a (South) African text that is at the same time a critique, a hybrid, and a transmutation of British (European) generic traditions. In this respect, *A Sport of Nature* is a postcolonial (and postmodern) text analogous to the postcolonial politics designated by the General as a "new combination" (266) and described by Sasha in his letter from prison: "I say there is unbeatable purpose expressed in the horrible mishmash of Marxism, Castroism, Gandhism, Fanonism, Hyde Park tub-thumping (colonial heritage), Gawd-on-our-sideism (missionary heritage), Black Consciousness jargon, Sandinistism, Christian liberation theology with which we formulate" (315). Both the General's and Sasha's heterogeneous politics and Gordimer's heterogeneous novel are answers to racist pretexts—for the General, colonial and neocolonial oppression; for Sasha, the major who interrogates him; for Gordimer, colonial discourse and apartheid society—and both exemplify the value of *métissage,*[24] a mixing of forms and categories that grafts transformed European traditions onto indigenous African ones.

A similar aesthetic is reflected in State House, the presidential residence where Hillela lives with the General when he once again becomes the head of state after defeating the military rulers who deposed him and governed his country with the help of the United States. In State House (Government House in the imperial era), the political aesthetic of *métissage* is subverted by eruptions of the kitsch that is most often identified with neocolonial political and cultural styles. While the General wants to install air conditioning and brick up old walls, the narrator tells us, Hillela insists that:

State House appropriate Government House, not destroy its architectural character. A style of living commensurate with the dignity of the State, she persuaded the President, is not expressed in the idiom of the Hilton and the Intercontinental (with which both have a strong emotional tie as the places where his return into his own was bargained for and planned). . . . Hillela would not touch, either, the collection of votary objects that surrounds the coat-of-arms that has replaced an imperial one: plaques beaten out of the country's copper, the carvings by local artists of heroic agrarian couples, faithfully but subconsciously reproducing as an aesthetic mode the oversize head and spindly legs of under-nourishment. (305–6)

If kitsch exemplifies what Andreas Huyssen has called the affirmative moment of postmodernism, the critical moment is implicit in the irony the narrator turns equally on the General's affinity for neocolonial kitsch and on Hillela's affinity for the "stylistic graces and charms of the past" (305), that is, the high colonial "good taste" she acquired under the tutelage of her elegant, antique-collecting Aunt Olga. Although Hillela dislikes the "idiom of the Hilton and Intercontinental," she values both European art and culture and the assemblage of styles that represent the African present; and the narrator implies that, like Hillela, we should not regard the latter with contempt. Indeed, in juxtaposing kitsch with *métissage* and holding them in tension, the novel elaborates an aesthetic of postcolonial pastiche analogous to Sasha's "horrible mishmash," his politics of revolutionary bricolage.[25]

This aesthetic extends the both/and strategy of female modernism. *A Sport of Nature* deploys not one but several sets of both/and pairs—Hillela and Sasha, the picaresque and the novel of consciousness, the affirmative and critical moments of postmodernism, revolutionary utopianism and political pragmatism, indigenous (South) African and borrowed political and cultural traditions, *métissage* and kitsch—that cannot be represented as points on a single Cartesian plane. Thus, *A Sport of Nature* presents itself at once as sui generis, a (South) African novel, and as a critique of colonial styles and codes. As an instance of cultural critique, the novel reproduces what is, for Roland Barthes, a central contradiction of (post)modern writing. In *Writing Degree Zero,* Barthes takes as his point of departure Marx's notion that men make their history but not under circumstances of their own choosing and transposes Marx's preoccupation with historical agency into a question of literary or linguistic originality. "The writer," Barthes says, "acknowledges the vast novelty of the present world but finds that in order to express it he has at his disposal only a language [*langue*] which is splendid but lifeless" (86).

In "The Essential Gesture" (the title is taken from *Writing Degree Zero*), Gordimer elaborates on Barthes's meditation on the politics of style. In this essay, she destabilizes the distinction between social responsibility and personal creativity by treating it as a product of the situation of Western European intellectuals in the era of high modernism. In addition, like Barthes, she undermines both the identification of social realism with political responsibility and the concomitant opposition between aesthetic innovation and political commitment, but at the same time she notes: "The kind of social responsibility writers have assumed at least since the beginning of the modern movement: to transform the world by style ... could not serve as the writer's essential gesture in countries such as South Africa or Nicaragua, but it has had its possibilities and sometimes proves its validity where complacency, indifference, accidie, and not conflict threaten the human spirit" (147–48).[26] In other words, Gordimer insists that, like responsibility and creativity, modernism is a historically and geographically specific category. If in *A Sport of Nature* Gordimer does not attempt to reanimate the classical (British, European) modern project and transform the world by style, she nevertheless exposes and transforms the dominant—and colonialist—styles of modernism. That is, she confronts the "vast novelty" of the postcolonial world by dismantling some of the styles and codes—among them, the dominant generic traditions and gender inscriptions of British fiction—that comprise the discourses of colonialism. At the same time, she raises the question of whether or how writing by English-speaking whites in South Africa can transmute the hybrid forms of cultural critique into an indigenous (South) African growth and help bring into being the utopian future imagined in different ways by Sasha, Barthes, Marx, and Mandela.

Notes

Parts of this essay began as papers delivered at a panel sponsored by the Division on Modern British Literature at the Modern Language Association meetings in 1987 and at the Comparative Literature: Modern Section at the Northeast MLA meetings in 1988. A slightly different version of this essay was presented at the Rutgers Center for Historical Analysis in 1990. I would like to thank the members of the center for their lively and rigorous response to my work, Celeste Schenck for her encouraging reading of early drafts of the essay, Karen Lawrence for her editorial generosity, and Dolores Greenberg for becoming the implied reader I addressed as I was writing.

1. As Glenn (75), Greenstein (227), JanMohamed (*Manichean Aesthetics* 265–66), and Cooke (181–83, 221), among others, have noted, these are the central questions posed by Gordimer's career.

2. Rabbi Hillel's best-known aphorism is an expression of an almost existential activism that makes him a model for Hillela, or more precisely for Gordimer herself: "If I am not for myself, who will be? If I am for myself only, what am I? If not now, when?"

3. Cf. Thomas Cartelli's notion that postcolonial writing revises our understanding of Shakespeare and the place of *The Tempest* in constructing colonial discourse. The distinction between colonial and postcolonial writing is not at all as clear as the distinction between Shakespeare and the latter, but colonial as well as explicitly postcolonial writing participates in the critique of the race plot I am concerned with here. I thank the members of the Rutgers Center for Historical Analysis for clarifying this for me.

4. See Gayatri Spivak and Laura E. Donaldson for discussions of this theme.

5. Critics who write about the classical (sixteenth to eighteenth century European) picaresque classify its protagonist as a rogue (Chandler), delinquent (Parker), half-outsider (Guillén) or vantage point (Alter). Bakhtin relates the picaresque to the travel novel and the "adventure novel of everyday life" and notes that the hero of the former is a "point moving in space," while the protagonist of the latter is a rogue or spy who reveals "through the device of 'not understanding'" the vulgar conventionality of everyday life ("Forms of Time and Chronotope" 184 and passim; "Bildungsroman" 10). Gordimer's postcolonial recuperation of the picaresque bears some resemblance to Martin Green's project in *Dreams of Adventure, Deeds of Empire*. In this study of imperialism shaped to fit a "situation of social and moral crisis," Green proposes to read critically the literature of adventure (empire) and uses "unconventional criteria" of seriousness to define as serious this literature which F. R. Leavis excluded from his tradition (xi–xii, 3). Cf. Green's essay in this volume.

6. In rewriting *Kim*, Gordimer recalls Woolf's *Orlando*, which asks, as Kipling does in *Kim* and as picaresque fictions do generally, whether identity is a function of costume: "He—for there could be no doubt of his sex, though the fashion of the time did something to disguise it—was in the act of slicing at the head of a Moor which swung from the rafters" (13). More important for our purposes is *Orlando*'s critique of colonialism (race). As Jane Marcus reminds us, Woolf implicates British culture in colonialism by connecting Orlando's slicing at the head of a Moor with his training to be an English poet.

7. As Edward W. Said points out, Kipling does not show the conflict between India and England because he does not consider India as unhappily subservient to imperialism (*"Kim"* 43).

8. For discussions of rogues and delinquents, see Alter, Chandler, and Parker.

9. See Donaldson on Miranda as a "feminine trope of colonialism" (68) and Susan M. Greenstein for an illuminating discussion of *Burger's Daughter* and *July's People* as (re)tellings of Miranda's story. In *A Sport of Nature* Gordimer travels farther from that paradigmatic colonial narrative than in the two preceding novels. Ironically, as an English-speaking Jew in South Africa, she writes from a position like that of the authors of the classic Spanish picaresque, many of whom, as Claudio Guillén points out (101), are thought to have been *conversos* who never fully assimilated into sixteenth-century Spanish society. The *conversos* were half-outsiders of a different sort from the characters they invented; as Jews, Gordimer and Hillela are also half-outsiders in the Afrikaner-Christian society of South Africa.

10. Said identifies the narrator's point of view with that of Colonel Creighton (54).

11. David Copperfield chooses "to begin my life with the beginning of my life" (chap. 1), but *David Copperfield* suggests that all such beginnings are arbitrary and constitute themselves by excluding something else. Hillela's conflicting accounts of her own beginnings disrupt the intention to begin that, according to Said, constitutes the classic bourgeois novel ("Novel as Beginning Intention").

12. Gordimer's notion of race as a political category recalls Frantz Fanon's argument against a naively racial or nationalist conception of anticolonial struggle. Fanon describes "settlers [who] . . . go so far as to condemn the colonial war[,] . . . go over to the enemy, become Negroes or Arabs, and accept suffering, torture, and death" (145). These settlers reappear as whites, like the Communist party leader and antiapartheid activist Bram Fischer, who are said to have given up being white (Gordimer, *Sport of Nature* 186).

13. Henry Louis Gates, Jr., takes a similarly deconstructive approach in the introduction to *"Race," Writing and Difference.*

14. The slippage effected by colonial discourses is discussed by Gilman, Lionnet, and Said (*Orientalism*), among others.

15. JanMohamed notes a "bifurcation of the paternal function: on the one hand, Kim's *personal* and *emotional* allegiance to the Indians and, on the other hand, his *impersonal* and *rational* relation to the Englishmen" ("Economy" 99). That is, JanMohamed divides Kim's fathers into English and Indian and assigns them gender traits accordingly.

16. Actually, the identification of the mother figure with colonial culture, noted by John Cooke in Gordimer's earlier novels (46), is superimposed on a pattern whereby the mother stands for the colonized "other," in the person of the black woman whose absence is, as Ian Glenn notes, a "critical lacuna" in Gordimer's work (77). Gordimer's revised family romance is an Oedipal story that is superimposed on a pre-Oedipal story, much as, Freud and his feminist interpreters explain, the girl's Oedipal situation is superimposed on the pre-Oedipal constellation it

reverses. Gordimer's Oedipal story recalls Fanon's version of the family romance which identifies the "mother-country" with the Oedipal mother; specifically, Fanon characterizes the former as a "bloodthirsty and implacable stepmother" (145).

17. Thanks to Deirdre David for clarifying this point for me.

18. On the conflict between the personal and the political in *Burger's Daughter,* see Meese.

19. This view derives from Ian Glenn, who commented on an early version of this essay.

20. For discussions of the picaresque as critique of romance, see Parker (21 ff.), and Alter (77). For female modernist delegitimation of romance, see DuPlessis (*Writing Beyond the Ending* 77–78 and passim).

21. Cf. Irving Howe, who notes that in political novels the characters themselves are "often aware of some coherent political loyalty or ideological identification .... They think in terms of supporting or opposing society" (19). Political novelists, Howe asserts, in terms reminiscent of Bakhtin's, must make "ideas or ideologies come to life, endow them with capacity for stirring characters into passionate gestures and sacrifices" (21).

22. Sasha's letters mention, among other figures, Ruth First, Breyten Breytenbach, and Jeremy Cronin (white South Africans imprisoned for their opposition to apartheid), and Antonio Gramsci, whose *Prison Notebooks* provided Gordimer with the epigraph to *July's People* and the title of a 1983 essay, "Living in the Interregnum."

23. The UDF is a broad, black-led, multiracial, antiapartheid coalition. It was banned in 1988 and unbanned in February 1990.

24. The term *métissage* and the concept it denotes come from Françoise Lionnet. I prefer the term to its nearest English equivalent, *miscegenation,* because it is less emotionally charged.

25. On bricolage as a process of formation of the multiple positions of "revolutionary subjects," see Radakrishnan (284).

26. Gordimer's remarks about high modernism recall Césaire's recuperation, as a critique of bourgeois society, of the work of such apparently apolitical poets as Lautréamont and Baudelaire (46–48). See Neil Lazarus for a discussion of the modernism of white oppositional writers in South Africa as a version of the "defiant negativity" (147) of Theodor Adorno.

Works Cited

Alter, Robert. *Rogue's Progress: Studies in the Picaresque Novel.* Cambridge: Harvard University Press, 1965.

Bakhtin, M. M. "The Bildungsroman." In *Speech Genres and Other Late Essays.* Trans. Vern W. McGee. Ed. Caryl Emerson and Michael Holquist. Austin: University of Texas Press, 1986, 10–60.

——. "Forms of Time and Chronotope." In *The Dialogic Imagination.* Trans. Caryl Emerson and Michael Holquist. Ed. Michael Holquist. Austin: University of Texas Press, 1981, 184–259.

——. *Problems of Dostoevsky's Poetics.* Ed. and trans. Caryl Emerson. Minneapolis: University of Minnesota Press, 1984.

Barthes, Roland. *Writing Degree Zero.* Trans. Annette Lavers and Colin Smith. New York: Hill and Wang, 1968.

Brown, Paul. " 'This Thing of Darkness I Acknowledge Mine': *The Tempest* and the Discourse of Colonialism." In *Political Shakespeare: New Essays in Cultural Materialism.* Ed. Jonathan Dollimore and Allan Sinfield. Ithaca: Cornell University Press, 1985, 48–71.

Cartelli, Thomas. "Prospero in Africa: *The Tempest* as Colonial Text and Pretext." In *Shakespeare Reproduced: The Text in History and Ideology.* Ed. Jean E. Howard and Marion F. O'Connor. New York and London: Methuen, 1987, 99–115.

Césaire, Aimé. *Discourse on Colonialism.* 1955. Trans. Joan Pinkham. New York: Monthly Review, 1972.

Chandler, Frank Wadleigh. *The Literature of Roguery,* 2 vols. 1907. New York: Burt Franklin, 1958.

Clingman, Stephen R. *The Novels of Nadine Gordimer: History from the Inside.* London: Allen and Unwin, 1987.

Cooke, John. *The Novels of Nadine Gordimer: Private Lives/Public Landscapes.* Baton Rouge: Louisiana State University Press, 1985.

Donaldson, Laura E. "The Miranda Complex: Colonialism and the Question of Feminist Reading." *Diacritics* 18 (1988): 65–79.

DuPlessis, Rachel Blau. *Writing Beyond the Ending: Narrative Strategies of Twentieth-Century Women Writers.* Bloomington: Indiana University Press, 1985.

DuPlessis, Rachel Blau, and Members of Workshop 9. "For the Etruscans: Sexual Difference and Artistic Production: The Debate over a Female Aesthetic." In *The Future of Difference.* Ed. Hester Eisenstein and Alice Jardine. Boston: Prentice-Hall, 1980, 128–56.

Fanon, Frantz. *The Wretched of the Earth.* 1961. Trans. Constance Farrington. New York: Grove, 1968.

Gates, Henry Louis, Jr., ed. *"Race," Writing and Difference.* Chicago: University of Chicago Press, 1986.

Gilman, Sander L. "Black Bodies, White Bodies: Toward an Iconography of Female Sexuality in Late Nineteenth-Century Art, Medicine, and Literature." In Gates, 223–62.

Glenn, Ian. "Hodiernal Hillela—Gordimer's Kim." Review of *A Sport of Nature. Contrast* 64 (1988): 75–81.

Gordimer, Nadine. "The Essential Gesture: Writers and Responsibility." *Granta* 15 (1985): 135–53.

——. *A Sport of Nature.* New York: Alfred A. Knopf, 1987.

——. "A Writer in South Africa." *London Magazine* (n.s.) 5 (1965): 21–30.

Green, Martin. *Dreams of Adventure, Deeds of Empire.* New York: Basic Books, 1979.

Greenstein, Susan M. "Miranda's Story: Nadine Gordimer and the Literature of Empire." *Novel* 18 (1984–85): 227–42.

Guillén, Claudio. "Toward a Definition of the Picaresque." *Literature as System: Essays toward the Theory of Literary History.* Princeton: Princeton University Press, 1971, 71–106.

Howe, Irving. *Politics and the Novel.* 1957. Freeport, N.Y.: Books for Libraries Press, 1970.

Huyssen, Andreas. "Mapping the Postmodern." *After the Great Divide: Modernism, Mass Culture, Postmodernism.* Bloomington: Indiana University Press, 1986, 179–221.

JanMohamed, Abdul R. *Manichean Aesthetics: The Politics of Literature in Colonial Africa.* Amherst: University of Massachusetts Press, 1983.

——. "The Economy of Manichean Allegory: The Function of Racial Difference in Colonialist Literature." In Gates, 78–106.

Jehlen, Myra. "Archimedes and the Paradox of Feminist Criticism." *Signs* 6 (1981): 575–601.

Kauffman, Linda, ed. *Feminism and Institutions: Dialogues on Feminist Theory.* New York: Basil Blackwell, 1989.

Kipling, Rudyard. *Kim.* 1901. New York: Signet Books, 1984.

Lazarus, Neil. "Modernism and Modernity: T. W. Adorno and Contemporary White South African Literature." *Cultural Critique* 5 (1986–87): 131–55.

Lionnet, Françoise. *Autobiographical Voices: Race, Gender, Self-Portraiture.* Ithaca: Cornell University Press, 1989.

Marcus, Jane. "Blood Narratives and Milk Narratives." Paper delivered at MLA, 1987.

Meese, Elizabeth A. "The Political Is the Personal: The Construction of Identity in Nadine Gordimer's *Burger's Daughter.*" In Kauffman, 253–75.

Monteser, Frederick. *The Picaresque Element in Western Literature.* University: University of Alabama Press, 1975.

Parker, Alexander. *Literature and the Delinquent.* Edinburgh: Edinburgh University Press, 1967.

Radakrishnan, R. "Negotiating Subject Positions in an Uneven World." In Kauffman, 276–90.

Said, Edward W. "*Kim,* the Pleasures of Imperialism." *Raritan* 7 (1987): 27–64.

——. "The Novel as Beginning Intention." *Beginnings: Intention and Method.* New York: Basic Books, 1975, 79–188.

———. *Orientalism.* New York: Pantheon, 1978.
Spivak, Gayatri. "Three Women's Texts and a Critique of Imperialism." In Gates, 262–80.

Oppressive Silence

J. M. Coetzee's Foe *and the Politics of the Canon*

> In the last corner, under the transoms, half buried in sand, his knees drawn up, his hands between his thighs, I come to Friday.
>
> I tug his woolly hair, finger the chain about his throat. "Friday," I say, I try to say, kneeling over him, sinking hands and knees into the ooze, "what is this ship?"
>
> But this is not a place of words. Each syllable, as it comes out, is caught and filled with water and diffused. This is a place where bodies are their own signs. It is the home of Friday.
>
> He turns and turns till he lies at full length, his face to my face. The skin is tight across his bones, his lips are drawn back. I pass a fingernail across his teeth, trying to find a way in.
>
> His mouth opens. From inside him comes a slow stream, without breath, without interruption. It flows up through his body and out upon me; it passes through the cabin, through the wreck; washing the cliffs and shores of the island, it runs northward and southward to the ends of the earth. Soft and cold, dark and unending, it beats against my eyelids, against the skin of my face. (157)

The final paragraphs of J. M. Coetzee's *Foe* achieve their power in large measure as a result of their relation to what has gone before, though even out of context they convey something of the resonating quality of Coetzee's distinctive style. Precise, vividly physical, but seldom concerned with the business of realistic description as cultivated in the novel through the eighteenth and nineteenth centuries, this style achieves its distinctive effects partly by means of the half-heard echoing of the literary tradition with which it thereby claims association. Here, for example, the first two scenes of *The Tempest,* with their memorable blending of loss and salvation, though never quite quoted, shimmer through the writing. The passage contains a number of words that occur, some of them several times, in these two scenes, all of them in speeches having to do with shipwreck: "sink," "ooze," "ship," "water," "cabin," "wreck," "washing," "shore," "island," "earth." But the allusiveness remains uncertain because these *are* single words: how can a single word be a quotation? One or two longer verbal fragments from these scenes may drift into the back of the reader's mind as well: "What, must our mouths be cold?" "Would thou mightst lie drowning / The washing of ten tides!" "'Tis beating in my mind. . . ." "Full fathom five thy father lies, / Of his bones are coral made."[1] Echoes other than Shakespearean ones play about the passage, too, such as the Book of Common Prayer's version of Psalm 45, which also concerns fears of shipwreck and the hope of safety: "Thou that art the hope of all the ends of the earth, and of them that remain in the broad sea." That note of hope will also be evoked for any reader who recalls the "gentle breeze" that, in the opening lines of Wordsworth's *Prelude,* "beats against my cheek / And seems half-conscious of the joy it gives."

There is also in this closing passage a continuation of the delicate play between a contemporary and an earlier literary style that characterizes all of *Foe.* An older rhetorical mode can be heard in the rhythmic and syntactic repetitions, many of them involving a successive phrasal lengthening—"I say, I try to say"; "without breath, without interruption"; "through the cabin, through the wreck"; "it flows . . . ; it passes . . . ; . . . it runs"; "against my eyelids, against the skin of my face"—and in the slight archaisms, like the prepositions "about" and "upon." The five qualifying phrases with which the passage begins—before the main clause of the sentence is reached—are also part of this highly deliberate and carefully paced rhetoric. But it is only when the passage is read as the conclusion of the novel that the force of this image and of these stylistic nuances can be fully felt; the narrator of the closing section (what name do we use—Susan Barton, Daniel Foe, Daniel Defoe, J. M. Coetzee, our own?) has made the last of many attempts to get Friday to speak, and the hauntingly allusive description of the soundless stream issuing from his body is a culmination of the book's concern with the powerful silence that is the price of our cultural achievements.

I begin at the end—not only of the novel but, at the time of writing, of Coetzee's output as a novelist—because what I wish to do is read back, back from this representation of a speechless speech endlessly covering the world to the ways in which Coetzee's words—and silences—are and are not heard by the institutions of our literary culture. The question I wish to address is that of access to the canon: What does it mean for novels like Coetzee's to claim canonic status, or for critics to make such a claim on their behalf? (That the phrase "novels like Coetzee's" is itself problematic indicates one dimension of the question.) What does it mean, culturally and politically, for this claim to succeed or fail?

If we characterize canonization in a fairly straightforward way, as widespread recognition within the institutions of publication and education that a body of texts by a single author constitutes an "important," "serious," "lasting" contribution to "literature" (a characterization I shall considerably complicate in due course), there are many signs that the process is well under way for Coetzee. He has published five novels since 1974, *Dusklands* (a pair of mirroring novellas), *In the Heart of the Country* (which has been made into a film), *Waiting for the Barbarians, Life & Times of Michael K,* and, in 1986, *Foe.* All are widely available in prestigious paperback editions, and among them they have won numerous literary awards. Recognition in the United States has been slower than in Britain, but most reviews have been highly respectful, and *Waiting for the Barbarians* and *Michael K* were named by the *New York Times* as among the best books of their years. In 1989 Coetzee was elected an honorary fellow of the Modern Language Association of America.

In South Africa, where Coetzee lives, the political determination of the canon has been more blatant, and the standing of his novels has been strongly affected by the degree to which they are perceived as hostile to the policies and practices of apartheid—and by the significance of this perception to different groups within the country. On the one hand, they have been subject to official scrutiny and delays, and ignored by the state-controlled media,[2] but they have not, like some more obviously antigovernment works, been banned; on the other hand, they have been championed by some of those in opposition and attacked by others for failing to engage directly in the political struggle. I shall return later to this complex array of responses.

What is it about these novels that has propelled them at least into the antechambers of the literary canon in the English-speaking world? The answers to this question are no doubt many and diverse; since canonization depends on the convergence of a multitude of separate decisions and actions, it is bound to be overdetermined. But one answer we have already glimpsed would be that through their *allusiveness* the novels offer themselves not as challenges to the canon but as canonic—as already canonized, one might say. They appear to locate themselves within an established literary culture, rather than present themselves as an assault on that culture. Sometimes the allusions are more overt than those in the last paragraph of *Foe,* and they run the risk of appearing as intrusive attempts to claim membership of the existing tradition. The narrator of *In the Heart of the Country* weaves into her text the words of canonic writers—notably Blake, whose *Proverbs of Hell* and *Songs of Experience* form a kind of subtext for the work—and as the novel draws to a close she hears, or believes she hears, fragments of the Western cultural encyclopedia descending to her from passing aircraft. *Waiting for the Barbarians* takes its title, and one aspect of its sociopolitical dynamic, from a poem of Cavafy's (*Collected Poems* 30–33) and alludes as well to Beckett's best-known play; while the name of the central character in *Michael K,* often referred to just as "K," cannot fail to recall Kafka.[3] However, it is in *Foe* that Coetzee has made canonic intertextuality a fundamental principle: the novel's manner of proceeding is to rewrite, and fuse together, the biography of Daniel Defoe and those of several of Defoe's fictional characters. The perpetuation of any canon is dependent in part on the references made to its earlier members by its later members (or would-be members); and in this respect Coetzee's novels could be said to presuppose and to reproduce the canonic status of their predecessors even as they claim to join them.

It might be argued that the *style* of Coetzee's novels also constitutes a claim to belong to an existing canonic tradition; the deliberate, chiseled prose has little to do with the exorbitance or casualness (however studied) by which texts we might characterize as "postmodern" frequently affront the traditional valorization of literary form. If Joyce is one of Coetzee's stylistic forebears, it is the Joyce who created the "scrupulous meanness" of *Dubliners;* more obvious are the affinities with Beckett, especially the meticulous prose, the present tense, the isolated figures of the Trilogy. Here, for instance, is an unmistakably Beckettian sentence from *In the Heart of the Country:* "I would have no qualm, I am sure, if it came to the pinch, though how it could come to this pinch I do not know, about living in a mud hut, or indeed under a lean-to of branches, out in the veld, eating chickenfeed, talking to the insects" (6). Coetzee's writing invites the reader to savor it, sentence by sentence, word by word, for its economy and efficiency; and although the style of each novel has its own unmistakable character, the reader receives the consistent impression in all of them of words chosen with extraordinary care. In fact, as with the use of allusions and citations, the very deliberateness of this highly literary language may for some tastes smack too obviously of canonic pretensions.

Also interpretable as consistent with the traditional humanist concerns of the canon is the *thematic focus:* for instance, the novels return again and again to the solitary individual in a hostile human and physical environment to raise crucial questions about the foundations of civilization and humanity. The American military propagandist during the U.S.-Vietnam war driven to the limits of sanity in "The Vietnam Project" and the hunter-explorer clinging to life in harsh country among "savage" people in "The Narrative of Jacobus Coetzee" (in the two parts of *Dusklands*); the self-tormenting farmer's daughter alone with her father's corpse on the isolated farm (in *In the Heart of the Country*); the well-meaning state official himself enduring the barbarism on which his "civilization" depends (in *Waiting for the Barbarians*); the nomadic victim of a racist society who manages to exist on the margins of death (in *Life & Times of Michael K*): these figures may appear as so many versions of Lear's experience on the heath—one poor, bare, forked animal after another. Or one might emphasize the repeated motif of masters (or mistresses) and servants—also important in *King Lear,* of course, and, in its yoking of a moral discourse of human bonds and rights with an actual relationship of economic exploitation, a recurrent source of tension in the bourgeois conscience and the novels that represent it. Once again, *Foe* foregrounds this relation to the tradition: not only is *The Tempest,* with its questioning of human culture's impingement on nature, a perceptible presence, but the novel of which *Foe* is a rewriting, *Robinson Crusoe,* is probably Western culture's most potent crystallization of its concern with the survival of the individual, the fundamentals of civilized life, and the dialectic of master and servant.

This account of the canonic claim made by the novels themselves needs to be complemented by factors external to the writing that also bear on the question of canonization. As a white male (like Daniel Defoe), Coetzee has a degree of privileged access to most canons, and as a South African, especially one who has chosen to remain in South Africa, he possesses a certain mystique: that country, for all its geographical marginality to the canonization processes of Western culture, has a notorious centrality in the contemporary political and ethical imagination which gives its writers a special claim on the world's attention. There is, of course, another side to this advantage: namely, the danger that writing emanating from South Africa will be read *only* as a reflection of or a resistance to a particular political situation,[4] whereas the high literary canon, in its most traditional form, is premised upon an assumption of universal moral and aesthetic values. But Coetzee's works seem expressly designed to escape that danger: of his five novels, only two and a half are set in South Africa, and then it is a South Africa distanced, by temporal or geographical displacement, from the one we read about in the newspapers. An apologist for the traditional canon might argue that Coetzee's novels are not about the South African situation per se, which would render them contingent and propagandist, but about the permanent human truths exemplified in that situation.

Within South Africa, however, this departicularization opens Coetzee to the accusation that he has abused his privileges as a member of the white elite in addressing not the immediate needs of his time but a mystified human totality. If the account I have given of his work's amenability to canonization is accurate and complete, this critique must stand as valid. The unproblematized notion of a canon is complicit with a mode of literature—and of criticism—that dehistoricizes and dematerializes the acts of writing and reading while promoting a myth of transcendent human truths and values. By the same token, however, a mode of fiction that exposes the ideological basis of canonization, that draws attention to its own relation to the existing canon, that thematizes the role of race, class, and gender in the processes of cultural acceptance and exclusion, and that, while speaking from a marginal location, addresses the question of marginality—such a mode of fiction would have to be seen as engaged in an attempt to break the silence in which so many are caught, even if it does so by literary means that have traditionally been celebrated as characterizing canonic art. A more careful reading of Coetzee's novels, I shall argue, shows just these qualities.

Foe came as something of a disappointment to many readers and reviewers.[5] The previous novel, *Life & Times of Michael K,* allowed itself to be read as, to quote the paperback's blurb, a "life-affirming novel" that "goes to the center of human experience," seeming to confirm those elements in *Waiting for the Barbarians* that could be taken as expressions of a spiritual and moral truth beyond politics or culturally determined structures of signification. Moreover, *Michael K* satisfied those who wanted Coetzee to deal more directly with the struggle in South Africa today (it is set during a war in that country in the not too distant future), while avoiding the adoption of a narrowly based political position.[6] But *Foe* is not only further removed in time and place from present-day South Africa; it has no character whose interior life is depicted in such a way as to evoke the reader's moral sympathy (as the magistrate's and K's do in the previous novels), and it seems to lack evidence of what one reviewer called, in discussing *Michael K,* Coetzee's "tender and unwavering faith in the individual."[7]

Instead of taking *Foe* as a swerve away from a clear and established mode of fiction and set of values, it is worth asking whether it can provide a perspective from which to reexamine the earlier works and their pertinence to the canon and to contemporary political and cultural life. We may do this by returning to the qualities of Coetzee's writing that I mentioned earlier and scrutinizing more carefully the argument that they constitute a straightforward, if dangerously self-conscious, claim to canonic status.

Although the overt intertextuality in Coetzee's novels can be read as an implicit claim to a place in the established canon, it is also possible to regard it as drawing attention to the way the text, like any text, is *manufactured* from the resources of a particular culture in order to gain acceptance within that culture, an operation that canonic works, and those who uphold the canon as an unproblematic reflection of inherent values, cannot fully acknowledge. (The most powerful upholders of the canon are, of course, those who do not acknowledge such a concept at all.) In *Foe* this process becomes inescapably evident, as the larger part of the novel consists of a memoir and several letters written by the newly returned castaway Susan Barton to the well-known author Daniel Foe, quotation marks before each of her paragraphs reminding us continually that this is not the mysterious immaterial language most fiction uses as its medium, nor even a representation of speech, but a representation *in* writing *of* writing. And it is written not as a simple day-to-day record of experience, as in a novel of letters or diary entries, but for the explicit purpose of proffering a narrative—the story of Barton's year on an island with another, earlier castaway named Robinson Cruso—for insertion into the canon of published English texts. When, toward the end of the novel, the quotation marks disappear, the reader is forced to ask questions that fiction seldom invites: On what occasion and by what means are *these* words now being produced? And to what audience are they being directed?

The intertextuality of *Foe* also works to unsettle any simple relation between historical report and fictional invention. The Cruso we encounter in this novel appears as the historical original of the fictional Crusoe we already know from our access to the canon,[8] yet even within the novel he is part of Susan Barton's narrative, which is clearly to some extent—but how much, and how deliberately?—a work of fiction on her part. At the same time, Barton herself is troubled by the repeated appearance of a girl claiming to be her daughter, whose reality, within the fictional world, is thrown into question by the reader's awareness that her story, and that of her maid, Amy, who often accompanies her, is told in another of Defoe's novels, *Roxana.*[9] From this perspective, the quotations in *In the Heart of the Country* and the name "Michael K" seem less like somewhat intrusive claims to belong to a tradition of great writing than determined reminders—working against the skillfully contrived immediacy of the narrators' thoughts—that all cultural work is a reworking, that all representations achieve vividness by exploiting culturally specific conventions and contexts.

Turning to my second point, Coetzee's chiseled style can be seen not as a bid for admission to the pantheon of great writers but as drawing attention to itself in a way that undermines the illusion of pure expression; the slight self-consciousness of its shaped sentences—what one critic has aptly described as "that style forever on its guard against itself" (Strauss 128)—goes hand in hand with the intertextual allusiveness to reinforce the awareness that all representation is mediated through the discourses that culture provides. Certainly in *Foe* it is no longer possible to regard this quality of the writing as an inadvertent one, an inability to achieve total unself-conscious limpidity. Whereas in the earlier novels a reader might decide that the echoes of Beckett's style are an excusable failure to evade a powerful precursor rather than a calculated effect, the tinges of eighteenth-century diction that characterize the language of *Foe* cannot be anything other than a distancing device rendering us conscious of the artifact we have before us—a device that, remarkably, does not diminish the writing's capacity to produce for the reader a powerful experience of reality. Reading is usually a more complex process than we allow for in our theories of it, and one of the pleasures of reading Coetzee is realizing this—and realizing that this realization need not spoil our more traditional literary pleasures. (The fact that the narrative of Jacobus Coetzee in *Dusklands,* presented with all the trappings of hyperrealism, gives two successive and totally different versions of a man's death, or that *In the Heart of the Country* consists of 266 numbered paragraphs, many of which contradict one another, seems guaranteed to shatter any sense of immediacy in the first-person accounts they claim to be; yet many readers have testified that there is no loss of the traditional power of storytelling in these novels.)

Lastly, with regard to the thematic concerns of Coetzee's fictions, one finds that whatever accommodation was possible between the earlier novels and the humanist tradition, the isolated individuals in *Foe* function—as I hope to demonstrate—not as representatives of the motif of naked humanity granted universal insight on the stormy heath but as compelling subversions of this motif. They demonstrate that what we call "insights" are produced and conveyed by the narrativizing agencies of culture; experience in itself is insufficient to gain credit as knowledge or truth. Even if the transmutation of experience into knowledge occurs in the privacy of the individual consciousness, it does so by virtue of internalized cultural norms, of which each of us is a repository; and without external validation, such "knowledge" must remain uncertain and insubstantial.

Every writer who desires to be read (and that is perhaps part of what it means to write) has to seek admittance to the canon—or, more precisely, *a* canon, since any group approval of a text is an instance of canonization; like languages, canons are not monolithic entities but complex, interrelated, and constantly changing systems that can be subdivided all the way down to individual preferences—"idiocanons," we might call them. Awareness of this necessity, conscious or not, governs the act of writing quite as much as the need for self-expression or the wish to communicate. What *Foe* suggests is that the same imperative drives our self-presentations and representations; unless we are read, we are nothing. And taking together the features of this and the earlier novels I have discussed, it would seem that it is not possible to separate the processes of canonization that operate within the domain of high, or for that matter popular, culture from the very similar processes that operate in our everyday experience. Constructing and sustaining an identity, making sense of one's own past, establishing an intelligible relationship with one's fellows, are all in part a matter of telling one's story (the story of who one is, was, and aspires to be) in such a way as to have it accepted and valorized within the body of recognized narratives—with their conventions of plot, character, symbolization, moralization, and so on—that are part of the cultural fabric and therefore part of our individual systems of judgment and interpretation. Acceptance into the canon is not merely a matter of success in the marketplace; it also confers *value,* although the value it confers is necessarily understood as not conferred and contingent but inherent and permanent. What is unusual about *Foe* is the way it simultaneously seeks admittance to the literary canon on these terms *and* draws attention to the canon's cultural and historical contingency, just as Barton, in seeking cultural acceptance for her story and through it an assertion of her unique subjectivity, shows an increasing awareness of the double bind that this implies.

If we extend the meaning of "canonization" to include these wider processes of legitimation, it might be said that the novel dramatizes the procedures and problems of canonization four times over. Cruso, who shows none of the practical ingenuity or the spiritual intensity we expect from the figure of bourgeois resourcefulness with whom we are familiar, has, by his isolation from culture, lost touch with its founding narratives and its need for narrative. Not only has he rescued very little from the wreck and made only minimal attempts to improve the quality of his life, but he has kept no journal (he doesn't even notch the passing days on a stick) and has no desire to leave the island. He spends most of his time leveling the island's hill into terraces—a parodic version of the canonic castaway's taming of nature, since he has nothing with which to plant them. Most interesting for my argument is that he appears to have lost any firm sense of the distinction between truth and fiction. Barton writes to Foe: " 'I would gladly now recount to you the history of this singular Cruso, as I heard it from his own lips. But the stories he told me were so various, and so hard to reconcile one with another, that I was more and more driven to conclude age and isolation had taken their toll on his memory, and he no longer knew for sure what was truth, what fancy' " (11–12). To her exhortation to Cruso to write a narrative of his experiences he makes two replies: " ' "Nothing is forgotten" ' " and " ' "Nothing I have forgotten is worth the remembering" ' " (17).

Barton herself, by contrast, feels that she lacks substance as an individual until the story of her year on the island with Cruso (who dies on the return journey) is written as a legitimated narrative yet she is barred from the domain of authorship by her gender, her social status, her economic dependence, and her unfamiliarity with the requirements of published narratives. It is not merely that publication of her story will bring fame and money; she has an obscure sense that her experience will remain lacking in reality until it is told as a publicly validated narrative:

> "Return to me the substance I have lost, Mr. Foe: that is my entreaty. For though my story gives the truth, it does not give the substance of the truth (I see that clearly, we need not pretend it is otherwise). To tell the truth in all its substance you must have quiet, and a comfortable chair away from all distraction, and a window to stare through; and then the knack of seeing waves when there are fields before your eyes, and of feeling the tropic sun when it is cold; and at your fingertips the words with which to capture the vision before it fades. I have none of these, while you have all." (51–52)

When Foe goes into hiding from his creditors, she waits for his return, reminding him that " 'my life is drearily suspended till your writing is done' " (63), and later takes up residence in his empty house. But the longer she waits, the more conscious she becomes that to depend for her identity on a process of writing is to cast doubt on that identity: " 'In the beginning I thought I would tell you the story of the island and, being done with that, return to my former life. But now all my life grows to be story and there is nothing of my own left to me' " (133). (One curious, but relevant, effect of Coetzee's strategy is that, for all the vivid first-person writing, Susan Barton does have an aura of insubstantiality, precisely because of the canonic success and consequent power of Defoe's novel.)

Foe, the professional author, makes little progress with Barton's story of her experiences on the island; he thinks of including it as one episode in the longer story of a woman in search of her daughter, or spicing it with additional material about cannibals and battles. She insists that he should concentrate exclusively on the story of the island, although she becomes increasingly aware of its unsuitability for the established canon: " 'I am growing to understand why you wanted Cruso to have a musket and be besieged by cannibals. I thought it was a sign you had no regard for the truth. I forgot you are a writer who knows above all how many words can be sucked from a cannibal feast, how few from a woman cowering from the wind. It is all a matter of words and the number of words, is it not?' " (94).

To assess how much rewriting Barton's story of the island requires to render it fit for the developing bourgeois canon of the early eighteenth century we need only turn from Coetzee's novel to the novel published in 1719 as *The Life and Adventures of Robinson Crusoe* by Daniel Defoe, the more aristocratic name adopted by plain Daniel Foe in 1695 as part of *his* assault on the British canon.[10] One of the striking absences from Defoe's highly successful novel, of course, is that of any female voice: the gender requirements of acceptable narrative forms allow for women heroines in certain roles (the entrepreneur in larceny and marriage exemplified by *Moll Flanders,* for instance), but these appear not to include stories of the mastering of natural forces and the colonizing of primitive cultures.[11] Within Coetzee's novel, Foe's decision to exclude Susan Barton from his published narrative is not represented; but we do witness how the professional author is much more attracted to Barton's own story before and after the period on the island, involving her lost daughter, and, we are encouraged to suspect from several hints thrown out, the colorful life of a courtesan. In other words, Barton's story—the one she does not want told—becomes Defoe's novel *Roxana.*[12]

It would be misleading to suggest that the novel uses a range of characters to lay out neatly a number of different attitudes to canonic narrative, for the novel is itself a narrative that offers strong resistance to the masterful reader or critic, frequently becoming opaque just when a systematic or allegorical meaning seems to be emerging. It may be possible, however, to think of Cruso and Foe as opposites, one who no longer has any use for narrative and the other who lives for, and through, narrative. Susan Barton, who, for all we are allowed to know, might be the author of the narratives of both Cruso and Foe, is aware of the constituting capacities of narrative and the emptiness of existence outside her culture's canonic stories, yet at the same time she is irresistibly (and understandably) attached to the notion of a subjectivity and a substantiality that do not have to be grounded in the conventions of narrative. She explains to Foe why she pursues him, instead of finding employment:

> "I could return in every respect to the life of a substantial body, the life you recommend. But such a life is abject. It is the life of a thing. A whore used by men is used as a substantial body. The waves picked me up and cast me ashore on an island, and a year later the same waves brought a ship to rescue me, and of the true story of that year, the story as it should be seen in God's great scheme of things, I remain as ignorant as a newborn babe. That is why I cannot rest, that is why I follow you to your hiding-place like a bad penny." (125–26)

Yet Barton attempts to resist, as she must, what is implied by this self-perception: that her story is determined not by herself but by the culture within which she seeks an identity. Thus, in refusing to tell Foe of her life before the shipwreck, she insists: " 'I choose not to tell it because to no one, not even to you, do I owe proof that I am a substantial being with a substantial history in the world. I choose rather to tell of the island, of myself and Cruso and Friday and what we three did there: for I am a free woman who asserts her freedom by telling her story according to her own desire' " (131).

At the end of her long debate with Foe, however, Barton appears to move toward his position: that there are no distinctions to be made between characters invented by an author and individuals with an independent reality. In answer to Foe's question about the substantiality of the girl claiming to be her daughter, the girl from the pages of *Roxana,* Barton concedes: " 'No, she is substantial, as my daughter is substantial, and I am substantial; and you too are substantial, no less and no more than any of us. We are all alive, we are all substantial, we are all in the same world' " (152). (For us, of course, that world is the world of Coetzee's novel.)

Foe might be read, then, as an exploration of a fact that is central to the processes of canonization, in the narrower as much as in the wider sense that I am giving it: human experience seems lacking in substance and significance if it is not represented (to oneself and to others) in culturally validated narrative forms, but those narrative forms constantly threaten, by their exteriority and conventionality, the substantiality of that experience. A similar concern could be traced in the earlier novels—in the different written versions of Jacobus Coetzee's journey beyond the Great River, for instance, or in the alternative stories Magda tells herself in *In the Heart of the Country,* or in the medical officer's attempts to get a story out of the man he calls "Michaels" in *Michael K.* One could thus base these novels' claim to canonic literary status in part on their critique of the traditional unproblematized notion of the canon, showing it to be the reflection of a transcendental humanism oblivious to the role of cultural production and historical materiality. This would suggest one of the ways in which these novels challenge the structures of apartheid, a political and social system whose founding narratives claim to reflect a prior and "natural" truth of racial superiority.

But Barton's reluctant conclusion that "we are all substantial, we are all in the same world" may be too hasty; and it is perhaps significant that it is Foe, the author, who raises the possibility of an exception to this generalization: " 'You have omitted Friday.' " The presence of this fourth major figure in the novel adds to, and considerably complicates, the account of Coetzee's fiction I have just given; it also constitutes the greatest risk Coetzee takes in the artistic and political project upon which he is engaged. One could say that the inner significance of Susan Barton's experience on the island, which she senses but cannot write down, and which she hopes (fruitlessly) will emerge when Foe's retelling achieves canonization, is most fully embodied neither in her story nor in Cruso's but in Friday's. Throughout the novel, Friday is presented not in his own terms—we have no sense of what they might be—but as he exists in relation to Susan Barton. Her memoir opens with his appearance to her on the shore of the island and his carrying her to Cruso's encampment in a " 'strange backwards embrace' " (6), and the narrative of her letters ends with a comparison of her importance to him with that of an unwanted child to a mother who has nevertheless reared it: " 'I do not love him, but he is mine. That is why he remains in England. That is why he is here' " (111).

Friday is a being wholly unfamiliar to her, in terms of race, class, gender, culture. He may be a cannibal. But Friday's story will never be known: he has had his tongue cut out and cannot even tell the story of the mutilation.[13] His silence, his absolute otherness to her and to her words, is at the heart of Barton's story, both motivating and circumscribing it: " 'On the island I accepted that I should never learn how Friday lost his tongue. . . . But what we can accept in life we cannot accept in history. To tell my story and be silent on Friday's tongue is no better than offering a book for sale with pages in it quietly left empty. Yet the only tongue that can tell Friday's secret is the tongue he has lost!' " (67). Later she tells Foe, " 'if the story seems stupid, that is only because it so doggedly holds its silence. The shadow whose lack you feel is there: it is the loss of Friday's tongue' " (117).

To put this experience of absolute otherness into words—at least any of the words Barton has been granted by her cultural experience—would be to reappropriate it within the familiar and to lose exactly that which makes it other, and therefore of the greatest possible significance, to her. She articulates this process of appropriation in her debate with Foe:

> "Friday has no command of words and therefore no defence against being re-shaped day by day in conformity with the desires of others. I say he is a cannibal and he becomes a cannibal; I say he is a laundryman and he becomes a laundryman. What is the truth of Friday? You will respond: he is neither cannibal nor laundryman, these are mere names, they do not touch his essence, he is a substantial body, he is himself, Friday is Friday. But that is not so. No matter what he is to himself (is he anything to himself?—how can he tell us?), what he is to the world is what I make him." (121–22)

Barton has, by this stage in the novel, made strenuous but unsuccessful attempts to teach Friday a language in which he might tell something of his story; even music proves to be a medium in which nothing approaching communication between the two can occur. Unlike her own silence about her experiences before the island, Friday's silence, Barton insists in this discussion with Foe, is not a concealment. (The same could be said of her silence about Friday's silence—which is also Coetzee's silence.) Yet its powerful *effects* are everywhere. Barton tells Foe: " 'when I lived in your house I would sometimes lie awake upstairs listening to the pulse of blood in my ears and to the silence from Friday below, a silence that rose up the stairway like smoke, like a welling of black smoke. Before long I could not breathe, I would feel I was stifling in my bed. My lungs, my heart, my head were full of black smoke' " (118).

In Foe's view, Friday's silence is simply a riddle that must be solved: " 'In every story there is a silence, some sight concealed, some word unspoken, I believe. Till we have spoken the unspoken we have not come to the heart of the story' " (141). He allegorizes this depth to be plumbed by means of an imaginative interpretation of Friday's mysterious act of paddling out on a log and dropping petals on the surface of the sea, an allegory that Barton takes up and revises, concluding: " 'It is for us to descend into the mouth (since we speak in figures). It is for us to open Friday's mouth and hear what it holds: silence, perhaps, or a roar, like the roar of a seashell held to the ear' " (142). For her, there can be no assurance that all silences will eventually be made to resound with the words of the dominant language and to tell their stories in canonized narratives—not because there is an inviolable core of silence to which the dominant discourse can never penetrate, but because the most fundamental silence is itself produced by—at the same time as it makes possible—the dominant discourse. The wordless stream that closes the novel runs to the ends of the earth, in a moment of loss that is also salvation.

Foe's most telling challenge to the literary canon is therefore not its insistence upon cultural construction and validation (an insistence to which we have become accustomed in postmodern writing) but its representation, through this most powerful of nonrepresentations, of the silence that is constitutive of canonicity itself. All canons rest on exclusion; the voice they give to some can be heard only by virtue of the silence they impose on others. But it is not just a silencing by exclusion; it is a silencing by inclusion as well: any voice we can hear is by that very fact purged of its uniqueness and alterity. Who is Friday's foe, who has cut out his tongue and made it impossible for his story to be heard? Is it perhaps Foe, the writer, the one who tells people's stories, whatever their race, gender, class, and who in writing, rewrites, driving into deeper and deeper silence that which his discourse necessarily excludes? Barton speculates near the end of the novel about Foe's efforts as an author: "But might the truth not be instead that he had laboured all these months to move a rock so heavy no man alive could budge it; that the pages I saw issuing from his pen were not idle tales of courtesans and grenadiers, as I supposed, but the same story over and over, in version after version, stillborn every time: the story of the island, as lifeless from his hand as from mine?" (151).

Yet it is important to remember that only from the point of view of his oppressors (however well meaning) does Friday figure as an absolute absence. Included among those oppressors are Coetzee and the reader, and hence it is only by indirection that the substantiality of Friday's own world (in which he is not, of course, "Friday"—perhaps not even "he") can be suggested. One example is the uninterpretable (though repeatedly interpreted) act of strewing petals on the sea's surface; another is the equally uninterpretable series of marks Friday makes on the slate when Barton tries to teach him—at Foe's bidding—to write. There is also the extraordinary final section, in which an unidentified first-person narrator makes two visits to Foe's hideaway, the second in our own time, since the house bears a blue-and-white plaque inscribed *Daniel Defoe, Author.* In the house are the bodies of Foe, Barton, the girl who claimed to be Barton's daughter, and Friday, but on both occasions it is Friday who commands attention. On the second occasion the narrative blends into Susan Barton's own story of the island, as we have heard it more than once, but the now multiple "I" achieves what neither Barton nor Foe had been able to achieve: the descent into the sunken wreck, "the home of Friday," which "is not a place of words" but "a place where bodies are their own signs," and the sight of the dark mouth opening to emit its wordless, endless stream.[14]

This moment answers to the moment when Jacobus Coetzee, in the second part of *Dusklands,* uses the words of Blake (whom, for reasons of chronology, he cannot have read) to speculate on the unknowability of the South African people he has moved among: "I am an explorer. My essence is to open what is closed, to bring light to what is dark. If the Hottentots comprise an immense world of delight, it is an impenetrable world, impenetrable to men like me, who must either skirt it, which is to evade our mission, or clear it out of the way" (106).[15] It answers (without answering) Magda's repeated questions in *In the Heart of the Country* about the others she cannot know, her father and her servants (and the other that is herself);[16] and it answers the questions the magistrate in *Waiting for the Barbarian* constantly asks the barbarian girl (" 'What do I have to do to move you?' . . . 'Does no one move you?' " [44]). It provides a reply, of a kind, to the despairing insistence of the medical officer in *Michael K*—the only novel in which Coetzee attempts at length an inner view of a character who remains opaque to those around him—trying, unsuccessfully, to get K to open his mouth, both to eat and to tell his story: "You are going to die, and your story is going to die too, for ever and ever, unless you come to your senses and listen to me. . . . no one is going to remember you but I, unless you yield and at last open your mouth. I appeal to you, Michaels: *yield!*" (207–8). (K, however, comes to think of himself as a mole, "that does not tell stories because it lives in silence" [248].)

It is a necessary property of any canon that it depends on what it excludes, and since culture as we understand it could not exist without canonic processes at all levels of its functioning—including, as we have seen, the constitution of individual subjectivity—there is no question of eradicating this source of exclusion. To be made aware of it, however, is to be reminded of the violence always implied in canonization, in the construction of cultural narratives, in the granting of a voice to one individual or one group, necessary and productive as that process is. In enforcing this awareness, Coetzee's fictions engage directly with the contemporary struggle in South Africa, doing so not primarily as political argument, vivid reportage, or moral allegory but as an exploitation of the traditions and potencies of the novel understood as a central form in Western culture. *Foe,* in particular, focuses on what might be considered the most fundamental narrative of bourgeois culture not only to examine the processes of canonization and legitimation implicit in it and in its popular success but also to bring forcefully to its readers' attention the silences that those processes generate and upon which they depend: in particular, a gender silence and a race silence.[17] At the same time, the novel refuses to endorse any simple call for the granting of a voice within the existing sociocultural discourses; such a gesture would leave the silencing mechanisms, and their repressive human effects, untouched.[18] Njabulo Ndebele speaks for black South Africans in these terms: "there have been diverse cultural interests to whom the challenge of the future has involved the need to open up cultural and educational centers to all races. Missing in these admirable acts of goodwill is an accompanying need to alter fundamentally the nature of cultural practice itself. It is almost always assumed that, upon being admitted, the oppressed will certainly like what they find" (223–24).

Coetzee's fiction, as I read it, brings out both the necessity and the difficulty of the process of genuine structural change in a society like South Africa's. Just as canonization inevitably involves, as a condition of the audibility of the canon, a continuous act of silencing, so political, cultural, and material domination of a social group produces, as far as the ears of the dominant class can determine, an impenetrable silence that is at the same time a necessary condition of the latter's power (and therefore a constant threat to it). Friday's tonguelessness is the sign of his oppression; it is also the sign of the silence, the absolute otherness, by which he appears to his oppressors and by which their oppression is sustained. Foe observes to Barton: " 'We deplore the barbarism of whoever maimed him, yet have we, his later masters, not reason to be secretly grateful? For as long as he is dumb we can tell ourselves his desires are dark to us, and continue to use him as we wish' " (148). What Foe is less conscious of is the cost of this inheritance of mastery, a cost of which Barton—herself subject to the logic of exclusion and silencing—is acutely aware.

For those who find themselves unwillingly in the dominant group—and Coetzee, like most of his readers, finds himself determined in advance as a member—there is no simple remedy to be understood in terms of investing Friday with speech. If he could have his tongue restored to him, he would melt into a class that is already constituted and socially placed by a pervasive discourse (Foe suggests that, even without the faculty of speech, Friday might join one of London's strolling Negro bands). Insofar as the oppressed *are* heard, it is as a marginalized dialect within the dominant language. Even those who speak against oppression from the position of the oppressed have to conform to the dominant language in order to be heard in the places where power is concentrated, as Susan Barton discovers. Effective social and political change, then, is not merely the granting or the seizing of a voice (and the power that goes with it) by one or another predetermined group; it also entails work on the part of members of both oppressed and oppressing groups to create breaks in the totalizing discourses that produce and reify that grouping itself. The burden of this work necessarily falls on the oppressed, who will themselves produce the discursive transformation that will allow them to be heard (as part of the process of effecting the material shift of power to which any lasting discursive shift is tied). But the members of the oppressing group who seek to secure change have a role, too; not Foe's project of teaching Friday to write the master discourse with which the main part of the novel ends (though there are indications—which could never, for us, be wholly legible— that Friday is in fact *subverting* the master discourse with his undecidable graphics), but Coetzee's project of representing the processes of authorship, empowerment, validation, and silencing in a narrative that is constantly aware of the problems inherent in its own acts of representation.

I observed earlier that the settings of Coetzee's novels render them less likely to be read as concerned exclusively with the South African struggle and that they may run the opposite risk of being taken as having little specifically to do with that struggle. There is clearly some significance in the fact that Friday is a black African in *Foe,* unlike Defoe's tawny-skinned creation, just as there is in the fact that the people who remain outside Jacobus Coetzee's or Magda's comprehension are South Africans excluded from white privileges. Nevertheless, the barbarians in *Waiting for the Barbarians* cannot be identified so clearly; they function as a less specifically historicized representation of otherness, upon whose necessary exclusion from its narratives, and occasionally from its physical spaces and economic resources, the civilization of the Empire depends. This absence of precise historical and geographical grounding is a necessary feature of Coetzee's fiction, I would argue, since the novels are addressed as much to those outside South Africa as to those within it (indeed, to be white and to write oppositional fiction in English is to restrict one's readership inside the country, making access to an international canon of peculiar importance[19]).

There are two relatively easy responses by outsiders to the issue of racial oppression in South Africa that Coetzee's writing inhibits: first, that what is at stake is a battle of universal human principles, a version of similar battles in every society and every period, another manifestation of the tragic complexity of the human condition[20]; and second, that the conflict is entirely a local matter of a particular history and a particular set of problems in need of urgent resolution by those on the spot. What Coetzee's novels work to suggest instead—and again, this is a task that falls peculiarly on the shoulders of the white South African writer in English—is that the South African struggle is *part* of a wider, and entirely concrete, struggle, that it has a particular history continuous with the particular histories of all other countries participating in the rise of Western capitalism and the ideology on which it depends, and that one requirement in moving toward a resolution of the struggle (one of many, but one in which works of art might have a special role) is an understanding of the ways in which the cultural formations we have inherited through those histories are, for all their indisputable value, complicit with the daily barbarities that occur in South Africa.

Turning back to the question of Coetzee's novels and the literary canon, the question that presses itself is this: can these works gain admittance to the canon without being in their turn reread (and thus rewritten) as stories—as the same story—of essential humanity and transcendent values, their textuality disguised, their otherness expunged, their political implications silenced? The novels themselves appear to give a negative answer, for the work of art is clearly in the same powerless situation as characters like the barbarian girl, K, or Friday: it is the subject of stories (both before and after it appears), and only through stories—commentaries, criticism, discussion, internal reflection—does it have meaning and value for us.[21] But anything like a "full" understanding of it would require an apprehension of what remains uncaptured in the critical and interpretive discourse by means of which we represent it to ourselves and others. It is important to recognize, however, that this is in no sense a mystical or Romantic notion; Coetzee's novels do not represent a yearning for some realm of richness and plenitude beyond language, a meaningfulness behind the emptiness of our conscious lives. They attempt strenuously to avoid both terms of the colonizer's contradiction I mentioned earlier (see note 15): that the other is wholly knowable, and that the other is wholly mysterious; that the other has no boundaries, and that the boundaries of the other are impenetrable.[22]

If Coetzee's novels do gain admittance to the canon, then, it will become increasingly difficult to read them *against* the canon, since their uniqueness will be dissolved by the ideologically determined voice that the canon grants; if they do not gain admittance, it will become increasingly difficult to read them at all, since the only voice available to them is the voice granted by one canon or another. This, we have seen, is the double bind dramatized in *Foe* at the level of the individual and inherent in any attempt to combat political and cultural repression. If I may end with a utopian thought, however, it would be that the canonization—however partial and uneven—of Coetzee's novels, along with other texts (fictional and otherwise) that question the very processes of canonicity itself, will slowly transform the ideology and the institutions from which the canon derives its power, so that new and presently unimaginable ways of finding a voice, and new ways of hearing such voices, will come into being. Instead of canons premised upon a notion of transcendental and inscrutable value, we can hope for cultural practices and formations that encourage an awareness of the historical production of value, of the part played by axiological systems in political domination and exclusion, of the necessarily provisional and historically contestable nature of any arrangement that allows some to speak and in that gesture renders others—and a part of themselves—silent. This project is a small component of a much greater struggle, currently taking a particularly violent form in South Africa, to fashion cultural and political structures and procedures that will allow us not just to hear each other's stories, as the liberal humanist dreams would have it, but to hear—and this will entail a different mode of hearing—each other's silences.

Notes

I would like to acknowledge the valuable contribution made to the revision of this essay by audiences at the Universities of Southampton, Leeds, and Toronto, to whom it was given as a paper. It was completed in 1988 and revised in 1989; it therefore takes no account of the political events in South Africa since February 1990, nor of J. M. Coetzee's latest novel, *Age of Iron* (London: Seckert & Warburg, 1990).

1. William Shakespeare, *The Tempest,* act I, scene i, lines 52, 56–57; scene ii, lines 176, 399–400. One could extend the verbal similarities to other parts of these two scenes, such as Miranda's reference to the "words" that Caliban has learned (I.ii.360), Ariel's promise to obey Prospero "to th' syllable" (I.ii.503), or even—by implication—Prospero's phrase "the fringed curtains of thine eye" (I.ii.411); but this would probably be more a product of conscious critical labor than an intertextual effect to which readers may respond without even being aware of it. As will emerge in the course of this essay, *The Tempest*'s status as one of the founding texts of English colonialism is also highly relevant to Coetzee's novel.

2. In an interview with Claude Wauthier in *Le Nouvel Observateur* (28 June–4 July 1985: 69), Coetzee comments on the fact that *Waiting for the Barbarians* and *Michael K* were not subject to the banning that works of black writers in particular have suffered but were held up by Customs delays. He goes on to observe that there are more subtle modes of pressure, such as the total overlooking by South African radio and television of writers hostile to apartheid.

3. One reviewer, at least, complained about the intrusiveness of these allusions: Christopher Lehmann-Haupt, in the *New York Times* (6 Dec. 1983: C22), noted the novel's "heavy debt to Franz Kafka," including the use of "K," the reference to the central military headquarters as "the Castle" (though anyone who has visited Cape Town knows that this is a real enough building, with just this significance), the frequent comparison of K to insects, and K's role as a hunger-artist. Lehmann-Haupt comments: "These are doubtless meant to be tributes to a master as much as borrowings from him, but they are overdone and call an unnecessary amount of attention to themselves."

4. Asked during an interview by Tony Morphet (*TriQuarterly* 69 [Spring/Summer 1987]: 454–60), apropos of *Michael K,* "Did you conceive of the novel as in any way a task presented to you by history—the history of South Africa specifically?" Coetzee replied: "Perhaps that is my fate. On the other hand, I sometimes wonder whether it isn't simply that vast and wholly ideological superstructure constituted by publishing, reviewing and criticism that is forcing on me the fate of being a 'South African novelist' " (460).

5. George Parker asserted in *The Nation* (28 Mar. 1987: 402–5) that *Foe* was a "wrong, if interesting step" in a novel-writing career concerned with "the fate of conscience in the face of its own oppressive power" while Nina Auerbach, writing in *The New Republic* (9 Mar. 1987: 36–38), complained that *Foe* "never quite

comes to life." In South Africa, the hostility was, if anything, more marked: Neil Darke of the *Cape Argus* (23 Oct. 1986) found the novel "often pointless, incomprehensible and tiresome," and one G.H., in *The Natal Mercury* (27 Nov. 1986), called it "a literary indulgence likely to prove too oblique for any but the converted to contend with, and to estrange even some of these."

6. The role of South African politics in the novel is far from simple: the opposing forces in the war are never identified, and there are no overt mentions of racial conflict. In fact, all indications of the race of the major characters are scrupulously avoided—one reason for the unspecific "K" and the namelessness of the medical officer who narrates part of the novel. Coetzee's "realistic" approach can leave out details just as purposefully as it can include them. Up to a point, this omission might be recuperable within realism by reading it as a sign of the irrelevance of race (for differing reasons) to the consciousnesses that dominate the novel, those of K and the medical officer; but the lack of even incidental references from which the reader might deduce racial types testifies to a willed exclusion. Race is revealed as the cultural-political construct that it is by the pressure it exerts, as an absence, upon the reader.

7. This quotation from Alan Ryan of the *Cleveland Plain Dealer* is used on the jacket of the 1987 Viking edition of *Foe*.

8. The spelling "Cruso" is that used by the Norwich family in the hosiery business that was Defoe's most likely source for his hero's name (see Bastian 90). Alexander Selkirk has no place in Coetzee's narrative, though Barton does speculate on Foe's possession of " 'a multitude of castaway narratives, most of them, I would guess, riddled with lies' " (50).

9. The hero of Defoe's *Colonel Jack* also makes an appearance in Coetzee's novel as the young pickpocket employed by Foe. Clearly, "the reader" alluded to here is one well-versed in Defoe's fiction: Coetzee exploits the canon's lack of definite boundaries by using allusions that range from the familiar to the scholarly. The novel does not depend upon the recognition of all its allusions by a single reader, however.

10. The events of *Foe* are not securely located at an identifiable moment in Defoe's life. It is likely that the historical author went into hiding from his creditors for a period in 1692, but Susan Barton has read *A True Relation of the Apparition of One Mrs. Veal* (written, she says, "long ago" [134]), Defoe's vivid report of the appearance of a ghost to a Canterbury woman in September 1705, which he published soon after the event. He was still trying to satisfy his creditors in 1706, and when he left for Scotland on a secret mission for Harley's ministry in that year, he allowed a story to circulate that he was fleeing because of debts (see Moore 97). However, *Robinson Crusoe* (his first substantial work of fiction—received by many as a factual report) was not published until 1719. Moreover, in imagining the papers that lie in Foe's chest, Barton describes materials on which a number of Defoe's works after *Robinson Crusoe* were based (including *The Dumb Philosopher,* about one Dickory Cronke, also published in 1719) (50), and she

mentions on more than one occasion the tales of thieves, courtesans, and grenadiers he has worked on. One effect of this chronological uncertainty, germane to
the novel's concerns, is that it remains unclear whether Foe's reputation is as a
reporter of fact or, as was the case later in Defoe's career, a creator of fiction.

11. I do not mean to suggest that the properties of texts accepted by the canon
are wholly determined in advance. Defoe is a good example of a writer whose
work, while it clearly answered to a growing need arising from changing economic and social conditions, played its own part, once it was admitted, in
transforming the literary canon. Some degree of resistance to canonic demands
can itself be a canonic requirement: I have already suggested that a possible
disability of Coetzee's novels as far as the canon is concerned is that they may
appear to conform too obviously to its requirements.

12. Roxana's real name is mentioned once in that novel: it is Susan, which is
also the name of the daughter who haunts her and who is murdered by her maid
Amy (205). (No surname is given for either of the Susans.) The daughter in *Foe*
says that her name is also Susan Barton, and her account of her mother's
desertion by a husband who was a brewer (76) tallies with the events of *Roxana*.

13. To be strictly accurate, our only reason for believing that Friday has been
mutilated is Barton's report of Cruso's statement to this effect; she herself has no
evidence of the cause of Friday's speechlessness, as she finds herself unable to
look into his mouth (85). This is of some importance to any allegorical reading of
the novel—an inevitable though problematic response to it—since it prevents any
simple assumptions about the *cause* of Friday's silence and thus provides a more
complex image of limited access to language than Michael K's harelip. It might be
thought of as connecting the *generalized* otherness produced by all representation
with the *specific* otherness produced by historical acts of oppression. The challenge of the novel is to acknowledge the former without weakening awareness of
the latter.

14. The narrator(s) of this final section is/are not invested with any greater
authority than earlier speakers in the novel; if anything, the uncertainties of
interpretation are increased by the sense of historical distance. We have already
noted that the final passage functions as a palimpsest of major documents of
Western culture, and we might add the affinities between the account of the
"home of Friday" and Montaigne's treatment of the body and language of the savage
in "Des Cannibales." See also the discussion of Montaigne's essay, and of the
place of the other in travel writing, by Michel de Certeau.

15. Jacobus Coetzee is not just an explorer but a writer, too, and much of his
writing is as destructive of the other as is his gun; it evinces the characteristically
self-contradictory claim of the colonizer, both to know everything that needs to be
known about the other and to find the other a wholly mysterious and unassimilable
entity. (On both counts the other—upon whom the colonizer in fact depends—is
regarded as dispensable.)

16. Part of Magda's anxiety concerns her sexual encounters with the servant

Hendrik, and there is much that could be said about the role of sexuality in Coetzee's novels. It usually remains resistant to the conventional narratives of eroticism or love; Magda's nightly dissatisfaction (she cannot, of course, know if there is satisfaction for Hendrik) finds an echo in the prostitute's masturbation of K and in Susan Barton's coupling with Cruso, which constitute moments of irreducibility in all these novels. Even Barton's sexual riding of Foe, which is given some narrative figuration, serves as a self-conscious allegory of the visitation of the Muse. And what in another novel might be a climactic revelation, Barton's description of Friday's robes flying up as he dances (119–20), finds no adequate language to state whether his genitals, like his tongue, have been mutilated.

17. Since my particular interest here is in Coetzee as a South African writer, I am focusing on the question of race rather than the question of gender, but I am conscious that this is to do less than justice to the novel. A longer discussion would consider the differences between the treatments of the two exclusions in *Foe,* as well as the connections that link them. (One would want to consider, for instance, the relationship between Friday's mutilation and that of female victims such as Philomela and Lavinia.) And this discussion could lead to other exclusions, such as those of class, religion, nationality. See also Gayatri Spivak's study of *Foe.*

18. See Jacques Derrida's demanding scrutiny of the question of the other (of philosophy, of politics, of literature) in "Psyche" (55–56, 59–62). For Derrida, to avoid programming the other into a version of the same, "one does not make the other come, one lets it come by preparing for its coming" (60); and this means preparing for its arrival by opening up and destabilizing the existing structures of foreclosure. The relevance of Derrida's discussion to Coetzee's fictional project would be clear even without the footnote that observes: "Racism is also an invention of the other, but in order to exclude it and tighten the circle of the same" (63).

19. To write "modernist" fiction is to limit one's audience further, of course. Lazarus argues interestingly that, since the modernist text resists reductive appropriation by the dominant discourse, "the relative underestimation, within South Africa itself, of the work of Gordimer and Coetzee ought to be taken as an index of the oppositional cogency of this work, and not, as it is usually taken, as an index of its irrelevance" (136).

20. This might be a significant difference between Coetzee and two of his most potent precursors, Kafka and Beckett: Coetzee's fiction is so directly concerned with the economic and political fabric of cultural existence that it is more difficult to derive from it general statements about the human predicament. There are moments, however, when the inadequacy of representation being dramatized appears to be not so much the inadequacy of a particular set of available discourses but that of language itself; notably, when the body feels or acts in ways that exceed or escape any possible conceptualization—as, for instance, in the magistrate's obscure physical desires in *Waiting for the Barbarians* or K's body's refusal to eat the food of the camps in *Michael K.* But this does not diminish the

importance of the more specific questions relating to the cultural validation of certain discourses at the expense of others, and of the price to be paid for cultural acceptance.

21. The most compelling (and therefore most occulting) of these stories are often those told by the authors themselves. It is notable that Coetzee observes a scrupulous reserve in relation to his texts, as is evident in his interviews with Morphet. For instance, in response to the question, "Friday has no tongue. Why?" Coetzee says, "Nobody seems to have sufficient authority to say for sure how it is that Friday has no tongue" (*TriQuarterly* 69 [Spring/Summer 1987]: 462). And later Coetzee remarks: "Your questions again and again drive me into a position I do not want to occupy. (But what legitimacy has that 'want'?) By accepting your implication, I would produce a master narrative for a set of texts that claim to deny all master narratives" (464). In *Foe,* Susan Barton discovers the simultaneous impossibility and necessity of metanarrative commentary: " ' "Alas, my stories seem always to have more applications than I intend, so that I must go back and laboriously extract the right application and apologize for the wrong ones and efface them" ' " (81).

22. Tournier's *Vendredi,* another modern rewriting of Defoe's novel that is in productive triangulation with Coetzee's work, offers a very different view of the other of colonialism: although in both reworkings the black servant represents a consciousness radically alien to the Western mind he serves, this otherness in Tournier's work is more easily assimilated to a Eurocentric primitivistic myth. Tournier's novel surfaces elsewhere—and is perhaps gently mocked—in Coetzee's oeuvre: Jacobus Coetzee, alone in the veld, tries to imitate the earth-fecundation of Tournier's Crusoe: "I bored a sheath in the earth and would have performed the ur-act had joy and laughter not reduced me to a four-inch dangle and helpless urination" (95).

23. After I completed this essay, Coetzee's *White Writing* was published. It contains a passage of tentative and self-critical speculation on reading as the hearing of silence, a passage in which there surfaces again the mistrust of an aesthetic (and ethic) that claims too easily to offer a voice to the voiceless, together with a utopian thought that may be a version of my own:

> Our ears today are finely attuned to modes of silence. We have been brought up on the music of Webern: substantial silence structured by tracings of sound. Our craft is all in reading *the other:* gaps, inverses, undersides; the veiled; the dark, the buried, the feminine; alterities. To a pastoral novel like *The Beadle* [by Pauline Smith] we give an antipastoral reading like the present one, alert to the spaces in the text. . . . Only part of the truth, such a reading asserts, resides in what writing says of the hitherto unsaid; for the rest, its truth lies in what it dare not say for the sake of its own safety, or in what it does not know about itself: in its silences. It is a mode of reading which, subverting the dominant, is in peril, like all triumphant subversion, of becoming the dominant in turn.

Is it a version of utopianism (or pastoralism) to look forward (or backward) to the day when the truth will be (or was) what is said, not what is not said, when we will hear (or heard) music as sound upon silence, not silence between sounds? (81)

Works Cited

Bastian, F. *Defoe's Early Life.* London: Macmillan, 1981.

Cavafy, C. P. "Waiting for the Barbarians." *Collected Poems.* Trans. Edmund Keeley and Philip Sherrard, ed. George Savidis. London: Hogarth Press. 1975, 30–33.

Certeau, Michel de. "Montaigne's 'Of Cannibals': The Savage 'I'." *Heterologies: Discourse on the Other.* Minneapolis: University of Minnesota Press, 1986, 67–79.

Coetzee, J. M. *Dusklands.* London: Secker & Warburg, 1982. (First published in South Africa by Ravan Press, 1974.)

——. *Foe.* London: Secker & Warburg, 1986.

——. *In the Heart of the Country.* London: Secker & Warburg, 1977.

——. *Life & Times of Michael K.* London: Secker & Warburg, 1983.

——. *Waiting for the Barbarians.* London: Secker & Warburg, 1980.

——. *White Writing: On the Culture of Letters in South Africa.* New Haven: Yale University Press, 1988.

Defoe, Daniel. *The Life and Adventures of Robinson Crusoe.* 1719. Ed. Angus Ross. Harmondsworth: Penguin Books, 1965.

——. *Roxana; or, The Fortunate Mistress.* Ed. Jane Jack. 1724. London: Oxford University Press, 1964.

Derrida, Jacques. "Living On/Borderlines." In *Deconstruction and Criticism.* Ed. Harold Bloom et al. London: Routledge, 1979, 75–175.

——. "Psyche: Inventions of the Other." In *Reading de Man Reading.* Ed. Lindsay Waters and Wlad Godzich. Minneapolis: University of Minnesota Press, 1989, 25–65.

Lazarus, Neil. "Modernism and Modernity: T. W. Adorno and Contemporary White South African Literature." *Cultural Critique* 5 (Winter 1986–7): 131–55.

Moore, John Robert. *Daniel Defoe: Citizen of the Modern World.* Chicago: University of Chicago Press, 1958.

Ndebele, Njabulo S. "The English Language and Social Change in South Africa." *From South Africa: New Writing, Photographs & Art.* Special issue of *TriQuarterly* 69 (Spring/Summer 1987): 217–35.

Shakespeare, William. *The Tempest.* Ed. Frank Kermode. (The Arden Shakespeare.) London: Metheun, 1958.

Spivak, Gayatri Chakravorty. "Theory in the Margin: Coetzee's *Foe* Reading Defoe's *Crusoe/Roxana.*" In *Consequences of Theory.* Ed. Jonathan Arac and Barbara Johnson. Baltimore: Johns Hopkins University Press, 1991, 154–80.

Strauss, Peter. "Coetzee's Idylls: The Ending of *In the Heart of the Country.*" In *Momentum: On Recent South African Writing.* Ed. M. J. Daymond, J. V. Jacobs, and Margaret Lenta. Pietermaritzburg: University of Natal Press, 1984, 121–28.

Tournier, Michel. *Vendredi ou les limbes du Pacifique.* Paris: Gallimard, 1967. (Trans. Norman Denny as *Friday.* New York: Pantheon Books, 1969.)

Wordsworth, William. *The Prelude.* Ed. Ernest de Selincourt, corrected by Stephen Gill. London: Oxford University Press, 1970.

PATRICK MCGEE

Texts between Worlds
African Fiction as Political Allegory

Discussions of third-world literature make clear the pitfalls of generalizing, even with progressive intentions, about such diverse and culturally complex phenomena as African, Indian, or South American fiction. For example, Fredric Jameson, in his essay on third-world literature, contends that such texts are "necessarily . . . allegorical" and should be read as "national allegories" (italics removed). Third-world fiction, he says, lacks one historical determinant of the Western realist and modernist novel: namely, "a radical split between the private and the public, between the poetic and the political, between what we have come to think of as the domain of sexuality and the unconscious and that of the public world of classes, of the economic, and of secular political power: in other words, Freud versus Marx" (69). Without this split, third-world fictions can all be reduced to the same fundamental narrative strategy: as Jameson states it, "the story of the private individual destiny is always an allegory of the embattled situation of the public third-world culture and society" (italics removed; 69). Ultimately, Jameson argues that third-world commitment to nationalist ideology is the only practical alternative to "some global American postmodernist culture" (65).

In response to Jameson's argument, Aijaz Ahmad claims that such sweeping generalization ignores the political allegory in American novels like Pynchon's *Gravity's Rainbow* and Ellison's *Invisible Man,* not to mention the political dimensions of personal experience in the work of Richard Wright and other black and feminist authors ("Jameson's Rhetoric" 15). But Jameson's argument actually relies on an assumption not about the presence or absence of allegory in different areas of contemporary fiction but about *the relation to* allegory; he argues that the allegorical structures of first-world texts are unconscious, while "third-world national allegories are conscious and overt: they imply a radically different and objective relationship of politics to libidinal dynamics" ("Third-World" 80). Several troubling assumptions underlie this generalization. According to Jameson, because first-world cultural texts are *unconscious* political allegories, they call for interpretive elaboration entailing "a whole social and historical critique of our first-world situation" (79). By implication, third-world texts would be transparent, conscious expressions of political desire, requiring no social and historical critique, apart from the determination of the author's intention. Jameson probably would not accept these assumptions as his own; but, as Ahmad suggests, they do follow from the rhetoric of "otherness" Jameson uses throughout his essay.

The slippage of Jameson's rhetoric into such a homogenized view of the cultures that we label "third-world" points toward a problem in articulating the social relation to language. For example, the works I discuss in this essay are mostly written in English, though one is in French and another is an English translation by the author of his Gĩkũyũ original. How does African literature in English and French relate to the languages in which it is written and the cultures from which those languages historically derive? In trying to answer such a question, the Western critic discovers the task Jameson set for himself: that of translating the experience of third-world literature into the critical language of the West. Such a gesture cannot avoid recapitulating the hegemonic structure of Western thought, though it also exposes that thought to dialogical response. In this case, Jameson's essay becomes the occasion for challenge and one possible opening for a discourse whose ends and political effects may exceed those of the initial position. If such critical language arguably subjects the "Third World" to Western ideologies, it also forces the radical thought of the West to open its ear to the discourse of the "Third World." The real question is whether Jameson's position is sufficiently dialogical, that is, whether it calls for an opening or a closing of discourse.

I think Ahmad's essay demonstrates that Jameson's discussion has become an opening in a much larger dialogue whose force is felt everywhere in world literature today. For example, with respect to African literature in French, Christopher Miller defines the situation of contemporary criticism in these terms: "The challenge now is to formulate a model of knowledge which, while remaining conscious of the lessons of rhetorical theory, recognizes European theory as a *local phenomenon*" ("Theories of Africans" 284). I want to agree with Miller that such a challenge points to the need for a "literary anthropology" influenced by the "facts" of ethnography and willing "to adopt modes of interpretation that might come out of the culture in question" (297). But in this return to anthropology it is essential that critics not use traditional African culture as the "final determining instance" of the African present: they should not silence African literature by situating its voice within a narrowly defined framework of their own design. As Miller knows, anthropology has a place in the history of ethnocentrism; and European theory remains a local phenomenon *even when it is conscious of its limits.* It would be naive to think that European theory could ever simply transcend those limits, which would be to transcend its history. Rather than evade his or her position within hegemonic culture, the Western critic should display it, expose it, and position it in relation to the third-world culture he or she needs to hear.

It is therefore not my intention to refute Jameson but to qualify and elaborate on one term of his discourse: namely, allegory. This term could be useful in describing the relation to language one finds in third-world and other oppositional literature. Classically, allegory is described for Western literature as the concrete representation of abstract ideas or values, that is, as Goethe suggested, a method of deriving the particular from the general. With the Romantics, however, allegory is challenged by the theory of the symbol, which derives the general from the particular, transcendent truth from the sensuous reality of nature. Several thinkers of the present century have analyzed the natural referent that grounds the Romantic symbol, showing it to be an illusion whose truth is a historically determined set of meanings and values. In other words, the symbol itself signifies through a process of *allegoresis.*

Walter Benjamin, in particular, has elaborated a theory of allegory that, according to Peter Bürger, owes something to the experience of the avant-garde work of art in the early twentieth century (68). Allegory, for Benjamin, reflects a cultural situation in which "any person, any object, any relationship can mean absolutely anything else. . . . In the field of allegorical intuition the image is a fragment, a rune" (*Origin* 175). Stated differently, allegory arises in a culture for which the real world has become meaningless, devoid of intrinsic value, fragmented yet mysterious. The allegorist merely arranges the fragments of this world, its images, to produce a meaning the fragments could not produce by themselves—a meaning not identical to the intention of the allegorist but reflecting his or her relation to the given historical context. As Bürger notes, "This is posited meaning; it does not derive from the original context of the fragments" (69). The result is not a finished whole but a process of signification that never reaches a final closure. Allegory possesses an "obviously constructed quality" because it is rooted in temporality, in the unfinished world of everyday life (Benjamin, *Origin* 179). Such writing expresses the critical relation to history of the nonorganic work; it shows history as a process of decay and ruin, the *facies hippocratica,* or deathmask, "a petrified, primordial landscape" (166). Allegory represents history as the concrete relation to death underlying the human situation. Though Benjamin describes this relation to history as one of melancholy, the more appropriate term is probably "alienation." But such alienation, as Marx understood, becomes the motive for social change, since it empowers the allegorist to ascribe new values and meanings to the things of his or her world: "If the object becomes allegorical under the gaze of melancholy, if melancholy causes life to flow out of it and it remains behind dead, but eternally secure, then it is exposed to the allegorist, it is unconditionally in his power. That is to say it is now quite incapable of emanating any meaning or significance of its own; such significance as it has, it acquires from the allegorist" (Benjamin, *Origin* 183–84).

In its allegorical potential, language is situated in the place of the Other, with a capital O. I use this Lacanian term because it has cropped up in criticism of African literature, particularly in the work of Christopher Miller and Abdul R. JanMohamed. But these writers, like Jameson, give the term a strictly binary interpretation that goes against the grain of Lacan's insistence that "there is no Other of the Other" (311), no metalanguage, no master narrative that governs it. In his theory of allegory, Benjamin describes the process by which language is emptied of "natural" meaning, abstracted from its ideological framework, and reduced to radical alterity: the substance of history as the support of any conceivable, historically determined meaning. As Bürger stresses, Benjamin's allegory "represents history as decline" (69); however, this is not a Spenglerian notion but a recognition of meaning's historicity. The signifier, in ceasing to be natural, becomes the field of historical intervention, the place from which radical meaning-production can take place in opposition to the hegemonic authority of some Western master-slave dialectic. Unlike the Hegelian other, which is only a detour from the subject, the Other is radical, irreducible alterity, underpinning every position insofar as it is historical. Such alterity dissolves even the distinction between first and third worlds, or rather reduces that difference to the historical dimensions that enable us to project the possibility of overthrow and change. It articulates the unity in difference that Indian philosophy would seem to privilege, and it is no accident that Lacan's Rome discourse concludes with references to the *Upanishads* (106–7). In relating to language as the Other, third-world writers enter into the "dialogic relation" with hegemonic discourse that JanMohamed specifies in the following terms: "The Third World's literary dialogue with Western cultures is marked by two broad characteristics: its attempt to negate the prior European negation of colonized cultures and its adoption and creative modification of Western languages and artistic forms in conjunction with indigenous languages and forms" (103–4).

Benjamin's theory, therefore, should not be a formula for the reductive generalization of all third-world writing. But it can be juxtaposed with the efforts of some third-world authors to confront and break through the wall of Western ideology with which colonialism has surrounded their specific cultures. For example, Wole Soyinka, resisting the sublimation of African into European culture, comments that his book *Myth, Literature, and the African World* "is engaged in what should be the simultaneous act of eliciting from history, mythology and literature, for the benefit of both genuine aliens and alienated Africans, a continuing process of self-apprehension whose temporary dislocation appears to have persuaded many of its nonexistence or its irrelevance . . . in contemporary world reality" (xi). These words anticipate the controversy that has recently surrounded his work, the attack on his "mythocentric/traditionalist" position by an overly dogmatic left-wing criticism from Africa and from Europe (see Gugelberger).

The object of this criticism has been Soyinka's reinterpretation of the Yoruba gods, particularly Ogun, the creator god of the hunt, fire, iron, and war. Soyinka has remarked: "I use the Yoruba gods as creative metaphors. Sometimes as metaphors for my own existence. One in particular called Ogun" ("Seminar on *Aké*" 512). The question as to whether he "believes" in African gods (in the Western sense of that word) hardly seems relevant to the larger context of his project—certainly no more relevant than the issue of Joyce's belief or disbelief in Catholicism to an understanding of his work. Ogun as creative metaphor functions within a particular matrix of thought, or symbolization, that derives not so much from some universal mind of Africa as from the symbolic material of Yoruba ritual, a fragment abstracted from the natural order and reinformed by personal and social desire. Ogun signifies not only African consciousness but the symbolic relation of Africans to the great historical shifts of the postcolonial era. In the context of Yoruba tragic drama, the past and the future are contained in the present, and tragic terror arises from the experience of severance or division within the temporal continuum. Ogun is the god who must create a bridge across the abyss that opens up in time: "The weightiest burden of severance is that of each from self, not godhead from mankind, and the most perilous aspect of the god's journey

is that in which the deity must truly undergo the experience of transition"
(Soyinka, *Myth* 153). This nontranscendent god is the first actor in the
battle against social dissolution; and "Yoruba tragic drama is the re-
enactment of the cosmic conflict" (149–50).

One can recognize the material autonomy of Soyinka's rethinking of
Yoruba mythology, and yet at the same time hear in it dialogical resonances with Benjamin's theoretical description of German tragic drama:
"Allegory established itself most permanently where transitoriness and
eternity confronted each other most closely" (*Origin* 224). In his fiction,
Soyinka transforms the Ogun figure, alienated by cultural imperialism,
into the warrior against Western hegemony; such a figure, crossing the
abyss of historical transition, is the main character of *Season of Anomy:*
Ofeyi employs the remnants of African communal culture to undermine
and wage war against the neocolonial Corporation. Ofeyi cannot separate
personal desire from collective action, as he searches for the kidnapped
Iriyise (who perhaps symbolizes the social regeneration of Africa?) in the
midst of class war: "I'm sure every man feels the need to seize for himself
the enormity of what is happening, of the time in which it is happening.
Perhaps deep down I realise that the search would immerse me in the
meaning of the event, lead me to a new understanding of history" (218).

Benjamin's concept of allegory, in other words, can be useful as an
instrument for analyzing the allegorical tendency of third-world literature—
one tendency among others. It enables us to hear resonances to which we
might not otherwise be open. Since my concern here is with African
writing, I want to set aside the term "third-world," while recognizing that
the term "African" lacks univocal meaning with reference to the fiction
under consideration. Even texts by Yambo Ouologuem from Mali, Ayi
Kwei Armah from Ghana, Ngũgĩ wa Thiong'o from Kenya, Wole Soyinka
from Nigeria, and Bessie Head from South Africa have been described by
Ngũgĩ not as "African" but as "Afro-European" because they are written
in the languages of the West. They are part of "an Afro-European literary
tradition which is likely to last for as long as Africa is under this rule of
European capital in a neo-colonial set-up" (*Decolonising the Mind* 27). In
this statement Ngũgĩ demonstrates the allegorical gesture that enables
him to reappropriate the term "African" from a dominating literary tradition and language and inform it with new value and meaning. Behind such
an act lies the historical alienation of the postindependence, neocolonial
intellectuals who have undergone the transformation that Frantz Fanon
described in *The Wretched of the Earth.* After having been shaped by
colonial education, which implants in their brains "a vigilant sentinel

ready to defend the Greco-Latin pedestal," they have entered into the struggle for liberation that turns "this artificial sentinel . . . into dust." In Fanon's words: "All the Mediterranean values,—the triumph of the human individual, of clarity and of beauty—become lifeless, colourless knick-knacks. All those speeches seem like collections of dead words; those values which seemed to uplift the soul are revealed as worthless, simply because they have nothing to do with the concrete conflict in which the people is engaged" (46–47). These words articulate the historical aliena-tion that Benjamin calls "melancholy"—a term having nothing to do with simple sadness or depression but with the perception of historical tran-sience and destruction. In the case of the colonial or neocolonial subject, it has to do with the perception of the historicity of those eternal truths and, most particularly, of those eternal values (including those called "aesthetic") that mask the hegemony of Western culture. It challenges the principle of canon ("the Greco-Latin pedestal") as reflective of a natural aesthetic order outside the realm of politics and desire.

At the end of Armah's novel *The Beautyful Ones Are Not Yet Born,* the central character, who is called simply *the man,* gazes upon an advertise-ment painted on the back of a bus. Forming an oval shape are these words: "The Beautyful Ones / Are Not Yet Born." Within the oval is "a single flower, solitary, unexplainable, and very beautiful" (183). This advertising slogan with its image is the signature of neocolonial power in Armah's home state of Ghana. After independence (1957), this power was supported by the bourgeois nationalists of the United Gold Coasts Convention, despite the socialist aspirations of Nkrumah and the Conven-tion People's party. Armah's novel paints a bitterly disenchanted portrait of the corrupting influence of that power on Ghana, where human goodness and autonomy, epitomized by *the man,* suffer from the overdeterminations of historical violence. *The man,* against pressure from family and colleagues, suffers throughout the novel, both physically and mentally, for his resis-tance to "the gleam" of commodity culture. In a final ironic gesture, he aids a corrupt official of the Nkrumah government to escape during the coup; in effect the victim is compelled by his own humanity to save the victimizer.

Another hope nevertheless emerges out of the ashes of disenchantment. The advertising slogan has become meaningless as a signifier of the social and economic order that produced it in the language of colonial power (with the "y" in "Beautyful" signifying the difference between the colonizer and the colonized); but in the gaze of *the man* it is transformed into the double-edged instrument of social criticism and revolutionary hope. The words and the emblematic flower are reinformed by *the man*'s vision. Earlier in the novel, after learning of the coup, he thinks: "Someday in the long future a new life would maybe flower in the country, but when it came, it would not choose as its instruments the same people who had made a habit of killing new flowers. The future goodness may come eventually, but before then where were the things in the present which would prepare the way for it?" (159–60). Although *the man* discovers no promises of future goodness outside himself, he does project his inward sense of beauty and social value into the dead and reified language of the advertisement, transforming the symbols of neocolonial domination into the emblems of future revolutions for African autonomy. As Neil Lazarus remarks, *the man*'s "sense of moral earnestness ought not . . . to be interpreted as idealistic, for it stems not from any abstract consideration as to how the 'good' or the 'just' life might be led, but rather from an appraisal of what was actually possible in Ghana after decolonization—of what seemed, indeed, to be prefigured in the style of the decolonizing movement itself" (147). Stated differently, *the man*'s utopian desire, though buried inside him, reflects social determinations that could bring about a transformation of the collective will under the right historical conditions. *The man* shows that the things that prepare the way for future goodness are in the brain of the neocolonial subject who can transform the dead letters of hegemonic culture into the hope for social revolution.

Revolutionary hope through pessimistic social vision also takes shape in the rewriting of African history. Two novels of considerable importance in this area are Ouologuem's *Bound to Violence* (*Le Devoir de violence*) and Armah's *Two Thousand Seasons*. Both novels project a vision of African history from the period of Arab domination of northern Africa in the thirteenth century to the postcolonial era. Ironically, Ouologuem, whose novel received the Prix Renaudot in 1968, was later accused of plagiarism for his so-called borrowings from André Schwartz-Bart, Graham Greene, and Guy de Maupassant; even so, Christopher Miller has usefully argued that the book is "an assault on European assumptions about writing and originality" (*Blank Darkness* 219). To my mind, Ouologuem engages in a compelling act of postmodern pastiche that attacks the authority of the Western master narrative by mirroring its violence and demystifying its claim to universal truth. As James Olney implies, Ouologuem not only inverts but displaces Western representations: "This stylistic pastiche, which combines elements from the historical traditions of family and village, from *griot* 'archives,' and from Arab chronicles, is matched . . . by a geographical and cultural pastiche, the elements of which Ouologuem draws from all over Africa; here again he freely mixes the real with the imaginary and the historic with the mythic to produce a new historic amalgam with a new interpretation." The result is the "symbolic autobiography of a continent" (241–42).

In *Bound to Violence,* Ouologuem not only does not condemn violence but he expresses the "duty of violence" as offering the only possibility of a solution to the social contradictions of African history; or, as Miller suggests, he "posits destructive violence and theft as origin itself" (*Blank Darkness* 219), not only of history but of any historical representation. In the end, Ouologuem's book is a ruse in a complicated game—like the game of chess between the black king Saif and the white bishop Henry in the last chapter, "Dawn." To Saif's remark, "You play the game. But you don't let yourself be made game of," Henry responds,

> "But keep your eye on the other man's play. . . . You must learn to know it and to know yourself in it. Say to yourself, . . . *I want to play as if they did not see me playing,* entering into my game without ostentation, appearing to be in accord with myself and with them, making use of their guile without ever seeming to face it head on or trying to divert it, exposing the intricate trap, but with caution, never touching anything until I have fathomed its hidden mechanism. Without such caution, my friend, can you hope to kill your adversary . . . in a game?" (176–77)

With a ruthless irony, Ouologuem puts these words into the mouth of a white Christian, and his work seems to imply that only through a sort of literary ventriloquism can the neocolonial subject subvert the voice of European culture, which has foreclosed African voices from symbolization—an appropriation that attempts to reverse the pattern of historical relations between Africa and the West. No doubt, Ouologuem's incorporation of fragments from writers like Greene and Maupassant, as well as his satirical portrayal of Western scholars like Frobenius (who appears in the book as Shrobenius), follows the same pattern of reversal and reappropriation—a strategy indicating the strength and the limitations of his achievement. As Jean-François Lyotard implies, the master narrative of Western culture, including its colonialist and neocolonialist chapters, can be viewed, in its symbolic dimension, as a game—indeed, a language game—that can be deconstructed by reducing it to the status of one language game among others. Ouologuem's "duty of violence" proposes the duty of African literature to strip all master narratives of their global authority by exposing them as allegories of power. But it remains silent as to the possibility of actually overthrowing cultural hegemony through the production of an authentic African voice.

In *Two Thousand Seasons,* through the style of "mythical realism," Ayi Kwei Armah tries to articulate that voice and the historical conditions of its coming to be. Although the book has been described as the fictional equivalent of Walter Rodney's *How Europe Underdeveloped Africa* (see Ngara 55), Armah concerns himself less with getting all the facts straight than with carving out a vision of the African past that creates the possibility of a future for the whole of Africa. In doing so, he fuses the personal voice of his social alienation with the more traditional voices of Africa, "a class of griots, poet-historians whose vision of their role has far more in common with that of the Yoruba Ijala singer or Ewe lyricist than with the self-conscious *angst* of many a Western artist" (Fraser 69). While consciously inverting the Manichean structure of colonial ideology—so that "whiteness" comes to signify the death-inflicting bestiality of colonialism and "blackness" the redemptive truth of African history—Armah also subverts in advance any naive relation to the past as pure origin: "How the very first of us lived, of that ultimate origin we have had unnumbered thoughts and more mere fables passed down to us from those gone before, but of none of this has any of us been told it was sure knowledge. We have not found that lying trick to our taste, the trick of making up sure knowledge of things possible to think of, things possible to wonder about but impossible to know in any such ultimate way" (*Seasons* 4).

So much for Hegel's absolute knowledge. For Armah, knowledge of the past is necessarily allegorical—that is to say, it arrives to us in fragments that must be arranged and for which a meaning must be posited through human agency. The past is not, as in the most common version of Christianity, the divine revelation of lost wholeness or unity of being: rather, "Of what is revealed, all is in fragments. Much of it was completely lost in that ashen time when loneliness, bringer of madness, nearly snapped the line of rememberers" (13). Revelation is a fragment; and out of these fragments Armah the allegorist constructs "the way" not simply as return but, in its "closer meaning," as "destruction's destruction" and "the search for paths to that necessary beginning" (233). The destruction of destruction means revolution and the "duty of violence," as well as revising the master-slave dialectic at the center of Western historiography by constructing a collective subject of African history that depends not on the recognition of the master but on the rearticulation of the present in constellation with a distinctly African past. Like Benjamin's historical materialist, Armah "recognizes the sign of a Messianic cessation of happening, or, put differently, a revolutionary chance in the fight for the oppressed past. He takes cognizance of it in order to blast a specific era out of the homogeneous course of history" (Benjamin, *Illuminations* 263).

Armah's book has been criticized for its racialism and negative depiction of Arabs and white Europeans, and there is no question that the author sees his book as a weapon and an antidote against the cultural domination of Africa both before and after the colonial era. In relation to such hegemonic culture, the book implicitly argues that Africa cannot sublimate or be sublimated; on the contrary, the destroyers must be destroyed before the roots of cultural autonomy can flower. Armah's "duty of violence," consequently, does not limit itself to the symbolic (as Ouologuem's appears to do) but calls for armed struggle and insurrection.

Soyinka's *Season of Anomy,* Ngũgĩ's *Petals of Blood,* and Bessie Head's *A Question of Power*—these novels employ an allegorical realism that projects African history onto the plane of contemporary postcolonial experience. The communalism of the African past is pitted against the violence of multinational capitalism in Ngũgĩ and Soyinka, while for Head the season of anomie stages itself in the mind of a woman struggling for a new communal life against the pull of history's nightmare, a scene of masculinist power and racist violence. The characters in these novels all find themselves "enmeshed in a surreal world," to cite the words of Munira in *Petals of Blood* (100), and the reader encounters another mode of surreality in the postmodern techniques of narration that decenter his or her position as knowing subject. Soyinka leaves out critical information that would tend to rationalize the brutal violence he depicts; Ngũgĩ employs multiple narrative techniques, combining detective fiction with historical epic, to challenge any linear view of social progress; Head refuses to make any strict divisions in narrating the contents of everyday reality and the unconscious. Perhaps Head articulates best the relation of these fictions to the cultural phantasmagoria of Western and Eastern gods and myths erected over African culture. In *A Question of Power,* the central character contemplates her own mental division as the result of colonial ideology: "So harsh was the present face-to-face view of evil that in a subconscious way Elizabeth found her mind turning with relief to African realism: a woman was simply a woman with legs; a man simply a man with legs, and if good and noble they earned a certain courteous respect, just as Christianity and God were courteous formalities people had learned to enjoy with mental and emotional detachment—the real battlefront was living people, their personalities, their treatment of each other" (66). Elizabeth struggles against the Manichean ideology implanted in her mind by colonial and patriarchal culture—an ideology that must be overthrown before she can reenter and help to re-create an African communal society for the future.

JanMohamed stresses that such an ideology, or *allegory,* reduces the African subject as "native" to his or her "exchange-value" in the colonialist symbolic—they are "fed into the manichean allegory, which functions as the currency, the medium of exchange, for the entire colonialist discursive system" (83). Of course, the Manichean allegory tries to hide its true character by denying its "constructed quality" and insisting that its "posited meaning" is universal and natural. African fiction, therefore, has to expose this "allegory" and open the symbolic field to ideological struggle. It must challenge the system of exchange values and overthrow the process of human commodification by redefining social ties, even those "courteous formalities" and languages taken over from the West, as incommensurable: that is, "African realism" against the Western canon. What counts is the bond between people, not their worth on a scale manufactured in Europe and America. But the evil remains, and the overthrow of its invisible system of values has to be repeated continually as a part of everyday life in Africa.

One of the most significant experiments in political allegory to have appeared in African fiction recently is Ngũgĩ's *Devil on the Cross.* The novel represents a genuine break in the development of Ngũgĩ's work and responds directly to the concrete historical situation of postindependence Kenya. I should make clear that in discussing this work, particularly in the context of "Afro-European" fiction, I aim not at an understanding of the original but of the translation, though a translation with a special claim to signatory status when we read below Ngũgĩ's name on the title page of the Heinemann edition, "Translated from the Gĩkũyũ by the author." As Ngũgĩ has declared, his decision to write his novel in the Gĩkũyũ language was a political one that arose out of regional (Kenyan) and more general (African) historical conditions. Originally, it was Ngũgĩ's work in a village cultural center that led him to write literature in his native tongue for the first time. After fifty peasants and factory workers in the Kamĩrĩĩthũ literacy program had learned how to read and write in Gĩkũyũ, "it was time . . . to enter the second phase of our program—that is, cultural development with theatre at the center." Ngũgĩ and his associate, having been asked to write a play, felt compelled to pose the question, "In what language were we going to write?" The answer was self-evident ("One writes in the language that the people use"), but that the question had even to be posed drove home to Ngũgĩ "how far gone we were." The play was written and performed; it became immediately popular with peasants and workers; and the "political result of this popularity was that the Kenyan regime reacted and after nine performances the play was stopped. I myself was put into political detention for a year in 1978." Realizing that the "whole point of a neo-colonial regime putting a writer into prison is really to keep him out of touch with the people," Ngũgĩ took the offensive and wrote *Caitaani Mũtharabainĩ* (Devil on the Cross) ("Tension" 5–6).

Elsewhere, Ngũgĩ has emphasized the importance of his decision to write Gĩkũyũ literature in the context of African culture as a whole. Those who question his decision have forced him to the conclusion that:

> in choosing to write in Gĩkũyũ, I was doing something abnormal. But Gĩkũyũ is my mother tongue! The very fact that what common sense dictates in the literary practice of other cultures is being questioned in an African writer is a measure of how far imperialism has distorted the view of African realities. It has turned reality upside down: the abnormal is viewed as normal and the normal is viewed as abnormal. Africa actually enriches Europe: but Africa is made to believe that it needs Europe to rescue it from poverty. Africa's natural and human resources continue to develop Europe and America: but Africa is made to feel grateful for aid from the same quarters that still sit on the back of the continent. Africa even produces intellectuals who now rationalise this upside-down way of looking at Africa. (*Decolonising the Mind* 27–28)

Ngũgĩ understands the act of writing Gĩkũyũ literature as part of the anti-imperialist struggle; and of course this struggle informs the content of his work, as it either directly or indirectly informs the work of all the writers I discuss in this essay. But by writing in his native tongue, Ngũgĩ positions himself in relation to a particular audience, or what American critics would call "interpretive community." He positions himself in relation to their world, their history, and their language. He need not produce a static image of that community; nor is he bound to reproduce any but a dynamic view of the African past or present. By writing in Gĩkũyũ, Ngũgĩ no longer translates Africa into a colonial tongue or oral narrative into the written idioms of English. At the same time, he has no reason to fear contamination by those components or fragments of Western and world culture that have become a part of the African experience in the colonial and postcolonial eras. Everything is grist for the mill of the postcolonial allegorist.

Ngũgĩ accepts even the influence of Conrad, apparent in all his novels, because "the story-within-a-story was part and parcel of the conversational norms of the peasantry. The linear/biographical unfolding of a story was more removed from actual social practice than the narrative of Conrad and Lamming" (*Decolonising the Mind* 76). Still, knowing what would be familiar to ordinary Kenyans impels him to borrow "heavily from forms of oral narrative, particularly the conversational tone, the fable, proverbs, songs and the whole tradition of poetic self-praise or praise of others. I also incorporated a biblical element—the parable—because many literates would have read the bible" (77–78). Most important, having long been intrigued by the Faust theme in literature, and suspecting that "the story of the good man who surrenders his soul to evil for immediate earthly gains of wealth, intellect and power was universal and was rooted in the lores of the peasantry" (80–81). Ngũgĩ is able to fuse the Christian embodiment of evil, the Devil, with more traditional figures of evil from Gĩkũyũ orature, such as the man-eating ogre: "Marimũ[s] were supposed to possess two mouths, one in front and the other at the back. The one at the back was covered with long hair. They were cruel, very greedy, and they lived on the labour of humans. What about the latter day Marimũs? Would the Marimũ characters provide me with the image I sought?" (80–81).

This work of fusion and reconstruction results in a novel of allegorical realism that identifies and analyzes the neocolonial setup while it displaces traditional African values toward a future beyond the present stage of imperialism. *Devil on the Cross* differs from Ngũgĩ's other novels in that its central character is a woman who must struggle against both the patriarchal structures native to Africa and neocolonial exploitation. Through flashbacks and stories within the story, we learn of Jacinta Warĩĩnga's history as the victim of wealthy men of the comprador class and we see her transformed by fantastic events into an autonomous figure (she becomes a mechanic and a student engineer) and finally into a revolutionary. The plot of the novel, however, focuses on the events taking place over a period of roughly twenty-four hours and it briefly discloses their aftermath two years later. Warĩĩnga loses her job in Nairobi when she refuses to become Boss Kĩhara's mistress, a repetition of her adolescent experience with a Rich Old Man. Her lover doesn't believe that she has been innocent in this relationship and he leaves her. She decides to go home to Ilmorog, but on the way to the *matatũ* stop she momentarily despairs and nearly steps in front of a city bus, another repetition from her past. She is stopped by a voice, and then a young student appears who eventually gives her an invitation to attend the Devil's Feast in Ilmorog where there will be a competition to choose seven experts in theft and robbery. She travels to Ilmorog on a *matatū* in which she meets a professor of music at the university, a worker, an unemployed woman, and a businessman. The driver of the *matatū* turns out to be a thug who will sell his treachery to the Devil for any price. In Ilmorog, Wariinga and the others discover that the Devil is really the capitalist class of Kenya and the international financiers who bankroll the capitalists and scoop off most of the profits from African labor. Each member of the competition elaborates on new and utterly fantastic techniques for expropriating the wealth produced by the people. Finally, the people rise up and throw the neocolonial devils out; but almost immediately the ringleaders, who turn out to be the working man and the unemployed woman from the *matatū,* are arrested and the status quo is reconfirmed. Two years later Wariinga has decided to marry the music professor. However, when she meets his father she recognizes the Rich Old Man who originally victimized her and almost drove her to suicide. After he threatens to do the same again, she shoots him with the gun handed to her for safekeeping by the revolutionary worker. This time Wariinga chooses revolution instead of suicide, and the future promises "the hardest struggles of her life's journey" (254).

This plot summary unfortunately cannot do justice to the stylistic force of the novel, which is constructed on the tension between the tragic shape of Wariinga's history and the satirical thrust of Ngũgĩ's depiction of the agents, both native and international, of neocolonialism. Wariinga achieves autonomy in the closing scenes, but the novel offers no illusion as to what the final price of her freedom may be. The history of postcolonial Kenya has become a nightmare, and Ngũgĩ depicts it as such, aiming in this book less at producing the effect of reality than at capturing the surreality of everyday life in a neocolony. Such a reality, "stranger than fiction," is "what confronts a novelist in a neo-colony vis-à-vis the audience most adversely affected by that reality" (*Decolonising the Mind* 78). In the case of Wariinga, Ngũgĩ creates a character whose revolutionary impulses reveal themselves unconsciously long before they are recognized by her consciousness. Throughout her life Wariinga has had a recurrent night-mare related to her early experience in Catholic churches. As a girl, when she looked at the pictures on the walls and windows of the church, she saw that the "Virgin Mary, Jesus and God's angels were white, like Europeans, but the Devil and his angels were black" (*Devil* 139). In her dreams, Wariinga reverses this Western symbolism: "Instead of Jesus on the Cross, she would see the Devil, with skin as white as that of a very fat European she once saw near the *Rift Valley Sports Club,* being crucified by people in tattered clothes—like the ones she used to see in Bondeni— and after three days, when he was in the throes of death, he would be taken down from the Cross by black people in suits and ties, and, thus restored to life, he would mock Wariinga" (139). This Devil on the cross eventually speaks to Wariinga in a waking dream and teaches her something that experience will confirm later. In addition to the two worlds she has witnessed, the worlds of "the oppressor and the oppressed, of those who eat what has been produced by others and the producers themselves" (186), there is a third world of "the revolutionary overthrow of the system of eating and being eaten" (188). Wariinga enters this world at the novel's end when she takes up for herself the "duty of violence." Like Soyinka's Ogun, she must progress through the abyss of transition, or history, to struggle against the agencies of economic and cultural hegemony.

Obviously, in spite of its popularity in Kenya (where it was absorbed through public readings in families as well as on buses, taxis, and in bars [*Decolonising the Mind* 83]), *Devil on the Cross* is not a work that can expect a popular reception in the West or even with those Africans deeply committed to Western culture and education. The work is polemical and committed and challenges Western aesthetic theory and its canon from every angle. So the question arises as to why Ngũgĩ bothered to translate it himself; that is: why does he give the translation signatory status for the Western reader? Since I began this essay with Benjamin's theory of allegory, it may be useful at this point to consider his theory of translation, for Benjamin understood that a translation possesses a different mode of intentionality from an original: namely, it does not reproduce the meaning of the original and, thereby, its social and historical context. The reader of Ngũgĩ's text in English cannot claim to grasp the full implications, the concrete value of the Gĩkũyũ original; he or she cannot claim to have entered the space of African literature, which remains irreducible and, to some extent, indecipherable to the purely Western viewpoint and methodology. But a translation can produce another effect that may have its own political significance, the effect of literalness that avoids "the desire to retain meaning" in any absolute sense. Benjamin describes this effect with an analogy: "Fragments of a vessel which are to be glued together must match one another in the smallest details, although they need not be like one another. In the same way a translation, instead of resembling the meaning of the original, must lovingly and in detail incorporate the original's mode of signification, thus making both the original and the translation recognizable as fragments of a greater language, just as fragments are part of a vessel" (*Illuminations* 78).

The greater language in which Gĩkũyũ and English are implicated—the whole of language that is not equal to the sum of its parts, that is, languages—could be called the Other: the material of language or mode of signification that remains beyond meaning. Stated differently, Ngũgĩ's translation of his work does not give his English-speaking reader the meaning of the original but rather shows the place of the original. The translation signifies the difference constituting what is incommensurable in the African experience, what cannot be translated into any other tongue and is irreducible to any other system of values. At the same time, the translation subverts the binary other with which a naively Western view wishes to locate and contain African history and culture. In effect, the English and the Gĩkũyũ are dialogically related to one another, in communication with one another, and contaminated by one another. But there is no question as to which language has the upper hand. It is the Gĩkũyũ text that governs the English text and that now impacts on the history of the English language. Ngũgĩ's translation is not reverse hegemony but a subtle displacement of the authority of English. It situates the original not as the transparent referent but as what Gayatri Spivak has called, after Derrida, "'the blank part of the text'": "that which is thought is, if blank, still *in the text* and must be consigned to the Other of history. That inaccessible blankness circumscribed by an interpretable text is what a postcolonial critic of imperialism would like to see developed within the European enclosure as *the* place of the production of theory. The postcolonial critics and intellectuals can attempt to displace their own production only by presupposing that *text-inscribed* blankness" (294).

By writing in Gĩkũyũ and translating into English, Ngũgĩ discloses and exploits his own contradiction as a postcolonial intellectual writing texts between worlds. He reveals the duality of his voice as both native Kenyan and Afro-European. In Gĩkũyũ, he does not speak *for* African subjects *to* a European or Eurocentric African audience. He does not *represent* them as the Other for the subject of Western culture. Rather, he speaks to Africans from the position of contradiction he occupies as a teacher and a writer—he represents them only in speaking as one of them but not for all of them. He engages in a symbolic exchange with the community whose language he shares. In English, by contrast, his text inscribes the Other of history as that which cannot be represented except as the "*text-inscribed* blankness." He does not present the English-speaking world with an

Africa to be assimilated to its ethnocentric concepts of humanity, human nature, and universal human characteristics. He presents them with *"the place of the production of theory"*—the place of the Other. Although this place cannot be assimilated or made transparent in the context of hegemonic culture, it can induce Western and Western-centered African intellectuals to question the transparency of their own positions as speaking subjects and to recognize the complicity of their theories with ideological processes. Ngũgĩ's translation *as text* articulates *the space between* ideological and cultural differences. As such, it epitomizes without prescribing the politically self-conscious relation of African writing to the hegemonic culture of Europe.[1]

Ngũgĩ's translation teaches that cultural, linguistic hegemony is never total—that it has the principle of reversibility inscribed within it. Translation foregrounds, to cite Derrida's reading of Benjamin, "the being-language, of the language, tongue or language *as such,* that unity without any self-identity" ("Tours" 201). Such a view defines language in its radical alterity, which enables the writer to take a critical relation to it and thus transform it. Through the pulverization of language informed by ideology, through its cadaverization as fragment, pastiche, myth, or allegory, the writer is able to seize language as the discourse of the Other, of collective human desire, which is reshaped and virtually translated. Thus, he or she transforms the substance of history, its raw signifiers, into the language of revolutionary hope and seeks the truth at which all languages, all cultures, aim beyond their immediate signification. The writer also speaks to the necessity of struggle, for culture can never be reshaped as long as the organs of social reproduction are monopolized by a hegemonic class.

Having cited English translations of three different languages (Ngũgĩ's Gĩkũyũ, Benjamin's German, and Derrida's French), I can do no more than suggest a relation to African fiction as world literature that future scholarship will either make concrete or reject. Crucial to this historical elaboration will be the recognition that what Western thinkers have termed the "postmodern condition" must be grounded in the "postcolonial condition" not only of the Third World but of those pockets of opposition within European and American culture.[2] Postcolonial African literature shares some common symbolic ground with postmodern oppositional writing in Europe and America. Whether the novels I discuss here are realistic or surrealistic, they are postmodern in their self-conscious understanding of the political functions of language and literature: to cite Lyotard, narrative "determines in a single stroke what one must say in order to be heard, what one must listen to in order to speak, and what role one must play (on the scene of diegetic reality) to be the object of a narrative" (21). Such a view challenges the ideologies of modernism, just as third-world literature as a whole exposes the Eurocentrism at the heart of modernist internationalism. It also challenges the aesthetic imperialism at the core of Western education. As Ngũgĩ points out, "In literature there have been two opposing aesthetics: the aesthetic of oppression and exploitation and of acquiescence with imperialism; and that of human struggle for total liberation" (*Writers in Politics* 38). Barbara Harlow writes that this distinction has important implications for literary criticism in the West, for it "contests the ascendancy of sets of analytic categories and formal conventions, whether generic, such as novel, sonnet, tragedy, etc.; national-linguistic as in French, German, or English literature; literary-historical; or even so simple a distinction as that which is still conventionally maintained between fiction and non-fiction" (9). To these formal or analytic categories, she argues, Ngũgĩ opposes a different organization of criticism, one that is " 'participatory' in the historical processes of hegemony and resistance to domination" (9).

In this redefinition of the political responsibility of the critic, another ground for dialogue between postmodern and postcolonial cultures opens up. Fredric Jameson's call for "a pedagogical political culture which seeks to endow the individual subject with some new heightened sense of its place in the global system" offers a prescription, no doubt utopian under the present organization of Western education, for the critical practice of radical teachers in America and Europe ("Postmodernism" 92). Although such a radical pedagogy will involve the teaching and disseminating of third-world texts, it also involves redefining the institution of criticism with its implicit assumptions about the nature and purpose of literature itself. It requires a challenge to the aesthetic hierarchies and systems of value that have been predominant in the West, particularly since Kant. Otherwise, teaching third-world texts becomes only another mode of assimilating the Other.

In summary, Jameson is not wrong to see an allegorical tendency in the postcolonial literature of Africa, but I think he makes a mistake in positing this as the condition of African or third-world otherness. The Afro-European texts I discuss here could and should be read in a dialogical relation to other writers, whether from the first or third worlds, who address and struggle against cultural hegemony: writers as different as Ishmael Reed, Kathy Acker, Monique Wittig, Salman Rushdie, or Gabriel García Márquez. None of these writers is free from contradiction; but

their works at least try to articulate the "*text-inscribed* blankness," what
global capitalist culture mystifies as its own self-reflection, by weaving a
texture of relations between irreducibly different worlds. Their works
could be thought of as the *discourses of the Other,* though in using the
term "Other" with a capital O I do not refer to the imaginary alterity of
binary logic but to the dialogical force of contemporary world literature
that calls into question such global distinctions as the Three Worlds
Theory. As Lacan suggested, the Other has no other. On the contrary, it
underpins every discourse as the place of the signifier before it enters into
the symbolic realm of signification. The Other is the ground of all
translation and the place from which the language of allegory emerges.

Notes

1. One reader of this essay in manuscript pointed out that I "fall into the trap
of assuming that writing in English means writing to an English/American audience,
ignoring or not realizing the enormous role English plays as a means of communication in countries like Kenya and across Africa." I was not aware that I made that
assumption, but this is an important issue to keep in mind. Ngũgĩ argues simply
that when he writes in English he writes in a language that is understood "by a
very tiny minority in each of the [African] nationalities." In Gĩkũyũ, by contrast,
he reaches "at least some peasants and workers" ("Interview" 163–64). Ngũgĩ
suggests elsewhere that by writing in English, African intellectuals contribute to
"the development of what could be called an Afro-Saxon literature" ("On Writing"
151). He is suggesting, I believe, that "Afro-Saxon literature" to some extent
supports and legitimates the authority of hegemonic Eurocentric culture. He also
insists that it is possible to reach more Africans by writing in native African
languages. Ngũgĩ's convictions are borne out by the commercial success of his first
Gĩkũyũ novel and play: "So in less than a year—from April to December of
1980—they [Heinemann] had to print about fifteen thousand copies of each of
these works, which for them was a record in the sale of any novel or play—be it in
English or any other language—for the same period of time" ("On Writing" 154).

The same reader informed me that Ngũgĩ has not translated his second
Gĩkũyũ novel, *Matigari,* into English. This does not surprise me, and I don't
think that it contradicts my argument. My point is that Ngũgĩ's translation of
his novel into English produces a particular symbolic effect, whether he intended
it or not. That effect has political implications; but it is certainly not the only effect
possible, nor should the English translation be privileged in any way over the
original or another translation. To my knowledge, Ngũgĩ has never underestimated
the importance of translation, though he has serious political reasons for wanting
to dethrone English from the position of mediator between different African
languages. As he comments, "You can write, let's say, in the Gĩkũyũ language, or

in Igbo language or in Luo. You can then have the work translated into other languages and for the first time, you will have the different languages of our different nationalities communicating within themselves instead of always having a foreign language to mediate between them" ("Interview" 164).

2. This connection, which I only suggest here, has been forcefully driven home to me by my former colleague and permanent friend, Prabhakara Jha. His forthcoming work on the "postcolonial condition" should illuminate and give new direction to research in this area.

Works Cited

Ahmad, Aijaz. "Jameson's Rhetoric of Otherness and the 'National Allegory.'" *Social Text* 17 (1987): 3–25.

Armah, Ayi Kwei. *The Beautyful Ones Are Not Yet Born.* London: Heinemann, 1975.

———. *Two Thousand Seasons.* Chicago: Third World, 1979.

Benjamin, Walter. "The Task of the Translator." In *Illuminations.* Ed. Hannah Arendt, trans. Harry Zohn. New York: Schocken, 1969, 69–82.

———. *The Origin of German Tragic Drama.* Trans. John Osborne. London: New Left Books, 1977.

Bürger, Peter. *Theory of the Avant-Garde.* Trans. Michael Shaw. Minneapolis: University of Minnesota Press, 1984.

Derrida, Jacques. "Des Tours de Babel." *Difference in Translation.* Trans. and ed. Joseph F. Graham. Ithaca: Cornell University Press, 1985, 165–207.

Fanon, Frantz. *The Wretched of the Earth.* Trans. Constance Farrington. New York: Grove, 1968.

Fraser, Robert. *The Novels of Ayi Kwei Armah: A Study in Polemical Fiction.* London: Heinemann, 1980.

Gugelberger, Georg M. *Marxism and African Literature.* London: James Currey, 1985.

Harlow, Barbara. *Resistance Literature.* New York and London: Methuen, 1987.

Head, Bessie. *A Question of Power.* New York: Pantheon, 1973.

Jameson, Fredric. "Third-World Literature in the Era of Multinational Capitalism." *Social Text* 15 (1986): 65–88.

———. "Postmodernism, or the Cultural Logic of Late Capitalism." *New Left Review* 146 (1984): 53–92.

JanMohamed, Abdul R. "The Economy of Manichean Allegory: The Function of Racial Difference in Colonialist Literature." In *"Race," Writing, and Difference.* Ed. Henry Louis Gates, Jr. Chicago: University of Chicago Press, 1985, 78–106.

Lacan, Jacques. *"Écrits": A Selection.* New York: W. W. Norton, 1977.

Lazarus, Neil. "Pessimism of the Intellect, Optimism of the Will: A Reading of Ayi Kwei Armah's *The Beautyful Ones Are Not Yet Born." Research in African Literatures* 18, no. 2 (1987): 137–75.

Lyotard, Jean-François. *The Postmodern Condition: A Report on Knowledge.* Minneapolis: University of Minnesota Press, 1985.

Miller, Christopher L. *Blank Darkness: Africanist Discourse in French.* Chicago: University of Chicago Press, 1985.

——. "Theories of Africans: The Question of Literary Anthropology." In *"Race," Writing, and Difference.* Ed. Henry Louis Gates, Jr. Chicago: University of Chicago Press, 1985, 281–300.

Ngara, Emmanuel. *Art and Ideology in the African Novel: A Study of the Influence of Marxism on the African Novel.* London: Heinemann, 1985.

Ngũgĩ wa Thiong'o. *Petals of Blood.* London: Heinemann, 1977.

——. *Writers in Politics.* London: Heinemann, 1981.

——. *Devil on the Cross.* London: Heinemann, 1982.

——. "The Tension between National and Imperialist Culture." *World Literature Written in English* 24, no. 1 (1984): 3–9.

——. "On Writing in Gĩkũyũ." *Research in African Literatures* 16, no. 2 (1985): 151–56.

——. *Decolonising the Mind: The Politics of Language in African Literature.* London: James Currey, 1986.

——. Interview by Hansel Nolumbe Eyoh. *Journal of Commonwealth Literature* 21, no. 1 (1986): 162–66.

Olney, James. *Tell Me Africa.* Princeton: Princeton University Press, 1973.

Ouologuem, Yambo. *Bound to Violence.* Trans. Ralph Manheim. London: Heinemann, 1977.

Soyinka, Wole. *Myth, Literature and the African World.* Cambridge: Cambridge University Press, 1976.

——. "Seminar on *Aké* with Wole Soyinka." *Southern Review* 23, no. 3 (1987): 511–26.

Spivak, Gayatri Chakravorty. "Can the Subaltern Speak?" In *Marxism and the Interpretation of Culture.* Ed. Cary Nelson and Lawrence Grossberg. Urbana: University of Illinois Press, 1988, 271–313.

GAY WILENTZ

English Is a Foreign Anguish
Caribbean Writers and the Disruption of the Colonial Canon

> You taught me language; and my profit on't
> Is, I know how to curse.
> > Caliban, *The Tempest*

The issue of canon revision and reconstruction goes well beyond the selection of texts, for as Cary Nelson states in "Against English: Theory and the Limits of Discipline": "The literary text is defended so as to distract attention from the real object to be protected—the profession of literary studies" (47). To examine Caribbean writers who write in English in relation to the British canon we must understand one of the basic tenets of this canon—that of colonialism and cultural domination. The authors of *Rewriting English: Cultural Politics of Gender and Class* comment that the whole construct of canon formation was developed "in the establishment of curriculum for imperial dominations. For 'English Literature' was born, as a school and college subject, not in England but in the mission schools and training colleges of Africa and India" (Batsleer et al. 23). This "academic terrorism," as they call it, clearly defines literary canons "not just as selections but as hierarchies. . . . Beneath the disinterested procedures of literary judgment and discrimination can be discerned the outlines of other, harsher words: exclusion, subjugation, dispossession" (29–30). In relation to the Caribbean, add "colonization and imperialism."

Bruce Woodcock, in examining Caribbean fiction's challenge to English literature, states that the "great" tradition of English literature ensured that these "emergent literatures . . . knew their place" and, moreover, that English literature itself constituted "powerful elements of ideological domination" (79). This cultural imperialism and domination came most forcefully in the form of language. Unlike the former colonies in Africa or India, for example, there was no language native to the Caribbean after the almost complete genocide of the Amerindians (the "nation" languages are creoles that blend European with African and other languages); literary language in the Anglophone Caribbean has been restricted, for the most part, to the use of English—the language of the oppressors. Barbadian novelist George Lamming calls the imposition of this foreign language "the first important achievement of the colonizing process" (109). But what we have learned from deconstruction (as well as from African and other philosophies before it) is that not only does a word contain its opposite but language can be the basis for its own opposition.[1]

In this essay, I examine how Caribbean writers have disrupted the colonial language and adapted it as a language of opposition, with specific references to first novels of the Guyanese writer Wilson Harris and the Jamaican writer Erna Brodber; moreover, with regard to the question of canonicity, I explore the dialectical relationship between the Caribbean novelists and modernism and how these so-called third-world modernists are exploding Prospero's myth by creating language afresh.

Much of the literature from the Caribbean has been considered difficult because of the lack of linear narrative, the fragmented quality of narrative voice, and the apparent obscurity of the language. Since this essay focuses on the use of language as a way of dismantling the cultural hegemony of the former colonialists, I concentrate on linguistic complexity. To examine language as a profound manifestation of this cultural hegemony, I use, in Raymond Williams's view, the concept of hegemony as beyond the "abstractions of 'social' and 'economic' experience"; rather, it is "a whole body of practices and expectations, over the whole of living: our senses and assignments of energy, our *shaping perceptions of ourselves*" (*Marxism and Literature* 110; emphasis added). Moreover, this cultural hegemony "has also to be seen as the lived dominance and subordination of particular classes [and races]" (110). For the Caribbean writer, the use of colonial English as linguistically dominant subordinates both the residual indigenous languages/cultures and the emerging "nation" languages/cultures. "Standard" English signifies a history of physical and intellectual servitude.

Certainly, one might conjecture that the difficulty of the writings from much of the Caribbean derives from a lack of knowledge of the Caribbean milieu. The imagery, the social history, and the divergent traditions of the Caribbean do not always offer easy access to the works for non-Caribbean readers, but that difficulty can often be allayed by study of the environment described. The oppositional difficulty of language interpretation in some of the writers, such as George Lamming, Jamaica Kincaid, Edward Brathwaite, and Derek Walcott, as well as Brodber and Harris, extends beyond access to this milieu to the basic contradiction in their use of English—a language, as the poet Marlene Nourbese Philip asserts, "which has sought to deny us" ("Earth and Sound"). John Guillory, in "Canonical and Non-canonical: A Critique of the Current Debate," sees the issue of language at the heart of class domination: "The internal differentiation of language produced by the classical education system as the distinction between a credentialed and a non-credentialed speech reproduces the social stratification on the model of the distinction between the tribe or nation and its sociolinguistic other, the 'barbarian' " (501). For the Caribbean writer, along with many other speakers of colonized English, there is complete identification with this dichotomy. They are the barbarians (well beyond class distinctions) who speak the noncredentialed language—these nation languages of pidgin/creole—and must, to be successful, write in the credentialed language of their oppressors.

Ironically, Shakespeare put forth the dynamics of this relationship in *The Tempest.* In Caribbean writings, as Susan Willis notes, "the plight of Caliban . . . has come to be associated with all artists from the Third World who must grapple with the languages of their domination" (96). For Caliban, the gift of language is a noose that keeps him enslaved and eternally subjugated. For these writers, the "gift" of Standard English is an internal colonizing tool far more effective than the weapons used for "pacification." Furthermore, the nation languages, emergent in the Caribbean, have been perceived solely as bastardized forms of English, not only by those who imposed their culture, but also by the colonial subjects who have been instructed by them. In *The Pleasures of Exile,* Lamming develops his case for Caliban as a symbol of the colonized, reading *The Tempest* as ideological construct. Clearly the gift that Prospero gives Caliban is no gift! Caliban "can never be regarded as heir of that Language, since his use of Language is no more than his way of serving Prospero; and Prospero's instruction in this language is only his way of measuring the distance which separates him from Caliban" (110). Furthermore, Lamming states that *"we shall never explode Prospero's old myth until we christen Language afresh"* (118; emphasis added). And this is precisely what Lamming and other Caribbean writers have attempted to do by disrupting the colonial language with its claims to linguistic and cultural superiority.

Marlene Nourbese Philip, born in Tobago, now lives in Canada. Her 1988 unpublished collection of poetry is dedicated to dismantling the colonial hold on her own and others' language, to "deuniversalize" the whole notion of literature, to discharge the canon. In the introduction to *She Tries Her Tongue, Her Silence Breaks Softly,* Philip refers to the poem "Discourse on the Logic of Language":

>The poem is sculpted out of the colonial experience—exploitative of people, destruction of mother tongues. . . . In "Discourse," by cramping the space traditionally given the poem itself, by forcing it to share its space with something else—an extended image about women, language and silence; with the edicts that established the parameters of silence for the African in the New World, by giving more space to descriptions of the physiology of speech, the scientific legacy of racism we have inherited, and by questioning the tongue as organ and concept, poetry is put in its place. . . . The canon of objectivity and universality is shifted—I hope permanently disturbed. (17)

In "Discourse" Philip pushes the colonial discourse of slavery, racial superiority, and language acquisition to the margins of the page, along with what has been formerly marginalized—the image of the mother cleaning her newborn child with her tongue. What is the center of the poem is Philip's own discourse—historically silenced by the cutting out of the tongue—now centered in the page, decentering the historical construct of colonialism and cultural imperialism:

>English
>is my mother tongue.
>A mother tongue is not
>not a foreign lan lan lang
>language
>l/anguish
> anguish
>-a foreign anguish. . . .
>
>I have no mother
>tongue
>no mother to tongue
>no tongue to mother
>to mother
>tongue
>me.   (24)

For Philip the lack of a "mother tongue" is related to the loss of a mother's love—witnessed in the tonguing of the newborn child. The silencing of this most primal voice (a mother's words) provokes profound anguish when learning to speak the patriarchal language of the colonial oppressors. Philip concludes this section of the poem, a painful attack on the dominance of Standard English, with the statement, "English / is a foreign anguish," but tacks on at the end a multiple-choice test forcing us to answer to the physical violence as well as the emotional destruction that has been perpetrated in the name of Western "civilization." One of the questions, "In man the tongue is—," demonstrates in the rational mode of Standard British English how biased the answers always are and compels us to reconsider this "scientific racism" by equating "the principal organ of articulate speech" and "the principal organ of oppression and exploitation" with "all of the above" (27). For Philip, as well as for Wilson Harris and Erna Brodber (whose work I discuss later in this essay), the aim is to "interrupt the text and make it totally unmanageable" ("Earth and Sound"). In this case the attack on the hegemony of English language is oppositional; it breaks down the linguistic control that keeps the natives manageable.

Readers versed in the canon of English literature that has symbolized the suppression of oppositional voices might notice a similarity to the modernist movement in Britain and America. And indeed there is a dialectical relationship between what the modernists were attempting to do and what these writers' intentions are. The modernists, through the disruption of narrative structure and often obscure language, aimed to deal with what they saw as a breakdown of culture and the emptiness of ritual. But Richard Poirier makes the point in *The Renewal of Literature* that some of the modernists saw English as an imperialist language (Joyce being the most obvious example). He comments further: "There is involved here something like a colonial protest against the shapes that language has assumed as it comes forth from England, still the seat of imperial cultural and political authority" (99). There may be a distinction between modernists like Joyce—whose impulse to write comes closer to those from other colonized environments—and High Modernists who bemoaned what they saw as a decline of cultural values. For Joyce, the language of colonial England was representative of the subordination of Irish culture under English control. But the historicity of the situation in Ireland belies easy comparison to imperialism in the New World, since the components of race and slavery do not enter into the colonization of European peoples. In any case, the High Modernists in particular wanted to express their reactions to the loss of culture in narrative structure and in language; the difficulty of modernist language comes out of their desire to "create language afresh," to use Lamming's term (118). And although the modernists may not have intended it that way, this decentering of these structures led the way for the "potential for dissolution of hierarchy, of rankings of inferiority and superiority" (Drake 171). This potential was taken up in the works of Caribbean writers who translated the concerns of modernism in terms of their own struggle against colonial power. But the relationship is dialectical because, unlike the High Modernists, Caribbean writers did not use modernist structures in their writings because they suffered from the loss of tradition but because they were in fact seeking to overturn that same Western (read: colonial) tradition that sought to subjugate and deny their own cultures' validity. Here antinarrative and modernist language translate into counterhegemonic, anticolonial opposition.

In overturning the imposition of the dominant culture, the Caribbean writers face their most challenging goal in dismantling the language. The correlation between the language developed out of a culture and that society's accepted sense of reality is clearly marked. What better way to ensure that the hegemony of the dominant culture has reached the very depth of being? For the people of the Caribbean, the writers in particular, there is clearly a distortion in this correlation. The literary language available to them reflects the internal domination inscribed in it. For example, the use of "black" as a negative metaphor in the English language is well documented; formerly colonized black people have felt the need to de-Anglicize and deracialize English, as well as find "imaginative coinings of alternative metaphors" (Mazrui 81). This break in the correlation of language and accepted reality—which is at once isolating and subjugating—necessitates revisionist metaphoric activity. The use of metaphor for these writers is directly related to the desire to disrupt the cultural hegemony of the language in which they write: "Metaphoric activity in post-colonial writing is thus likely to be more culturally functional than poetically decorative, more self-consciously concerned with the problem of expressing the new in the language of the old, and more concerned with the importance of language, art, literature not just as expressions of new perception or paradox, *but as active agents in the reconstitution of the colonial psyche, fragmented, debilitated, or apparently destroyed by the imperial process*" (Tiffin 16; emphasis added).

Both Wilson Harris in *Palace of the Peacock* and Erna Brodber in *Jane and Louisa Will Soon Come Home* have chosen to use the novel, a bourgeois construct, as their medium to question the hegemony of the language in which they write. Like the modernists, they have chosen to disrupt the basic tenets of this genre, but with a difference: these novelists reflect the concerns of their non-Western, ethnically diverse and colonized cultures by rejecting the conventions of the novel in narrative structure, time/space relations, and the use of language. Harris, a Guyanese novelist, philosopher, and critic who has lived much of his adult life in

Britain, is clearly a "Third World modernist," as Sandra Drake terms it (6), who gathers up aspects from all the cultures that form the Caribbean and disrupts the hegemony of the colonizer's dominant ideology. His eclectic portrayal of the Guyanese landscape and society illustrates modernist attributes; he is considered a very difficult writer because his language, structure, and thematic concerns attempt to dislodge the hegemony of the European culture to expose what is "other" in the dominant ideal. In his critical essay "A Talk on the Subjective Imagination," Harris states that "to a major extent, we are dominated by what I would call a homogeneous imperative. We are dominated by that, and therefore we fail to see that the homogeneous imperative very often masks or conceals from us the 'heterogeneous roots' of a community" (*Explorations* 57). By focusing on these heterogeneous roots of colonized cultures, Harris dislodges hegemonic discourse that attempts to "homogenize all differences" (JanMohamed 10). Moreover, he thrusts together the dominant, the residual, and the emergent cultures that make up the controlling and oppositional modes encoded in what Abdul JanMohamed calls "hegemonic colonialization" (8). Harris makes considerable effort in his writings not to project an emergent culture as the answer to hegemonic colonialism—a culture that would become yet another hegemony, denying its own heterogeneous roots.

In examining *Palace of the Peacock,* Anthony Boxill misses the subtlety of Harris's vision by commenting that, while other West Indian writers are concerned with issues such as "racial prejudice and colonialism," Harris takes "the time to think about the deeper meaning of human existence" (383). For him, the meaning of human existence is directly tied to the trauma of the Middle Passage and the cultures that disappeared under the oppression of the European colonists. In his imaginative fiction, Harris strives to break through the conventions of Western thought to unmask what has heretofore been suppressed. This apparent metonymic notion of what he calls "partiality" underscores the limitations of a unified vision.[2] By disrupting this vision and exposing the other, he reveals the potential for a "meaningful dialogue" between oppressed and dominant cultures.

In "The Complexity of Freedom," Harris emphasizes the necessity of a new language within literature to begin a dialogue of mutuality between formerly hierarchized groups: "What is required at a certain level—if a new dialogue is to begin to emerge—is a penetration of partial images, not a submission to the traditional reinforcement of partiality into total or absolute institution; partiality may begin to declare itself for what it is and to acquire a re-creative susceptibility to otherness in a new and varied evolution of community within a fabric of images in fiction and drama" (*Explorations* 116). Harris's literary technique, mirroring his worldview, disrupts linear narrative and expresses through his language and imagery the possibility of a world in which no image is sovereign, no culture supreme, and no word a static fact.

Palace of the Peacock is Wilson Harris's first novel, and it was in writing this novel that he initially grappled with the problem of presenting the Guyanese landscape in the language of Britain. For the reasons discussed above, as well as the violent difference of the geographic world he hoped to write about, Harris found himself forced to disrupt and transform the imperial language of the colonizers. He explained during a seminar at the University of Texas in 1982: "I had to unlearn what I had learned. I could not just write 'The river is dark; the trees are green.' One of the tasks that began to haunt me personally is how to write that."[3] Here is an example of how Harris is relearning the language to convey the depth of this landscape and worldview he perceived within the rich Caribbean forest:

> The solid wall of trees was filled with ancient blacks of shadow and with gleaming hinges of light. Wind rustled the leafy curtains through which the masks of living beard dangled as low as the water and the sun. . . . The whispering trees spun their leaves to a sudden fall wherein the ground seemed to grow lighter in my mind and to move to meet them in the air. The carpet on which I stood had an uncertain place within splintered and timeless roots whose fibre was stone in the tremulous ground. I lowered my head a little, blind almost, and began forcing a path into the trees away from the river's opening and side.
>
> A brittle moss and carpet appeared underfoot, a dry pond and stream whose course and reflection and image had been stamped for ever like the breathless outline of a dreaming skeleton in the earth. (*Palace* 26–27)

In relearning the language, Harris works out of a conviction that the sovereign notion of a nature that "man" can understand and control limits our vision. For Harris, metaphor is a force that mediates "with 'unstructured' intensity between all partial structures" denied in the dominant vision ("Myth and Metaphor" 2). The imagery of this scene described by the I-narrator (who is nameless and half-blind) reflects the very partiality of the ground on which we stand—partial because, like the narrator, human vision of the universe is necessarily limited and because the homogeneous imperative has further tunneled our vision. Harris disrupts our constructs of earth and sky as he writes of the ground growing lighter and meeting the falling leaves in the air. The hanging moss becomes "living beard" and takes on another life that the men of the crew must deal with, disturbing the order they have imposed on the forest. Furthermore, the lost, betrayed, and vanquished worlds remain imprinted—"the breathless outline of a dreaming skeleton in the earth."

For Harris, this awareness of the partiality of nature mediates our vision and also shows us how to bear the beauty and the infinite terror that surrounds us. Much of the background and memory of the novel comes from Harris's own voyages into the Amazon basin as a surveyor. The landscape is excruciatingly beautiful yet treacherous; a small stone jutting above the water might conceal jagged rocks to tear a boat and its inhabitants to pieces. This affinity of beauty and terror led Harris to question sovereign views of nature and humanity. The conquistador presumption that nature is there to be ravaged is violently shaken by the river's response. In this world, clarity is deceptive; the conquering notion is turned in on itself, since it is the power of nature to ravage those who appear dominant. On a symbolic as well as a literal level, in the novel it is precisely the deceptive moment of calm—unexpected—that is most treacherous. In fact, the appearance of calm and the image of dominancy is only partial. This partiality reflects the gap in hegemonic colonialism, since "no dominant culture in reality exhausts the full range of human practice," no matter how complete the appearance of hegemony (Williams, "Base and Superstructure" 386). Each one of the partial images, residual within the dominant ideal, betrays a world barely glimpsed and contains traces of vanquished cultures, since the reduction of nature coalesces with the domination and virtual genocide of the Amerindians. Undefined by either a sovereign view or a linear sense of time/space, the landscape becomes a lived resistance that maps out the potential for dialogue between oppressed and dominant cultures where before there was merely conquest.

In the novel, the dialectic of conquest and potential dialogue is replayed. An ethnically mixed crew under the leadership of the conquistador Donne follows the Amerindian folk, the Arawaks (an ethnic group practically exterminated by the Europeans), upriver to force them to work as cheap labor on Donne's plantation. Throughout the treacherous journey, the crew, including Donne and his weakened half-brother, the narrator, are stripped of their imperialist desires, and they must search for spiritual self-realization and for the "other" that is in them. At the end of the journey is the Palace of the Peacock, a towering waterfall. In this section, "Paling of Ancestors," Harris disrupts the hierarchical associations of dominant discourse by "miniaturizing" the symbols of European hegemony and elevating those of the vanquished cultures so that there is mutuality.[4] His language is fluid and open-ended, resisting static interpretation. Symbols purported to be absolute in Western culture become partial images in the palace, toppling this false hegemony without replacing it with another. Seen through one of the waterfall windows of the palace is the carpenter Christ painting the world. In the next window are the madonna and child—but the language reconstructs and, on second look, the madonna is Donne's abused mistress, Mariella of the folk, as well as a venerable Arawak woman muse, both old and young, who is forced to guide the crew on its journey. This deity of Amerindian mythology shares the palace with the son of Christianity, as does Anancy, the West African spider figure (Anancy, whom I examine more fully in relation to *Jane and Louisa,* is an archetypal figure in West Africa and the Caribbean). What has hitherto been perceived as hegemonic becomes merely one strain in the heterophony of cultural discourse. For Harris, these symbols represent interrelationship of the dominant and the repressed inscribed in our language, and they are blended, breaking through the bonds of a hegemonic worldview. His language is not "hierarchized explanation but non-hierarchized parallel possibility"; through it he "seeks to 'wrench the world out of its old status'" (Drake 178, 184).

It is of paramount importance to Harris to resist the linguistic impulse to allow a residual or emerging culture to become the dominant one—thus reformulating an imposed unity, replacing one hegemonic structure by another. By forcing the language to include not only its opposite but other variations of itself, Harris compels us to perceive our world (all our worlds) as partial, without a governing dominant ideal. This move toward mutuality, which Harris sees played out within a linguistic context, calls into question the Hegelian notion of the "unified spirit" as well as the dichotomy of subject and object.[5] Implicit in this worldview, although Harris does not mention this specifically, is a total disruption of even the notion of a canon, since its hegemonic method of selection serves to hierarchize and to exclude.

For Harris, even the indigenous cultures of the Caribbean have encoded within them the possibility for another hegemonic absolute; therefore, his discourse is eclectic, expansive, and unresolved. But other writers, resisting the anguish of colonial imposition, see their opposition as centered in residual African culture and the emerging indigenous "nation" cultures.

Erna Brodber, a Jamaican sociologist and novelist, has been compared to Harris in both the difficulty and significance of her work. "Probably no one else in the West Indies, apart from Wilson Harris," claims reviewer Jean Pierre Durix, "has revolutionized the art of fiction as much as Erna Brodber in *Jane and Louisa.*" Brodber's work is grounded in the Jamaica in which she was brought up and still lives. Over a decade after Harris's novel was published, Brodber's examination of cultural conflict, the hegemony of European culture, and the reconciliation of self and society is more specific, less theoretical than his. Moreover, her own resistance to hegemonic colonialism arises from her identification with the indigenous Jamaican cultural milieu and its nation language.

Jane and Louisa Will Soon Come Home, Brodber's first novel, has similarities with others by Afro-Caribbean novelists, particularly women; it is semi-autobiographical and features a young woman narrator, Nellie, who comes to terms with the conflict of cultures through an understanding of personal and community history—in her case, through violently fragmented childhood memories. The novel reflects the feminist adage that the personal is the political, and Nellie's growth as a woman and sexual being mirrors the development of her identity, as Jimmy Cliff sings it, as "a true-born Jamaican." Furthermore, this growth is connected to her throwing off the disfiguring mask of the dominant culture. Brodber, who is an activist, sees her fiction writing as "part of my sociological methods" ("Fiction"). She says that through her fiction she provides "information with which those of the diaspora can find out about themselves."

The few critics who have written on *Jane and Louisa* point to the personal development of the character of Nellie in relation to the theme of "alienation and historical trauma" (Cobham 33). The novel is a layered bildungsroman that centers on the transformation of Nellie's confused sexual and cultural identity at the beginning to her growing understanding of her own, her family's, and her country's trauma of separation from the African aspects of their heritage and the glorification of the dominant European ones. Particularly at the beginning, the novel is extremely difficult to understand since it is narrated by Nellie, who is having a psychological breakdown. It becomes more coherent toward the end as Nellie begins to tie in all the strands of her past life with the help of her Rastafarian friend Baba's "folk psychiatry." This movement toward wholeness, which reflects the changes in Nellie's personal development, also functions linguistically in terms of Brodber's disruption of the alien use of English as her medium for writing. Like the works of Wilson Harris and others, Brodber's novel lacks a coherent notion of chronological time. It makes extensive use of metaphor—especially the image of the kumbla, the cocoon of the august worm—and for the most part presents us with disembodied voices of the Jamaican scene that we as readers must unravel.

As Harris's work focuses outward to wrestle with the partiality of our universe by dislodging notions of cultural hegemony, Brodber turns inward and strips away layers of domination to reconstruct a language determined by cultures formerly denied. The opening paragraph of "Voices," the first section of the novel, presents no specific characters and little of the narrator Nellie, just an undetermined "we" whose colors are metaphors for the class and race conflicts in Jamaica: "So we were brown, intellectual, better and apart, two generations of lightening blue-blacks and gracing elementary schools with brightness. The cream of the earth, isolated, quadroon, mulatto, Anglican. But we had two wiry black hands up to the elbows in khaki suds" (*Jane and Louisa* 7). As readers, we are unclear who the "we" are, and whether the "two wiry black hands" belong to one of the "we" or to a darker-skinned mother/grandmother whose hands wash clothes in dirty water the color of these children's skin (ironically, khaki is a name for the light-skinned). But it is evident, without our knowledge of who is speaking or where the scene takes place, that light-skinned children are privileged, on the one hand, yet their coloring is metaphorically that of dirty water, on the other. The disembodied "we" of the opening paragraph speak in Standard English, but much of the language of the novel is in Jamaican pidgin or "nation" language. It is one way the reader divines who is speaking, but it is also representative of the class- and race-bound society of Jamaica.

This linguistic spectrum, related to the class structures imposed by the former colonialists and the neocolonialists, illustrates Brodber's resistance to the dominance of Standard Jamaican English. The tension between the upwardly mobile khakis whose English is a source of pride and the darker-skinned folk who detest the pretension of these speakers, yet are painfully aware of their privilege, is played out in the narrator's consciousness. Here the incoherence of the language and the disembodied voices present English as an anguish to the narrator. Nellie's movement toward psychic wholeness also is one toward a less disruptive, more holistic language—at once Carib-centric and feminist—blending oral traditions and childhood memories, as Nellie takes her first tentative steps out of the kumbla.

The main character takes us along a spiral backward into her life—from her detached memories of Jamaica and overseas, to her breakdown while working with a activist Marxist group, and finally to her spiritual healing through the help of her childhood friend Baba. As readers we have to reconstruct the narrative as Nellie reconstructs the language. What has been learned—the privilege of "correct" English, which is also a curse—must be unlearned. And it is this unlearning that begins to free Nellie as it confounds the reader. Her childhood memories are metaphors that sift through disjointed scenes. The safety of the mother's love becomes evident although there is no mention of a mother: "Ever see a fowl sitting on eggs in cold December rain. We knew the warmth and security of those eggs in the dark of her bottom" (9). The image also calls forth the precariousness of their position, perched between two hostile cultures. Her awakened sexuality is twisted into horror by repressive Anglican values and her confused sense of cultural identity: "You feel shame and you see your mother's face and you hear her scream and you feel the snail what she sees making for your mouth. One long nasty snail, curling up, straightening out to show its white underside that the sun never touches" (28).

The sexual metaphor of the snail is clear enough, but what adds to the linguistic complexity of this passage, whether what it represents is real or imagined, is that the underside of the snail also exposes another penetration—that of white domination. Throughout the novel, the adult Nellie and the child Nellie clash; only in the final section, which shares the book's title, does a strong, clear voice emerge. This section is Nellie's generational, historical recounting of her family's and her nation's past.

The central metaphor of the final section is the kumbla, presented in the traditional Anancy story "Go eena Kumbla." Anancy, the trickster spider who shares Harris's Palace with Christ, has a powerful presence in the Caribbean. In "The Metaphor of Anancy in Caribbean Literature," Helen Tiffin comments that for Caribbean writers, Anancy "becomes a very complex metaphor and archetype for the Caribbean experience" (17); on the one hand, Anancy represents "the fossilized past of the colonized," and on the other, it is "a possible source of fresh creative energy" (35). The Anancy story of the kumbla creates a similar dialectic in *Jane and Louisa.* In the story, Anancy and his children are caught stealing fish from the powerful Dryhead. To save his children from being eaten, Anancy hides the others and takes only his eldest son with him to face their captors. Anancy calls forth his "children," one at a time; each time the eldest son comes forward disguised as one of his siblings, and each time Anancy shouts a supposed curse, "You face favor . . . go eena kumbla," which means for the son to "change colour" and disguise himself as yet another of the "children." Dryhead finally allows Anancy to leave *only* with his eldest son, but in fact all the children are saved (123–30).

In the Anancy story, the kumbla works as a protective covering that fools the enemy. Nellie's kumbla, a symbolic rendering of the worm's white cocoon, is also a disguise; it is a "round seamless calabash that protects you without caring" (123). It is a metaphor for the way that Caribbean women protect their children against the pain of their existence—against the poor and darker, as well as the well-off and lighter. For young girls, the kumbla is also used as a way to protect them against the onslaught of male aggression (or even their own sexual yearnings). But while the kumbla protects, it can also "disfigure" (Cobham 34). After narrating the Anancy story, Nellie exposes the kumbla's limitations: "But the trouble with the kumbla is the getting out of the kumbla. It is a protective device. If you dwell too long in it, it makes you delicate. Makes you an albino: skin white but not by genes. Vision extra-sensitive to the sun and blurred without spectacles. Baba and Alice urged me out of mine. Weak thin, tired like a breach baby" (*Jane and Louisa* 130). The dialectic of this protective, yet disfiguring, device reflects Nellie's predicament as a middle-class Caribbean woman. As Yakemi Kemp notes, "Nellie wants both the oneness with the community and the affluence of the middle-class but cannot reconcile the conflicting values represented by the two" (26). And this conflict is most clearly played out in relation to language, and in some instances to the lack of words.

Nellie receives no valid explanation from her family about her noticeable growth into womanhood, protected by the kumbla of cryptic words. The silences of her family's past, particularly the half-told story of her Aunt Beca, who aborts her baby because it may come out too dark, weigh on her ability to communicate. The image of the snail, as noted above, evokes violent sexual objects—tongues and penises; the response to Nellie's sexual awareness is "Vomit and bear it!" (*Jane and Louisa* 28). All around her, Nellie witnesses the silences imposed by the conflict of gender, color, and class-bound language, determined by the standard dialect of schooled Jamaican English, and as she returns from abroad she sees people "waiting. Perhaps for language" (41). She is disturbed by these silences and by the lack of a language to represent her nation, a language that is not class and race bound. Even the words of liberation from her political group come in "an unknown tongue . . . words like 'underdevelopment', 'Marx', 'cultural pluralism' " (46). The dichotomy of the community-born pidgin, informed by residual African languages, and the dominance of the colonial Standard English leaves no voice for Nellie to speak as herself.

This dis-ease is most evident in her great-grandmother Tia who marries the white William, "spouting khaki children" (136). Tia represents the most damaging aspects of European hegemonic colonialism in that she "had built a fine and effective kumbla out of William's skin" (142). The kumbla, initially used to protect, becomes a symbol of deformed cultural identity. Tia helps develop a new hegemony—that of upper-class, light-skinned Jamaicans—from which she is excluded. She makes herself disappear so that her children (the khaki ones) can make their way into this dominant culture. The white, finely spun kumblas she builds for her children isolate them from her, and she rejects the one daughter who refuses to deny her maternal heritage. Tia's success in spinning kumblas around her children is evident in the use of language: "Tia wanted it so that with a snap of her fingers she could disappear and her children would loom large in their place in the sun. *The stranger the words her children spoke, the happier she felt*" (139; emphasis added). Their place in the sun, obviously the world of the aspiring bourgeois Jamaicans, has no room for the black Tia, thus severing the most primal bonding of mother to child as well as denying African heritage and community.

Nellie, a direct descendant of these generational kumblas, has to re-create language to be able to reintegrate into her culture without losing other aspects of herself. Nellie's reordering of language and history is the linguistic thrust of the novel. Her ability to feel comfortable in a language is like her first tentative steps out of the kumbla. She lets Baba guide her healing process because "I knew Baba's past. He knew mine. On this we shared a common language" (67). Her aim to have her language reflect her cultural identity and break away from the imposition of the dominant culture's loaded words echoes Caliban's. In response to Baba's prodding Nellie out of her kumbla, she reacts and curses at him. She stops and says, "I have been talking aloud. Is that me? with such expressions. Am I a fishwife?" Baba answers, "Yes it is you. You have found your language" (71). Nellie's growth is directly related to her ability to speak language anew.

By the end of the novel, Nellie is retelling her family history/herstory in her own personal/"nation" language. Unlike Harris, Brodber moves toward reconciliation, rejecting the idea that new ways of speaking may produce new hegemonies. The oral traditions of her African ancestors blended with the English (subdued, nonhierarchical) of her European ancestors produces a language and structure that is the most cohesive in the novel. But the readers have had to relearn the language as well to hear Nellie's story. "Vulnerable as a premature worm," Nellie finds her story strengthened by the now known "wiry black hands" of her Granny Tucker (146). Nellie reconciles the khaki and black ancestors, moving deftly from Standard Jamaican English to the nation language of Creole. This movement toward reconciliation of the different aspects of her culture is inscribed in a language that has been feminized and Africanized. The end of the novel is chantlike, partial (to use Wilson Harris's term); and the last line, "We are getting ready" (147), implies an open resolution—a stepping out of the kumbla, not just for Nellie, but for her nation.

From Caliban to the Caribbean writers, the domain of language as dialectically encoded domination and resistance is of paramount importance. Whether returning to residual cultures to liberate the language, like Brodber, or drawing from the whole universe of inscribed meanings, like Harris, these writers present language as integral to the creation of emerging culture(s), counterhegemonic and nonhierarchical. Learning this language of opposition is part of the mandate of these Caribbean writers—language that is no longer Anglo-supreme, no longer supportive of empire. The power of English as a canonical language may have appeared as a kumbla with some protection and possibility of publication, but in fact it has been a suffocating cocoon that disfigured some and silenced others, marginality inscribed in its discourse. The language that so carelessly structures our ways of thinking and seeing—and my own words here—is transformed by the Caribbean writers so as to contain their own world(s) by disrupting the domain of Prospero. By questioning the hegemonic colonialism of the very language we write in, Philip, Harris, and Brodber, among others, force confrontation with the dominant structures of new-world societies and create language afresh as a way of dehierarchizing it.

Notes

1. See, for example, Jacques Derrida's "Difference" (129–60). For an excellent discussion of this opposition within the context of Igbo cosmology, see Achebe.

2. Although Harris's concept of partiality appears to be a form of metonymy, it actually deconstructs the terms since, for Harris, no "whole" exists.

3. I am extremely grateful to Wilson Harris for helping me formulate my thoughts on this novel through long conversations and two formal seminars at the University of Texas, spring 1982 and 1983.

4. For a more in-depth examination of this aspect of the novel, see Wilentz.

5. Like Marxist philosopher Theodor Adorno, Harris implicitly critiques Hegel's dialectics and the notion of the transcendent. For a further examination of the constant sense of nonidentity in identity, the other in the dominant ideal, see Adorno.

Works Cited

Achebe, Chinua. *Morning Yet on Creation Day.* London: Heinemann, 1975.

Adorno, Theodore. *Negative Dialectics.* London: Routledge, 1973.

Batsleer, Janet, Tony Davies, Rebecca O'Rourke, and Chris Weedon. *Rewriting English: Cultural Politics of Gender and Class.* London: Methuen, 1985.

Boxill, Anthony. "Wilson Harris's *Palace of the Peacock:* A New Dimension in West Indian Fiction." *College Language Association Journal* 14 (June 1971): 381–84.

Brodber, Erna. "Fiction in Science and Politics." Paper delivered at the First International Conference on Women Writers from the English-speaking Caribbean, Wellesley, Mass., 9 April 1988.

———. *Jane and Louisa Will Soon Come Home.* London: New Beacon Books, 1980.

Cobham, Rhonda. "Getting Out of the Kumbla." *Race Today* 14 (December 1981/January 1982): 33–34.

Derrida, Jacques. "Difference." *Speech and Phenomena: And Other Essays on Husserl's Theory of Signs.* Trans. David B. Allison. Evanston: Northwestern University Press, 1973, 129–60.

Drake, Sandra E. *Wilson Harris and the Modern Tradition.* Westport, Conn: Greenwood Press, 1986.

Durix, Jean-Pierre. "A Reading of 'Paling of Ancestors.' " *Commonwealth Newsletter* 9 (January 1976): 32–40.

Guillory, John. "Canonical and Non-canonical: A Critique of the Current Debate." *English Literary History* 54 (1987): 483–527.

Harris, Wilson. *Explorations.* Mundelstrup: Dangaroo, 1981.

———. "A Talk on the Subjective Imagination." *Explorations,* 57–67.

———. "The Complexity of Freedom." *Explorations,* 113–24.

———. "Myth and Metaphor." In Selleck, 1–14.

———. *Palace of the Peacock.* London: Faber & Faber, 1960.

JanMohamed, Abdul. "Dominance, Hegemony and the Task of Criticism." *Griot* 6, no. 2 (1987): 7–11.

Kemp, Yakemi. "Woman and Womanchild: Bonding and Selfhood in Three West Indian Novels." *Sage* 2, no. 1 (1985): 24–27.

Lamming, George. *The Pleasures of Exile.* London: Allison & Busby, 1960, 1984.

Mazrui, Ali. *The Political Sociology of the English Language: An African Perspective.* The Hague: Mouton, 1975.

Nelson, Cary. "Against English: Theory and the Limits of the Discipline." In *Profession* 87 (New York: MLA, 1988), 46–52.

Philip, Marlene Nourbese. "She Tried Her Tongue, Her Silence Breaks Softly." Ms., 1988.

———. "Earth and Sound: The Place of Poetry." Paper delivered at the First International Conference on Women Writers from the English-speaking Caribbean, Wellesley, Mass., 9 April 1988.

Poirier, Richard. *The Renewal of Literature*. New York: Random House, 1987.

Selleck, Robert, ed. *Myth and Metaphor*. Adelaide, Australia: Center for Research in the New Literatures in English, 1982.

Tiffin, Helen. "The Metaphor of Anancy in Caribbean Literature." In Selleck, 15–52.

Wilentz, Gay. "Wilson Harris's Divine Comedy of Existence: Miniaturizations of the Cosmos in *Palace of the Peacock*." *Kunapipi* 8, no. 2 (1986): 56–66.

Williams, Raymond. "Base and Superstructure in Marxist Cultural Theory." In *Contemporary Literary Theory*. Ed. Robert Con Davis and Ronald Schleifer. New York: Longman, 1989, 378–90.

———. *Marxism and Literature*. London: Oxford University Press, 1977.

Willis, Susan. "Caliban as Poet: Reversing the Maps of Domination." In *Reinventing the Americas*. Ed. Belle Gale Chevigny and Gari Laguardia. London: Cambridge University Press, 1986, 92–105.

Woodcock, Bruce. "Post-1975 Caribbean Fiction and the Challenge to English Literature." *Critical Quarterly* 28, no. 4 (1986): 79–95.

Notes on Contributors

DEREK ATTRIDGE is a professor of English at Rutgers University, New Brunswick. Among his books are *Peculiar Language: Literature as Difference from the Renaissance to James Joyce* (1988) and, as coeditor, *Post-structuralism and the Question of History* (1987). He is currently editing a selection of Jacques Derrida's texts in English translation.

RACHEL BOWLBY is a senior lecturer in English at Sussex University and the author of *Just Looking* (1985), on femininity and consumerism in turn-of-the-century novels, and *Virginia Woolf: Feminist Destinations* (1988).

ROBERT L. CASERIO teaches English and American literature at the University of Utah. He is the author of *Plot, Story and the Novel* (1979) and of numerous critical essays. "The Novel as a Novel Experiment in Statement" is part of a work-in-progress on the history and theory of the British novel in the twentieth century.

MARTIN GREEN is the Fay Professor of Literature at Tufts University and the author of numerous books, including *The Robinson Crusoe Story* (1991). He is currently writing a study of the New Age phenomenon in three centuries.

KAREN R. LAWRENCE is a professor of English at the University of Utah. She is the author of *The Odyssey of Style in Ulysses* (1981), *Penelope Voyages: Women and Travel in the British Literary Tradition* (forthcoming), and numerous articles on nineteenth- and twentieth-century literature.

JANE MARCUS is Distinguished Professor of English at the City College of New York and presently director of women's studies at the Graduate Center. She is the author of *Art and Anger* (1988) and *Virginia Woolf and the Languages of Patriarchy* (1987).

PATRICK MCGEE is an associate professor of English at Louisiana State University. He is the author of *Paperspace: Style as Ideology in Joyce's "Ulysses"*

(1988) and has published articles in *The Faulkner Journal* and *James Joyce Quarterly,* among others. He is currently completing a book entitled *Writing and Symbolic Exchange.*

MARILYN REIZBAUM is an associate professor of English at Bowdoin College. She is currently completing a manuscript, "James Joyce's Judaic 'Other': Text and Contexts." Her essay in this volume will be part of a manuscript on "Nationalism, Feminism, and the 'Minor' Literatures of Scotland and Ireland."

LILLIAN S. ROBINSON is a visiting scholar in residence at the Harry Ransom Humanities Research Center, University of Texas, Austin. Her books include *Sex, Class, and Culture* (1986) and, as coauthor, *Feminist Scholarship: Kindling in the Groves of Academe* (1985).

CELESTE M. SCHENCK is an associate professor of English and Ann Whitney Olin Fellow at Barnard College. She is cofounder of "Women Poets at Barnard," a series of readings and publications featuring the work of new women poets, and general coeditor of "Reading Women Writing," a series in feminist criticism published by Cornell University Press. She is the author of *Mourning and Panegyric: The Poetics of Pastoral Ceremony* (1989) and coeditor of *Life/Lines: Theorizing Women's Autobiography* (1988). She is currently finishing *Corinna Sings: Women Poets and the Politics of Genre.*

GAY WILENTZ is an assistant professor of English at East Carolina University, a constituent institution of the University of North Carolina. She received her Ph.D. in African, African-American and Caribbean Literatures from the University of Texas, and was a Fulbright Scholar to Nigeria. Her teaching and research interests include women's studies, ethnic studies, and world literature in English. She is the author of *Binding Cultures: African and African-American Women Writers* (forthcoming).

LOUISE YELIN is an associate professor in the Literature Board of Study at SUNY, Purchase. She is at work on a book entitled *From the Margins of Empire* on twentieth-century (English) colonial and postcolonial women writers.

Index

Rosetti, Ana, 58
Rosmarin, Adena, 139, 141
Roxana (Defoe), 219, 222
"Rule, Britannia!" (Thomson), 140
Rushdie, Salman, 257

Saga adventure tales. *See* Viking adventure tales
Said, Edward, 138, 165, 166
Santayana, George, 91
Sappho, 40, 45, 46, 47–48, 181
Sartre, Jean-Paul, 91
Sati: in *The Waves,* 137–38, 159
Schenck, Celeste, 11, 12, 37–69
Schwartz-Bart, André, 246
Schwob, Marcel, 76, 78
Scots language, 183–84
Scott, Walter, 79–80, 83, 86, 168
Scottish Literature (Smith), 172
Scottish writers: of adventure tales, 79–80; women, 165–90
Seagle, William, 119
Season of Anomy (Soyinka), 244, 249
Seillière, Ernest, 81–82
Selby, Hubert, 135n.36
Self-canonizing: by modernists, 89; by Coetzee, 214–37
Sexton, Anne, 53–54, 57–58
Sexuality: Gordimer's politicizing of, 199–203; in Coetzee's works, 235n.16. *See also* Epithalamium
Sexual Politics (Millett), 13, 128
"Shakespeare, Judith," 33, 38
Shakespeare, William, 33, 44, 196, 263
Shaw, George Bernard, 130–31, 168
Shelley, Mary, 168
Shelley, Percy Bysshe, 137–38, 145, 155
Sheppard, David, 135n.36
She Tries Her Tongue, Her Silence Breaks Softly (Philip), 263–64
"Sibling Mysteries" (Rich), 56
Silence: in *Foe,* 213, 217, 225–26, 228–29, 236n.23. *See also* Silencing
Silences (Olsen), 33
Silencing: and women's experience of the canon, 33; in epithalamia, 41, 42, 47; in *The Waves,* 139, 143, 146; of Caribbean writers, 264–65. *See also* Language(s); Silence
Sinfield, Alan, 5, 15n.1, 16n.2
Sitwell, Edith, 45, 114, 142
Slavery, 265, 267
Smith, Barbara, 185n.1

Smith, David C., 88
Smith, Gregory, 172
Smith, Stevie, 114
Smyth, Ailbhe, 178
"Snapshots of a Daughter-in-Law" (Rich), 37–38
"Social Darwinism and Upper Class Education in England" (Mangan), 84
Song of Songs, 57
Songs of Experience (Blake), 215
Sonnets, 39, 44
South Africa. *See* Gordimer, Nadine; Coetzee, J. M.
Soyinka, Wole, 31, 243–44, 249, 254
Spanish-American War, 74
Spectator, The, 124
Spenser, Edmund, 40, 42, 54, 59–60
Spivak, Gayatri, 8, 10, 17n.7, 138, 165–66, 255
Sport of Nature, A (Gordimer), 14, 191–211
Spying: in Kipling and Gordimer, 195–96
Stallybrass, Peter, 156–57
Stanford, Ann, 53
Stein, Gertrude, 45, 91
Stephen, Dorothea, 149, 155
Stephen, Fitzjames, 84, 152
Stephen, J. K., 146, 149, 151–53
Stephen, Leslie, 75, 148, 151, 152
Stephen, Thoby, 151, 153
Stephen family: and imperialism, 147–49
Stevenson, Robert Louis, 74, 75–76, 78, 79, 82, 86, 168
Stewart, Pamela, 52
"Still Practice" (Marcus), 33
Storace, Patricia, 59, 61–63
Story of Rolf and the Viking's Bow (French), 83
Strachey, Lytton, 150–51
Studies in Early Indian Thought (D. Stephen), 149, 155–56
"Study of Poetry, The" (Arnold), 115
Styrbiorn the Strong (Eddison), 83
Sulieman, Susan, 165, 166
Surfacing (Atwood), 32
Swan, Jim, 157
Swift, Jonathan, 90
Symbolist writings, 76–77

Tadié, Jean-Yves, 76, 79
"Tale, A" (Finch), 46
Tales from the North (Dasent), 84